Essays on the Greek Historians
and Greek History

Essays on the Greek Historians and Greek History

H. D. WESTLAKE

Hulme Professor of Greek in the
University of Manchester

MANCHESTER UNIVERSITY PRESS
BARNES & NOBLE, INC., NEW YORK

MANCHESTER UNIVERSITY PRESS
316–324 Oxford Road,
Manchester, M13 9NR
England

Published in the U.S.A.
1969
Barnes & Noble, Inc.
105 Fifth Avenue,
New York, N.Y. 10003

G.B. SBN 7190 0366 0

Printed in Great Britain by
Butler & Tanner Ltd,
Frome and London

Preface

Of the eighteen essays assembled in this volume all except the first and longest essay are reprinted from periodicals. No division is made between those on the Greek historians and those on Greek history: all are, to some degree at least, concerned with both. The volume includes most of my publications in periodicals, apart from reviews, since 1942. I have excluded work published before that date, not because it seems to me to be necessarily inferior to my more recent publications, but because papers written more than twenty-five years ago tend to have a somewhat old-fashioned air, even to their author. In accordance with what appears to be normal practice in collections of this kind, I have confined alterations to the correction of minor errors and some modernisation of references.

Nos. 2, 4, 5 and 11 were first published in the *Classical Quarterly*, in vols. n.s. 5 (1955), 41 (1947), 39 (1945) and n.s. 8 (1958) respectively; no. 3 in *Classical Philology*, vol. 45 (1950); nos. 6 and 14 in *Historia*, vols. 9 (1960) and 2 (1954); nos. 7, 9 and 10 in *Hermes*, vols. 90 (1962), 84 (1956) and 86 (1958); no. 8 in the *Proceedings of the Cambridge Philological Society*, n.s. vol. 7 (1961); nos. 12, 13 and 18 in the *Bulletin of the John Rylands Library*, vols. 41 (1958), 49 (1966) and 37 (1954); no. 15 in the *Durham University Journal*, n.s. vol. 7 (1946); no. 16 in the *American Journal of Philology*, vol. 70 (1949); no. 17 in the *Cambridge Historical Journal*, vol. 7 (1942). I wish to thank the publishers of these Journals for giving their permission for me to reproduce these essays here.

H.D.W.

University of Manchester

Contents

1

Irrelevant notes and minor excursuses in Thucydides

In his selection of subject-matter, as in many other respects, Thucydides was an innovator. To have chosen a contemporary war as his theme was a novelty; to have chosen to concern himself with this war, with politics in so far as they influenced its course, with general lessons to be learned from it, and with hardly anything else, was even more strikingly original. Specialisation, which was largely the outcome of the intellectual movement in Periclean Athens, had only recently begun to develop in prose literature. Thucydides was the first specialist in historiography in the sense that historical works before his were to a large extent collections of interesting stories and of interesting information on a wide variety of subjects.

His predecessors, to whom his own somewhat indefinite term 'logographer' (1.21.1) is traditionally applied, were innocent of specialisation, and even Hellanicus, an older contemporary, was evidently not affected by its growing influence to the extent that he was. Because the works of the logographers are known only from meagre fragments or from observations made about them by authors writing centuries later,[1] their characteristics remain very uncertain. There is, however, no doubt that these works covered a wide range of subjects, which is an additional reason why it is hazardous to generalise about them. Among the topics with which they dealt were mythology, genealogy, local history, geography and ethnography, in many cases apparently several of these together in the same work. Their arrangement was as loosely knit as their style, and they were to a large extent uncritical. Designed to propagate as widely as possible information hitherto unknown or little known, they were unscientific and had an essentially popular appeal.[2]

[1] The *locus classicus* on the logographers is a statement by Dionysius of Halicarnassus (*De Thuc.* 5), which provides valuable evidence, though not all of it is necessarily accurate, cf. T. S. Brown, *Amer. Hist. Rev.* lix (1954), 834–8.
[2] Although the Hippocratic *Airs, Waters, Places* is in theory a scientific

Herodotus differed from his predecessors in at least one fundamental respect: he chose to write a single, comprehensive work on a great and noble theme, the conflict between East and West. Nevertheless, his inexhaustible passion for ἱστορίη led him to incorporate in his account of that conflict a mass of information on the topics with which the logographers were accustomed to deal. It is true that he turned more and more from geography and ethnography to history, in the modern sense, as his work progressed.[3] Fortunately for his readers, however, his conversion was never complete, and he belongs essentially to the tradition of the logographers.[4]

Thucydides broke away from this tradition, which he considered to be meretricious and unsound. He decided from the outset to write a historical work of a very different character. Not only did he expressly exclude τὸ μυθῶδες (1.22.4), but he also tacitly omitted information which might have been valuable in helping posterity to understand contemporary situations and problems.[5] Yet, even though normally he maintained this break with tradition by observing his self-imposed limitations in the choice of subject-matter, he did not entirely abandon the practice of including more or less irrelevant information which seemed to merit attention. A considerable number of passages may be

treatise, the second half (12–24), which discusses the physiological characteristics of various races, is largely popular ethnography and seems to reflect the tradition of the logographers.

[3] Cf. K. Latte, *Entretiens Fondation Hardt* iv (1956), 6–7.

[4] A. Momigliano, *Studies in Historiography* (1966), 130–1 (a paper originally published in 1958), suggests that Thucydides did a disservice to historiography by imposing upon his successors 'the idea that contemporary political history was the only serious history' and thus caused Herodotus to be unjustly slighted. While this view has much to recommend it, it seems to me to overrate the influence of Thucydides (which certainly did not induce later historians to confine their subject-matter to war and politics) and to underrate that of Herodotus. *Inter alia*, geography, which was an incidental element in the work of Thucydides (see below, n. 16) but a major interest of Herodotus, continued for centuries to play a large part in historical writings; cf. the insistence of Polybius (3.57–9; 12.25 e 1) on its importance to the historian and on the value of autopsy.

[5] An example is his omission of biographical detail about major personalities, cf. A. W. Gomme, *Historical Commentary on Thucydides* i (1945), 26–8. It is noteworthy that Dionysius of Halicarnassus (*Ad Pomp.* 3.11–12), writing from the standpoint of a rhetorician, criticises Thucydides for lack of variety in subject-matter.

found in his *History*, most of them brief,[6] in which particulars are given on some topic largely or wholly unconnected with the war or of a kind not normally included in his work—and apparently for no other reason than that this information interested him and seemed likely to interest his readers. In some instances he may conceivably have sought to correct errors by his predecessors contained in works now no longer extant. There seems, however, to be no evidence or indication that such was his motive; and indeed, if it had been, he might have been expected not merely to have stated what he believed to be true but also to have tried to substantiate his view by means of supporting arguments.[7]

Many scholars have drawn attention to the existence of passages in the *History* containing more or less irrelevant material.[8] Apparently, however, it has not been observed that they are by no means evenly distributed throughout the work; that far more of them occur in what may loosely be termed the first half (1.1–5.24), which deals with the Archidamian war and its causes, than in the second half (5.25–8.109), covering the period from 421 to 411.[9] This unevenness of distribution can hardly be fortuitous, since the number of passages in the first half is quite substantial. Unless there are other grounds on which it can be

[6] Major excursuses, which will be briefly discussed below (pp. 4–5), seem to me to belong to a different category.

[7] As in fact he does in his major excursuses.

[8] For example, W. Schadewaldt, *Die Geschichtschreibung des Thukydides* (1929), 33–4 and 69–73; L. Pearson, *C.Q.* xxxiii (1939), 48–54 and *Local Historians of Attica* (1942), 27–48.

[9] The division of the *History* into two halves is discussed in my *Individuals in Thucydides* (1968), 1–2. The existence of a very marked break in the structure of the work at 5.25, to which many scholars have drawn attention, seems to be hardly disputable, since Thucydides himself, on completing his account of the Archidamian war, makes a fresh start (5.26.1, γέγραφε δὲ καὶ ταῦτα ὁ αὐτὸς Θουκυδίδης ᾿Αθηναῖος) and inserts a passage commonly known as the second introduction (26.1–6). Yet this passage, though undoubtedly marking a *structural* division in the *History*, does not provide cogent evidence that he substantially completed the first half a considerable time before he embarked upon the second half. The interval could have been quite short. Hence the existence of this second introduction makes a contribution of only limited value to the long-standing controversy about the composition of the *History*. For the same reason no attempt will be made in the present paper to show that my conclusions about irrelevant notes and minor excursuses, if valid, contribute anything to this controversy, though they might perhaps be deemed to do so.

3

satisfactorily explained, it suggests the conclusion that in the second half Thucydides adopted even stricter standards of relevance than in the first; that he became even less dependent upon the tradition established by his predecessors and moved even further in the direction of specialisation. The purpose of this paper is to try to establish that such a change of attitude did in fact take place, marking a step of some significance in his development as a historian.

The passages conveying more or less irrelevant information vary very considerably both in length and in the degree of their irrelevance. Many consist of only a few words, though they are not necessarily any less significant on that account, while others amount to minor excursuses. Before embarking upon a survey of these passages and noting their distribution, a necessary preliminary is to discuss briefly five major excursuses and to explain why they will be excluded from the survey. Although their subject-matter is remote enough from the Peloponnesian war, they are not designed primarily to provide information likely to be of interest to the reader. It is true that they do provide interesting information, by no means all of it being strictly relevant to the main theme of the excursus, but this function is incidental. Their primary purpose is to expound and substantiate the personal convictions of Thucydides on controversial, or potentially controversial, issues. He seeks to establish a novel theory of his own or to correct widely accepted beliefs which were in his opinion mistaken. Above all, he wishes to demonstrate that he is right and that anyone holding contrary views is wrong.

The first of these major excursuses, the 'Archaeology' (1.1–23), is an attempt to prove that the Peloponnesian war was the greatest war of all time, the basic argument being that earlier generations were prevented from waging wars on a comparable scale by the inadequacy of their material resources. This highly original doctrine challenges traditional views, and in applying a new technique to the study of the distant past Thucydides is also challenging the uncritical methods of his predecessors.[10] The main purpose of his excursus on the Pentecontaetia (1.89–118) is, as he himself makes clear, to corroborate his personal view on the causes of the war (1.89.1; 97.2;

[10] J. de Romilly, *Histoire et raison chez Thucydide* (1956), 240–98, analyses this technique.

118.2). To provide an account of a period neglected by other writers is only a secondary aim. The excursus on Cylon, Pausanias and Themistocles (1.126–138) is largely the outcome of a conviction on the part of Thucydides that the accounts of earlier writers were unsatisfactory and required correction.[11] The ostensible purpose of the excursus on barbarian and Greek settlements in Sicily (6.2–5) is to show that, when the Athenians planned to conquer the island, they were undertaking an enterprise little inferior in scale to the war against the Peloponnesians (6.1.1) Chronology is, however, the main theme of the excursus, and there is hardly any doubt that Thucydides has adopted a chronological system which he found in a little known *History of Sicily* by Antiochus of Syracuse.[12] Hence he seems to be deliberately challenging the generally accepted scheme of Sicilian chronology contained in the standard chronological work of the time, the *Priestesses of Hera at Argos* by Hellanicus. This excursus, like the other four, is essentially an essay in controversy. The excursus on the Peisistratidae (6.54–59) is the most obviously polemical of the five. Here Thucydides insists that he is right on some basic facts relating to the last years of the tyranny and that both the Athenians themselves and 'the others' are wrong (54.1; 55.1). Undoubtedly these non-Athenians include Hellanicus, whose *Atthis* contained an account of the tyranny, and the reference may be to him alone.[13] Thucydides is supporting the version of Herodotus, supplemented by the fruits of his own research, and is rejecting the popularly accredited version, which was accepted, and may indeed have been influenced, by Hellanicus.

The last two of these major excursuses show that in the second half of the *History* Thucydides continued his practice of inserting discussions on controversial subjects more or less unconnected with the war where he felt himself able to make a valuable contribution by putting forward views of his own or refuting those of others. In some respects the influence exerted upon him by the intellectual movement of Periclean Athens seems to have

---

[11] On Cylon see F. Jacoby, *Atthis* (1949), 186–8. For the treatment of Pausanias and Themistocles see below, pp. 51–5.

[12] K. J. Dover, *Maia* vi (1953), 1–20; R. van Compernolle, *Étude de chronologie et d'historiographie siciliotes* (1960), 437–500.

[13] Jacoby, *Atthis* 159.

5

faded somewhat as the years of his exile lengthened.[14] He did not, however, lose his zest for intellectual discussion, which was natural to a man of his upbringing. Another manifestation of it, namely his habit of including pairs of speeches presenting opposing points of view, though less prominent in the second half than in the first, is very effectively maintained in his account of the Sicilian expedition. It is perfectly natural that, when he threw off the influence of Ionian ἱστορίη, as will be shown below, by drastically reducing irrelevant notes and minor excursuses introduced for their general interest, he did not at the same time discontinue the inclusion of major excursuses: the latter had a totally different and far more serious purpose.

The irrelevant notes and minor excursuses may now be examined and their distribution noted. They will be divided into two groups, those belonging to the first half of the *History* (I) and those belonging to the second half (II). Because the former group of passages is comparatively large, it will be subdivided into those relating to geography and antiquarianism (A), those relating to natural phenomena (B), and those containing biographical information and anecdote (C).[15] In some instances passages in both halves dealing with the same locality or the same topic will be discussed together and compared in order to show that those in the second half tend to be more relevant to the history of the war. A few comparisons with passages by other authors will also be made.

I. THE FIRST HALF

(A) *Geography and antiquarianism*

Most of the geographical information contained in the *History* is unquestionably relevant to its main theme and does not call for discussion here. Normally when referring to remote or insignificant places and occasionally when referring to better known places, Thucydides briefly defines their location, though he is not at all consistent in this respect. There are also plenty of passages in which geographical information is provided, some of it detailed, with the evident intention of helping the reader to

[14] Cf. *Individuals in Thucydides*, 318–19.
[15] The passages in subdivision C are not necessarily irrelevant, but their subject-matter is of a kind not normally found in the *History*.

6

understand how, or why, historical events took place. There remains, however, a much smaller but by no means negligible number of geographical passages in which the subject-matter is largely or wholly irrelevant and cannot legitimately be claimed to make the historical context more intelligible.[16] Because mythology and early history, which were indistinguishable to Thucydides, are sometimes linked with geography in the same passage, as they were by his predecessors, it will be convenient to discuss together in a single section the passages concerned with these subjects. This section, being a relatively large one, will be divided into five subsections (i–v), each containing the passages relating to one geographical area.

(i) *Sicily*

Included in the very brief account of the Athenian intervention in Sicily during the Archidamian war are two notes which throw little or no light upon the campaign. The first, amounting to a brief excursus, describes the Lipara islands, against which the Athenians made an expedition in collaboration with their Rhegine allies in the winter of 427/26 (3.88). Thucydides dismisses the military operations, which were unsuccessful, in a few words (88.4). He supplies much more information on the interesting characteristics of these volcanic islands and their inhabitants, including a reference to the local belief that the smithy of Hephaestus lay beneath Hiera (88.2–3). One feature of the islands, namely their lack of water, is relevant, since it explains why the attack was made in winter (88.1). In other respects the passage is sheer logography.[17] The second note is

[16] F. Sieveking, *Klio* xlii (1964), 73–179 (which came to my notice after the first draft of this paper was written) has made a detailed analysis of geographical passages in Thucydides and has discussed their function. As a general principle his conclusion is undoubtedly valid that Thucydides did not include geographical information for its own sake but in order to elucidate the historical narrative. He seems to me, however, to be unjustifiably reluctant to acknowledge that there are any exceptions. He tends to use unconvincing arguments when attempting to establish the relevance of passages which in fact have little or none (cf. 126–8 on 2.68.3–8; 130–1 on 4.24.5; 170 on 2.102.2–6).

[17] There are good reasons for believing that the substance of this minor excursus is derived from Antiochus of Syracuse (van Compernolle, op. cit., 473–9), though not the account of the Athenian campaign in Sicilian waters, which is more likely to have been based on reports by Athenians who served in it (Gomme, op. cit., ii. 389 and 392; iii. 521–2).

concerned with the straits of Messana (4.24.5). Thucydides has stated that the Syracusans had expectations of capturing Rhegium and would thereby prevent the Athenians from controlling the straits (24.4). It would have been logical if he had then proceeded to explain their strategic importance, but instead he supplies some information which is largely irrelevant, though doubtless interesting to his readers. He identifies the straits with the Homeric Charybdis and explains why they were considered to be dangerous.

It is noteworthy that these two largely irrelevant passages are inserted in a narrative of military operations written in his bleakest manner: he expressly states that he intends to record only the most memorable actions in which the Athenians were involved (3.90.1).[18] In the far more detailed account of the later and greater Athenian expedition to Sicily, to which the sixth and seventh books are almost exclusively devoted, there are, as will be seen below, hardly any notes of a similar kind, though Sicily and Italy were geographically interesting areas and also rich in legend.

(ii) *North-western Greece*

In his account of the conflict between Corcyra and Corinth arising from the dissensions at Epidamnus Thucydides includes two notes of very questionable relevance. He refers to the Illyrian neighbours of the Epidamnians, the Taulantii, who are not mentioned by name anywhere else in his narrative of this episode or indeed in the whole *History* (1.24.1).[19] Later he describes the neighbourhood of Cheimerium in Thesprotia, where the Corinthians anchored and encamped before the battle of Sybota (46.3–5). This passage contains a surprising amount of detail

---

[18] On Athenian aims in Sicily see below, pp. 101–22.

[19] Pearson, *C.Q.* xxxiii (1939), 51. Sieveking, op. cit., 122, claims that the reference is relevant, since the Taulantii are to be identified with the barbarians mentioned later (24.4–5; 26.4). This argument is unconvincing. Thucydides could have postponed his reference to the Taulantii until he had occasion to mention Epidamnian relations with the barbarians. Moreover, the passage might have made some contribution to its immediate context, which is concerned with the site of Epidamnus, if he had explained precisely where the Taulantii lived; but he does not.

which is interesting geographically but makes a negligible contribution to the historical narrative.[20]

Notes of a similar kind are found in his accounts of the campaigns in Amphilochia, Acarnania and Aetolia from 430 to 426. The area was one about which most of his readers were doubtless ill-informed, but these notes are of hardly any value in helping them to understand the developments of the military situation there. Interposed between the two parts of a very brief report on an abortive attempt by the Ambraciots to take Amphilochian Argos in 430 (2.68.1 and 9) is a considerably longer sketch of Amphilochian history from the period immediately after the Trojan war, when Amphilochus is said to have settled there, down to the time of this attack (68.2–8). It is true that the local feuds between the peoples of the area became a factor of some importance when the Athenians and the Peloponnesians were soon afterwards involved in a struggle for control of north-western Greece. It is also true that the account of the first Athenian intervention (68.7), which took place not very many years before the outbreak of the Peloponnesian war, is neither irrelevant nor unduly detailed. On the other hand, much of the information given concerning the foundation of Amphilochian Argos, the origin of its name, and its early history seems to have been included only because Thucydides found the subject attractive.

An even more striking passage is attached to his account of an expedition to Acarnania in the winter of 429/28 by an Athenian force from Naupactus under Phormio, who landed his troops at Astacus and led them into the interior with the object of strengthening Athenian influence there (2.102.1). In order to explain why Phormio did not attack Oeniadae, the only Acarnanian city which had always been hostile to Athens, Thucydides states that the inundations caused by the Achelous rendered military operations impossible there in winter (102.2). He describes the peculiar features of the Achelous estuary and the Echinades islands much more fully than the context demands, and he makes the prediction, which remained unfulfilled, that all these islands would shortly become attached to the mainland (102.2–4). Finally, he turns to the myth of Alcmaeon and recounts

---

[20] Gomme, op cit., i. 179–81 and ii. 365, who draws attention to the inaccuracy of the passage. That Thucydides may have derived its substance from Hecataeus does not make it any less irrelevant.

a part of it, explaining how it was that Alcmaeon made his home on newly-formed land in the Achelous estuary (102.5–6). The geographical and mythological sections of this minor excursus are together much longer than the account of the Athenian expedition. The closing sentence of the excursus, τὰ μὲν οὖν περὶ ᾿Αλκμέωνα τοιαῦτα λεγόμενα παρελάβομεν is thoroughly Herodotean in tone.[21]

Two brief notes giving information unconnected with the war are included in the narrative of the military operations conducted by Demosthenes in north-western Greece in 426. When the Messenians urged him to invade Aetolia, they suggested the order in which he should attack three Aetolian tribes. The last of these were the Eurytanes, described by Thucydides as ἀγνωστότατοι γλῶσσαν καὶ ὠμοφάγοι ὡς λέγονται (3.94.5). This description does not appear to have any military significance, since he certainly did not subscribe to the view that the troops of uncivilised tribes were necessarily more formidable than those of less backward peoples.[22] There is possibly a hint that the judgement of Demosthenes, of which Thucydides is critical in his account of this campaign (3.97.2), was at fault when he allowed himself to be persuaded to attack semi-savages. The note seems, however, to be purely ethnographical. Later, when Demosthenes was about to launch his invasion, he encamped in the precinct of Nemean Zeus near the Aetolian border. Thucydides adds that Hesiod was said to have been murdered there, and he alludes to, but does not record in full, the story of the misleading oracle by which Hesiod was told that he would die 'at Nemea' (3.96.1). This note has no topographical value, since it does not help the

---

[21] Thucydides does not use παραλαμβάνω elsewhere in the sense of ascertaining facts in the course of enquiry, but the verb is so used quite commonly by Herodotus (cf. 1.55.1 and 126.4; 2.19.1, 19.3 and 148.6; 4.27).

There seems to be no reason to believe, as suggested by Sieveking, op. cit., 170, that Thucydides had in mind a passing reference to the Achelous by Herodotus (2.10.3) and wished to improve upon it. It is a mistake to imagine that Thucydides frequently challenges Herodotus; and doubtless other passages about the Achelous, which was geographically interesting, occurred in works known to Thucydides but subsequently lost. It is, however, noteworthy that, while both Herodotus and Thucydides have occasion to refer to the Achelous, the latter interrupts his narrative in order to include a minor excursus on the subject, but the former does not.

[22] Cf. the contemptuous observations attributed to Brasidas in Macedonia (4.126.3–6), which were confirmed by the subsequent fighting (127.1–128.3).

10

reader to identify the site of the precinct. The story is of a kind characteristic rather of Herodotus than of Thucydides.[23]

A less significant passage relating to the same area lists ten village communities in Ozolian Locris from which the Peloponnesians obtained, or sought to obtain, hostages in 426 when they were threatening Napactus (3.101.2). None of the ten is mentioned again in the account of the military operations in this period or indeed elsewhere in the *History*. The list contributes very little to the historical narrative and seems to have been included mainly for its geographical interest.

(iii) *Attica and central Greece*

When describing the abandonment of Attica to devastation by the Peloponnesians in 431, Thucydides develops the theme that this withdrawal to the city caused the Athenians great distress because most of the population had always been accustomed to live in the country (2.14.2–16.1). He first discusses political conditions in Attica when it was occupied by separate and largely independent communities (15.1). He then records the union of Attica on the initiative of Theseus, mentioning the festival known as ξυνοίκια (15.2); he goes on to argue that at Athens only the acropolis and an area south of it were inhabited in ancient times and finds confirmation of this view in the fact that many of the oldest sanctuaries and the fountain Callirrhoe were situated there (15.3–6). He is accounting for the bitterness of contemporary feeling by seeking its origin in long-established tradition (16.1), and in accordance with his normal procedure when writing about the past, he cites his evidence most scrupulously. It is, however, evident that the abundance of detail in this minor excursus is the outcome of interest in the early history of Attica. The practice of living in the country was not so strange to other Greeks as to demand a lengthy and complex explanation, and he could have established much more briefly his conclusion that this practice was a legacy from the distant past.

In the same summer of 431 the Athenians made an alliance with the Thracian Sitalces, whose father Teres founded the

---

[23] A close parallel is the story told by Herodotus (3.64.3–5) about the oracle predicting the death of Cambyses 'at Ecbatana', cf. Plut. *Pel.* 20.7 on the oracular warning to the Spartans 'to guard against the vengeance of Leuctra'.

Odrysian kingdom (2.29). When outlining the course of the negotiations leading to this alliance, Thucydides refers to the story of Tereus and Procne, daughter of the Athenian king Pandion, with which he assumes his readers to be familiar. He maintains that there was no connection between Teres and Tereus and that Tereus, the husband of Procne, though a Thracian, lived in Daulia, a district in what was later Phocis; and he adds arguments in substantiation of this view (29.3). It may be that contemporary propaganda sought support for the proposed alliance between Athens and the Odrysian Thracians by referring to an alleged marriage tie in ancient times,[24] or that some Athenian writer made use of the story in order to pay a compliment to Sitalces.[25] Hence there is a possibility, though no more than a possibility, that in this instance the main purpose of Thucydides in inserting a discussion on early history may have been to correct a contemporary error.

Another passage of questionable relevance is the description, which precedes the Funeral Speech, of the burial ceremony held in accordance with ancestral custom at the end of 431 to honour Athenians killed in the first year of the war (2.34.2–7). If this description is a mere peg upon which to hang the Funeral Speech, it is a surprisingly long peg; and its tone is even more remarkable than its length. Thucydides might have been expected to have stated how many Athenians have fallen in 431 and were now honoured, but he does not give this figure, which he could doubtless have ascertained without much difficulty. He was interested in the ceremony rather for its own sake and for reasons largely unconnected with the history of the war.[26] He doubtless witnessed it himself on this or some other occasion, and it evidently impressed him as a spectacle. It attracted his attention to an even greater extent as an exceptional custom, out of keeping with Greek tradition, since the armies of other

[24] Steup, n. ad loc.

[25] Gomme, op. cit., ii. 90. n. 1.

[26] F. Jacoby, *J.H.S.* lxiv (1944), 59, is perhaps right in maintaining that he selects for mention features of the ceremony illustrating Athenian characteristics described in the Funeral Speech, but not, in my opinion, in believing that he shows little interest in the antiquarian details. The main contention of this paper, ibid., 37–66, namely that Thucydides was wrong in thinking the ceremony to be of ancient origin, has been vigorously contested by Gomme, op. cit., ii. 94–101.

states habitually buried their dead on the battlefield. His account of the ritual has a tinge of Ionian ἱστορίη[27] and recalls Herodotean descriptions of strange customs in barbarian countries.[28] It is almost anthropology. A significant contrast may be drawn between this passage and a passage in the second half of the *History* on the mutilation of the Hermae. He explains in a parenthesis what the Hermae were and where they stood (6.27.1), but he gives no information about the cult or its origin.

In his account of the Athenian attack on Corinthian territory led by Nicias and two colleagues in 425 (4.42–45) Thucydides mentions a hill named Solygeios which overlooked the beach where the Athenians landed. He adds that during the Dorian invasion the hill was used as a base by the Dorians when making war on the Aeolians of Corinth (42.2). Some scholars believe that this reference to the distant past throws light upon the aims of the Athenians in 425: that they intended to establish a fortified post on Solygeios and, like the Dorians long before, to conduct raids from it on Corinthian territory.[29] While some elucidation of Athenian aims, which are left obscure by Thucydides,[30] would have been very welcome, this explanation is unconvincing.[31] The two occasions when Solygeios was militarily important were by no means comparable. No one understood better than Thucydides, as is clear from the 'Archaeology', that warfare at the time of the Dorian invasion was totally different from that of his own day; and whereas the Dorians had relied upon infiltration by land only, the Athenian attack was seaborne. The reference by Thucydides to the use made of Solygeios by the Dorians is irrelevant and seems to have been included solely for its antiquarian interest.

Another brief note of a similar kind occurs in the account of the elaborate plans laid by Hippocrates and Demosthenes for attacking Boeotia in 424 (4.76.2–5). Thucydides remarks that Orchomenus was formerly called Minyan but was now called Boeotian (76.3). Even if he felt that he must remove any danger

---

[27] Cf. ἐπὶ τοῦ καλλίστου προαστείου τῆς πόλεως (34.5), which is not named.
[28] Cf. Hdt. 4.71–3 on Scythian burial rites.
[29] G. Busolt, *Gr. Gesch.* iii. 2 (1904), 1114 n. 3, cf. Sieveking, op. cit., 102–4.
[30] *Individuals in Thucydides* 89.
[31] It is, rightly in my view, rejected by Gomme, op. cit., iii. 494.

of confusion with Arcadian Orchomenus, which is virtually excluded by the context, he could have referred merely to 'Boeotian Orchomenus', as he does in an earlier passage (3.87.4). His reference to the term used to define it in ancient times, which occurs in the Homeric Catalogue (*Il.*2.511, cf. *Od.*11.284), is irrelevant here.[32]

(iv) *Macedonia, Chalcidice and Thrace*

Thucydides was intimately acquainted with the northern coast of the Aegean (cf. 4.105.1) and possessed a knowledge of its hinterland and which very few of his Athenian contemporaries can have matched. He provides his readers with exceptionally abundant information about this area, some of it being of questionable relevance to his main theme. Much of this information is included in a passage describing at considerable length the invasion of Macedonia and Chalcidice by Sitalces and a 'mixed horde' of Thracians at the end of 429 (2.95–101). It has been designated by some scholars as a single continuous major excursus,[33] but without justification, since the military narrative at any rate does throw a little light upon the course of the Peloponnesian war. Admittedly the results of the expedition were almost negligible, and neither the Athenians nor the Peloponnesians were actively involved in it, but it was directed by an ally of the former against an ally of the latter. The narrative is also instructive in underlining a general military principle to which Thucydides evidently subscribed, namely that the armies of barbarian peoples on the fringes of the Greek world tended to be so ill organised that they were of little value as allies.[34] At two points, however, the military narrative is interrupted, and information is given in considerable detail about the kingdoms then at war, Odrysian Thrace and Macedonia. The section on the former supplies a full account of its extent, prosperity and financial organisation

[32] Although neither geographical nor antiquarian, the information given in 3.68.3 about the buildings and dedications on the site of Plataea after the city had been destroyed may be noted here. It is not perhaps wholly irrelevant but seems unnecessarily detailed.

[33] Cf. K. Ziegler, *Rhein Mus.* lxxviii (1929), 58. Gomme, op. cit., ii. 241, is inclined to accept this view with some qualification.

[34] Cf. Aristoph. *Acharn.* 134–73.

(97).[35] This analysis, though bearing a superficial resemblance to many ethnographical passages in Herodotus, shows a more penetrating and scientific understanding of the economic factors upon which military power was based.[36] The section on Macedonia traces the progress of Macedonian expansion through the expulsion of neighbouring tribes over a long period dating back to the foundation of the monarchy (99.2–6). These two sections, which show that Macedonia was a more unified kingdom than Odrysian Thrace because of its policy of expelling conquered tribes, help to explain why Sitalces was able to mobilise a vast army and yet accomplish so little. This point could, however, have been established much more briefly. Thucydides evidently welcomed the opportunity of instructing his readers about an area on which he was himself a specialist. Both inside and outside the two sections there are notes on districts beyond the boundaries of Thrace and Macedonia. One of these notes is concerned with the Scyths: Thucydides comments that their military resources were much superior to those of the Thracians and that they could, if united, have proved irresistible but were handicapped by their lack of εὐβουλία and ξύνεσις (97.5.–6).[37] This comment is the most irrelevant section of a passage containing a remarkable amount of digression.

The next major episode in the north-east was the mission of Brasidas, of which Thucydides gives a very full account. In it he includes some notes on topics somewhat tenuously connected with his narrative. Before describing the fall of Amphipolis he inserts a brief historical sketch of the three attempts to establish a Greek settlement there (4.102.2–3). Attached to this sketch is some topographical detail which helps the reader to understand the ensuing narrative. On the other hand, the historical material, especially the references to the two abortive attempts to found a colony, is not strictly relevant here,[38] even though it shows that the site of Amphipolis was considered to be an attractive one for colonisation. Much of it has already been included

---

[35] The section might be deemed to begin at 96.3.

[36] J. de Romilly, *Thucydide* ii¹ (Budé, 1962), xxxix–xl.

[37] Gomme, op. cit., ii. 245–6, is probably right in rejecting the view that Thucydides is here criticising Herodotus.

[38] Sieveking, who examines the passage in detail (op. cit., 113–19), has to acknowledge that the reasons why Thucydides includes it can only be guessed.

in the major excursus on the Pentecontaetia (1.100.3), where it is much more appropriate. An exceptional feature of these notes is that the events to which they refer belong to the fifth century and not to the distant past.

After the fall of Amphipolis, Brasidas made an expedition to the peninsula of Acte with the intention of winning over the small towns there (4.109.1). The outcome of this unimportant and not wholly successful expedition is recorded in one short sentence (109.5), which is preceded by a much longer passage consisting of geographical and ethnographical notes on Acte. They include some very interesting but totally irrelevant information about its extraordinarily mixed population (109.2–4). Of the six small towns listed by Thucydides (109.3) only three are mentioned again by him, Sane in a document quoted verbatim (5.18.6) and Thyssus and Dium in brief historical notes (5.35.1; 82.1).[39] Finally, his narrative on the revolt of Scione is prefixed by a reference to a local tradition that the city was founded by Pelleneans from the Peloponnese, whose ships were driven there by the celebrated storm which inflicted so much damage upon the Greeks returning homewards from Troy (4.120.1). He normally names the mother-city when mentioning a colony, and this practice can hardly be deemed to involve irrelevance, since often the link between a colony and its mother-city influenced the course of history centuries after its foundation.[40] Here, however, he provides more detail than usual, presumably because the circumstances leading to the foundation of Scione, though entirely unconnected with its revolt in 423, seemed to him to be especially interesting.[41]

[39] He was evidently familiar with the description of Acte by Herodotus (7.22.2–3) and may, as Sieveking, op. cit., 173, suggests, have been prompted thereby to produce a more accurate version, though in fact the differences are slight. Two further suggestions are made by Sieveking, loc. cit., namely that the catalogue of towns shows how successful Brasidas was and that the reference to the mixture of population explains why resistance was slight: both are unsound, since Brasidas failed to reduce Sane and Dium (109.5–110.1) which seem to have been among the more important of the six towns.

[40] A. J. Graham, *Colony and Mother City in Ancient Greece* (1964), 9–12, concludes that Thucydides was not exceptional among his contemporaries in believing in the importance of these relations.

[41] In 4.107.3 he refers to the death of an Edonian king at the hands of conspirators including his own wife. This event was apparently advantageous to Brasidas in causing the town of Myrcinus to join him, but Thucydides

16

(v) *Delos*

Four passages concerning Delos, two being from the first half of the *History* and two from the second half, may conveniently be considered together at this point, because a distinction of some significance may be drawn between the two pairs. The first passage of the first pair is concerned with the purification of Delos by the Athenians at the end of 426 and their institution of a quadrennial festival there. It amounts to a minor excursus (3.104). The measures taken to purify the island are described rather briefly, but Thucydides also refers to its associations with the tyrants Peisistratus and Polycrates (104.1–2). He then proceeds to discuss at some length the great Ionian festival held there long ago, which had to a large extent been discontinued; he explains that the Athenians were in effect restoring it, with additions, when they established their quadrennial festival (104.3–6). In order to substantiate his information about the old Ionian festival he quotes as evidence two passages, amounting together to thirteen lines, from the *Homeric Hymn to Apollo.* His only reference to the motives of the Athenians in purifying Delos in 426 is remarkably brief and vague: he notes merely that the decision was taken 'because of a certain oracle' (104.1).[42] It is very probable that the purification of the island and the revival and extension of the Ionian festival were to a large extent acts of political propaganda; that the Athenians by claiming to be the heirs and preservers of old Ionian traditions sought to justify and reinforce their domination of the Ionian cities.[43] Thucydides, who is fond of putting ideas into the minds of his readers by various subtle means, perhaps intends to suggest here that political issues connected with the war were involved. He does not, however, expressly link the actions of the Athenians with contemporary events, and most of the passage is devoted

---

perhaps mentions it, and names the very obscure persons involved, largely because of its dramatic character. One is reminded of the similar story about the murder of Alexander of Pherae told in much greater detail by Xenophon (*Hell.* 6.4.35–37).

[42] κατὰ χρησμὸν δή τινα, where δή seems to suggest that in his view the Athenians were too much influenced by superstition.

[43] Gomme, op. cit., ii. 414, makes the excellent point that 'the opportunity was taken to assert Athenian interest in Apollo, who at Delphi seemed now almost exclusively Peloponnesian and Dorian'.

to antiquarian discussion on the history of Delos and its festival in the more or less distant past.[44] On the other hand, Diodorus (12.58.6), doubtless following Ephorus, adopts a totally different viewpoint: he reports that the Athenians undertook the purification to placate the gods, who were believed to have been responsible for the plague. A similar disagreement with the version of Diodorus may be noted in the second passage about Delos from the first half of the *History*, which records the expulsion of the Delians from their island by the Athenians in 422 (5.1). Thucydides ascribes the Athenian action to religious motives, which are carefully explained, whereas Diodorus (12.73.1) states that the Delians were charged with negotiating a secret alliance with Sparta.

Both references to the Delians in the second half of the *History* are expressly linked with the war. In 421 the Athenians restored the Delians to their homes: Thucydides explains that this reversal of policy was due partly to uneasiness arising from military defeats and partly to a Delphic oracle (5.32.1). The last passage about the Delians is a reference back to an incident which occurred while they were living at Atramyttium in Aeolis after their banishment by the Athenians (8.108.4–5). In 411 the Antandrians with Peloponnesian assistance expelled from their acropolis the troops commanded by a Persian officer named Arsaces because of their distrust of him, which was largely due to his treacherous massacre of some Delians at Atramyttium some years earlier. This massacre is described more fully than is strictly necessary, and the passage is among the very few references in the eighth book to events of the past, even the recent past.[45] Nevertheless, the treachery of Arsaces in his treatment of the Delians does help to explain why the Antandrians enlisted the support of the Peloponnesians, thereby aggravating the already vexed relations between the latter and Tissaphernes.

Delos and the Delians were politically and militarily unimportant during the Peloponnesian war. It is, however, interesting, and not perhaps purely fortuitous, that in the two passages

---

[44] A. Heubeck, *Wien. Stud.* lxxix (1966), 148–57, examines the whole passage minutely. In my opinion he overrates (156) the extent to which it is designed to reflect the political aims of the Athenians, and he underrates the antiquarian element, which is substantial.

[45] See below, p. 31.

about them in the first half of his work Thucydides allows himself to discuss matters belonging to the history of religion, whereas in the two passages in the second half he takes pains to show that the information which he gives belongs to the history of the war.

(B) *Natural phenomena*

Because Thucydides was deeply influenced by his association with the intellectual movement of Periclean Athens, he recognised eclipses, earthquakes and eruptions as natural phenomena, rejecting the popular view that they were manifestations of divine power.[46]

Of the two eclipses mentioned in the first half of the *History* the first, which was solar, occurred in the summer of 431 (2.28). Thucydides gives some scientific details, probably based on autopsy, and states rather tentatively (δοκεῖ) that solar eclipses could take place only νουμηνίᾳ κατὰ σελήνην, which is true and was believed to have been the view of Anaxagoras.[47] This eclipse is also mentioned by Cicero and Plutarch, who describe how at first it aroused superstitious fears among the Athenian populace; these were later dispelled when Pericles gave a scientific explanation of it.[48] It is not the practice of Thucydides to include picturesque anecdotes of this kind, but Athenian morale, especially in the first years of the war, is a subject to which he devotes much attention, evidently considering it to be a factor of great importance.[49] When mentioning the eclipse, he could well have referred to its effect on morale. He does not, however, link it with the war at all and chooses to regard it purely as a physical phenomenon worthy of mention because of its scientific interest. His treatment of the second eclipse, also solar, which occurred in the early spring of 424, is similar, though briefer (4.52.1). It is mentioned in the same sentence as an

[46] A passage referring to the prevalence of earthquakes and eclipses during the war (1.23.3) might possibly be thought to point to the opposite conclusion. There is, however, some lack of clarity here, and, since Thucydides is normally contemptuous of anything verging on superstition (cf. 7.50.4), he is probably reporting public opinion and not expressing his own views (Gomme, op. cit., i. 151).

[47] Cic. *Rep.* 1.16.25, cf. Plut. *Nic.* 23.3.
[48] Cic. loc. cit.; Plut. *Per.* 35.2, cf. Val. Max. 8.11 ext. 1.
[49] Cf. 2.59.1–2; 65.2 and 9; 3.3.1.

earthquake, neither being associated in any way with the war.[50] The only eclipse mentioned in the second half of the *History* is the famous eclipse of the moon in August 413 which led to the postponement of the Athenian withdrawal from Syracuse, thereby influencing the fate of the whole expeditionary force (7.50.4) and indirectly endangering the existence of the Athenian state.

The significance of this evidence on eclipses must not be exaggerated. It appears that in the period covered by the first half of the *History* there occurred three solar and seven lunar eclipses visible in Greece, in the period covered by the second half two solar and ten lunar eclipses.[51] Doubtless some of these were not observed by the Greeks, but one, to which Thucydides does not refer, certainly was, and it belongs to the period covered by the first half of the *History*. This was a total eclipse of the moon in 425, which is mentioned by Aristophanes[52] and can hardly have been unknown to Thucydides. Hence it cannot be maintained that when, writing the first half of the *History*, Thucydides felt himself to be under an obligation to record as a noteworthy event every eclipse known to him. It must also be pointed out that in his only reference in the second half of the *History* to an eclipse, the momentous lunar eclipse of 413, he adds a few words of scientific explanation (7.50.4, ἐτύγχανε γὰρ πασσέληνος οὖσα). The fact remains, however, that the first half contains two notes in which eclipses are reported as natural phenomena, whereas the second half does not contain any notes of the same kind.

References to earthquakes, which are more numerous than references to eclipses, are also instructive in suggesting some change of outlook. An earthquake might influence the course of the war either by causing damage which affected military

---

[50] There is a reference to the same eclipse in Aristoph. *Clouds* 584–6, where the sun is said to have threatened not to appear again to the Athenians if they elected Cleon strategos.

[51] F. K. Ginzel, *Handbuch der mathematischen und technischen Chronologie* ii (1911), 526 (solar) and 537–8 (lunar). Similar but not identical figures are given in the same author's earlier work, which seems to be more easily accessible, *Spezieller Kannon der Sonnen und Mondfinsternisse* (1899), 58–9 (solar) and 137 (lunar).

[52] *Clouds* 584 with schol. It occurred about six months before the solar eclipse mentioned in the same passage (above n. 50).

operations or, as happened much more frequently, by arousing superstitious fears which led to the cancellation or modification of military plans or political discussions. Whereas in both halves of the *History* Thucydides mentions the effect of earthquakes upon the course of the war, it is only in the first half that he shows unmistakable scientific interest in them as natural phenomena. Of the three references in the first half the earliest is to an earthquake which occurred at Delos shortly before the war began (2.8.3).[53] He notes that it 'was said and thought' to foreshadow coming events. Although he expresses himself very cautiously here, it is scarcely credible that he can himself have subscribed to this superstitious view. On the other hand, the popular reaction to the earthquake contributed to the general tension throughout Greece which he is describing (2.8.1–3), so that he evidently considered it to have been historically significant.[54] The next reference is not to a single earthquake but to a whole series. They occurred in the winter of 427/26 and in the following spring at various places on the mainland of central Greece and on islands near the coast (3.87.4; 89.1–5). The earthquakes in the spring of 426 influenced the military situation by causing the Peloponnesian army assembled at the isthmus for an invasion of Attica to be disbanded (89.1). Thucydides proceeds, however, after mentioning the cancellation of this expedition, to describe at far greater length the effect of the earthquakes, and of the tidal waves caused by them, upon several insignificant places of little or no military importance (89.2–4). He adds his own explanation of the connection between the earthquakes and the tidal waves (89.5), which shows that his interest in them is mainly scientific. A further earthquake in the spring of 424 is mentioned with a solar eclipse which immediately preceded it (4.52.1), as was noted above; there is no suggestion that it influenced military or political events.

In the second half of the *History* Thucydides refers to five earthquakes. All five had at least some influence upon the course of events, and it is evidently for this reason that he

[53] The great earthquake at Sparta in 464 must be excluded because it occurred so long before the outbreak of war in a period on which Thucydides writes very briefly (1.101.2, cf. 1.128.1 and 2.27.2).

[54] It may be that in stating that this was the first recorded earthquake at Delos he was correcting a passage in Herodotus (6.98.1–3).

mentions them and not because of their scientific interest. The first occurred in 420; it caused a meeting of the Athenian assembly to be adjourned at which Alcibiades played his celebrated trick upon envoys from Sparta (5.45.4). The second led to the abandonment of negotiations in the same year at Corinth in which rival missions from the Argive alliance and from Sparta were taking part (5.50.5). The third brought about the withdrawal of a Spartan army sent to attack Argos in 414 when it had already reached Cleonae and was evidently about to march down into the Argive plain (6.95.1). The fourth was responsible for a change of plan on the part of the Spartans in 412; presumably on the recommendation of soothsayers consulted because of the earthquake, they cancelled their decision to send ten ships to Chios under their *nauarchos* Melanchridas and prepared to send five ships later under Chalcideus (8.6.5). It is only in the fifth and last instance that there is any mention of material damage caused by an earthquake, and here it affected military operations. In the winter of 412/11 when the Peloponnesian forces in Asia under the leadership of Astyochus sacked Cos, their task was made easier because the town was unwalled and had recently been devastated by an earthquake. The population sought refuge in the mountains (8.41.2). Thucydides notes that the earthquake was the most violent of any known to him. This observation may have been prompted by scientific interest, but he seems concerned to make clear that, in view of the circumstances which played into the hands of Astyochus and the Peloponnesians, their reduction of Cos to submission did not deserve much credit as a military achievement.[55]

Thucydides mentions only one volcanic eruption, and, so far as is known, no others occurred during the Peloponnesian war. Hence it is not possible to adopt the same comparative method as has been applied to his references to eclipses and earthquakes. Nevertheless, his note on an eruption of Etna which took place early in 425 and so is recorded in the first half of his work (3.116.1–2), does not contain information relevant to the war but is purely seismological. He states that Catana suffered damage to its agricultural land, that the preceding eruption was said to have occurred fifty years earlier and that there were

[55] The unfavourable presentation of Astyochus is discussed in *Individuals in Thucydides*, 290–307.

believed to have been three eruptions since the Greek colonisation of Sicily.[56] He may well have consulted a member of the
Athenian expeditionary force operating in Sicily when the eruption of 425 took place, but there is no suggestion that it affected
the course of the campaign there in any way.[57]

(C) *Biographical information and anecdote*

Thucydides certainly does not underestimate the influence of
leading individuals upon the course of history, and there is at
least a case for believing that he sets more store by this influence
in the second half of his work than in the first.[58] In both halves,
however, he is normally rigorous in excluding biographical detail.[59]
In some of the major excursuses, where he is writing about great
men of the past, he allows the personal element to play a prominent role,[60] but he gives no information about the private
lives or personal habits of contemporary leaders unless, as in the
case of Alcibiades (6.15.3-4), political or military situations
were manifestly affected thereby. Although information of this
kind must have been accessible in abundance to Thucydides, he
doubtless discarded it because he felt it to be inconsistent with
his aims in a work which, unlike those of others such as Herodotus and the gossip writers Ion and Stesimbrotus, was to provide
not entertainment but instruction.

There is perhaps only one passage in the *History* in which
Thucydides permits himself a considerable amount of biographical detail, much of it not strictly necessary in the context,
about a contemporary leader. This passage, which might be
classed as a minor excursus, belongs to the first half of the
History. Its subject is the exile and restoration of the Spartan

---

[56] The note is somewhat carelessly written and lacks precision (Steup,
n. ad loc.). It seems to have been jotted down hastily and never revised.

[57] Interest in natural phenomena is also shown in a very brief note on
spontaneous forest fires, containing an explanation of their origin, which is
inserted in the account of the siege operations at Plataea in 429 (2.77.4).

[58] This theme is the principal conclusion of my *Individuals in Thucydides*.

[59] Cf. the illuminating comments by Gomme, op. cit., i. 26-8, cited above,
p. 2 n.5.

[60] Especially in the excursuses on Cylon, Pausanias and Themistocles and
on the Peisistratidae, but parts of the excursus on the Pentecontaetia have an
almost equally personal colouring, cf. below, pp. 48-51.

king Pleistoanax, the son of Pausanias (5.16.1–17.1);[61] and it is inserted to explain why, when the Peace of Nicias was being negotiated, Pleistoanax was its principal advocate on the Spartan side. He felt that, if peace were concluded, he would no longer be subjected to attacks by his personal enemies, who held him responsible for Spartan failures in the war: for he was alleged to have secured his restoration by dishonest and impious means, thereby exposing Sparta to divine anger (16.1–3). While it is characteristic of Thucydides to seek to account for the eagerness of Pleistoanax to bring about the conclusion of peace with Athens, the explanation has some very exceptional features. The motives attributed to Pleistoanax, and also to the more famous leaders mentioned here—Cleon, Brasidas and Nicias—are unusually personal, indeed egoistical (16.1).[62] It is even more remarkable that the passage continues with a report on the chequered career of Pleistoanax containing a number of interesting and picturesque details which have not much relevance and are Herodotean rather than Thucydidean in tone. These include a paraphrase of the oracle leading to his restoration, a note that the house in which he lived during his exile lay partly within a sanctuary of Zeus, and a reference to the similarity between the ceremonies at his reinstatement and those performed when the Spartan kingship was first established (16.2–3). No passage of Thucydides outside the major excursuses strikes quite the same note,[63] and it is strange that its subject is a man whose influence upon the course of the war was apparently, except on this one occasion, almost negligible.[64]

In the summer of 423 the Argive Heraeum was destroyed by a

[61] The circumstances in which he was banished are mentioned briefly, and independently, in 1.114.2 and 2.21.1 (where the parenthetical reference to his banishment and to the charge brought against him is an irrelevant note).

[62] The treatment of Nicias in this passage is surprising for other reasons as well, cf. *Individuals in Thucydides*, 93–6.

[63] It is a plausible guess that the personal information about Pleistoanax is derived from the same source as the personal information about his father Pausanias in the first book. The source could have been Pleistoanax himself. On pp. 58–9 below, I have suggested that Thucydides completed his research on the career of Pausanias during the early years of his exile and used Peloponnesian sources.

[64] That much of 5.15–17 is the work of an interpolator has been argued by Steup in an elaborate appendix (*Anhang* 249–53). His arguments are rightly rejected by Gomme, op. cit., iii. 665–6. The passage is, however, somewhat

24

fire accidentally caused by Chrysis the elderly priestess, who at once fled through fear of the consequences, thereby vacating her office after a long tenure (4.133.2–3). Modern scholars have been interested in this passage mainly because it is deemed to throw some light upon the relationship between Thucydides and Hellanicus, who, as has already been noted,[65] wrote a chronographical work entitled *Priestesses of Hera at Argos*.[66] It is true that an earlier reference to Chrysis is purely chronological (2.2.1) and that here Thucydides mentions that her tenure of office included eight and a half years of the war. He would, however, hardly have recorded so graphically the circumstances in which she ceased to be priestess if his interest in the episode had been confined to its relevance to chronology. Nor should its inclusion be attributed to the fact that it occurred during the year of truce when there was not much else to record.[67] Thucydides did not fill his *History* with padding. The story about Chrysis has an almost journalistic flavour.

A few passages of a more or less anecdotic character are attached to military narratives in the first half of the *History*. An example is the story that, when the Athenians withdrew from their raid on Corinthian territory in 425, they failed to find the bodies of two men killed in action; later they went to the length of negotiating a truce in order to recover the two bodies (4.44.5–6).[68] Another passage which is virtually an anecdote, though it might be thought to shed a little light upon a leading character, describes how Brasidas dedicated to Athena a reward promised to the first man to scale the wall of a fortified position at Torone. He took this action because the collapse of some defence works, which led to its capture, seemed to have been caused by superhuman agency (4.116.2). More significant perhaps are two accounts of conversations between unnamed persons who do not seem to have held any high office. The first conversation is between an Ambraciot herald and

lacking in coherence: it gives the impression of having been hastily put together and never fully integrated.

[65] See above, p. 5.

[66] Widely differing conclusions have been drawn from the passage about Chrysis: cf. Pearson, *Local Historians*, 42; Dover, *Maia* vi. 4; Jacoby, *F. Gr. Hist.*, iii b Suppl. i (1954), 5.

[67] It is strange to find this suggestion made by Gomme, op. cit., iii. 624.

[68] Plutarch (*Nic.* 6.5–7) uses the story to illustrate the piety of Nicias.

c

someone, presumably an Athenian,[69] at the camp of Demosthenes after the two Ambraciot defeats in Amphilochia in the winter of 426/25 (3.113.1–5). The second is between one of the Spartans who had surrendered on Sphacteria and someone from a city allied to Athens (4.40.2). Neither anecdote is wholly irrelevant. Both throw some light upon factors of importance to which Thucydides wishes to draw the attention of his readers: these are the extreme severity of the Ambraciot losses (3.113.6) and the shocked reaction throughout Greece to the surrender of the Spartans, who were expected to fight to the death(4.40.1). It is, however, very remarkable that Thucydides in these two instances introduces comment on past events in the form of private and unofficial conversations which have a tinge of colloquial gossip.

A passage in the second half of the *History* which might at first glance appear to belong to the same category occurs in the account of the manœuvres preceding the battle of Mantinea in 418. When Agis was on the point of engaging the Argives drawn up in a very strong position, an elderly Spartan shouted out a comment which amounted to censure of his generalship. Thereupon Agis hastily withdrew his army without making contact with the enemy (5.65.2). Thucydides, confessing ignorance of the reason for this last-minute reversal of plan, suggests that Agis may either have been convinced by the shouted criticism or have independently changed his mind in the same direction (65.3). This incident is not, however, reported merely to lend colour to the narrative. Thucydides is evidently quoting all the evidence available to him on a disputable point of considerable importance, and if the first of his two explanations is accepted, the remark of the elderly Spartan may well have influenced the outcome of a campaign which was vital to Spartan interests.[70]

[69] Cf. N. G. L. Hammond, *Epirus* (1967), 503, who maintains, convincingly in my opinion, that Thucydides did not visit this area.

[70] Steup, n. ad loc., has suggested with good reason that this Spartan was one of the ten commissioners who had been appointed to advise Agis because of the outcry against him for agreeing to a truce at an earlier stage of the campaign (63.4). If so, the shout of protest amounted to official advice. Part of the Spartan army, including the older and younger men, had been sent home from Orestheum (64.3). Hence, although some older men are later found defending the Spartan camp (72.3), it is difficult to understand why τῶν πρεσβυτέρων τις (65.2) was within hailing distance of Agis unless he were a member of the commission.

26

Many anecdotes relating to the Athenian expedition to Sicily must have been current when Thucydides was writing his account of it, and indeed some have been preserved by other authorities. According to Plutarch (*Nic.* 19.4), when Gylippus, on arriving at Syracuse, offered the Athenians a truce on condition that they withdrew at once from Sicily, Nicias did not deign to reply, but some soldiers gave the herald a scornful and insulting answer which is reported in full. Thucydides, on the other hand, states only that the Athenians treated the offer with contempt and sent the herald away unanswered (7.3.2). A similar contrast may be noted in the treatment of other events by Plutarch and Thucydides, including the arrival at Athens of the news that the Athenian forces in Sicily had been annihilated. Plutarch (*Nic.* 30.1–3)[71] tells a characteristically colourful story describing how the first report reached Athens through a stranger who, after landing at the Piraeus, began to talk about the disaster in a barber's shop there, assuming that it was already known; the barber rushed up to Athens with the news, where he was questioned and eventually tortured because he was unable to give a satisfactory account of what he had learned. Thucydides, after mentioning briefly that the Athenians remained incredulous even when reports were brought by survivors of the expedition, proceeds to give a detailed and penetrating analysis of Athenian reactions to the situation created by the disaster (8.1.1–3). Anecdotes recorded by Plutarch and other late authors but not by Thucydides are not necessarily apocryphal; some are doubtless derived ultimately from Philistus.[72] Such stories may well have been known to Thucydides but are not found in the *History* because, however attractive they might have been to the reader, they did not seem to him to be essential to the narrative or to illustrate any factor in the situation to which he wished to draw attention.[73]

[71] Plutarch gives a more detailed version in *Mor.* (*De garrulitate*) 509 a–c.

[72] Plutarch cites Philistus twice in the *Nicias* (19.6; 28.5) and probably made direct use of his work, cf. Jacoby, *F. Gr. Hist.*, iii b Komm. (1955), 502 and 512. That the Sicilian tradition included personal detail not recorded by Thucydides is suggested by fragments of Timaeus, cf. *F. Gr. Hist.*, 566 F 100 for gossip about Gylippus.

[73] In 6.104.2 it is noted that the father of Gylippus had become a citizen of Thurii. The point is relevant, since Gylippus evidently hoped that the association between the Thurians and his father would cause them to support

II THE SECOND HALF

Passages in the second half of the *History* referring to topics not directly connected with the war are so few that they may most conveniently be considered in the order in which they appear. In hardly any instances does information seem to have been given solely because of its inherent interest.

The disturbed situation in Greece, and especially in the Peloponnese, in the period after the Peace of Nicias gave rise to a long series of negotiations and disputes which Thucydides records in some detail. In three passages describing contemporary relations between Greek states he refers to events of the past—in two cases the distant past—which affected these relations. He accounts for the hostility of Elis towards Sparta in 421 by referring to relations between the Eleans and their neighbours the Lepreates in the past. Some time ago (ποτε) an agreement has been concluded between the two states in circumstances which are explained. When after the outbreak of the Archidamian war a dispute arose in regard to this agreement, Sparta arbitrated in favour of the Lepreates and sent a military force to protect them, thus incurring Elean resentment (5.31.1–5). The date of the agreement with Lepreum cannot be accurately dated, but it probably belongs to the middle of the fifth century.[74] Thucydides evidently felt that, if the decision of the Eleans to break away from the Peloponnesian League and to join the Argive coalition was to be fully understood, their feud with Sparta must be traced back to its origin.

The second reference to the past occurs in a passage reporting an extraordinary proposal by some Argive envoys at Sparta in the summer of 420. They were willing to conclude a peace treaty for fifty years but stipulated that, subject to certain conditions, either side should be entitled to challenge the other to a battle with agreed rules for a disputed frontier-district 'as on a previous occasion when both sides claimed to be victorious' (5.41.2). This phrase refers to an episode fully described by Herodotus (1.82.3–6) when three hundred Argives fought three hundred

---

him. No additional details are given, though the circumstances in which Cleandridas became an exile from Sparta and migrated to Thurii must have been known to Thucydides (cf. 2.21.1).

[74] F. Bölte, *R.E.* vii A (1939) 197–8; F. Kiechle, *Historia* ix (1960), 21 n. 3.

Spartans: its date seems to be about 550.[75] This contest was undoubtedly mentioned by the Argive envoys, and there may well have been a reference to it in the draft agreement to which the Spartans, after first dismissing the proposal as absurdly archaic, eventually gave their consent. A third reference to the past immediately follows the second. In the same summer the Boeotians, when compelled by Spartan pressure to comply with a demand for the restoration of the border-town of Panactum to the Athenians, claimed to be justified in having destroyed it before handing it over on the pretext that long ago both parties had sworn to leave the site unoccupied (5.42.1). The agreement cited by the Boeotians, though its date is very uncertain, was probably concluded towards the close of the sixth century.[76]

In the second and third of these passages Thucydides is reporting references to events of the past by one of the parties involved, and he may well be doing the same in the first passage, since the Eleans must have reviewed the history of their grievance against Sparta while conducting negotiations at Corinth and Argos (5.31.1).[77] In none of these three passages does he mention historical events of earlier times merely because he found them interesting and expected them to interest his readers.[78]

The narrative of the great Athenian expedition to Sicily is magnificently relevant.[79] Hardly any notes are included on topics

[75] V. Ehrenberg, *R.E.* xviii (1942), 1871–2.

[76] K. J. Beloch, *Klio* xi (1911), 438–9, seems to be right in maintaining that the agreement must be assigned to a date before Plataea first became an ally of Athens. Unfortunately the date of that alliance is also uncertain. If the evidence of Thucydides (3.68.5) is accepted, its date is 519, but the text is somewhat suspect (cf. Gomme, op. cit., ii. 358, who denies that the passage is corrupt). E. Kirsten, *R.E.* xx (1950), 2284–6, defends the traditional dating, but A. French, *J.H.S.* lxxx (1960), 191, rejects it on the ground that the Peisistratidae are unlikely to have made such an alliance.

[77] In Greek diplomatic exchanges references to relations in the past between states involved in disputes were very common, as may be seen from many Thucydidean speeches: for example, those of the Corcyrean and Corinthian envoys at Athens (1.32–43).

[78] At the Olympic festival of 420 the owner of a winning chariot-team was disqualified, after being assaulted by the stewards, on the ground that as a Spartan he had no right to compete (5.50.4). The incident well illustrates the tension arising from the antagonism of the Eleans towards Sparta, but it is perhaps described with more wealth of graphic detail than is strictly essential.

[79] The two major excursuses in the sixth book and the reasons for their inclusion have been briefly discussed above, p. 5.

not directly connected with the course of the war.[80] An account of an Athenian raid on the neighbourhood of Sicilian Megara in the spring of 414 begins with a statement that the Syracusans had expelled its inhabitants in the time of Gelon (6.94.1). Thucydides here inserts a cross-reference to a passage in his major excursus at the beginning of the sixth book where the expulsion of the Megarians has already been mentioned (6.4.2). He evidently wishes to remind his readers that no town of Megara existed at the time of the Athenian raid and that the district belonged to Syracuse.[81] A passage in the seventh book describes how nine hundred hoplites from Sparta and Boeotia, who had sailed for Sicily in the early spring of 413 on merchant ships by the direct route over the open sea, found themselves in Libya and after a series of adventures there finally landed at Selinus in the late summer (7.50.1-2, cf. 19.3-4). They were troops of high quality, and the military situation at Syracuse must have been affected first by their long delay in reaching their destination and then by their eventual arrival in time to play a part in the last stages of the struggle. It must, however, be acknowledged that their experiences in Libya are recorded more fully than is necessary. On the other hand, Thucydides confines his account to these experiences: he includes no information on Libyan geography or ethnology, though the area was one of great interest to most Greeks, nor does he explain the origin of the war between the Libyans and the Euhesperitans. A reference to the frequency of thunderstorms in late summer, which occurs in his account of the Athenian withdrawal from Syracuse (7.79.3), is not inserted because of his interest in natural phenomena but in order to make the point that the superstitious fears of the despondent Athenians, who felt that divine powers were seeking their destruction, was based upon ignorance.[82]

Two passages of some length in the seventh book (27.3-28 and 57-58) are digressive in that they interrupt the continuity of the narrative, but they are not excursuses in the sense in which the term is used in this paper. The substance of both passages is entirely relevant to the war and indeed of great value in

---

[80] On the absence of anecdote see above, p. 27.

[81] As Dover points out (n. on 94.2), Thucydides seems to have forgotten his reference in 75.1 to a Syracusan φρούριον on the site of Megara.

[82] A somewhat similar point is made in 6.70.1.

helping the reader to understand its development. The first
(27.3–28) discusses the difficulties, mainly financial, in which the
Athenians became involved through the occupation of Decelea.[83]
It looks back to the Archidamian war and forward to the period
after the Athenian disaster in Sicily. Its abruptness and compression, which lead to some lack of clarity, may well have arisen
partly because the focus of attention is on Sicily. The second
passage (57–58) is the catalogue of the forces fighting on each
side in the final struggle at Syracuse. It is inserted, doubtless
for dramatic reasons, at the point at which all the contingents
of allies had arrived (59.1), and it explains how each contingent
came to be supporting the Athenians or the Syracusans, in some
cases against their own kin. Although perhaps somewhat rhetorical, it is not at all irrelevant.[84]

The eighth book is a detailed record of events written, it
appears, soon after they occurred[85] and subsequently, for some
reason, left unaltered. It looks neither backwards nor forwards
but concentrates upon the task, not always successfully accomplished, of guiding the reader through an obscure, complex and
rapidly changing period. It contains no excursuses of any kind
and only a minute number of passages providing information
which is not strictly relevant.[86] One of these occurs in a discussion
of Chian policy in 412 (8.24.3–5), where Thucydides attributes
the prosperity of the island to its immunity from devastation
ever since the Persian wars and to wise government during a
long period of peaceful development. The purpose of this discussion is to establish that, although the Chians were hard pressed
by the Athenians, their decision to revolt had not been foolhardy.
It is not altogether clear why he chooses to make this emphatic
defence of the Chians against charges of rashness which might be,

---

[83] The passage is analysed by H. Erbse, *Rhein. Mus.* xcvi (1953), 38–46; see
also Dover, n. ad loc.

[84] It may well have been added at or after the end of the Peloponnesian
war (Dover, n. ad loc.) to a narrative which was probably completed, apart
from minor revisions, some years earlier.

[85] F. E. Adcock, *Thucydides and his History* (1963), 84–8, maintains that it
was completed not later than 410.

[86] Pearson, *Local Historians*, 47, makes the excellent point that in this book
Thucydides mentions Colonus (67.2) and the fortifications of the Piraeus
(90.4–5) without adding notes on mythology in the case of the former or on
earlier history in the case of the latter.

and perhaps already had been, brought against them. Yet, whatever his reason may have been, his reference to their past record of prosperity and wisdom is a natural prelude to his argument. Another brief reference to the period of the Persian wars seems to be entirely irrelevant: when describing how in the spring of 411 the Athenians made Sestos their operational headquarters in the Hellespont, he mentions that the Persians once held it (62.3).[87] A note on the massacre of some Delians at Atramyttium has already been discussed.[88]

III CONCLUSION

The foregoing survey of irrelevant notes and minor excursuses, if it has any validity, does seem to have established that such material is far more abundant in the first half of the *History* than in the second. This difference between the two halves is one of sufficient importance to call for some investigation of its origin, which will now be considered. Can some satisfactory explanation of it be offered which does not involve concluding that Thucydides has modified his criteria in the selection of subject-matter? Or does it point to a modest but not inconsiderable change in his interpretation of his function as a historian?

One factor to which this difference might appear to be attributable is the following. During the period of a little less than five years covered by the sixth, seventh and eighth books of the *History* the tempo of war became greatly accelerated. Military operations were more continuous and tended to be on a larger scale and to have more unity than those of the Archidamian war. In these books, therefore, Thucydides might be expected to confine himself strictly to his central theme and to be disinclined to touch on topics not directly connected with it, however interesting he might find them; in the first half, on the other hand, he cannot have felt himself under the same pressure.

[87] Possibly Thucydides, who in this book does not always indicate the sequence of thought very clearly, may mean that the Sestians, remembering the former occupation of their city by the Persians, could be trusted not to revolt because they might fall into the hands of the Persian satrap Pharnabazus, now supporting the Peloponnesians in this area (62.1).

[88] See above, p. 18. A note that the Cnidian promontory of Triopium was a sanctuary of Apollo (35.2) may well have been added in order to help the reader to locate it (cf. 1.29.3 and 7.26.2, where temples of Apollo are mentioned for this reason).

This explanation is almost entirely unacceptable. It is indeed true that in the Archidamian war the defensive strategy adopted by the Athenians on land and by the Spartans at sea tended to reduce military operations to a series of isolated episodes, many of them brief and very few bringing into action more than a fraction of the armed forces which either side could mobilise. If, however, this feature of the Archidamian war has affected the extent to which irrelevant notes are introduced, it is strange to find several of them attached to accounts of episodes in the first half which are most fully reported, such as the missions of Demosthenes to the north-west and of Brasidas to the north-east. A much weightier objection is that the intensity with which the war was being waged was only a small element in determining the scale on which Thucydides chose to write about it. He was not a mere annalist, and the political, moral and legal issues raised by the war, as well as the general strategy of both sides, interested him at least as much as its military actions. It would be unjust to him, and even rather absurd, to suggest that he included irrelevant notes when he had little to report about the progress of the war and excluded them when he had plenty to report.[89] His practice in the first half of the *History* is to select for detailed treatment certain episodes which seemed to him to be especially important or instructive and to confine himself to essentials when recording the rest. Although sometimes hampered by the difficulty of obtaining trustworthy reports (1.22.2–3), he must, in common with other writers of contemporary history, have normally been embarrassed by the volume of information available to him and at almost every point have known much that he has chosen to omit. To cite a single example where there can be no doubt, he could certainly have included far more detail about the fall of Amphipolis, which he himself failed to prevent; and yet he prefixes to his account a note, which is largely irrelevant, on unsuccessful attempts long ago to establish a colony there.[90] Another reason, which is indeed rather obvious, may be added for rejecting the view that the second half of the *History* contains hardly any irrelevant material because the period covered by it was so packed with military action. In the latter part of the fifth book (25–116), which deals with the years of

[89] See above, p. 25 with n. 67.
[90] See above, pp. 15–16.

uneasy peace from 421 to 416, such material is as sparse as in the sixth, seventh and eighth books.

A different approach might be made by suggesting a combination of two explanations to account for the paucity of irrelevant notes throughout the entire second half of the *History*, the first explanation being applicable to the sixth and seventh books and the second to the latter part of the fifth book and to the eighth book. In the main narrative of the Athenian expedition to Sicily there might appear to be no place for irrelevant notes on geography and antiquarianism because information of this kind has already been included in the major excursus on Sicilian colonisation at the beginning of the sixth book (6.2–5). This argument is valid only to a very limited degree. The principal motive of Thucydides in inserting an account of barbarian and Greek settlements in Sicily is, as has already been noted,[91] with good reason thought to have been to challenge the generally accepted scheme of chronology by producing what he believed to be a more accurate scheme based on the work of the Syracusan historian Antiochus. The excursus contains few details about Sicilian geography. It dismisses briefly and contemptuously the traditions about the Cyclopes and the Laestrygonians, who were believed to have been the earliest inhabitants, as too shadowy to have any historical value (6.2.1). It is not concerned with Sicilian history in general but only with a single aspect of it during a limited period, namely the circumstances in which each site or area was occupied and, in a few cases, subsequently abandoned. Notes of the kind not uncommon in the first half of the *History* could well have been inserted in the main narrative of the sixth and seventh books without necessarily duplicating information already given in the excursus on barbarian and Greek settlements, and also, it may be added, without impairing the dramatic effectiveness of these books. The very brief passages on Sicily in the first half of the *History* afford a significant contrast, to which attention has already been drawn: they contain two geographical notes which have little relevance to their context, each including a mythological allusion,[92] and there is also a reference to an eruption of Etna.[93]

The latter part of the fifth book (25–116) and the eighth book have at least one feature in common. They are adjudged to be

[91] See above, p. 5.   [92] See above, pp. 7–8.   [93] See above, pp. 22–3.

inferior in quality to the rest of the *History*, an assessment almost universally accepted in modern times. The eighth book is palpably an unrevised draft. Whether the latter part of the fifth book is also an unrevised draft of a somewhat different kind, a provisional stop-gap linking more finished sections of the *History*, is a very large question, too large to be more than touched upon here.[94] To deal with it at all adequately would necessitate a general discussion of the old controversy, which has many offshoots, whether the *History* was written in stages over a long period or continuously in a relatively short period. Since, however, the latter part of the fifth book has been thought to be unrevised like the eighth book, the possibility must be considered that the sparsity of irrelevant material in both cases has the same origin, namely lack of revision. If the *History* passed through several stages of development, it is natural to believe that the speeches belong to a later stage, and their absence from the eighth book lends support to this view.[95] On the other hand, it is highly improbable that the irrelevant notes and minor excursuses are late additions. There can be little doubt that the information on natural phenomena not affecting the course of the war is based on records compiled at the time of their occurrence, and the few anecdotes are likely to have found their way into the *History* in the same manner. It is also difficult to believe that irrelevant material on geography and antiquarianism can have been introduced only at a late stage of composition. To imagine that Thucydides went over his *History* inserting here and there Herodotean passages designed to appeal to

[94] There is, in my opinion, no good reason to believe that Thucydides intended to rewrite this part of his work so as to give a much more detailed account of events during the years of uneasy peace. The scale on which he has reported these events seems to me to correspond with his estimate of their importance. He may, however, have been handicapped in one respect when he came to write his account of this period: because the war appeared to be ended and his *History* to be ended with it, he may well have discontinued his practice, adopted when the war began (1.1.1), of collecting evidence about each episode as it occurred. In a more limited sense there is a good case for believing the fifth book to be unrevised, namely that obscurity and confusion is more common than in any other part of the *History* apart from the eighth book.

[95] The statement of Cratippus, *F. Gr. Hist.*, 64 F 1, that Thucydides changed his mind about the appropriateness of including speeches is foolish and must be rejected, cf. A. W. Gomme, *C.Q.* iv (1954), 54-5.

readers who, like Dionysius of Halicarnassus,[96] found the narrative monotonous is an unconvincing and almost ludicrous hypothesis. Such passages are far more credibly assigned to a very early stage in the process of composition, especially as there is reason to think that before his banishment he conducted research into the past.[97] Accordingly it would not be valid to conclude that the fifth and eighth books contain hardly any irrelevant material because perhaps the former and certainly the latter has been preserved in the form of an unrevised draft.

Yet another explanation might be offered to account for the disparity between the first half and the second in the amount of irrelevant material included. It might be suggested that the irrelevant notes were in most cases contributed by informants who supplied Thucydides with the substance of the narrative in which these notes are found; and that informants from whom he obtained material for the first half of the *History* happened to be more inclined to include irrelevances in their reports than those from whom he obtained material for the second half. Such an explanation would be unconvincing. It would presuppose that his method of composition was to incorporate in the *History*, without much pruning on his part, the bulk of what each informant told him. He certainly did nothing of the kind. If the celebrated passage in which he defines his own methods is to be believed (1.22.1–3), he consulted large numbers of eyewitnesses drawn from both sides (cf. 5.26.5; 7.44.1), sifting and comparing their reports and fully recognising that oral evidence might be inaccurate. Furthermore, for the period before his banishment he was evidently able to use to a considerable extent the evidence of his own eyes and ears (cf. 1.22.1–2), which he valued more highly than reports from others; and yet most of his irrelevant notes are found in his account of this period. Thus, while possibly in a few instances such notes may have been incorporated in his text because they occurred in reports which he had compiled when questioning eyewitnesses, it is very difficult to believe that many can have had this origin.

Thucydides is contemptuous of logographers in general (1.21.1). He expressly criticises Hellanicus in the excursus on the

---

[96] *Ad Pomp.* 3.11–12, where (as noted above, p. 2 n. 5) he criticises Thucydides for lack of variety.

[97] See below, pp. 56–7.

Pentecontaetia (1.97.2) and seems to be tacitly criticising him in other major excursuses[98] and probably elsewhere.[99] Although he agrees with Herodotus on some controversial issues, he is thought to be correcting him in a number of passages,[100] and he differed fundamentally from him in his general approach towards the methods and aims of historical writing. Nevertheless, despite this attitude of contempt towards his predecessors and contemporaries, most of the irrelevant notes examined above are concerned with the very subjects with which these predecessors and contemporaries chose principally to deal, namely geography and mythology. Hence it may with some confidence be inferred that, when he wrote the first half of his *History* in which irrelevant notes are relatively abundant, his choice of what was appropriate for inclusion in a historical work was influenced in some degree by the tradition of Ionian ἱστορίη, perhaps unconsciously and doubtless more deeply than he would have been willing to admit. That this influence had almost disappeared when he wrote the second half of the *History* is suggested by the striking decline in the number of irrelevant notes. The principal reason for this change is perfectly clear; he had meanwhile made further progress in the direction of specialisation, which caused him to focus his attention even more closely than before upon the war and to resist any temptation to digress on other topics, however interesting he might find them.

An indication of the same development towards specialisation is also provided by the distribution of irrelevant notes on natural phenomena, to which attention has been drawn in the foregoing survey.[101] The interest shown by Thucydides in the scientific aspects of eclipses and earthquakes was doubtless kindled by the work of great physicists active in his youth, notably Anaxagoras, who was a close associate of Pericles.[102] The study of physics was a major preoccupation of intellectuals at

[98] See above, p. 5.

[99] O. Lendle, *Hermes* lxxxviii (1960), 38–40, and xcii (1964), 129–43.

[100] The clearest instance is 1.20.3 (cf. schol. ad loc.). Other passages are: 1.89.2 and 126.8; 2.8.3 and 97.6.

[101] See above, pp. 19–23.

[102] There is evidence that Anaxagoras studied eclipses (DK 59 A 42.9–10, A 77) and earthquakes (A 1.9, A 42.12, A 89). Democritus is known to have been interested in eclipses (DK 68 A 75) and earthquakes (A 97–8), and Archelaus in earthquakes (DK 60 A 16 a).

37

Athens in this period. Hence Socrates could be presented to a popular audience in the *Clouds* as primarily a physicist. Indeed Socrates declares in the *Phaedo* that as a young man he developed a passion for the subject,[103] though the historical accuracy of this statement may be doubted. The influence of the Sophists tended to stimulate intellectual study in other fields, but there is evidence that Antiphon was interested in eclipses and earthquakes.[104] In the first half of the *History* Thucydides includes a number of largely or wholly irrelevant notes on natural phenomena; in the second half his references to such phenomena are concerned only with their effect upon the course of the war. During his long exile he can have had few opportunities for contact with educated Athenians, and his taste for physical science, as for other subjects previously of interest to him,[105] may well have gradually faded because the stimulus of discussion with others brought up in the same intellectual climate was denied to him. Here again, however, the contrast between the first half of the *History* and the second is doubtless chiefly the outcome of even more rigorous concentration upon his main theme.[106]

[103] *Phaedo* 96 a, θαυμαστῶς ὡς ἐπεθύμησα ταύτης τῆς σοφίας ἣν δὴ καλοῦσι περὶ φύσεως ἱστορίαν.

[104] DK 87 B 28 (eclipses), B 30–1 (earthquakes).

[105] See above, pp. 5–6 with n. 14.

[106] Attention has often been drawn to the remarkable interest in, and knowledge of, medicine which Thucydides shows in his account of the Athenian plague (as well as to the influence of contemporary medicine upon his methods of historical investigation). The account of the plague belongs to the first half of the *History* (2.47–54), but to use it as evidence of his attitude towards his choice of subject-matter would be unwarranted, though there is a reference in the second half to sickness in the Athenian camp at Syracuse containing no mention of symptoms (7.47.2). The plague was an altogether exceptional event, and his account is equally exceptional. It has perhaps some affinity with his five major excursuses, and there is at least a possibility that it has an element of controversy (2.48.3).

I am deeply indebted to Mr D. M. Leahy for valuable criticism of this essay when it was in draft.

2

Thucydides and the Pentekontaetia

It was at one time almost universally believed, and is still believed by some scholars,[1] that Thucydides cannot have written his account of the Pentekontaetia (1.89–118.2) before his return from exile because he refers in it (97.2)[2] to the *Ἀττικὴ ξυγγραφή* of Hellanicus, in which an event belonging to the year 407/6 was mentioned. This argument in favour of a late date for the composition of the excursus has been disputed and is now much less widely supported. It has been suggested that the reference to Hellanicus in 97.2,[3] or the whole of that section,[4] was added by Thucydides to a part of his work written much earlier, or that an edition of the *Ἀττικὴ ξυγγραφή* including an account of the Pentekontaetia may have been published long before 406 and the work have been subsequently continued.[5] Of these three suggestions the first is perhaps the most convincing: the brief sentence in which Thucydides refers to the work of Hellanicus disturbs the balance of the passage, which would be clearer and more logical without it.[6] If this sentence is a later insertion, it supplies, as F. E. Adcock has pointed out,[7] a *terminus ante quem* instead of a *terminus post quem* for the composition of the excursus. At all events the reference to the work of Hellanicus can no longer be accepted as incontrovertible proof that Thucydides wrote his account of the Pentekontaetia after his return from exile.

This conflict of opinion on the conclusions to be drawn from 97.2 well illustrates the weakness of relying upon short passages,

[1] H. Patzer, *Das Problem der Geschichtsschreibung des Thukydides* (1937), 104; J. de Romilly, *Thucydide et l'impérialisme athénien* (1947), 23–4; Schmid-Stählin, *Gesch. der griech. Literatur*, i. 5 (1948), 131.

[2] Throughout this essay the references to Thucydides by chapter and section only are to Book 1.

[3] K. Ziegler, *Rhein. Mus.* lxxviii (1929), 66, n. 2.

[4] N. G. L. Hammond, *C.Q.* xxxiv (1940), 149–50.

[5] A. W. Gomme, *Historical Commentary on Thucydides*, i (1945), 6, n. 3, 280, 362, n. 2. Gomme also (op. cit., 264–6) disposes of the arguments that references to the walls of Athens (93.2) and of the Piraeus (93.5) were written after 404.

[6] Ziegler, loc. cit.   [7] *J.H.S.* lxxi (1951), 11.

or even single clauses, believed to be 'early' or 'late' as evidence of the date at which Thucydides wrote substantial sections of his work. Datable passages, provided that they really are datable, throw a certain amount of light on the problem, but their contribution is very limited and has been much exaggerated.[8] A list of 'early' and 'late' passages compiled by H. Patzer is not a long one,[9] and some of them are disputable; it provides a very slight and insecure basis for general conclusions on the composition problem. The 'early' passages show only that Thucydides began to compile notes while the war was in progress, a fact much more securely authenticated by the opening sentence of his work (1.1), the 'late' passages only that, if he composed the bulk of his earlier books long before the end of the war, he subsequently made a few additions. Other methods of approach may appear to be based on less secure foundations because they are necessarily more subjective. There has, however, been a tendency in recent discussions of the Thucydidean problem, or of parts of it, to rely less on datable passages and more on broader considerations, and though disagreement on every aspect of the problem remains as wide as ever, this change of emphasis has yielded very interesting results.[10]

The excursus on the Pentekontaetia is remarkable in several ways. It falls into two parts, of which the first (89–96) is strikingly different from the second (97–118.2) in scale and general tone, including the treatment of leading characters; neither part can be deemed to fulfil altogether satisfactorily the purpose for which the excursus was evidently written; the first part has affinities with the excursus on Pausanias and Themistocles which occurs towards the end of the same book (128–38); the second part has an introduction of its own (97), which is longer than that of the first (89.1). Of these characteristics the last has played some part in discussions on the date of composition of the excursus,[11] but though attention has been drawn to the others,

[8] de Romilly, op. cit., 12, points out that a single phrase referring to Aegina in 7.57.2 is believed by Schadewaldt to date two entire books, by Schwartz to date two chapters, and by Rehm to date only the reference to Aegina.

[9] Op. cit., 103–9.

[10] Cf. the admirable study by J. H. Finley, *Harv. Stud.*, *Suppl. Vol.* i (1940), 255–97, though I do not agree with his conclusion that Thucydides wrote his history wholly after 404.

[11] Cf. G. B. Grundy, *Thucydides*, i[2] (1948), 441–4.

they do not appear to have been generally considered to be relevant to this problem. Gomme, however, in an interesting note,[12] writes: 'it is a not unnatural inference that 89–96 is in fact the beginning of a rewriting of the whole excursus'. This view will presumably be developed in the appendix to the third volume of his *Commentary* in which the composition problem is to be discussed.[13] As briefly stated in this note, it does not seem to be wholly convincing. He maintains that the two prefaces, namely 89.1, οἱ γὰρ Ἀθηναῖοι τρόπῳ τοιῷδε ἦλθον ἐπὶ τὰ πράγματα ἐν οἷς ηὐξήθησαν, and 97.1, τοσάδε ἐπῆλθον πολέμῳ τε καὶ διαχειρίσει πραγμάτων μεταξὺ τοῦδε τοῦ πολέμου καὶ τοῦ Μηδικοῦ κ.τ.λ., 'both cover all the ground'. Most editors, however, consider the first of these passages to be an introduction to 89–96 alone,[14] and it can be made to introduce 97–118.2 as well only by interpreting ηὐξήθησαν as equivalent to a pluperfect,[15] which seems unnatural. It is also questionable whether 97.1 could stand as a preface to the whole excursus. The opening words ἡγούμενοι δὲ αὐτονόμων τὸ πρῶτον τῶν ξυμμάχων καὶ ἀπὸ κοινῶν ξυνόδων βουλευόντων, which precede the part of the sentence quoted by Gomme, show that Thucydides is introducing an account of Athenian achievements after the foundation of the Delian Confederacy. The phrase ἀπὸ κοινῶν ξυνόδων clearly refers to the meetings of League representatives at Delos mentioned in 96.2; hence 97.1 is closely linked to the preceding narrative, as Gomme himself points out,[16] and is in no sense an alternative preface to the whole excursus.[17] An even stronger objection is that, if Thucydides had rewritten 98–117 on a scale

[12] Op. cit., 363, n. 1.
[13] Op. cit., 113. (Lamentably he did not live to finish his work.)
[14] So Stahl, Classen, Forbes and Maddalena.
[15] So Gomme, op. cit., 256 (n. ad loc.), but it is surely preferable to regard the aorist as virtually ingressive, cf. 6.33.6 where ηὐξήθησαν is similarly used.
[16] Op. cit., 363, n. 1. He also draws attention to another difficulty, namely that 'we should expect the longer preface, with the reason given for the whole excursus (97.2), to be the later one, or, if it had already been written for the earlier and shorter form of the excursus, that it would have been transferred to the beginning of the later form at 89.1'.
[17] μεταξὺ τοῦδε τοῦ πολέμου καὶ τοῦ Μηδικοῦ in 97.1 is a convenient phrase, which is only slightly inaccurate. The first event recorded in 98.1 occurred about two and a half years after the end of the Persian war. In 118.2, which certainly refers to the whole excursus, the limits of time are much more accurately defined.

approximately equal to that of 89–96, his excursus would have become of unmanageable length and thrown out of balance his carefully constructed explanation of the causes of the Peloponnesian war.[18]

My own conviction is that the two parts of the excursus were not composed separately at different dates but that, except for the reference to Hellanicus (97.2), the whole excursus as it now stands was put together at the same time, the marked difference between the two parts being due to the limitations of the sources then available to Thucydides. Gomme argues from the chronological deficiencies of the excursus that 'Thucydides had not any list of archons readily accessible' and therefore 'wrote it when absent from Athens either when in command in Thrace or after his exile'.[19] The arguments upon which this conclusion is founded do not seem to me to be entirely cogent. If the criticism of Hellanicus for inaccurate chronology is a later addition, as Ziegler suggests,[20] Thucydides must have written his excursus before he read the narrative of Hellanicus on the Pentekontaetia, and a desire 'to correct chronological errors'[21] was not necessarily among his objects in writing it. Apart from the reference to Hellanicus, there is nothing in the excursus to indicate that the chronology of the Pentekontaetia, which is barely relevant to the growth of Athenian power and Spartan fears, was a subject of special interest to him.[22] On the other hand, there do appear

[18] 89–96, which cover a period of two years or a little more, amount to little less than half the length of 98–117, which cover a period of nearly forty years.

[19] Op. cit., 362. He evidently refers to 97–118.2 and not to 89–96, which, as stated above, he believes to be 'the beginning of a rewriting of the whole excursus'.

[20] See above, p. 39 with n. 3.   [21] Gomme, loc. cit.

[22] 'He gives a few figures for the duration of events and a few others for intervals between events' (Gomme, op. cit., 361). Some of these figures illustrate characteristics of the Athenians which might be deemed to have contributed to the rapid expansion of their power: for example, that they invaded Boeotia on the sixty-second day after the battle of Tanagra (108.2) and that they continued their campaign in Egypt for six years (110.1). On the other hand, to have established the precise date of any given event in the Pentekontaetia could scarcely have helped Thucydides to substantiate his main thesis. He undoubtedly knew some dates which he has not chosen to mention in his excursus (Gomme, op. cit., 362 and 389–91), and it is arguable that he omits them because in this context they did not seem to him to be important.

42

to me to be good reasons for believing the excursus to have been written when Thucydides was absent from Athens. Because my reasons are unconnected with its chronological deficiencies and based upon its distinctive features mentioned above, it will be necessary to attempt to substantiate my view by an examination of these features. Thucydides appears to have been severely handicapped. For the first part of the excursus his information, though relatively abundant,[23] seems to have been of a largely personal character and adapted *faute de mieux* for use in a context to which it was not ideally suited. The second part of the excursus contains many indications that, as in his narrative on the last three years of the Archidamian war,[24] he was very inadequately informed on Athenian activities and plans about which he could surely have obtained more evidence if he had been at Athens. The entire process of composition,[25] including the preliminary assemblage of material, seems to belong wholly to the period of his exile.[26]

In examining the excursus it will be convenient to begin with the second part (97–118.2). This part, in contrast to the first, gives remarkably little prominence to individuals, especially to Athenian leaders who contributed to the rise of Athenian power. Decisions are made and action taken by 'the Athenians' or 'the Lacedaemonians'. References to individuals are few except in formal genitive absolutes as the commanders of fleets or armies.[27]

[23] It is significant that his complaint that his predecessors had neglected the Pentekontaetia (97.2) occurs in the preface to the second part of the excursus.

[24] Grundy, op. cit., i² 479–83.

[25] His statement that he began his work on the war as soon as it broke out (1.1), which must refer to the compilation of notes, applies only to the events of the war itself and its immediate antecedents. A point to be remembered is that during the years of uneasy peace between 421 and 413 he could, and doubtless did, consult Athenians travelling abroad, but they did not necessarily include any whose knowledge for the Pentekontaetia was greater than his.

[26] The possibility that he wrote the excursus during the period of his command in Thrace is perhaps sufficiently remote to be discounted. This period was probably not a long one, and he can scarcely have imposed upon himself the handicap involved by absence from Athens when there was every reason to expect that he would soon return.

[27] With στρατηγοῦντος where they are Athenians (98.1; 100.1; 102.1; 105.2 and 4; 108.2 and 5; 111.2; 112.2; 113.1; 114.3; 116.1) and ἡγουμένου where they are Spartans (107.2; 114.2). In 117.2 a different formula is adopted in

Individuals appear in the nominative only in the accounts of the Athenian expeditions to Egypt and Thessaly and of the Samian revolt, and only one of them is an Athenian. The list is: Inaros (104.1; 110.3), Artaxerxes (109.2–3), Megabazus (109.3), Megabyzus (109.4), Orestes the Pharsalian (111.1), Pericles (114.1; 116.3), and Stesagoras the Samian (116.3).[28] If Thucydides is believed to have deliberately chosen to limit his narrative at this point to a bare summary, it was naturally impossible for him to dwell upon the part played by the leading personalities of the period. It is, however, remarkable that he is entirely silent on the vitally important foreign policies of Cimon, to whom he was probably related, and of Pericles, whose personality was to dominate a large section of his work, and that the military leadership of both, except that of Pericles in the Samian revolt, is given so little prominence. More information might also have been expected about Myronides and Tolmides; the former was long afterwards remembered as a hero by Aristophanes,[29] while both seem to have been somewhat extravagantly praised by Ephorus.[30] Although it may be arguable that the achievements of the period were largely the outcome of collective effort by the whole citizen body, Thucydides nowhere expresses this view. He cannot have assumed that his readers would already be well informed about these Athenian leaders; for one of his reasons for writing on this period is that historians had neglected it (97.2). It is not unnatural to infer that he lacked adequate information about Athenian leaders, or at least information believed by him to be trustworthy.

Another unexpected feature of these chapters points in the same direction. Only a single sentence is devoted to each of four major Athenian victories, at the Eurymedon (100.1), off Aegina (105.2), at Oenophyta (108.3), and off Salamis in Cyprus (112.4), and except that in the first two instances the losses of the enemy are mentioned, no details are provided. Nor does Thucydides

---

listing Athenian commanders of fleets sent to Samos. In 112.3 and 4 and 114.1 individuals are mentioned in genitive absolutes but not as commanders.

[28] Some of the same persons appear in other cases (cf. 104.1; 109.2 and 3; 110.2; 111.1), also Amyrtaeus (110.2) and Pissuthnes (115.4 and 5).

[29] *Lys.* 801–4; *Eccles.* 303–5.

[30] Diod. 11.81–4. It is possible that Diodorus may himself be partly responsible for these eulogies and their extravagance.

explain why the Athenians embarked upon the campaigns in which these victories were won. It is also noteworthy that, where his accounts of military operations or diplomatic exchanges become more than a bare catalogue of events, as they do in a number of cases, the Athenians, though invariably involved in the events described, do not, except in the chapters on the Samian revolt (115-17), dominate the narrative to the extent that might have been expected if the bulk of the narrative had been derived from Athenian sources. Nor can the episodes recorded rather more fully be considered to be conspicuously relevant to the growth of Athenian power or especially significant for any other reason.[31] It appears that here, as in the far more detailed narrative on the Archidamian war, Thucydides is selecting for somewhat fuller treatment episodes on which the amount of trustworthy information available to him was relatively large.

There are three passages in this part of the excursus in which he includes detailed information very probably derived from Spartan sources.[32] In his account of the revolt of Thasos he states that the Spartans, when urged by the Thasians to assist them by invading Attica, ὑπέσχοντο μέν κρύφα τῶν ᾿Αθηναίων καὶ ἔμελλον, διεκωλύθησαν δὲ ὑπὸ τοῦ γενομένου σεισμοῦ (101.2). It is significant that he expresses himself so confidently about an unfulfilled intention of the Spartans which was not disclosed at the time and cannot have been known at Athens at least two years later when Cimon was sent to Ithome.[33] Some scholars have rejected this statement,[34] though without adequate reason. The second passage is his account of the Helot revolt (101.2-103.3). Here he explains in some detail the undisclosed reasons why the Spartans dismissed their Athenian allies (102.3), whereas he is silent on the question whether the Spartans were justified in

---

[31] Gomme, op. cit., 363.

[32] That he used Peloponnesian sources during his exile is attested by his own statement in 5.26.5, though it refers only to evidence on the events of the Peloponnesian war.

[33] In 58.1 he asserts almost as positively that the Spartan magistrates promised an invasion of Attica if Potidaea were attacked; but this information was probably communicated to him by the Corinthian Aristeus (cf. below, pp. 74-83), who may well have been among the Corinthians sent with the Potidaean envoys to Sparta.

[34] Cf. Maddalena, n. ad loc.

suspecting the Athenians and does not seem to have been in possession of sufficient information from Athenian sources to enable him to assess the validity of these suspicions. While the revolt was both important and relevant to the main theme of the excursus because it led to the first open breach between Athens and Sparta, some details included by Thucydides in his account are of local and even antiquarian interest (101.2; 103.2). Somewhat less striking is a passage on the events leading to the battle of Tanagra (107.2–7). He dwells upon the apprehensions of the Spartans, after they had concluded their campaign against Phocis, about the difficulties in which they would be involved if they attempted to return home by sea or by way of the Isthmus. These apprehensions are not wholly deducible from their decision to remain temporarily in Boeotia. The abortive plot of some Athenian traitors (107.4) must have been better known to the Spartans, to whom they communicated their subversive intentions, than to the Athenian authorities, who only suspected a conspiracy. On the other hand, the chapter presents a somewhat puzzling account of Spartan actions,[35] and it contains at least some material probably derived from Athenian sources, namely, the figures of the Athenian and allied army (107.5) and perhaps the reasons why the Athenians marched into Boeotia (107.6), though these reasons could have been inferred from information already given. It is, however, noteworthy that, after Thucydides has recorded the Spartan return to the Peloponnese, his narrative reverts to a bare summary, and, as already mentioned, he does not explain how the battle of Oenophyta came to be fought.

The account of the Athenian expedition to Egypt (104 and 109–10) is noteworthy both for what it includes and for what it omits. The campaign impeded and did not advance the growth of Athenian power, but it illustrated the restless and adventurous spirit of the Athenians, which was an important factor in evoking Spartan fears. These chapters, though richer in detail than most in this part of the excursus, are not altogether satisfactory if judged solely as a record of an Athenian enterprise. Thucydides does not state the purpose of the Athenians in supporting the revolt or in persevering in their support, nor does he give the name of any Athenian or allied commander in a campaign lasting six years. There are also reasons for believing

[35] D. W. Reece, *J.H.S.* lxx (1950), 75–6.

him to be mistaken in implying, as he certainly does, that the losses of the Athenians and their allies amounted to considerably more than 200 ships with most of their crews.[36] On the other hand, he gives more information than would seem to be strictly necessary about Egyptian geography (cf. 104.1; 109.4; 110.2), about measures taken by the Persians to suppress the revolt, and about the fortunes of the rebel leaders. As already pointed out, individuals are more prominent in the chapters on the Egyptian revolt than elsewhere in this part of the excursus, and they are all barbarians. Whatever the sources of the narrative may have been, they cannot have been wholly Athenian. It is tempting to conjecture that much of it was obtained from some Greek, or Greeks, who, like Herodotus, had travelled in Egypt and had been in contact with Egyptians and Persians alike.

Apart from the chapters on the Samian revolt, the only other passage in the second half of the excursus in which the narrative becomes more than a bare summary is the account of the campaign against the Corinthians in the Megarid (105.3–106.2). While this expedition illustrates the temperament of the Athenians in that they decided to use their reserve force of 'the oldest and youngest' outside Attica rather than raise the siege of Aegina, neither the indecisive battle nor its sequel, which is described in detail, seems to have been of great importance.[37] This sequel involved the Corinthians in what is described as πάθος μέγα because a detachment of troops was annihilated, but the main body escaped. There is no reason why Thucydides could not have obtained his relatively detailed information about these operations from Athenians who took part in them, but his statement that the Corinthians returned to the battlefield κακιζόμενοι ὑπὸ τῶν ἐν τῇ πόλει πρεσβυτέρων (105.6) perhaps points rather to a Corinthian source. At all events, these chapters exemplify the fact that the scale of his narrative in this part of his

[36] I discuss this point, and others in which I believe his narrative to be defective, below, pp. 61–73.
[37] Gomme, op. cit., 309–10, argues that 'the activities of this year, culminating in the victory of the Athenian reserves over the Corinthians, were memorable—hence the much greater detail with which Thucydides narrates the campaign in the Megarid'. This view is not wholly convincing: it is surely more natural to expect Thucydides to enlarge upon the most important event of a memorable year than upon the last.

47

excursus is by no means determined by the importance, or the relevance, of its content.

The Samian revolt was the outstanding episode of the decade between the conclusion of the Thirty Years Peace and the battle of Leukimme. It was, however, of no greater importance than the revolts of Naxos, to which Thucydides devotes only one sentence (98.4), and of Thasos, which is also described very briefly (100.2; 101.1 and 3). These two earlier revolts may in fact be deemed more relevant than that of Samos to the growth of Athenian power and the development of Spartan fears because they occurred before the transformation of the Delian Confederacy into an Athenian ἀρχή and were the first major examples of 'enslavement'. The fuller treatment of the Samian revolt cannot legitimately be explained on the assumption that it was especially interesting to Thucydides because Pericles played a leading part in its suppression. Other operations where Pericles was in command are recorded briefly (111.2–3; 114), while his expedition to the Euxine and other enterprises for which he was certainly or probably responsible are not even mentioned in the excursus.[38] The only reason why Thucydides describes the Samian revolt so fully seems to be that, probably alone among the major episodes of the Pentekontaetia, it lay within the limits of his own adult recollection.[39] If this explanation be accepted, it suggests that his brevity in dealing with earlier events was dictated by lack of trustworthy evidence.

The first part of the excursus (89–96) is on a very different scale and of a very different character. After an introduction consisting of a single sentence (89.1), which has already been discussed, Thucydides briefly refers to the return of Leotychidas and the Peloponnesians after the battle of Mycale and to the siege and capture of Sestos by the Athenians with the aid of their allies from Ionia and the Hellespont (89.2).[40] He then embarks upon a lengthy account of two episodes, the rebuilding of the wall round Athens (89.3–93.2) and the completion of the Piraeus wall (93.3–6). The former was carried out in great haste and occupied only a few months; the duration of the latter is not precisely determinable but probably did not much exceed a

---

[38] Gomme, op. cit., 366–9.   [39] Cf. Adcock, op. cit., 12.

[40] His brevity is doubtless influenced by the fact that Herodotus (9.114–18) had given a full account of these events.

year.[41] Both these building operations were historically important because they were essential prerequisites to the development of Athenian sea-power, but it may be doubted whether it is for this reason alone that the scale of the narrative is here so much more generous than in other parts of the excursus. Themistocles dominates these chapters, which have a personal colouring so marked that they might almost have been written by Herodotus or Plutarch.[42] The story of the stratagems whereby he frustrated the attempt of the Spartans to prevent the rebuilding of the Athenian wall, though it recalls the trick played by Alcibiades upon a Spartan embassy in 420 (5.44.3–46.1), has an almost romantic flavour encountered in very few passages of Thucydides, and its authenticity has been doubted. While these doubts are probably unfounded,[43] there is reason to suspect that on points of detail the trustworthiness of his evidence is here not above suspicion and that popular tradition, of which he is elsewhere contemptuous,[44] has to a large extent provided the basis of his account, though he has probably rationalized this tradition. The episode occurred long before his own time, and the number of persons to whom all its complex details were accurately known can never have been large. He can scarcely have possessed altogether trustworthy evidence on the final speech of Themistocles at Sparta, of which he gives a circumstantial report in *oratio obliqua* (91.4–7). The passage on the completion of the Piraeus wall is briefer but similar in character: it attributes to Themistocles the unfulfilled intention of having the wall raised to double the height that it actually reached (93.5), a detail that may be authentic but is unlikely to have been known for certain after an interval of so many years. At the beginning (93.3–4) and attached to the end (93.7) of this passage on the Piraeus wall stand a few observations on the aims of Themistocles, which together amount to a summary of his naval policy combined with a personal estimate by Thucydides (ὡς ἐμοὶ δοκεῖ) of the

[41] According to the confused narrative of Diodorus the work was speedily done (11.43.2). He records the building operations at Athens under 478/7, those at the Piraeus under 477/6, and his chronology may be correct (Gomme, op. cit., 262).

[42] Plutarch (*Them.* 19) in fact follows a different tradition.

[43] E. Meyer, *Hermes*, xl (1905), 561–9.

[44] Cf. 20.2. Characteristically, however, he confirms that the wall was hastily built by reference to its appearance in his own day (93.2).

motives that caused him to adopt it. This summary supplies the key to the opening chapters of the excursus: Themistocles is here presented as the initiator of the naval policy responsible for the rise of Athens to the greatness of the Periclean age.[45] The claims of Themistocles to this distinction were by no means unchallenged,[46] and Thucydides here seeks to substantiate these claims, although the controversy is not strictly relevant to the main purpose of his excursus. The even more personal chapters on the last years of Themistocles contained in another excursus (135–8) have a similar aim, and their relation to chapters 89–93 will be discussed below.

The first part of the excursus concludes with three chapters (94–96) which do not differ from the second part to the same degree as the chapters on Themistocles, though they cover a period of little more than a year. The expeditions of the allied Greeks under Pausanias to Cyprus and Byzantium (94) are recorded as briefly as the first successes of Cimon (98), though somewhat more prominence is given to their leader. The concluding chapter (96) explains very summarily the organisation of the Delian Confederacy: it is parallel to a later chapter (99) dealing with the causes of revolts in the Confederacy and, despite its position, may be deemed to belong rather to the second part of the excursus than to the first, being probably derived from sources of a similar character. On the other hand, the second of these three chapters (95), which considerably exceeds the combined length of the other two, is much more personal and resembles in general tone, though not in scale, the chapters on Themistocles. The decision of the Ionians and the other Greeks to invite the Athenians to assume the leadership of the allied forces is attributed wholly to the behaviour of Pausanias (95.1), and one of the reasons given for the subsequent acquiescence of the Spartans in this transference of command is their apprehension that other Spartan generals might be similarly corrupted (95.7). The recall and first trial of Pausanias (95.3–5) influenced the relationship between Athens and Sparta only to a very limited degree; they did not affect the transference of command because the invitation to the Athenians was issued while he was still at Byzantium, and Thucydides evidently dwells upon them here because of his interest in the controversy raised by the

---

[45] Cf. 14.3. [46] See below, pp. 57–8.

various accusations made against Pausanias, which he later discusses in much greater detail (128.3–135.1). Pausanias dominates the excursus at this point in much the same way as Themistocles dominates its opening chapters and for similar reasons. The few passages dealing with matters in which neither was directly involved have the same conciseness as is general in the second part of the excursus. Accordingly it may be inferred with some confidence that, whereas the volume of evidence available to Thucydides on the Pentekontaetia generally was limited, he did possess plenty of information about Themistocles and, to a lesser degree, about Pausanias.[47] Not all this information was altogether suitable for inclusion in an excursus on the growth of Athenian power, for much was personal in character and apparently collected in the first instance for use in the long-continued debates on the merits of these two controversial figures.

This conclusion is to some extent confirmed by the substantial excursus on the last years of Pausanias and Themistocles inserted towards the end of Book 1 (128–38) on the somewhat flimsy pretext of the Athenian demand that the Spartans should drive out τὸ τῆς Χαλκιοίκου ἄγος (128.2). This excursus is thus relevant to the problems under discussion and must accordingly be examined. Its two sections are not precisely continuations of the chapters dealing with Pausanias and Themistocles in the opening chapters of the excursus on the Pentekontaetia: in the one case there is an overlap,[48] in the other a hiatus of some years. Nevertheless the presentation of Pausanias and Themistocles, though divided between two excursuses, is essentially a unity, as E. Schwartz has shown.[49] The second excursus (128–38) is remarkable in that

---

[47] It is clear from 128.3–135.1 that he was in fact equally well informed about Pausanias.

[48] It is true that 128.3 takes up the story of Pausanias at the point where 95.5 left it, but 128.5–130.2 deals with his behaviour in the course of his first visit to the Hellespont and therefore covers the same period as 95.1–5, though in greater detail and from a more exclusively personal angle.

[49] *Das Geschichtswerk des Thukydides* (1929), 155–6. His whole chapter (154–67) is instructive, though his late dating of these excursuses is based on the view, no longer widely accepted, that Thucydides embarked upon a fundamental revision of his work after the fall of Athens. H. Münch, *Studien zu den Exkursen des Thukydides* (1935), 16–17, points out that the first excursus deals with political, the second with personal, activities of the two leaders, but this fact does not destroy the unity to which Schwartz draws attention.

Thucydides here allows himself to describe the personal experiences of two individuals whose careers as leaders in their own states had already ended. It would, however, be a mistake to imagine that his interest in them was exclusively biographical. He evidently felt that Herodotus, and perhaps other writers, had erred in their estimates of Pausanias and Themistocles, especially the latter, and one of his aims in this excursus was to correct the errors of which he believed his predecessors to have been guilty.[50] While Herodotus draws a largely favourable picture of Pausanias as commander of the Greek forces at Plataea and is inclined to be sceptical about the stories of his subsequent intrigues (5.32), Thucydides seeks to convict him on all the charges brought against him. The cleavage of opinion is even sharper in the case of Themistocles. To Herodotus he was a cunning, self-seeking, and untrustworthy intriguer, whereas Thucydides insists that he was a man of outstanding natural ability who did not medise until he had become the victim of false charges and had been relentlessly hounded from one place of refuge to another through the spite of his ungrateful fellow-countrymen. The famous passage in which Thucydides analyses the genius of Themistocles (138.3) is remarkable both for its elaborateness and for its warmth of feeling. Hence this excursus develops and corroborates the views implicit in the passages dealing with Pausanias and Themistocles contained in the account of the Pentekontaetia.

The distinctive features of this excursus are approximately the same as those of the chapters at the beginning of the excursus on the Pentekontaetia. The difference is one of degree, the personal element and the romantic colouring being considerably more marked. Here also, to an even greater extent than in the narrative on Themistocles and the wall-building, there is reason to suspect that Thucydides has accepted popular tradition somewhat uncritically.[51] Though the excursus is packed with details

---

[50] Grundy, op. cit., i.[2] 451; Münch, op. cit., 17–18; de Romilly, *Thucydide* i (Budé, which has been published since this article was written), *Notice*, xliv, n. 3. Among his objects in inserting the excursus here was doubtless to contrast the two leaders as representatives of Sparta and Athens (Schwartz, op. cit., 158–61).

[51] G. Méautis, *Ant. Class.* xx (1951), 297–304, has recently discussed the general character of the narrative describing the flight of Themistocles, cf. R. Flacelière, *R.É.A.* lv (1953), 14. F. M. Cornford, *Thucydides Mythistoricus* (1907), 137 with n. 2, goes too far in asserting that 'what he has left is

about secret negotiations and private conversations which took place long ago, he gives scarcely a hint that the authenticity of any of them might be suspect.[52] Nor is it at all likely that after a lapse of so many years he can have possessed wholly trustworthy evidence on undisclosed and unattained aims of Pausanias (128.3; 131.2), which seem to be merely inferred from the sequence of events, a practice from which he normally refrains when writing contemporary history.[53] Other points are notably un-Thucydidean: the versions of two rival traditions on the death of Themistocles are mentioned, and the source of the story that his bones were secretly buried in Attica is cited.[54] A further remarkable and indeed unique feature of this excursus is the inclusion of three personal letters: from Pausanias to Xerxes (128.7), from Xerxes to Pausanias (129.3), and from Themistocles to Artaxerxes (137.4). Thucydides gives what evidently purports to be the full text of each, except that a portion of the last is omitted and the content of this portion summarised in a parenthesis. The disputed question whether these letters are genuine lies outside the scope of this paper and cannot be fully discussed.[55] It is, however, evident that only by a singular stroke of good fortune, or rather by three singular strokes of good fortune, can Thucydides have had access to the texts of personal and secret letters written many years before he began to devote himself to historical research.[56] That he may have been so fortunate is not

---

dramatized legend, not the historical facts out of which it was worked up' (on Pausanias) and that the chapters on Themistocles are 'rationalized Saga-history influenced by drama'.

[52] Only ὡς λέγεται in 132.5 and 138.1 and λέγεται in 134.1 suggest uncertainty.

[53] See below, p. 79, where I do not refer to these two passages because they do not belong to the period of the Peloponnesian war or its immediate antecedents.

[54] 138.4, νοσήσας δὲ τελευτᾷ τὸν βίον· λέγουσι δέ τινες καὶ ἑκούσιον φαρμάκῳ ἀποθανεῖν αὐτόν, and 138.6, τὰ δὲ ὀστᾶ φασὶ κομισθῆναι αὐτοῦ οἱ προσήκοντες οἴκαδε.

[55] Schwartz, op. cit., 30, n. 1, and Münch, op. cit., 23–4 (cf. Méautis, op. cit., 298, n. 2), believe that Thucydides wrote them himself. M. van den Hout, Mnemos, ii (4th series, 1949), 34–6 and 144, maintains that they are authentic, though somewhat altered by Thucydides.

[56] H. Schaefer, R.E. xviii. 4 (1949), 2577, seeks to defend the authenticity of the letters by referring to the treaties between Sparta and Persia of which

impossible, but it seems far more probable that he composed them himself. Some phrases in the letter from Xerxes to Pausanias which have an oriental ring and are paralleled in Persian documents[57] do not prove its genuineness. Thucydides may well have based them on similar phrases used by Herodotus,[58] and he had almost certainly seen at least one official letter from a Persian king.[59] It was surely not beyond his powers to compose a letter sufficiently oriental in phrasing and tone to satisfy Greek readers that it could have been written by Xerxes. Very few readers can have been fully or accurately informed about Persian manners.

In the chapters on Pausanias and Themistocles the personal tone, the romantic treatment, the rapid flow of the narrative, and the ready acceptance of evidence that can scarcely have been authenticated beyond any reasonable doubt are all characteristics of Herodotus rather than of Thucydides. Nowhere else is the influence of Herodotus nearly so marked. It is therefore natural to believe that, whatever the date may have been at which Thucydides inserted this excursus in his account of the events leading to the outbreak of the Peloponnesian war, he wrote the substance of it before he developed the unique style and technique of historical writing which are so alien to the Ionian tradition. It is true that some scholars, including Schwartz,[60] believe that Thucydides wrote the excursus towards the end of his life. This late dating, however, is based upon general views about the development of his work to which not many scholars now subscribe:[61] if the account of the Pentekontaetia were held to be late, this excursus, which is clearly related to it, would naturally be

---

the texts are reproduced in Book 8. The analogy is, however, misleading: copies of contemporary official documents are far more likely to have been accessible to Thucydides than copies of personal letters written many years ago.

[57] A. T. Olmstead, *Amer. Journ. of Semitic Languages*, xlix (1932–3), 156–61.

[58] Cf. the parallels cited by Gomme, op. cit., 432 (note on 129.3).

[59] 4.50.1–2, where he records the substance of a letter from Artaxerxes to the Spartans intercepted by the Athenians.

[60] Op. cit., 162, 'sie (sc. the accounts of Pausanias and Themistocles) sind ein Experiment des greisen Schriftstellers', cf. Münch, op. cit., 28. Grundy, op. cit., i.² 450–1 (cf. 489), does not consider that the date at which the chapters on Pausanias were written is determinable, but he is inclined to assign the chapters on Themistocles to what he believes to have been the first draft.

[61] See above, p. 51, n. 49.

held to be late also.[62] No cogent reason suggests itself to explain why if he wrote the excursus in his last years he should have chosen to abandon his own manner and principles of composition and to revert to those of his predecessors.

K. Ziegler has attempted to show that all the excursuses of Thucydides dealing with past history, including those on the Pentekontaetia and on Pausanias and Themistocles, are the fruits of research conducted by him before the outbreak of the Peloponnesian war and were designed for inclusion in a general history of Greece, this projected work being abandoned because the greatness of the war caused him to devote himself to contemporary events.[63] While it is true that Thucydides is much more likely to have felt himself impelled to write a history of the Peloponnesian war if he had previously carried out historical research than if he had not,[64] this hypothesis is unconvincing as a general explanation of the excursus. It is altogether too simple; the excursuses, and the problems raised by them, are too diverse to be explained by a single comprehensive hypothesis of this kind. So far as the excursus on the Pentekontaetia is concerned, Adcock raises the objection that 'it seems too selectively relevant not to be written, or at least re-written, for purposes concerned with the causes of the war'.[65] This objection is certainly valid for the greater part of the excursus, which, despite its inadequacies as an exposition of its main theme, can scarcely be even a drastically revised version of a narrative originally composed to form part of a general history of Greece. The chapters on the activities of Themistocles (90–93) and, to a lesser degree, the chapter on the

---

[62] The further contention of Schwartz, op. cit., 161–2, that Thucydides, when writing about the treatment of Pausanias and Themistocles by Sparta and Athens respectively, must have had in mind the treatment of Lysander and Alcibiades is over-subtle. It is not the practice of Thucydides to draw parallels, directly or by implication, between the events of different periods. There were instances of injustice and ingratitude on the part of the Athenian democracy during the Archidamian war, cf. 2.65.3 and 4.65.3–4.

[63] Op. cit., 58–67.

[64] Ziegler, op cit., 63. The view of W. Jaeger, *Paideia* (Eng. trans., 1939), i. 382, that 'it was the war that made Thucydides a historian' seems to me to overestimate the dependence of Thucydides the historian upon Thucydides the statesman and admiral, though it was probably the war that caused him to create a new kind of historical writing.

[65] Op. cit., 11 (cf. Grundy, op. cit., i.[2] 442, 'it does not deal with a single incident which is unconnected with Attic history').

recall of Pausanias (95) are very different: their distinctive features do suggest that they were written in the first instance for accounts of these two leaders composed for a purpose other than that of explaining the causes of the Peloponnesian war, and that they were adapted for use in this context because Thucydides lacked information of a less personal and more suitable character on the first stages in the development of Athenian power immediately after the Persian wars.[66] The excursus on the last years of Pausanias and Themistocles (128–38) seems to have the same origin. Because the chapters on Pausanias are somewhat tenuously linked with the narrative of events leading to the Peloponnesian war and the chapters on Themistocles are even less relevant, Thucydides was perhaps content to leave them largely unaltered. Hence they preserve, to a greater extent than the corresponding chapters in the excursus on the Pentekontaetia, the frankly biographical tone and partisan attitude which may be believed to have pervaded the original work, as well as traces of early composition, especially the clear and rapid style.

One of the sources used by Thucydides thus seems to have been a work, published or unpublished, dealing specifically with the careers of Pausanias and Themistocles, or with the later stages of their careers, and seeking to establish the guilt of the former and to vindicate the latter.[67] Such a work might have been written by someone other than Thucydides and merely used by him because it contained information of value to him. This possibility is, however, a very remote one: he disparages the historical research of others,[68] and in the *Archaeology* he clearly is not attempting to improve upon accounts of early Greece written by his predecessors but to create an entirely new one by employing his own methods of investigation. It is scarcely credible that he here accepted unquestioningly the polemical views of another and reproduced them in his own work. Accordingly there is some reason to believe that this source was an early piece of research conducted by himself, which was probably never published and may not even have been completed but was preserved with his notes on the Peloponnesian war and thus available to him while

[66] See above, pp. 48–51.

[67] It is immaterial whether this source consisted of a single work or of two separate works, the one devoted to Pausanias and the other to Themistocles.

[68] Cf. 20.3–21.1.

in exile, whereas an abundance of evidence on other aspects of the Pentekontaetia evidently was not.[69]

That Thucydides may have written a minor work of this kind at some time before his exile is by no means improbable. Stesimbrotus published, probably soon after the death of Pericles, a work entitled περὶ Θεμιστοκλέους καὶ Θουκυδίδου καὶ Περικλέους, of which some fragments survive.[70] It seems to have been written with the object of attacking Athenian democracy or Athenian imperialism or both; at all events, though its outward form was apparently that of biographical memoirs, it was essentially a political pamphlet.[71] Stesimbrotus drew an unsympathetic picture of Themistocles, denying him originality and probably damning his character on moral grounds as he certainly damned that of Pericles.[72] The surviving traces of this work show that highly polemical accounts of leading statesmen, including those of the past, were written at this time, being in some cases doubtless designed to influence contemporary political opinion. It may indeed have been the strictures of Stesimbrotus, in addition to the unflattering account of Herodotus, that prompted Thucydides to present Themistocles in what he believed to be a true light.[73] A much disputed question affecting the reputation of

[69] It cannot be legitimately argued that if Thucydides had studied the career of Themistocles he would have been better informed about Athenian activities between 477 and 470 (which seems to be the most probable date for the ostracism of Themistocles). It does not appear that Themistocles played any part in the foreign relations of Athens in these years, and Thucydides is not concerned with the internal history of the period (cf. 97.1, and Gomme, op. cit., 385–7).

[70] F. Jacoby, F. Gr. Hist., 107 F 1–11 (ii. B 516–19).

[71] R. Laqueur, R.E. iii A (1929), 2466–7; Jacoby, op. cit., ii D 343–4; Schmid-Stählin, op. cit., i. 2 (1934), 676–7.

[72] Ion of Chios also may have been unsympathetic towards Themistocles (cf. F. Gr. Hist., 392 F 13), but Jacoby, C.Q. xli (1947), 12, concludes that his Epidemiai cannot have dealt with Themistocles in any great detail. Nothing is known of the work in which Charon of Lampsacus (F. Gr. Hist., 262 F 11) referred to the relations of Themistocles with Artaxerxes after his flight to Asia.

[73] In 138.3, οἰκείᾳ γὰρ ξυνέσει καὶ οὔτε προμαθὼν ἐς αὐτὴν οὐδὲν οὔτ᾽ ἐπιμαθών, Thucydides seems to be contesting the view that Themistocles was deeply indebted to the teaching of others, as G. B. Kerferd, C.R. lxiv (1950), 9, maintains. Stesimbrotus referred to the teachers of Themistocles (F 2) and, because he depreciated him, is likely to have been among the advocates of this view and perhaps was its originator. Gomme, op. cit., 442 (n. ad loc.), denies that these words refer to what Themistocles was said to have learned from others,

E

Themistocles was whether he was personally responsible for framing and putting into execution the naval policy that contributed so much to the expansion of Athenian power. As has been pointed out above, Thucydides strongly supports the claims of Themistocles,[74] while Stesimbrotus, though apparently disapproving of this naval policy, held a similar view (F 2). There are, however, traces of a tradition which assigned this distinction not to Themistocles but to Aristeides,[75] and though no evidence dating from the fifth century survives, this controversy must have originated from their rivalry in their own lifetime and was very probably a political issue in the period of the Peloponnesian war.

The family connections of Thucydides with leading politicians, together with the political and military experience that are likely to have preceded his election to the *strategia*, provided him with excellent qualifications for writing a work in defence of Themistocles. The date at which he may have composed such a work must remain uncertain. If it were the outcome of a desire to correct the pictures drawn by Herodotus and Stesimbrotus, it is not likely to have been written before the outbreak of the Peloponnesian war, though Thucydides may have had knowledge of their works before they were published. It can scarcely have been written after his period of exile had begun because he must surely have had access to Athenian sources while writing it. There is, however, no justification for assuming that between 431 and 424 he was so fully occupied by military duties and by the compilation of notes on the events of the Peloponnesian war that he was precluded from undertaking any other literary composition. It is even more difficult to reach any conclusion about the date of his research on the fall of Pausanias. He perhaps became interested in this controversial subject while he was working on Themistocles, who was accused of treasonable collaboration with

---

and H. T. Wade-Gery, *J.H.S.* lxix (1949), 84, seems inclined to agree. There is, however, evidence that the question whether Themistocles owed his success to his teachers or to natural ability was much debated (Xen. *Mem.* 4.2.2, cited by Kerferd, loc. cit.), and contemporary readers of Thucydides, being familiar with this controversy, would probably have no hesitation in interpreting these somewhat obscure words as a contribution to it.

[74] See above, p. 50; cf. Aristoph. *Eq.* 813–19, 884–5.

[75] Arist. Ἀθ.πολ. 24.1–2, cited by Gomme, op. cit., 262, cf. C. Hignett, *History of the Athenian Constitution* (1952), 184.

Pausanias (135.2). It seems likely, however, that he did not complete his research on Pausanias until the early years of his exile when he was probably able to obtain information from Spartan sources.

If the results of the foregoing investigation have any validity, they throw a little light upon the wider problem of the date at which Book 1 assumed its present shape. It is beyond doubt that the purpose of the excursus on the Pentekontaetia is very largely, if not wholly, to substantiate the view of Thucydides on the ἀληθεστάτη πρόφασις of the Peloponnesian war.[76] The chain of argument, though strengthened by the inclusion of this excursus, would not be broken if it were absent. While it is credible that Book 1 could have existed with the ἀληθεστάτη πρόφασις included but without the excursus, it is incredible that Book 1 could have existed with the excursus included but without the ἀληθεστάτη πρόφασις.[77] If Thucydides wrote the excursus while he was in exile, he must have completed Book 1, substantially as it now exists, before his return to Athens at the end of the war.[78] If this conclusion be accepted, it is impossible to maintain that in the period between his return and his death he either fundamentally revised an earlier draft of Book 1, as was once very widely believed, or composed ab initio his entire work, having hitherto written nothing except notes, as is believed by some scholars including Finley.

I have refrained from expressing any opinion on the question at what stage of his exile, which lasted twenty years, Thucydides wrote his excursus on the Pentekontaetia. My arguments, if valid, show only that he was absent from Athens; they do not serve to define the date of composition more precisely. It is, however,

---

[76] Cf. 23.6 with 118.2 (and the last sentence of 97.2).

[77] Cf. de Romilly, *Thucydide et l'impérialisme athénien*, 23–8, who dates the excursus late but maintains (23) that 'rien ne permet de supposer que l'idée de l' ἀληθεστάτη πρόφασις en ait jamais été absente'.

[78] The brief account of the Pentekontaetia in 18.2–19 perhaps suggests that when he wrote it Thucydides did not contemplate his excursus (Grundy, op. cit., i.² 422–3); but the two accounts were written to support different theses. They have no real point of contact unless the disputed αὐτοῖς in the last sentence of 19 refers to the Athenians alone, and A. Delachaux, *Notes critiques sur Thucydide* (1925), 29–30, seems to me to have shown conclusively that it refers to both the Athenians and the Spartans.

unlikely that he wrote the excursus in the last years of his exile. Book I contains nothing that must have been written after the beginning of the Decelean war, with the probable exception of the reference to Hellanicus (97.2); it seems to have been designed to introduce the Archidamian war only, a conclusion to which the existence of the 'second preface' (5.26) lends support. It is natural to believe, though obviously not provable, that in the earlier years of his exile, perhaps not long after the Peace of Nicias, Thucydides embarked upon the task of writing a history of the Archidamian war and its causes which he based mainly on notes compiled at Athens between 431 and 424. He then perhaps found that his principal thesis on the causes of the war could be strengthened by the inclusion of an excursus on the Pentekontaetia. When he came to assemble material for this excursus, a further reason for writing it occurred to him, namely, that the period had been neglected by historians (97.2) and that his readers could not be assumed to possess any knowledge of it as they could of the period of the Persian wars. Thus the inclusion of the excursus may be considered to be an afterthought but only in the sense that he did not envisage that he would wish to write on the Pentekontaetia when he began to collect notes on the Peloponnesian war at its outbreak (1.1) and did not decide to do so until he was in exile, when his explanation of the causes of the war began to assume its present shape. After he returned home and again had access to Athenian sources, he doubtless intended to revise the excursus, but though he probably added his reference to Hellanicus, he evidently did not live to undertake this task.

3

Thucydides and the Athenian disaster in Egypt

The subject of a fifth-century inscription from Samos published in 1939 by W. Peek is a naval engagement between Greeks and Persians very probably belonging to the Athenian expedition to Egypt.[1] It cannot be said that the new evidence makes any substantial addition to our knowledge of the campaign, which remains as obscure as ever. It does, however, throw a little fresh light upon the merits of the literary authorities and suggests that some reassessment of their credibility and completeness is required.

The two principal accounts of the expedition, the one by Thucydides in his sketch of the Pentecontaetia (1.104 and 109–10) and the other by the epitomator of Ctesias' *Persica* (32–7), have little in common except their brevity.[2] Ctesias evidently narrated this episode from the Persian point of view and derived his material from Persian sources, but he seems elsewhere to have drawn freely upon his own imagination,[3] and there has been a tendency, on the whole well-justified, to prefer the account of Thucydides. On one important point, however, the version of Ctesias is now confirmed: the naval engagement to which the Samian inscription refers is almost certainly to be identified with the crushing defeat of the Persian fleet at the beginning of the

---

[1] Peek, *Klio* xxxii (1939), 289–306. The restoration [Μέμ]φιος ἀμφ' ἐρατῆς in the second line is convincing. The article is not easily obtainable in this country, and it is only through the kindness of Professor F. E. Adcock that I have been able to see a copy. I am also indebted to him for having read a first draft of this paper and for having made valuable criticisms and suggestions.

[2] The longer account by Diodorus (11. 74–75 and 77.1–5) is founded upon an attempt by Ephorus to reconcile the accounts of Thucydides and Ctesias (Meyer, *G. d. A.*, iv², 1, 552, n. 3; Beloch, *Gr. Gesch.*, ii², 1, 173, n. 1). It has a little independent authority because Ephorus must have read the *Persica* unabridged; he was, however, far too eager to defend Athenian honour at all costs.

[3] Antiquity considered Ctesias to be thoroughly untrustworthy (cf. Plut. *Artax.* 1.4), but the Photian epitome probably does him less than justice.

campaign mentioned by the epitomator of the *Persica* (*Pers.* 32). Thucydides, on the other hand, merely states that the Athenians and their allies sailed up the Nile and were in control of the river when they captured most of Memphis and began their investment of the White Castle (1.104.2). It is true that he chooses to confine his narrative to the barest summary when dealing with the middle years of the Pentecontaetia and that the campaign in Egypt is not altogether relevant to the principal theme of his excursus, which is the growth of Athenian power.[4] Nevertheless, the virtual omission of a major battle is not wholly explained by these considerations.[5] Together with other deficiencies, which will be discussed below, it may well be due not to compression but to ignorance.

It is remarkable that Thucydides nowhere states the total extent of the losses sustained in Egypt by the Athenians and their allies. His narrative, as it stands, seems to imply clearly enough that the enterprise cost, from first to last, considerably more than two hundred ships with the greater part of their crews. From shortly after his own time[6] until the end of the nineteenth century every reader apparently accepted this implication without hesitation, and such is the impression that his account would undoubtedly convey if studied *in vacuo*. Eduard Meyer seems to have been the first to feel misgivings when he suggested, somewhat tentatively, that part of the fleet may have been withdrawn after its initial successes.[7] More recently, in consequence of the substantial progress made in reconstructing this period, several scholars have argued that losses in Egypt on a scale approximately equal to those of the Sicilian expedition cannot be fitted into the pattern of Athenian history in the middle of the fifth century. A disaster of such magnitude must have had most

[4] Momigliano, *Aegyptus*, x (1929), 191.

[5] A much less serious omission by Thucydides is the victory of Inaros at Papremis. It is mentioned by Herodotus (3.12.4, cf. 7.7) and was probably known to Thucydides, who must have chosen to omit it because it took place before the arrival of the Athenian fleet (Diod. 11.74.3 is palpably mistaken on this point).

[6] Cf. Isocr. 8.86 (the whole of this passage seems to be founded upon a casual study of Thucydides).

[7] Op. cit., iv², 1, 570, n. 1 (iii. 606 in the first edition). Busolt, *Gr. Gesch.*, iii, 1, 331, n. 3, had rather earlier mentioned the possibility of such a reduction but concluded that it must have been almost negligible.

damaging repercussions, of which there is scarcely any trace,[8] upon Athenian interests both in Greece and in the Delian Confederacy. The arguments whereby it has been shown that the Athenian losses can have amounted to only a fraction of the figure implied by Thucydides have been widely, though not unanimously, accepted,[9] and will not be reconsidered here. If, however, the implication of Thucydides is rejected, it is necessary to explain its origin. On this question there have been two rival views. Some scholars believe readers of Thucydides to have been at fault in concluding that as many as two hundred Athenian and allied ships were sent to Egypt from Cyprus;[10] others believe Thucydides himself to have been at fault in omitting to mention, because his account of the Pentecontaetia is sketchy and incomplete, that a large proportion of the Athenian fleet was withdrawn from Egypt for service elsewhere.[11] Both views involve the assumption that he possessed full information on the actions of the Athenians throughout the campaign and did not intend to create the impression that his narrative has created. This assumption is surely unwarranted. The error could, and perhaps does, lie neither with his readers nor with himself but with his sources. It may be that, because he had no information of any Athenian withdrawal, he mistakenly believed the entire fleet of two hundred ships to have remained in Egypt throughout the six years of the campaign and thus to have been involved in the final disaster.

A fatal objection to the first of the two explanations mentioned above is that the meaning of the sentence in which Thucydides records the Athenian response to the appeal of Inaros, οἱ δέ (ἔτυχον γὰρ ἐς Κύπρον στρατευόμενοι ναυσὶ διακοσίαις αὐτῶν τε καὶ

---

[8] Meiggs, *J.H.S.* lxiii (1943), 21–34, finds evidence of disaffection, especially in Ionia, in the years preceding 450. Some of this unrest may, as he suggests, have been encouraged by the disaster in Egypt; it does not, however, appear to have been very serious or widespread.

[9] Cary, *C.Q.* vii (1913), 198–201; Adcock, *Proc. Camb. Phil. Soc.*, 1926, 3–5; Wallace, *T.A.P.A.*, lxvii (1936), 252–60. Cloché, *L'antiquité classique*, xi (1942), 219, n. 1, who himself expresses a cautious acceptance of this view (ibid., 220), points out that a few have rejected it; others appear to have ignored it.

[10] Cary, loc. cit., followed by Peek, op. cit., 301–2.

[11] Adcock, op. cit., 4–5; Gomme, *Historical Commentary on Thucydides*, i, 322, 'the general sketchiness of the *Pentakontaëtia* must account for it' (cf. his long list of omissions, op. cit., i, 365–9).

τῶν ξυμμάχων) ἦλθον ἀπολιπόντες τὴν Κύπρον (1.104.2), is ambiguous only to those determined to find ambiguity. It undoubtedly means that all, or almost all, the two hundred ships operating off Cyprus were sent to Egypt.[12] No moderately careful historian could have written the sentence in this form if the greater part of the fleet had remained off Cyprus. The alleged parallel of the later expedition to Cyprus under Cimon,[13] when only sixty ships from a fleet of two hundred were sent to help Amyrtaeus in Egypt (1.112.2–3), is not a true parallel. The Egyptian revolt had in 450 been reduced to a mere smoulder, and little advantage was likely to be gained by lending support to the rebels on a large scale. It is true that according to Ctesias the Athenian fleet assisting Inaros amounted to only forty ships (*Pers*. 32). This statement is a valuable piece of information, especially as the Persians are unlikely to have understated the strength of their opponents, and may well be correct for most of the period of six years during which the operations in Egypt continued.[14] A fleet of forty, probably enjoying an advantage in seamanship, might well have defeated a Persian fleet of eighty, but the very heavy losses sustained by the Persians, amounting to twenty ships captured and thirty destroyed according to Ctesias, are more easily credited if they were inflicted by a fleet of nearly two hundred. Support for the view that a large proportion of the two hundred Athenian ships did not sail to Egypt has also been sought in the Erechtheid inscription with its record of Athenian casualties in Cyprus, Egypt, and Phoenicia in a single

---

[12] Adcock, op. cit., 3. Ephorus (Diod. 11.74.3, cf. 71.5 and 13.25.2) and Aristodemus (*F. Gr. Hist.*, 104 F 11.3–4) interpreted this passage as meaning that the whole fleet operating off Cyprus sailed to Egypt.

[13] Peek, op. cit., 302.

[14] The Athenian commander was an otherwise unknown Charitimides (*Pers*. 32); he was still in command some four years later when Megabyzus defeated the Athenians and Egyptians (ibid., 33). It was unusual for the Athenians to renew a command several times unless the holder were a well-known figure. In this case the fleet was operating far from home, but communications with Athens must have remained uninterrupted throughout the siege of the White Castle. Hence Ctesias or his epitomator may well have known that when Megabyzus invaded Egypt the Athenian fleet consisted of forty ships under Charitimides and have mistakenly assumed that the same fleet under the same commander defeated the Persians at the beginning of the campaign.

year.[15] It does not, however, point to this conclusion. The year in which these casualties occurred is not necessarily the first year of the Egyptian expedition,[16] and those sustained in Cyprus and Phoenicia, which may have been very few, do not necessarily imply operations involving a considerable number of ships. At all stages of the Egyptian campaign it was in the interest of the Athenians to divert Persian attention from the main theatre of war. Raids on the Phoenician coast, and perhaps on Cyprus as well, may have been conducted by ships detached from the fleet in Egypt, and these ships may subsequently have sailed either back to Egypt or home to Athens. Many hypotheses suggest themselves, all equally conjectural. Nor does the new inscription from Samos, with its reference to a naval battle [Μέμ]φιος ἀμφ᾽ ἐρατῆς, indicate that the Athenian and allied fleet is more likely to have numbered about forty than two hundred. It is true that the Nile at Memphis is not sufficiently broad for a fleet of two hundred ships to have fought an action on conventional lines there.[17] Topographical accuracy is not, however, to be expected in a dedicatory epigram of this kind, and the author evidently found difficulty in hammering his material into most uninspired verse. He could have written as he did if an Athenian fleet of two hundred defeated the Persians at the mouth of the Nile (κατὰ θάλασσαν, Pers. 32) and a section of it, including the Samian contingent, had pursued the fugitives upstream as far as Memphis,[18] where the prizes to which he refers were secured, perhaps in co-operation with land forces under Inaros.[19]

[15] I.G., i,[2] 929, 1–4.

[16] Gomme, op. cit., i, 311 and 412, n. 2; Meiggs, op. cit., 29, n. 42.

[17] Peek, op. cit., 301.

[18] It is by no means impossible that the entire fleet may have sailed as far as Memphis (cf. Thuc. 1.104.2). The Persian fleet of Megabyzus, said to have numbered 300 (Pers. 33; Diod. 11.77.1), apparently did, and Persian fleets sent to operate in Egypt in the fourth century were very large (Diod. 15.41.3, cf. 43.1 where Iphicrates planned to sail up the Nile to attack Memphis; 16.40.6).

[19] Peek, op. cit., 299, argues that Inaros, whose participation in the battle is implied by Ctesias (Pers. 32), would not have proceeded northwards leaving the enemy in the rear. But Inaros apparently had no ships, and Ctesias surely means only that the naval battle resulted in a victory for the rebel cause, of which Inaros was the leader, and not necessarily that he was present. It was natural that he should remain in the neighbourhood of Memphis and equally natural that the Persians should send their fleet downstream to prevent the Athenians from establishing contact with him.

The narrative of Thucydides is very differently, and somewhat more convincingly, interpreted by those who maintain that, while the Athenians sent to Egypt the whole fleet of two hundred operating off Cyprus, they withdrew some three-quarters of it not long after the victory mentioned by Ctesias, which gave them the undisputed control of the Nile mentioned by Thucydides.[20] Large naval forces could not hasten the reduction of the White Castle; they could be, and evidently were, employed to much better effect in home waters. Hence it is maintained that the squadron retained in Egypt and eventually blockaded at the island of Prosopitis amounted to not more than about forty ships, the figure given by Ctesias. This reconstruction of events, though by no means complete or beyond doubt, is more consistent than the other with what is known of Athenian military history in this period.[21] It also receives a little additional support from a reference in Justin, who records that, while the resources of the Athenians were weakened by the despatch of a fleet to Egypt, they suffered a naval defeat at home,[22] but *interiecto deinde tempore post reditum suorum aucti et classe et militum robore proelium reparant* (3.6.6–7). Although the chapter in which this passage occurs bristles with the grossest blunders, Justin may have preserved an authentic point of some importance.[23] The failure of Thucydides to refer to the reduction of the Athenian fleet in either section of his narrative on the Egyptian expedition, or at some point between them, is attributed by advocates of this reconstruction to his extreme brevity in dealing with the middle years of the Pentecontaetia. They point to other omissions of greater or less importance, and it is undeniable that he could have been guilty of such an oversight here. On the other hand, there is no demonstrable hiatus in his account or between its two sections; indeed,

[20] The suggestion of Meyer, loc. cit., that some of the fleet was withdrawn has been developed by Adcock, op. cit., 4, Wallace, op. cit., 257 and Gomme, op. cit., 322.

[21] For example, Wallace, op. cit., 259, points out that the Athenians had to use the 'oldest and youngest' to defend the Megarid in 458 (Thuc. 1.105.3–4) and yet could muster a large army for the battle of Tanagra in the following year (1.107.5).

[22] Apparently the Corinthian victory at Halieis (Thuc. 1.105.1).

[23] Trogus (*Prol.* 3) in the book here epitomised by Justin apparently gave an account of the Egyptian revolt recorded from the Persian point of view and perhaps derived from the unabridged *Persica* of Ctesias.

he begins his second section with the words οἱ δ᾽ ἐν τῇ Αἰγύπτῳ Ἀθηναῖοι καὶ οἱ ξύμμαχοι ἐπέμενον (1.109.1). It is difficult to reconcile his use of this phrase with the assumption that he was aware of the Athenian withdrawal but omitted to mention it. He would scarcely have stated so categorically that the Athenians stayed on if he had known that most of them withdrew. If, as is possible, the withdrawal took place before the last event mentioned in the first section of his account, namely the investment of the White Castle (1.104.2), he would surely have written 'those of the Athenians and their allies left in Egypt' or 'not withdrawn from Egypt'.[24]

Confirmation of the view that he had no knowledge of an Athenian withdrawal may be found in the language and arrangement of the chapter in which he describes the end of the campaign (1.110). In contrast to his usual practice of understatement, he lays great emphasis both upon the magnitude of the expedition and the magnitude of the disaster. His closing words are τὰ μὲν κατὰ τὴν μεγάλην στρατείαν Ἀθηναίων καὶ τῶν ξυμμάχων ἐς Αἴγυπτον οὕτως ἐτελεύτησεν (1.110.4). It happens that the phrase μεγάλη στρατεία occurs nowhere else in his work, and his use of it here is the more striking in that he tends to depreciate the scale of naval expeditions anterior to the Peloponnesian war.[25] In recording the operations at the Eurymedon (1.100.1), off Cyprus in 450 (1.112.2–4) and against Samos (1.115–17), all involving the employment of two hundred ships by the Athenians, he does not use similar language, though admittedly these were enterprises of much shorter duration than the expedition to Egypt. In the Peloponnesian war itself the expedition of Sitalces with his huge army is not described as great (2.101.6, τὰ μὲν οὖν κατὰ τὴν Σιτάλκου στρατείαν οὕτως ἐγένετο), while the first Athenian intervention in Sicily, conducted initially by twenty ships, later by sixty, and lasting about three years, did not impress him greatly (3.90.1). His insistence on the magnitude of the disaster in Egypt is striking: he uses terms closely parallel to those with which he ends his account of the great Sicilian expedition (cf. 1.110.1, οὕτω μὲν τὰ τῶν Ἑλλήνων πράγματα ἐφθάρη ἓξ ἔτη

---

[24] As his text stands, οἱ ἐν τῇ Αἰγύπτῳ Ἀθηναῖοι καὶ οἱ ξύμμαχοι in 1.109.1 are surely identical with those whose achievements are described in 1.104.2.

[25] Of the expedition against Troy he expresses the opinion τὴν στρατείαν ἐκείνην μεγίστην μὲν γενέσθαι τῶν πρὸ αὐτῆς, λειπομένην δὲ τῶν νῦν (1.10.3).

πολεμήσαντα· καὶ ὀλίγοι ἀπὸ πολλῶν πορευόμενοι διὰ τῆς Λιβύης ἐς Κυρήνην ἐσώθησαν, οἱ δὲ πλεῖστοι ἀπώλοντο with 7.87.6, καὶ ὀλίγοι ἀπὸ πολλῶν ἐπ' οἴκου ἀπενόστησαν).[26] A campaign conducted throughout most of its course by a fleet of some forty ships was considerable, and a disaster involving the whole of this fleet with most of the crews and also part of a further squadron was serious enough, but it may be doubted whether either would have evoked from Thucydides this abnormal emphasis in a largely irrelevant section of a highly compressed excursus. His arrangement of material in describing the fate of the Athenians is equally significant. The sentence quoted above in which he stresses their losses (1.110.1) is the climax of the drama. Yet it does not occur at the end of the whole tragedy but after the debacle at Prosopitis, which is evidently the most important episode. To it are appended notes on two subsidiary episodes, the fate of the Egyptian rebels and their leader Inaros (ibid., 2–3) and the fate of an Athenian squadron, amounting to fifty ships, which arriving in the mouth of the Nile after the fall of Prosopitis was surprised by the enemy and lost a large proportion of its strength (ibid., 4). The arrangement of this chapter may have been influenced by Greek dramatic practice, but it surely suggests that the losses sustained by the squadron of fifty, which perhaps amounted to some thirty-five ships with their crews,[27] were far less serious than those of the fleet destroyed at Prosopitis. If Thucydides had believed the latter to have consisted of only about forty ships, some of the crews escaping to Cyrene, he would have arranged his narrative differently, for the two defeats would have seemed to him at least comparable in their cost to Athens.

Some information provided by Ctesias perhaps explains how Thucydides came to overestimate the extent of the disaster. The epitomator states that more than six thousand Athenians surrendered to the Persians (*Pers.* 34), a figure consistent with his earlier statement that the Athenian fleet amounted to forty

---

[26] Pearson, *T.A.P.A.*, lxxviii (1947), 48, n. 24, draws attention to the similarity of the language used in these two passages. Cf. also 3.112.8, ὀλίγοι ἀπὸ πολλῶν ἐσώθησαν (the Ambraciot disaster at Idomene).

[27] 1.110.4. Both ancient and modern scholars have magnified the losses of this squadron, cf. Schol. ad loc. and Wallace, op. cit., 258, 'a relieving squadron . . . was almost wiped out'. Thucydides does not imply that much more than half the squadron was lost.

ships.[28] He adds that Megabyzus undertook to allow these men to return home unharmed.[29] Diodorus also refers to this surrender (11.77.4–5); evidently Ephorus, reading Thucydides and Ctesias together, concluded that all the survivors from the two hundred ships originally sent to Egypt were permitted by agreement with the Persians to reach Cyrene in safety.[30] There is every reason to accept the surrender as authentic: it is difficult to understand why the Persians should have invented it. Their chief aim was to rid themselves of the Athenians in order that they might complete the suppression of the revolt. They probably had no wish to provoke reprisals, and their action may mark a first step towards the Peace of Callias. There is also every reason to believe that Thucydides was ignorant of the surrender, which was far from creditable in that the survivors had bought their safety at the price of abandoning Egypt; it may even have been repudiated. Despite the compression of his narrative he could scarcely have failed to mention this vital point if he had been aware of it.[31] On the other hand, he could well have known the number of those repatriated by way of Cyrene, namely six thousand, and omitted it as a detail of subsidiary importance. This knowledge, combined with ignorance that the Athenian fleet had long before been reduced from two hundred to about forty, would lead him to infer a loss of more than thirty thousand men and thus to write ὀλίγοι ἀπὸ πολλῶν . . . ἐσώθησαν, οἱ δὲ πλεῖστοι ἀπώλοντο (1.110.1).

The sentence in which Thucydides records the arrival of the fifty Athenian ships in the Nile after the fall of Prosopitis raises a further difficulty and probably contains another error (1.110.4,

[28] Cary, op. cit., 199–200. Busolt, loc. cit., assumes that this figure includes Athenian citizens only, but surely the Persians, from whom Ctesias derived his material, would have drawn no distinction between citizens and non-citizens.

[29] His story that the Athenian prisoners were taken with Inaros to the Persian court where 50 of them were executed (*Pers.* 35–6), if it has any foundation, probably refers to men from the squadron surprised in the Nile. They would not be protected by the local agreement made with Megabyzus by the commanders of the other Athenian fleet.

[30] The mention of this surrender by Diodorus is surely fatal to the view of Momigliano, op. cit., 199–205, that Ephorus did not use the *Persica*.

[31] Although he does not expressly deny that any Athenians surrendered, it is difficult to understand the view of Busolt, op. cit., iii, 1, 331, n. 1, that a surrender is not incompatible with his account.

ἐκ δὲ τῶν Ἀθηνῶν καὶ τῆς ἄλλης ξυμμαχίδος πεντήκοντα τριήρεις διάδοχοι πλέουσαι ἐς Αἴγυπτον ἔσχον κατὰ τὸ Μενδήσιον κέρας, οὐκ εἰδότες τῶν γεγονότων οὐδέν). There is no doubt that διάδοχοι means 'relief' or 'substitute' and not 'reinforcement'.[32] In the fifth and fourth centuries διάδοχος and διαδοχή seem to have invariably contained the idea of taking over some function, or more rarely of inheriting some property, from another; they imply succession, not assistance and co-operation.[33] Thucydides thus means that the squadron of fifty ships was sent to replace part of, possibly all, the fleet operating in Egypt, which was to have then sailed home.[34] It is, however, difficult to believe that the Ecclesia can have voted such a replacement at this stage. The blockade of Prosopitis lasted eighteen months (1.109.4), and when the squadron of fifty was despatched, the Athenians must either have known that their troops had been defeated and were being invested or, having received no news for more than a year, have felt serious anxiety for their safety. Their decision was surely the outcome of bad news or no news, very probably the former.[35]

[32] Adcock, op. cit., 4; Peek, op. cit., 302.

[33] The other passages of Thucydides in which διάδοχος (3.115.2; 7.15.1; 8.85.1) and διαδοχή (2.36.1; 4.8.9; 7.27.3 and 28.2) occur all point to this interpretation. There are many similar examples in fourth-century prose. Isaeus 7.14 and Isocr. 19.43 illustrate the legal sense.

[34] According to Adcock, loc. cit., (cf. Peek, loc. cit.) διάδοχοι πλέουσαι ἐς Αἴγυπτον contains a hint that the Athenian fleet in Egypt at this time amounted to only about fifty ships, the relieving force of fifty being sent to replace a force of approximately equal size. Very probably the fleet in Egypt did not exceed this figure at the end of the campaign, but the words used here by Thucydides surely admit of two other interpretations. He could mean (and whether he was right or not is immaterial) either that the relieving force of fifty was sent to replace part of a fleet of 200 or that the relieving force of fifty was sent to replace the whole of a fleet of 200 (i.e., a substantial reduction was intended). Elsewhere he uses διάδοχος in the singular only, but approximate equality of function appears to be a much stronger ingredient in this word than approximate equality of numbers. For example, the plural occurs twice in a passage where Herodotus (9.21.2–3) describes how at Plataea an Athenian force of 300 relieved a Megarian force of 3,000 (ibid., 28.6); although his account is not above suspicion, what matters is that he can use διάδοχοι despite the disparity of numbers. In the legal sense Isocrates (19.43) uses διαδόχους τῆς κληρονομίας where several persons are to succeed to the estate of one man.

[35] With most of Egypt in sympathy with the Athenians single messengers can have had little difficulty in evading the Persians. Even the large forces of Megabyzus can scarcely have maintained a complete blockade of Prosopitis

In either case the situation clearly demanded that the fleet should be extricated from its present dangers,[36] known or suspected, and not that any part of it should be replaced, an operation likely to be hazardous and unlikely to be profitable. During the siege of the White Castle reliefs may perhaps have been sent to replace ships no longer fit for active service. In the critical period after the victory of Megabyzus, just as in the Sicilian campaign after the Syracusans had gained the initiative, only assistance and reinforcement can have been contemplated. Here again Thucydides seems to have been misled by faulty information.

As has been suggested in the foregoing pages, there is reason to believe that on no less than four points of substance Thucydides' account of the Athenian expedition to Egypt is defective. He was probably ignorant of the naval victory won at the outset, ignorant of the subsequent withdrawal involving a substantial reduction of the Athenian fleet, ignorant of the surrender by the survivors of the blockade at Prosopitis and misinformed on the

---

(Mallet, *Les rapports des Grecs avec l'Égypte*, 38–9). The island was of considerable extent (Hdt. 2.41.5), and the Athenians could hardly have continued their resistance so long unless they had been able to replenish their stocks of food. The ignorance that caused the squadron of fifty to be surprised by the enemy (οὐκ εἰδότες τῶν γεγονότων οὐδέν) was surely not of the blockade at Prosopitis but of the final disaster there. Thucydides deems worthy of mention the fact that its commanders chose the Mendesian arm of the Nile, which was not one of the three major branches; their purpose may have been to evade the Persian fleet and reach Prosopitis without being intercepted, but the Persians learned of their approach, possibly from a captured despatch, in time to concentrate large forces against them.

[36] It is difficult to understand why Cloché, *Revue belge de philologie et d'histoire*, xxv (1946–7), 67, believes that the blockade was considered at Athens to be '*sans péril grave*'. Even though the information available to the Athenians may have been incomplete, it must have been obvious that their troops, surrounded by superior forces at a point many miles from the open sea, were in a very dangerous situation. The complacency ascribed to the Athenian commanders by De Sanctis, *Pericle* 122, is hardly credible unless the statement of Thucydides that their forces were blockaded and besieged (1.109.4) is dismissed as false or grossly exaggerated; even if they felt confident of being able to evade the Persian land forces whenever they chose, the likelihood of an encounter with the Phoenician fleet mentioned by Thucydides (1.110.4) could not be ignored.

71

sailing orders issued to the squadron of fifty sent out at the end of the campaign. The deficiency of his information is not at all surprising if his difficulties in collecting material on this period are fully appreciated. They were probably at least as great as those of Herodotus in collecting material on the invasion of Xerxes. To obtain accurate information on the Peloponnesian war was, as he points out, a laborious task because eyewitnesses were untrustworthy (1.22.3); to reconstruct τὰ παλαιά with any certainty was almost impossible (1.1.3 and 20.1).[37] The Pentecontaetia occupies an intermediate stage to which he does not happen to refer in his introduction, though he does remark later that it was a neglected period (1.97.2). Both in quantity and in quality the available material must have been even less adequate than for the events of the Peloponnesian war: to a much greater extent the passage of time had thinned the ranks of potential informants and increased the risk of distortion on their part. The question when and where he wrote the sketch of the Pentecontaetia is a particularly controversial part of a controversial issue, which lies outside the scope of this essay.[38] If, however, as was once generally agreed and is still believed by many scholars, he added it after his return from exile, very few survivors of the Egyptian expedition can have then been alive. If, as has been recently maintained and seems very probable, he wrote it not long after 424, while he was absent from Athens,[39] he can hardly have had the opportunity of consulting Athenian sources, oral or documentary. He could have revised it after his return, but there is good reason for believing that it never received a thorough revision. Yet his greatest handicap perhaps was that he was here without the immense advantage, which he mentions among his

[37] In both these passages he appears to refer to all Greek history before the Peloponnesian war, but scholars have doubted with good reason whether he intends to include the Pentecontaetia in either case, and the text of the first passage may be defective (Gomme, op. cit., i, 91–2 and 135–6).

[38] Almost all problems connected with the work of Thucydides are in some degree affected by the major problem of its origin and growth (J. de Romilly, *Thucydide et l'impérialisme athénien*, 10).

[39] Gomme, op. cit., i, 362–3, cf. Hammond, *C.Q.* xxxiv (1940), 146–52. This view is, in my opinion, much more convincing than that of Ziegler, *Rh. Mus.*, lxxviii (1929), 58–67, who dates the sketch of the Pentecontaetia, with other excursuses, very early (cf. the very brief summary in *Proc. Camb. Phil. Soc.*, 1912, 9, of a paper by Harrison).

principal qualifications for writing on the Peloponnesian war, of having lived through the period αἰσθανόμενος τῇ ἡλικίᾳ.[40]

Thucydides was probably not more than about six years old when the news of the disaster in Egypt reached Athens. The consternation with which it was received may have been among his earliest recollections, doubtless making a deep impression upon him at a time when he was far too young to assess its true significance for himself. There is also good reason to believe that he was related to the Philaidae,[41] and he is likely to have been brought up in a family circle where the seriousness of the Athenian losses was overrated because the expedition had been undertaken and conducted by the political opponents of Cimon.[42] Hence a mistaken preconception may have been added to the probable inadequacy of his information.

[40] 5.26.5. One reason why he describes the Samian revolt at greater length than earlier episodes of no less importance may be that he was probably passing from boyhood to manhood when it occurred.

[41] Finley, *Thucydides*, 9–10 and 29.

[42] The attitude of Pericles towards the expedition is unknown, and there is no indication whether Thucydides approved of his policy before 445 (cf. 2.65.5).

4

Aristeus, the son of Adeimantus

The chapters in which Thucydides describes the revolt of Potidaea and the subsequent operations there (1.56–65) have often been criticised for their lack of clarity and precision.[1] Their unevenness suggests an inadequate mastery of technique, and it seems very probable that they were written in the earliest years of the Peloponnesian war and never revised.[2] Although opportunities to interrogate Peloponnesian prisoners must occasionally have come his way (cf. 1.22.3), his accounts of military operations which took place long before his banishment are founded very largely upon evidence derived from Athenian sources; but the chapters on Potidaea do not suffer from this disadvantage, and their faults are in no way attributable to a dearth of information from Peloponnesian sources, which seem, strangely enough, to have provided him with much of his material. His narrative is written as much from a Peloponnesian as from an Athenian point of view, and indeed it achieves warmth and colour only where its subject is the Corinthian Aristeus, whose plans and even motives are described in some detail, though they did not substantially influence the course of events. His treatment of Aristeus is suf-

---

[1] The chronology is obscure and confused (Grundy, *Thucydides*, 439; Gomme, *C.R.* lv (1941), 59–67, and *Historical Commentary on Thucydides*, i. 222–4). Among faults of detail (discussed by Steup, *Thukyd. Studien*, ii. 31–5 and in the notes of his edition, cf. the notes of Gomme's *Commentary*) the following are perhaps the most important: though Perdiccas is mentioned in 56.2, he is not fully defined until 57.2; other Macedonians are named without any explanation of their relationship to Perdiccas or to one another (Derdas, 57.3; Pausanias, 64.4; Iolaus, 62.2); and there is no record of the Potidaean reaction to the first Athenian demands (56.2). Grundy, op. cit., 372, is also dissatisfied with the narrative on more general grounds.

[2] Grundy, op. cit., 439–40, believes that these chapters were composed early, but he is sceptical about the conclusions drawn by Steup from the use of the present tense οἰκοῦσιν in 56.2 (*Thukyd. Studien*, ii. 35 and n. ad loc., cf. Gomme, n. ad loc., who promises further discussion in a later volume). This isolated use of the present in a geographical parenthesis does not prove that the whole narrative was completed before the fall of Potidaea, but it does indicate that these chapters were not revised years later when its inaccuracy would have struck the eye.

74

ficiently remarkable to merit examination with the object of seeking an explanation of its peculiarities.

Aristeus is introduced as the leader of the expeditionary force organised at Corinth for the relief of Potidaea. Two personal details are at once noted, and both are creditable: it was owing to his popularity at home that most of the Corinthian volunteers were willing to enlist for this enterprise, and his long-standing friendship with the Potidaeans was responsible for his appointment (1.60.2).[3] That he arrived on the fortieth day after the revolt (1.60.3) is a minor point on which the Athenians can scarcely have had precise information. The aims of his tactical plan at the battle of Potidaea, which involved holding back part of his forces to attack the Athenian rear from Olynthus (1.62.3), are carefully defined, although this unorthodox disposition did not affect the result because one wing of his main army was routed before the detachment at Olynthus could be brought into action (1.63.2). His intentions were anticipated by the opposing generals, but it is unlikely that Thucydides merely inferred them from the movements of the defending army and the counter-movements of the Athenians. If his information had been derived exclusively from Athenian sources, he could not have known that Aristeus and not Perdiccas, who was in command of the cavalry (1.62.2), was responsible for the plan. The success of the wing commanded by Aristeus, which pursued the enemy for a considerable distance, is contrasted with the rout of the Potidaeans and Peloponnesians on the other wing (1.62.6).[4] The sentence in which Thucydides describes the hesitation of Aristeus whether to try to fight his way towards Olynthus or back to Potidaea (1.63.1 ἠπόρησε μὲν ὁποτέρωσε διακινδυνεύσῃ χωρήσας, ἢ ἐπὶ τῆς Ὀλύνθου ἢ ἐς τὴν Ποτείδαιαν) is perhaps the most remarkable of the whole narrative. His doubts recall those of Homeric heroes in dangerous situations (cf. *Il.* 13.455–7), and Thucydides can have learned only through Aristeus himself or from a privileged informant closely associated with him that he ever

---

[3] It is tempting to conjecture that he had served as Corinthian ἐπιδημιουργός at Potidaea (1.56.2).

[4] Aristeus may have been at fault in allowing his men to carry the pursuit too far instead of turning to support the other wing, but no such criticism is implied by Thucydides, who does not appear to have studied the technique of hoplite battles thoroughly until he wrote his account of Mantinea.

contemplated the less obvious course of trying to reach Olynthus. The account of his feelings and actions when the arrival of Phormio with reinforcements had enabled the Athenians to complete the blockade is also significant. Believing that there was little prospect of prolonged resistance unless the number of mouths to be fed were to be drastically reduced, he proposed to retain a garrison of only 500 and to evacuate the remainder of the defenders by sea. He failed, however, to secure the adoption of his plan.[5] His reasons for making this proposal, and perhaps even the proposal itself, were probably communicated only to local officials and not to the assembly, whose morale would have been adversely affected thereby,[6] and in any case his views cannot have been widely known outside Potidaea. Events proved his military appreciation of the situation to have been too pessimistic; despite strenuous efforts by the Athenians (2.58.1–2) and the absence of any direct assistance from the Peloponnese, resistance was continued until the winter of 430–429. His motive in leaving the city secretly after the rejection of his proposal is stated somewhat vaguely (ὅπως τὰ ἔξωθεν ἕξει ὡς ἄριστα): he doubtless hoped to relieve the pressure upon the defenders, but he may also have felt that, as the situation at Potidaea was apparently so hopeless, he could best serve the interests of Corinth by avoiding capture and stirring up trouble for the Athenians elsewhere. The rejection of his plan is likely to have caused some friction between him and the leading citizens. The end of his career is fully described in a later chapter. In the late summer of 430, when he was a member of an embassy sent to obtain Persian aid for the Peloponnesian cause, he and his fellow-envoys were arrested in Thrace by Sadocus, the son of Sitalces, and handed over to the Athenians (2.67, cf. Hdt. 7.137). They were then conveyed to Athens, where they were executed on the day of their arrival without being granted a trial or even

[5] 1.65.1. There seems no reason why Thucydides should have mentioned this rejected scheme at all, and its inclusion appears to be entirely due to his interest in its author. In stating that Aristeus was prepared to remain with the reduced garrison Thucydides is evidently making a point in his favour, and the general tone of this chapter gives the impression that the Potidaeans acted short-sightedly in refusing to accept his recommendation.

[6] A similar plan was adopted at Plataea (2.6.4 and 78.3), but the Plataeans were hardly in a position to reject any decision reached by the Athenians and may not even have been consulted.

76

a hearing. Thucydides attributes this decision, which he records with barely concealed repugnance, to Athenian fears of Aristeus μὴ αὖθις σφᾶς ἔτι πλείω κακουργῇ διαφυγών, ὅτι καὶ πρὸ τούτων τὰ τῆς Ποτειδαίας καὶ τῶν ἐπὶ Θρᾴκης πάντα ἐφαίνετο πράξας (2.67.4). The treatment of Aristeus exhibits two features seldom encountered by readers of Thucydides—its tone of undisguised admiration and its wealth of information about unfulfilled plans and undisclosed motives. Because Aristeus is nowhere directly praised, he is not normally included among characters, such as Pericles and Antiphon, who won the admiration of Thucydides, but just as his activities in the north-east foreshadow the part played by Brasidas in the same area, so his qualities are suggested by similar methods. Yet the record of his brief career compares most unfavourably with that of Brasidas, whose expeditionary force was somewhat smaller (4.78.1), and seems scarcely to warrant the high estimate implied by Thucydides. Aristeus played a minor part in the development of the quarrel between Athens and the Peloponnesian powers, and his achievements were unimpressive. Except for his initial success in reaching Potidaea at all, which was not necessarily a praiseworthy accomplishment and is ignored by Thucydides,[7] and a minor victory at Sermylia, which then revolted,[8] he failed to secure

[7] In discussing how Aristeus and his army reached Potidaea editors seem to have exaggerated the difficulties involved. That they marched overland throughout is almost certain (Gomme on 1.60.3 and 61.3). No obstacles were likely to be encountered in time of peace by a body of volunteers—even in Thessaly, where, though the κοινόν was in alliance with Athens, the influence of Perdiccas with the aristocracy was strong (4.78.2 and 132.2). Parts of Macedonia bordering on Thessaly may have been controlled by rebel princes supported by the Athenians, but Perdiccas could doubtless secure the safe passage of the Corinthian force by one of the several alternative passes and thereafter by routes unlikely to be cut by the enemy. The Athenian operations at Therma and Pydna (1.61.2–3) were part of the campaign against Perdiccas (1.59.2), and it is a mere guess to assume that they constituted an attempt to intercept Aristeus. The silence of Thucydides on the route followed by the Corinthian force may be attributable to carelessness or ignorance, since Athenian movements are also inadequately recorded, but in view of his general attitude towards Aristeus a more probable explanation is that the march was unopposed.

[8] 1.65.2. The revolt of this town is inferred from its failure to pay tribute in the following years (Gomme, n. ad loc.). That Aristeus effected so little after leaving Potidaea was doubtless due to the efforts of Phormio and his force of hoplites.

77

any of his principal aims. It does not appear either that his past associations with Potidaea were in any way responsible for the revolt, which was largely the work of Perdiccas, or that, if his own picked troops had not defeated the opposing wing of the Athenians, the city would have fallen at once by direct assault. His scheme to reduce the garrison, though clearly approved by Thucydides, involved obvious dangers in view of the overwhelming Athenian superiority at sea. While it might have increased the chances of prolonging the siege until the Peloponnesians could organise direct or indirect assistance, it would also have enabled the Athenians to release more of their troops for operations against other rebels in this region (1.65.2). When he was brought to Athens as a captive, the Athenians had every reason to feel resentment against him for contributing to the trouble and expense caused by the operations at Potidaea,[9] but it may well be that personal admiration has led Thucydides to give an exaggerated picture of their fears.[10]

The abundance of information about the plans and motives of Aristeus affords a striking contrast to the general objectivity of the chapters on Potidaea. The interest felt by Thucydides in Aristeus is doubtless responsible for its inclusion, but it is remarkable that, if writing some years before his banishment, he was able to acquire it. Except where the motives of individuals

[9] The choice of the word κακουργεῖν in 2.67.4 (quoted above) is noteworthy. While it is used of legitimate plundering in war (cf. 3.1.2, 6.7.3, 7.19.2), it was a technical term of criminal law and is applied by Thucydides in one of his most outspoken passages to the malefactions of Cleon (5.16.1, cf. 1.37.2 and 134.4, 6.38.2). Aristeus had fought against the Athenians before they were formally at war with Corinth and was evidently classed as a criminal by those who secured his execution, perhaps the extreme democrats (cf. the treatment of the Thebans captured in the attack on Plataea before the declaration of war). Thucydides may have had in mind some decree or speech defending this flagrant breach of international law, especially as he goes on to explain that the Athenians claimed to be within their rights in taking reprisals for the treatment of merchants whom the Spartans had executed as criminals. As Aristeus and his colleagues were travelling to a non-belligerent country and would not be accompanied by a herald, they could not claim sacrosanctity, but they could claim the rights accorded to ordinary prisoners of war.

[10] 2.67.4. There is no evidence that Aristeus became, like Brasidas, a sort of bogy in Attic comedy. It is true that no comedy survives from the first years of the war, but Athenian jokes were remarkably durable. Potidaea was still topical in 424 (Aristoph. *Knights*, 438).

are entirely obvious or may legitimately be inferred from sub-sequent developments,[11] it is not his practice to record them unless he is in possession of material derived from a trustworthy informant. He never guesses undisclosed motives, and very seldom even deduces them from his general estimate of a man's character,[12] but rather applies to them the same searching methods as he claims to have devoted to historical events (1.22.2). The rarity of passages dealing with the plans and motives of individuals is especially marked in his first three books. Before the closing chapters of Book 3, where he describes the campaigns of Demosthenes in the north-west, there is only one passage, apart from those on Aristeus, in which he records undisclosed motives, and in this instance the subject is an Athenian (3.33.3 on Paches).[13] On some of the episodes fully recounted in these books, notably the events at Corcyra, he evidently possessed first-hand evidence of the highest quality, but though some of his informants must have been eyewitnesses, there is no indication that they included persons closely associated with the leading characters. That he became acquainted with the plans and motives of Aristeus must almost certainly have been due to some lucky accident which put him in possession of confidential and reliable information. His picture of Aristeus hesitating between alternative courses of action after the battle of Potidaea appears to have no parallel elsewhere in his work.[14]

The use of Peloponnesian sources during his exile is attested by Thucydides himself (5.26.5, cf. 7.44.1), and his high opinion of Aristeus, as well as the passages on plans and motives, might be founded upon material collected after 424. Acceptance of this explanation would not necessarily involve the assumption that the whole story of the events at Potidaea was written in exile. Some of the details about Aristeus are easily detachable

[11] For example, the motives of Perdiccas in urging his Greek neighbours to revolt from Athens (1.57.5) are so obvious that they might well have been left to the intelligence of the reader.

[12] The discreditable motives ascribed to Cleon (4.27.3-4 and 28.2; 5.16.1), which cannot be based on wholly reliable evidence, are exceptional.

[13] In some cases, where the evidence was deficient or untrustworthy, he states frankly that he is expressing his own opinion or quoting hearsay (cf. 5.65.3 on Agis).

[14] 7.48.3 (on Nicias) has some affinity with this passage but is much less striking.

from the main narrative (1.60.2, 65.1 and the first sentence of 2) and could have been inserted after 424 in chapters composed soon after the outbreak of war. But the account of the battle of Potidaea (1.62-3), which is the corner-stone of the whole episode, would be unintelligible if deprived of its details about the aims of Aristeus:[15] it must have been entirely rewritten to give prominence to his thoughts and actions, and a fundamental revision of this kind would surely have led Thucydides to remove some of the blemishes in other chapters noted by modern scholars. Moreover, his well-known reluctance to trust the accuracy and good judgement of others would scarcely have permitted him to accept so enthusiastically the opinion of an informant on the virtues of an unimportant character who had died some years earlier and had achieved very little success.

The treatment of Aristeus is sufficiently unusual to suggest that it is founded upon personal contacts. To determine precisely where and when these contacts can have been established is rendered difficult by the reticence of Thucydides on his own career, but some negative conclusions may be stated with some confidence. A series of interviews at Athens in 430, when Aristeus was a prisoner, is out of the question, since all the envoys were put to death on the day of their arrival (2.67.4, αὐθημερόν). It is arguable that the admiration felt by Thucydides might be the outcome of meetings with Aristeus in the north-east some years before Potidaea revolted and that the information about plans and motives might have been obtained later from someone whose qualifications to supply it were above suspicion. As had been noted above, the associations of Aristeus with Potidaea were of long standing, while Thucydides owned silver-mines on the mainland opposite Thasos (4.105.1) and is so well informed about the geography of the northern Aegean area that his knowledge must be based largely on autopsy.[16] The interest aroused by earlier contacts would naturally lead him to make

---

[15] Only 1.63.1 could well be a later insertion. It may also be noted that the account of the Potidaea αἰτία, if shorn of the material on Aristeus, would be reduced to a bare summary and could hardly have been used by Thucydides to balance the Corcyra αἰτία even in an unrevised draft.

[16] The neighbourhood of Potidaea was well known to him (1.63.2). Gomme, n. ad loc., observes that 'a not unimportant detail in the topography is missing', but this omission seems to be due rather to compression than to ignorance of the terrain.

searching enquiries about the part played by Aristeus during the revolt, but it is difficult to see how he could have secured his information on plans and motives from any trustworthy source other than the two Athenian ambassadors, Learchus and Ameiniades, who persuaded Sadocus to hand over the Peloponnesian envoys and conveyed them to Athens (2.67.2–3),[17] or someone who had served under Aristeus at Potidaea. It is, however, most unlikely that Learchus and Ameiniades took the trouble to interrogate Aristeus closely about his aims in the conduct of operations which had occurred two years earlier and could no longer provide military intelligence useful to the Athenian *strategoi*. Nor is it at all probable that in the first years of the war Thucydides had an opportunity of meeting and questioning anyone associated with Aristeus in the defence of Potidaea. A staff officer accompanying Aristeus on his mission to Persia might have supplied valuable information, but Greek envoys normally travelled almost unattended, especially on long journeys by land; there is also every reason to believe that all the captives brought to Athens from Thrace, including any subordinates or servants, were executed at once.[18] Most of the Corinthian volunteers at Potidaea evidently remained there when Aristeus slipped away (1.66 and 67.1), and these may have included officers who had enjoyed his confidence. When, however, the city finally capitulated on terms which permitted the entire garrison and the civil population to go wherever they wished (2.70.3–4), the Corinthian volunteers, instead of becoming prisoners of war, must have made their way homewards or to territories not controlled by the Athenians.[19] Moreover, if

---

[17] Unfortunately neither Learchus nor Ameiniades is mentioned elsewhere.

[18] 2.67.4. The number of merchants for whose execution by the Spartans the Athenians were taking reprisals must have far exceeded that of the envoys and their following. The modest expenditure incurred by even the most important embassies (Dem. 19.158) shows that they were not elaborate. The comic ambassador in the *Acharnians* (65–7 and the following scene) succeeded in making his leisurely mission to Persia both remunerative and comfortable, but there is no suggestion that he and his colleagues took a train of Athenians with them.

[19] In 2.70.3 τοὺς ἐπικούρους seems at first sight to refer only to the Peloponnesian mercenaries mentioned in 1.60.1 and to exclude the Corinthian volunteers, but the word is evidently used in its wider sense of 'allies' (cf. 1.40.3, 3.18.1–2).

Thucydides had been able to interrogate an officer who had served at Potidaea throughout the siege, he would surely have described its later stages more fully and from a less exclusively Athenian standpoint (2.58 and 70). Some Corinthian officers doubtless left Potidaea with Aristeus and may have continued his work in Chalcidice when he joined the embassy to Persia, but it is difficult to imagine circumstances in which any of them might have fallen into Athenian hands in the early years of the war:[20] apart from the siege of Potidaea and the subsequent defeat of the Athenians at Spartolus (2.79), there were no important operations involving Athenian troops in the north-east in this period.[21]

All these factors, together with the general impression created by the chapters on Potidaea,[22] combine to make a strong case for believing that Thucydides secured his material about the plans and motives of Aristeus by interrogating him personally in captivity. Athens cannot have been the scene of this interrogation, as has already been noted, so that it can have taken place only in Thrace or during the voyage to Attica. That Thucydides was probably in the north-east in the late summer of 430 is a conclusion of some interest. He almost certainly heard the last speech of Pericles (2.60–4), which was probably delivered in August, and he may have suffered from the plague about this time, though his experience of its effects upon himself and others (2.48.3) may have been gained after the first outbreak (cf. 3.87.1). There is certainly nothing to suggest that he remained at Athens throughout this summer. As he is so well informed about the circumstances in which the Peloponnesian envoys were handed over to the Athenians (2.67.1–3) and shows so much interest in Sitalces (2.29 and 95–101), he may even have been serving in some capacity under Learchus and Ameiniades, who almost certainly travelled to Thrace by sea and seem to have had no

[20] Desertion to the Athenian side by an officer who had been sufficiently closely associated with Aristeus to be aware of his motives is a possibility so remote that it may safely be discounted.

[21] They maintained a garrison at Potidaea (Dittenberger, *S.I.G*[3]. 75.27–9, and 77.44), but they failed to implement their promise to support Sitalces with a fleet and army when he invaded Chalcidice at the end of 429 (2.95.3 and 101.1).

[22] The generally accepted view that Thucydides met and questioned Brasidas rests upon impression alone.

difficulty in securing a guard for their captives, possibly drawn from the crew of their ship. Alternatively, he may have been engaged on some other business, perhaps the management or protection of his Thracian property, and have had the good fortune to return home on the ship conveying the captured envoys. His admiration for Aristeus may date only from this time; on the other hand, he may merely have confirmed in 430 an estimate based upon associations with him in the north-east some years before the outbreak of war. On this relatively unimportant point it would be hazardous to speculate.

In conclusion, it is an interesting coincidence, but no more than a coincidence, that the treatment of Aristeus by Thucydides and that of his father Adeimantus by Herodotus are so strikingly different. The malicious Athenian tradition reproduced by Herodotus, which charges Adeimantus with cowardice at Artemisium and Salamis (8.5 and 94, cf. 59 and 61), is believed by some scholars to owe its origin to the exploits of his son before and during the Peloponnesian war.[23] This hypothesis has nothing to recommend it. The Athenian tradition must have taken shape many years before the revolt of Potidaea,[24] and, as suggested above, the impression made upon the Athenian populace by the achievements of Aristeus may have been exaggerated by Thucydides and was certainly not sufficiently deep to evoke distortions of past history. Conversely, it would be doing an injustice to Thucydides to imagine that his picture of Aristeus is a favourable one merely because popular tradition followed by Herodotus had traduced Adeimantus. He is, however, fond of exposing the gullibility of his predecessors, and he may well have derived a certain amount of satisfaction from reinstating the house of Adeimantus in Athenian esteem.[25]

---

[23] *Inter alios*, How and Wells, *Commentary on Herodotus*, Introduction 39 and note on 8.94. Plutarch, *De Mal. Herod.* 39, produces a thoroughly convincing defence of Adeimantus.

[24] Macan, *Herodotus Books vii–viii–ix* n. on 8.94. In *J.H.S.* lvi (1936), 23–4, I attempted to disprove a parallel view that Herodotus condones the medism of the Thessalians because they were later allied with the Athenians.

[25] I am much indebted to Professor F. E. Adcock, whose criticisms and suggestions have been of the greatest value to me.

5

Seaborne raids in Periclean strategy

Although the decision of Pericles to abandon Attica to devastation in 431 has often been severely criticised, the conviction of Thucydides that his defensive strategy was sound has been widely accepted during the last half-century.[1] On the other hand, the offensive side of his strategic plan, consisting mainly of using his fleet to raid coastal districts of the Peloponnese, has tended to be dismissed as unimportant by modern writers, while a few have condemned it as pointless and wasteful.[2] Because Thucydides devotes so little space to these raids, it is tempting to regard them as minor operations, but his careful record of the naval and military resources engaged, together with his statement that the force which Pericles commanded in 430 was approximately equal to that sent to Sicily in 415 (6.31.2–3),[3] shows that they were on a substantial scale. Their influence upon the course of the war was slight, but if Periclean strategy is to be fully appreciated, it is clearly important to enquire why they were undertaken.

The story of these operations in Thucydides does not make impressive reading, as a brief summary will show. The first expedition sent out by Pericles sailed towards the end of June 431, while the Peloponnesians were still in Attica. It consisted of 100 Athenian ships carrying 1,000 hoplites and 400 archers and was joined by 50 ships from Corcyra with some unspecified contingents from other western allies. Landings were made at several places in the Peloponnese, including Methone, the Messenian town inhabited by Laconian Perioeci, which was narrowly saved by Brasidas, and Pheia in Elis, which was

[1] Busolt, *Gr. Gesch.* iii. 2.901–2; Meyer, *G. d. A.* iv. 297–9; Adcock, *C.A.H.* v.195–6; Miltner, *R.E.* xix.781. Even Beloch, who leads the attack on Periclean strategy (*Gr. Gesch.* ii.1.300 with n. 1, cf. his earlier *Att. Politik*, 22–4), agrees that he was right in refusing to fight a pitched battle in Attica.

[2] Grundy, *Thucydides*, 354–5; Beloch, loc. cit.; Henderson, *Great War between Athens and Sparta*, 62 ('These naval parades round the Peloponnese were extraordinarily futile'); De Sanctis, *Storia dei Greci*, ii.268.

[3] De Sanctis, loc. cit., apparently ignores this passage when he writes of 'piccoli sbarchi sulle coste del Peloponneso'.

stormed; more attention seems to have been paid to systematic plundering than to assaults on cities. Sollium and Astacus in Acarnania were then captured, and Cephallenia was won without bloodshed (2.17.4, 23.2, 25, 30).[4] The Athenian ships on their return voyage landed troops in the Megarid, where they cooperated with the invading land-army under Pericles (2.31.1). In the same year a second fleet of 30 ships raided the coast of eastern Locris at several points with some success and established a permanent fort on the uninhabited island of Atalante (2.26, 32). In 430 Pericles himself took command of a fleet of 100 Athenian ships, on which 4,000 hoplites and 300 cavalry were embarked, the Chians and Lesbians contributing a supplementary squadron of 50 ships. Sailing at the end of June, this force landed near Epidaurus, plundered the country extensively, and almost succeeded in capturing the city; it then plundered the territory of Troezen, Halieis, and Hermione and landed at Prasiae in Laconia, where after still more plundering of the country the small town was captured and sacked. Pericles then withdrew somewhat abruptly from Peloponnesian waters and sent this force immediately to Potidaea under Hagnon (2.56, 58.1).

The expedition to Locris does not present any difficulties and may be dismissed in a few words. The landings on the coast and the occupation of Atalante were both designed to deter the Locrians, who were notorious for piracy, from ravaging Euboea, whose importance to Athens is often stressed (3.93.1; 7.28; 8.1.3, 95.2; Aristoph. *Wasps*, 715–18). Thucydides states that this was the object of these operations, and there is every reason to believe him, especially as hostages were taken. These police measures were essentially defensive: their resemblance to the more ambitious operations round the Peloponnese is only superficial, and the establishment of a fortified post manned by Athenian troops is most unusual at this stage of the war.[5]

Before attempting to discover the motives of Pericles in undertaking the raids on the Peloponnese it will be convenient to

[4] Throughout this essay all references where the author is unspecified are to Thucydides.

[5] A secondary object of the Locrian operations may have been to safeguard communications with the Thessalians, whose cavalry gave some support to the Athenians in the first year of the war (2.22). The interest shown by both sides in this area is illustrated by the Spartan foundation of Heraclea in 426.

examine the attitude of Thucydides towards them. Clearly he did not know what objects they were intended to gain, and as it was his custom to record motives only where he had reliable evidence, he has preferred silence to guesswork.[6] While Pericles saw advantages in publishing the main principles of his defensive strategy before the outbreak of the war, to have disclosed details of his offensive plans in advance was obviously undesirable, and there is no good reason for believing that Thucydides ever served on the board of strategoi with him or had access to any secret information on his designs. One of the reasons why these expeditions seem so aimless and haphazard is that Thucydides has merely summarised the operations at each point where an important landing was made. His bleak notes have none of the lively interest of the pages on the campaigns of Demosthenes in the north-west or of Brasidas in Chalcidice, in which the forces engaged were smaller. Lack of information on their purpose, together with a conviction that, as they resulted neither in triumph nor in disaster, their effect was inconsiderable, may account largely for his treatment of these raids. Yet is is hard to resist the impression that he disapproved of them, believing them to be neither a necessary part of Periclean strategy nor sufficiently effective to compensate for the heavy expenditure which they must have involved.[7] This impression receives some support from his famous eulogy of Pericles, in which he has expressed his personal opinions more openly than in any other passage (2.65.6–13). He approved unreservedly of concentration upon defence and believed that, if maintained, it would have led to ultimate victory, but his silence on any offensive measures and his condemnation of the ambitious enterprises undertaken by others suggest that he himself favoured a more than Periclean strategy which excluded even expeditions around the Peloponnese.[8] It is also significant that the last speech of Pericles (2.60–4)

---

[6] Grundy, op. cit., 317–18, though it seems unlikely that Thucydides was so incurious about matters which he leaves unexplained.

[7] Plutarch (*Per.* 35.3) concludes—apparently from the narrative of Thucydides—that the operations of 430 were abortive, though he expresses very different views on those of 431 (ibid., 34.4). Thucydides treats the expeditions of Nicias, about which he is likely to have been well informed through having served at least once as his colleague, in much the same way as those of Pericles (Westlake, *C.Q.* xxxv (1941), 59–60).

[8] 2.65.7, ἡσυχάζοντάς τε καὶ τό ναυτικὸν θεραπεύοντας, cf. 2.13.2.

contains no reference to the seaborne raids of 431 and 430; if Thucydides had considered them to be effective or even likely to lead to an eventual improvement of the situation, he would surely have caused them to be used as an antidote to Athenian depression. That a favourable peace could have been won by allowing the Peloponnesians to exhaust their strength and their patience in Attica without retaliation is at least a plausible view, in which Thucydides may have had implicit faith, but the facts which he records prove that Pericles was far from content to remain on the defensive.

It is also conceivable, if most improbable, that lack of information or his personal disapproval of these raids may have led Thucydides to obscure an important and immediate result achieved by them. Diodorus (12.42.7–8) states that the expedition of 431 caused the Peloponnesian army to withdraw from Attica, thereby saving the country from further devastation.[9] His later statement that the expedition of 430 had the same result is palpably false and must be dismissed as one of his many doublets (ibid. 45.3): in this year the Peloponnesians remained for forty days in Attica, their longest invasion in the Archidamian war (2.57.2), and it is inconceivable that the Athenians should have promptly lost confidence in Pericles if there had been any grounds for believing that his diversion had caused the enemy to withdraw.[10] For the operations of 431 Diodorus may possibly have had access to evidence on the reactions of the Spartan High Command derived ultimately from an author better informed than Thucydides, who merely states that the Peloponnesians remained as long as they could feed their troops (2.23.3). The hasty retreat of Agis from Attica in 425, as soon as he learned that Pylos had been occupied, may be cited in support of Diodorus, though other factors were involved (4.6). Since, however, his narrative on this stage of the war is no more than a feeble echo of Thucydides, it is far more probable that he has made some mistake or been misled by his source,[11] and

[9] The same point is made in a brief and inaccurate note by Frontinus (*Strat.* 1.3.9).

[10] In 2.57.1 Thucydides quotes a report, in which he does not seem to have had much confidence, that the withdrawal was hastened by the plague.

[11] The earlier statement of Diodorus in 42.7–8 may possibly be a doublet of 45.3, the latter being a false inference from a sentence in Thucydides stating

that the Athenian raids did not influence the movements of the Peloponnesian army in either year.

Pericles has been credited with the intention of blockading the Peloponnese, and his expeditions in the first two summers of the war have been connected with this alleged design.[12] This view is surely untenable. The Peloponnese has a long coastline containing many harbours easily accessible to ancient ships, and whereas triremes, not being designed to carry large quantities of food and water, normally hugged the shore and did not remain long away from their bases, merchant ships did not share these limitations and could, if necessary, cross the open sea.[13] By stationing fleets at Naupactus, Salamis, and Aegina the Athenians might hope to maintain a partial blockade of the Isthmus,[14] though the channel between Aegina and the peninsula of Methana could not be effectively closed until the occupation of the latter, while in the Corinthian Gulf a merchant ship skirting the southern shore had an excellent chance of slipping past Naupactus, especially at night. If the Athenians were to intercept a large proportion of the ships sailing to and from Peloponnesian harbours, they would require a vastly increased navy and well-equipped bases on the coasts or nearby islands. Fleets operating off the Peloponnese for a few weeks at the height of the summer could not hope to interfere decisively with the movement of merchant shipping. In 427, when corn was reaching the Peloponnese from Sicily, the Athenians used their fleet against the sources of supply instead of trying to intercept it (3.86.4). A blockade of the Peloponnese is mentioned only once in Thucydides: Alcibiades declares in his speech at Sparta that the Athenians intended, after they had conquered Sicily, to build additional triremes from Italian timber and use them to blockade

---

that, when the expedition of 430 returned from Prasiae, the Peloponnesians had already left Attica (2.56.6). It is strange that Diodorus, when describing the occupation of Pylos, does not mention the fact that it induced Agis to withdraw his army from Attica (12.61.1; cf. Thuc. 4.6).

[12] Busolt, op. cit., 3. 2.899–901 with 892 n. 6; Beloch, loc. cit.; Kromayer in Kromayer and Veith, *Heerwesen und Kriegführung*, 152–3; Miltner, loc. cit.

[13] Gomme, *Essays in Greek History and Literature*, 190–203.

[14] 2.69.1 (Corinthian Gulf—though the squadron under Phormio was not sent to Naupactus until the winter of 430–429); 2.93.4 (Nisaea).

the Peloponnese (6.90.3, τὴν Πελοπόννησον πέριξ πολιορκοῦντες).[15] It is at least debatable whether the Athenian strategoi ever entertained all the ambitious designs described by Alcibiades, but even if he is speaking the truth, he acknowledges that an increase in Athenian naval strength would be required and that the blockade would be supplemented by extensive operations on land. His words suggest that the Athenians would be embarking upon an entirely new venture in seeking to blockade the Peloponnese.[16] Certainly the brief sorties in 431 and 430 were not planned with this intention.

Developments in the later years of the Archidamian war suggest that the Periclean raids may have been designed to lead to the occupation of fortified posts (φρούρια) in coastal areas, from which the neighbouring country could be harried throughout the year. ἐπιτειχισμός by seaborne troops was a strategy upon which any power enjoying command of the sea might embark at will, and Pericles mentions the possibility of such operations in the speech which he delivered shortly before the outbreak of the war, though only as a retaliatory measure if the enemy established a φρούριον in Attica (1.142.4). The passage is obscure and perhaps deliberately vague, but even if the evidence which it provides is of somewhat doubtful value, this method of exhausting the enemy can scarcely have been overlooked until 425, when Demosthenes suddenly had a happy inspiration while weatherbound at Pylos. The scorn with which Eurymedon and Sophocles received his proposal to fortify the headland (4.3.2–3) suggests rather that they had no faith in ἐπιτειχισμός than that they had never heard of it. From the outset Pericles doubtless considered the adoption of ἐπιτειχισμός,

[15] 2.7.3 does not refer to blockade, as Corcyra, Cephallenia, Acarnania, and Zacynthus were too far from Laconia to serve as bases for blockading the whole Peloponnese. On the other hand, they would be most useful to Athenian fleets making seaborne raids against points west of Cape Taenarum, as is shown by the operations of 431.

[16] Grundy, op. cit., 358, interprets this passage rather differently, inferring from the construction of additional ships that a blockade had been attempted before (i.e. after 425, when bases had been occupied), but had failed because the fleet was too small. It is difficult to believe that, even when they held Pylos and Cythera, the Athenians aimed at an effective blockade of the Peloponnese, but this difference of interpretation is immaterial so far as the operations of Pericles are concerned.

G

but the withdrawal of the Athenians after the capture of Pheia in 431 and of Prasiae in 430 without leaving a garrison[17] indicates that, for the present at least, he rejected it as a contributory means of shortening the war. That he might have adopted it later, if signs of disintegration were apparent in the Peloponnese and all his resources could be thrown into the offensive, is by no means improbable, though the occupation even of small plundering bases is not strictly reconcilable with his cardinal principle that new conquests should not be attempted during the war (1.144.1, 2.65.7).[18] From 425 onwards ἐπιτειχισμός proved a very effective weapon: it led the Spartans to sue for peace soon after the fall of Sphacteria (4.41.2–3), contributed to the grave decline of Spartan morale (4.55), might have caused serious disturbances among the Helots if Brasidas had not achieved his successful diversion in Chalcidice (4.80), and was partly responsible for the willingness of Sparta to make peace in 421 (5.14.3), though anxiety to recover the prisoners lost at Sphacteria was doubtless a stronger motive (4.117.2). In 431, however, long before the offensive power of the enemy had been so much weakened by the somewhat fortuitous capture of these prisoners together with the Peloponnesian fleet, the disadvantages of ἐπιτειχισμός must have appeared to outweigh its advantages. Pericles has been severely criticised for not seizing Cythera at once,[19] but the establishment of garrisons at points in enemy territory which were far from the nearest

[17] The case of Sollium does not affect the present enquiry, as it lay outside the Peloponnese; but it was handed over to the Acarnanians after the Corinthians had been expelled and was not occupied by Athenian troops. The object of the operations at Sollium and Astacus is clear: it was to damage Corinthian interests in the north-west and to gratify the Corcyreans, who contributed to the allied fleet in this year.

[18] Gomme, *Historical Commentary on Thucydides*, i. 462 (n. on 1.144.1), considers that Pericles would not have disapproved of operations such as those at Pylos and Cythera, but the fact remains that he did not attempt to occupy Peloponnesian bases, though his raids afforded at least two excellent opportunities.

[19] Beloch, op. cit., ii.1.300, n. 1, and 330; Henderson, op. cit., 63. It is not by any means certain that the occupation of the island would have been easy; in 424 the end of resistance was hastened by secret negotiations which Nicias had conducted in advance with a disaffected party (4.54.3), and the Spartans may have withdrawn their governor and garrison, fearing a recurrence of the disaster on Sphacteria (Busolt, op. cit., iii.2.1126, n. 4).

friendly port and could not be supplied or reinforced at short notice was an extremely hazardous undertaking. A φρούριον on Cythera might well be attacked and overrun by large forces from Laconia before help could be summoned, while forts on the mainland would be even more vulnerable.[20] The extent and reliability of the support which might be obtained from Messenians and Helots could not be assessed in advance,[21] and the bulk of each garrison might have to consist of Athenian citizens. Unless man-power were to be diverted from the more vital task of defending Athens and the empire, these garrisons could scarcely be large enough to inflict much damage and to resist heavy attacks. If they were small, they could accomplish little more than privateering[22] and might be overwhelmed seriatim. It is both likely from the course which Pericles pursued at the beginning of the war and consistent with his principles that he resolved not to attempt ἐπιτειχισμός, at least until Athens had gained a decisive advantage.

A somewhat more convincing, though by no means satisfactory, explanation of these raids is that they were undertaken for the sake of their effect on morale, Athenian, allied, and Peloponnesian. The evidence of Thucydides (2.21. 2–22.1) and the *Acharnians* shows that a large section of the Athenian populace was severely shaken by the devastation of Attica, and no one knew better than Pericles how easily a change of popular feeling might frustrate his entire plan. Retaliation against the coasts of the Peloponnese, even if it secured no military or political advantages, might at least raise the spirits of Athenians who had lost their property.[23] A display of Athenian sea power would

[20] The first reaction of the Spartan government to the occupation of Pylos was that it could be recovered with ease (4.5.1).

[21] One of the aims of the raid on Methone may have been to test the reactions of the Messenians. In the absence of modern methods of communication the establishment of contact with an underground movement must have been extremely difficult. Pericles can hardly have anticipated how useful and how loyal the Messenians from Naupactus would prove.

[22] When Thucydides states before the occupation of Pylos the Spartans were ἀμαθεῖς ἐν τῷ πρὶν χρόνῳ λῃστείας καὶ τοῦ τοιούτου πολέμου (4.41.3), he implies a distinction between the damage inflicted by seaborne raids, which the Spartans had experienced, and the almost continuous petty privateering conducted from fortified posts, of which they had had no experience hitherto.

[23] Grundy, op. cit., 331, inclines to this view, though without much conviction (cf. Plut. *Per.* 34.3).

also discourage the allies from seeking to use the opportunity afforded by the war to regain their freedom. Morale in the Peloponnese, where the decision to go to war had been secured only by a majority vote, might be weakened, especially in coastal districts where the fear of having homes and farms destroyed must have been highly demoralising. These considerations doubtless influenced Pericles in some degree, but they would have been satisfied by operations on a much less ambitious scale than those which he undertook. In 428 during the dark days of the Mytilenean revolt the Athenians improvised a fleet of 100 ships and sent it to raid Peloponnesian districts near the Isthmus with the express object, so Thucydides believed (3.16.1–2), of parading their strength and impressing the enemy, but the circumstances were very different from those of 431 and 430, and the achievements of this force were not sufficiently important to be noted separately. As Pericles differed from others in leading the populace rather than being led by it (2.65.8), it is most unlikely that he allowed a part of his strategy to be dictated wholly by public opinion. As an experienced and at least competent soldier, he must also have learned long ago the short-sightedness of undertaking operations designed only to provide propaganda.

The most striking feature of the two expeditions to the Peloponnese is the amount of plundering which they accomplished. Wherever troops were landed on Peloponnesian shores they ravaged the country, and in some cases apparently attempted nothing more. Plundering by organised bodies of troops, who either marched or were transported by sea to enemy territory, was a practice so well established in Greek warfare that it was officially distinguished from attempted conquest on the one hand and from mere privateering on the other.[24] It was often entirely aimless and sometimes enabled an incompetent or

[24] Distinguished from attempted conquest, 5.23.1–2 and 47.3–4 (documents of the peace terms and the alliance between Athens and Sparta); from privateering, above p. 91, n. 22 Gomme, op. cit., 10–24, in an interesting summary of conditions of warfare does not refer to seaborne raids. This omission arises from his dichotomy between land warfare and naval warfare, which are surely inseparable in this period. As both sides refused to fight a decisive battle where they were weak, the Athenians on land and the Peloponnesians at sea, most operations undertaken by the Athenians and some undertaken by the Peloponnesians were amphibious.

pusillanimous general, who could not or dared not bring the enemy to battle, to satisfy himself and his home government that he had at least achieved something.[25] As the Greeks were so backward in developing siege technique, a direct assault upon a walled town was most unlikely to succeed, but systematic devastation of the surrounding country would cause the enemy some injury and might even provoke him to come out and fight. Operations of this kind seem sterile, and frequently were, but it is a commonplace that the pillaging of agricultural land was far more damaging in the small coastal plains and narrow valleys of Greece than in richer countries where a normal pro- portion of the total area was cultivable.[26] In raids such as those of 431 and 430 the year's harvest would be burnt,[27] and more lasting injury would result from the destruction of farm buildings and villages, of as many olives and vines as could be dealt with, and of such stock as had not been driven to safety. If, as hap- pened at Pheia and Prasiae, a small town could be stormed without waste of time on siege operations, the distress caused to the whole district would be substantially greater. Conditions of famine could in few cases be relieved by friendly neighbours, who would be unlikely to have any surplus available and would be hampered by the difficulties of transport, especially by land. The area to which each raid brought disaster must be small, and the sufferings of a few thousand Eleans, Epidaurians, or even Laconian Perioeci would scarcely induce Sparta and the Peloponnesian League to discontinue their invasions of Attica and agree to terms which left the Athenian empire intact. Nevertheless, the cumulative effect of continued and intensified

[25] A typical example is that of Alcidas, who in 427 refused to fight a second engagement off Corcyra, much to the disgust of Brasidas, and salved his con- science by plundering the promontory of Leucimme (3.79.3).

[26] The potential destructiveness of such pillaging is illustrated by the suggestion made in the *Republic* (5.470a–471c) that Greeks should refrain from ravaging the land and burning the houses of other Greeks and should content themselves with carrying off the crops.

[27] The expeditions of 431 and 430 both sailed towards the end of June, when Peloponnesian corn would already be cut and could be more easily destroyed than while it was still growing. The Peloponnesians, on the other hand, had to adopt the more laborious method of destroying standing crops in Attica, as the Athenians, if given time to gather their harvest, could have removed the bulk of it to safety behind the Long Walls.

93

raids might have contributed substantially towards the attainment of this aim, so that in this case a well-designed experiment in strategy may lie behind plundering which appears to be so pointless. Pericles, who calculated the resources of Athens so carefully at the outbreak of the war (2.13.2–9), was not likely to squander them on haphazard retaliation for the devastation of Attica and certainly intended his offensive operations to serve some useful purpose in supplementing his more vital defensive strategy.

The injury which seaborne raids could inflict upon the Peloponnese was far smaller in aggregate than that caused by the Peloponnesian invasions of Attica.[28] The landing-force carried by the expedition of 431 was a modest one, and even the larger numbers engaged in the following year compare most unfavourably with the full levy of the Peloponnesian League, while the absence of shore bases limited the maximum duration of each raid. Pericles maintained, however, that, because the Athenians enjoyed the advantages of an overseas empire and control of the sea, their sufferings from the total devastation of Attica would be less severe than those of the enemy from a limited amount of plundering in the Peloponnese (1.143.4).[29] Evidence on economic conditions in the Peloponnese is scanty, but this claim may well be true. The invasions of Attica, however carefully timed to interfere as little as possible with the gathering of the harvest, must have diverted man-power from agriculture and probably reduced the production of foodstuffs.[30] Whereas the Peloponnese may have been largely self-supporting in time of peace except for the states near the Isthmus,[31] wheat was imported during the war from Sicily (3.86.4), and probably from

[28] Beloch, op. cit., ii.1.300; De Sanctis, loc. cit.

[29] It is perhaps the misinterpretation of this passage by some unknown historian that leads Justin (3.7.5–6) and Polyaenus (1.36.1) to declare that the Athenians actually inflicted greater damage than the Peloponnesians (cf. the more cautious statement of Plut. *Per.* 34.3–4). The same tradition, exaggerating the effect of the Athenian raids, may have misled Diodorus (see above, pp. 87–8). Contemporary public opinion, represented by Aristoph. *Peace* 625–7, envisaged the sufferings of Peloponnesian farmers from Athenian raids as severe (Ehrenberg, *People of Aristophanes*, 68).

[30] Gomme, op. cit., 26, mentions this point as one on which Thucydides supplies no information. The only hint is 3.15, where he states that the allies of Sparta resented the proposal to make an additional invasion in 428, because they were busy with their autumn harvest.

[31] Tod, *C.A.H.* v. 14; Michell, *Economics of Ancient Greece*, 49.

Egypt and Libya as well (4.53.3). As the maintenance of an effective blockade was impossible, this traffic could not be stopped, but the devastation of coastal areas might so increase the demand for imported food and other materials that the limited resources of Peloponnesian states in shipping and finance could not bear the strain. Even the inhabitants of inland districts, such as Arcadia, would suffer hardship: as the Corinthians had warned them before the outbreak of the war, the normal flow of their exports and imports might be seriously interrupted by Athenian sea power if they failed to support the cities of the coast (1.120.2). The Peloponnese was economically vulnerable, and since a disaffected opposition existed in nearly every Greek city and the subject populations in Laconia and Messenia were bitterly hostile to Sparta, economic distress might lead to political upheavals. The process whereby Pericles may have hoped to bring about the defection of coastal cities was perhaps somewhat as follows, though any reconstruction of his unfulfilled plans must be hypothetical: first, a seaborne raid (or, if necessary, a series of raids in consecutive summers) leading to acute distress, both physical and psychological; then the emergence of an opposition party, normally democratic, which would take advantage of the state of popular feeling to open negotiations with Athens; finally, the overthrow of the existing régime, possibly with military support from outside. The preliminary stages of this technique nearly brought about the capture of Epidaurus in 430, if, as seems highly probable, a dissident faction was narrowly prevented from betraying the city to Pericles.[32] Movements of the same kind produced valuable results some years later at Megara—though the final step was successful only in securing the capture of Nisaea (4.66–9)—at Troezen (4.118.4) and at Halieis.[33] Admittedly these cities were within easy reach of the Piraeus, and there were other circumstances which would not apply to most Peloponnesian states: Megara had been blockaded with some success and had suffered invasion by land from Attica twice each year, while Troezen and Halieis had been subjected

---

[32] Adcock, *C.A.H.* v. 200.
[33] Meritt and Davidson, *A.J.P.* lvi (1935), 65–71, interpreting *I.G.*i².87. In 412 the devastation of rich agricultural land at Chios nearly caused a revolution led by a faction wishing to come to terms with Athens (8.24.2–5, 38.2–3), but here too ἐπιτειχισμός was used.

95

to ἐπιτειχισμός since the establishment of a fortified post at Methana by Nicias (4.45.2). Moreover, all three places seem to have been garrisoned and treated as Athenian conquests in violation of the principle of Pericles mentioned above. Nevertheless, if the plague had not frustrated the offensive part of Periclean strategy and carried off its author, similar results might have been achieved farther afield by intensive raiding alone, and the structure of the Peloponnesian League might gradually have been undermined.

This method could not be expected to produce quick results, but there is evidence that Pericles envisaged a war lasting several years (1.141.5), and indeed his defensive strategy was based on this assumption. The operations of 431 were perhaps largely experimental, being designed to test enemy reactions, and they seem to have disclosed certain tactical weaknesses which led to changes in the size and composition of the landing-force embarked for the expedition of 430. While the number of ships engaged was 100 Athenian and 50 allied in both summers, the hoplite force was increased from 1,000 to 4,000, and 300 cavalry were substituted for 400 archers. Pericles may have felt in 431 that he must maintain a strong reserve in Attica during the Peloponnesian invasion, as an assault on the Long Walls might be attempted, whereas in 430 this possibility could be ignored owing to the plague. It is, however, more probable that the raids of 431 disclosed the need for stronger and more mobile landing-parties if the work of devastation was to be sufficiently thorough and cover a sufficiently wide area. Cavalry could operate only in moderately unbroken country and would be useless where even the most primitive fortifications were encountered, but the difficult feat of transporting horses by sea, on which Thucydides comments with interest (2.56.2), was undertaken for the first time in order that it should be available. Doubtless even a small body of cavalry would enable the area which could be pillaged in a short raid to be substantially enlarged. Further increases could have been made in the raiding forces after the fall of Potidaea if the plague had not caused the abandonment of such operations.

The demands which these raids would make upon the resources of Athens in man-power, ships and finance must have been carefully studied by Pericles. They took place when the army of the Peloponnesian League, amounting to two-thirds

96

of its strength, was absent in Attica and the forces left in the Peloponnese were small and scattered. Although the Athenian fleet would be known to be off the coast, the objective of each raid could only be guessed, and initial surprise could almost always be achieved.[34] The only resistance likely to be met at the outset was from the local 'oldest and youngest', who could not be expected to put up much opposition against trained hoplites. At Methone Brasidas, forcing his way into the town with only 100 hoplites while the attention of the Athenians was distracted, so stiffened the defence that the assault was abandoned (2.25.2). At Pheia, however, even after two days had been spent in plundering, the Eleans could muster only a striking force of 300 picked men from neighbouring districts, who, being heavily outnumbered, suffered defeat. It was not until a further unspecified period had elapsed, during which the town was captured, that the main force of the Eleans, or such parts of it as were not serving under Archidamus, approached the scene of operations. The Athenians then withdrew, their fleet enabling them to avoid a pitched battle against a superior enemy (ibid. 3–5).[35] The tactics adopted by the Athenians show that they were unwilling to risk substantial losses, and the battle casualties sustained in raids of this kind, provided that they were competently directed, must have been almost negligible. Hence the Athenians would be able to conserve their hoplite strength, in which they were so much inferior to their enemies, even if the absence of commitments elsewhere allowed them to increase their raiding forces beyond the figures of 430. In ships also these operations must have been very economical, as there was little prospect that the Peloponnesians could ever afford to fight a sea battle in defence of their coasts despite their sanguine hopes of assembling huge fleets with assistance from Italy and Sicily (2.7) or by means of loans from Delphi and Olympia (1.121.3, 143.1) The financial burden, on the other hand, must have been heavy,[36] since to keep fleets at sea, especially with large forces

[34] The technique of such raids is admirably summarised by the 'Old Oligarch' (Ps.-Xen. *Ath. Resp.* 2.4).

[35] The home army, i.e. a third of the total hoplite strength, may have amounted to at least 1,500 men, excluding light-armed troops (Beloch, op. cit., iii.1.281–2).

[36] De Sanctis, loc. cit. Records of some payments made for the expedition of 431 are preserved in *I.G.*i².296, ll. 30–40.

97

of troops on board, was very costly. Thucydides comments on the heavy expenditure incurred in one of the early years of the war, when the number of ships in commission was at its maximum (3.17); the year to which he refers is uncertain, but may be 430,[37] when the siege of Potidaea was still in progress. The siege, which cost 2,000 talents in all (2.70.2), was doubtless responsible for the bulk of this expenditure, as it involved winter campaigning, whereas the expedition to the Peloponnese lasted only a few weeks. If Potidaea could soon be reduced and no further revolts occurred, the defensive action required of the Athenian armed forces was unlikely to prove expensive. Pericles had devoted much attention to balancing the possible cost of the war against his available resources (2.13.3–5), and his reserves, judged by ancient standards, were more than adequate.[38] Financial considerations would not prevent the continuance of operations at least as ambitious as those of 430.[39]

It would be absurd to claim that seaborne raids, however successful they might be, could ever have led to the conquest of the Peloponnese, or even of a large part of it. The offensive operations of Pericles were intended only to hasten the attainment of his defensive aims. It has often been pointed out that, unlike his successors, he was content to maintain the *status quo*, and his goal was the limited one of destroying the enthusiasm of the Peloponnesians for the war and persuading them that they could not break up the Athenian empire. The Athenians were

[37] Adcock, *Camb. Hist. Journ.* i (1925), 319–22, who gives reasons for believing that 3.17 has been misplaced and should be inserted after 2.56.

[38] Ferguson, *Treasurers of Athena*, 166–7, lays emphasis on the remarkable feat of accumulating a large reserve and of later recreating a considerable part of it.

[39] Thucydides' treatment of finance is unsatisfactory to modern scholars (Gomme, op. cit., 26), and the amount of information which can be extracted from inscriptions by the labours of epigraphists is insufficient to make good this deficiency. It is strange that there has been so much discussion on the adequacy of Pericles' financial provision for the war when his offensive plans have tended to be underrated and were certainly modest in comparison with those of the Pentecontaetia and of the period after his death. The report of Thucydides in 2.13, which has no parallel elsewhere, is doubtless responsible. There is every reason to believe that Pericles, who had not scrupled to use the funds of the Confederacy for his building programme, would have been prepared to press the allies for heavier tribute if he had thought that a decisive advantage in war could have been gained thereby.

almost universally believed to be the weaker side. It is a favourite motif of Thucydides that not only the Peloponnesians but also most of the Greek world expected them to capitulate soon (1.121.2; 4.85.2; 5.14.3; 7.28.3), this belief being based upon the advantage held by the enemy in far superior man-power (1.121.2) combined with unhindered access to Attica by land. The view expressed by Pericles and shared by Thucydides that, as sea power and finance were the twin foundations of political ascendancy,[40] Athens would prove the stronger was something of a heresy and did not win easy acceptance even at home. Pericles himself may have felt occasional misgivings, but it is natural that he should seek to apply his principles by using sea power and finance to the best advantage. Whether or not his offensive strategy would have helped him to achieve his aim within some five or six years is a question upon which it would be rash and unprofitable to speculate. It was, however, an experiment which might well be successful and could not seriously weaken Athenian resources.

Three explanations of the seaborne raids directed against the Peloponnese have been examined and rejected: that they formed part of a design to blockade the whole peninsula, that they were the immediate prelude to the establishment of fortified bases round the coast, and that their sole object was to influence morale. It is scarcely necessary to debate whether, while Pericles successfully devised a method of thwarting the Spartan plan to force a decision by orthodox land attack, his offensive action was a mere *pis aller* adopted because he could think of no better way of using his fleet, or was the outcome of a vague ambition to rival the exploits of Tolmides in 455.[41] There remains the view that the devastation of enemy territory, which was the chief achievement of these operations, was also their chief object, being designed to cause so much economic distress that political consequences would ensue and the Peloponnesian League would have no

---

[40] That the conventional Archidamus also held this view is perhaps not very probable. The sentiments attributed to him in 1.80–1 have a somewhat Periclean flavour: Thucydides may have known only that he opposed a declaration of war and himself supplied τὰ δέοντα (1.22.1). The attitude of Pericles and Thucydides towards sea power is discussed by Momigliano, *C.R.* lviii (1944), 2–3.

[41] Henderson, op. cit., 62–3, believes that he attached far too great a value to his recollection of Tolmides' voyage and its results.

heart to continue the war. Because the plague caused the early abandonment of his counter-offensive, the motives of Pericles were not disclosed and apparently remained unknown to Thucydides. Although so many generals of the fifth and fourth centuries plundered enemy territory without forming a clear conception of the advantages which they hoped to secure, Pericles was not necessarily one of them.

6

Athenian aims in Sicily, 427–424 B.C.

A STUDY IN THUCYDIDEAN MOTIVATION

The first Athenian expedition to Sicily is among the most puzzling episodes of the Archidamian war. The evidence is virtually
confined to the account of Thucydides[1] which is tantalisingly
meagre and does not explain at all fully the motives of the
Athenians in this venture.[2] There have been many modern
attempts to reconstruct Athenian relations with the west before
the great expedition of 415–413,[3] and these have necessarily included some consideration of Athenian aims in sending out, and
later reinforcing, the first expedition. It seems to me that some
light may be thrown upon the problem of Athenian aims by an
examination of certain passages in the narrative of Thucydides.
A preliminary requirement, however, is to try to account for
features of the narrative that have caused readers to find it
somewhat unsatisfactory as a record of an interesting and not
unimportant episode.

I. THE GENERAL LESSON OF THE EPISODE

To Thucydides the function of a historian, though almost
wholly didactic, is not by any means confined to imparting
factual information. To instruct his readers by expounding
to them the general lessons to which historical events give rise is,
as has often been observed, at least as important to him as to

---

[1] Diodorus (12.53–4) and Justin (4.3.4–7) add nothing of value. The former
gives some rather untrustworthy information about the mission of Gorgias to
Athens (53.2–5), while the account of Justin is full of characteristic blunders.
A papyrus fragment from an unknown historical work, possibly that of
Philistus (*F. Gr. Hist.*, 577 F 2), is much more reliable: it includes some details
about the campaign not recorded by Thucydides, and these seem to be
authentic.

[2] The relevant chapters are: 3.86, 88, 90, 99, 103, 115; 4.1–2, 24–5 (cf. 48.6),
58, 65.

[3] Cf., apart from general histories of Greece or of Sicily, H. Droysen, *Athen
und der Westen* (1882), and H. Wentker, *Sizilien und Athen* (1956). I have not
seen G. M. Columba, *La prima spedizione ateniense in Sicilia* (1889).

provide them with a reliable record of these events.[4] The desire to establish the general principles by which the course of history was guided is, very naturally, seen most clearly in the speeches, but it also pervades his narrative, though here his conclusions are more often implied than expressed and in some instances emerge only after careful examination.[5] In the two sentences with which he ends his account of the first Athenian expedition to Sicily he voices with exceptional forthrightness his personal conviction on an issue of very wide significance. After recording the condemnation of the Athenian generals on their return from Sicily, Pythodorus and Sophocles being banished and Eurymedon fined, he adds that the Athenians οὕτω τῇ παρούσῃ εὐτυχίᾳ χρώμενοι ἠξίουν σφίσι μηδὲν ἐναντιοῦσθαι, ἀλλὰ καὶ τὰ δυνατὰ ἐν ἴσῳ καὶ τὰ ἀπορώτερα μεγάλῃ τε ὁμοίως καὶ ἐνδεεστέρᾳ παρασκευῇ κατεργάζεσθαι. αἰτία δ᾽ ἦν ἡ παρὰ λόγον τῶν πλεόνων εὐπραγία αὐτοῖς ὑποτιθεῖσα ἰσχὺν τῆς ἐλπίδος (4.65.4). He thus finds in the treatment of the generals an illustration of the irresponsibility shown by the Athenians under the influence of bad leadership by the successors of Pericles.[6] The over-optimism to which he refers became less widespread after the defeat at Delium, but in his opinion extreme democracy was at all times liable to make grave mistakes, and he is seeking here to expose one of its inherent defects for the enlightenment of his readers. His own condemnation after the loss of Amphipolis could have been cited in support of his thesis and was perhaps in his mind, but characteristically he has not chosen to cite it.

The wish to teach a lesson, which may be detected in so many Thucydidean narratives, naturally influences the way in which the facts are presented. A good example is the account of the naval engagements in 429 in which the small Athenian squadron under Phormio showed how immensely superior the Athenians

---

[4] Cf. R. G. Collingwood, *The Idea of History* (1946) 29–31, who, in comparing him with Herodotus, is severely critical of him because his mind 'is constantly being drawn away from the events to some lesson that lurks behind them'; J. H. Finley, *Thucydides* (1942), 296–7.

[5] The minute analysis of several narrative passages by J. de Romilly, *Histoire et raison chez Thucydide* (1956), 21–106, is most instructive.

[6] Cf. 2.65.7, which was probably written long after 4.65.4. F. Jacoby, *F. Gr. Hist.* iii b, Suppl. i (1954), 135–6, discusses this deterioration in connection with the condemnation of Phormio, who was perhaps its first victim.

ATHENIAN AIMS IN SICILY, 427–424 B.C.

were to the Peloponnesians in enterprise and in naval technique (2.83–92). Thucydides makes this superiority the keynote of his narrative. Although Phormio was apparently guilty of a serious error before the second battle, this point is not stressed,[7] the reason surely being not that Thucydides is over-indulgent towards Phormio but that he is anxious not to prejudice the main lesson of his narrative. The impact of a general lesson upon his account of the first expedition to Sicily is less obvious, partly because the narrative is not continuous but broken up to an abnormal extent through strict application of his chronological system. Here too, however, the same influence may be seen at work throughout his account of the expedition. His presentation of it, which is remarkable in some respects, seems to have been largely determined by a desire to use the episode to substantiate the validity of the general lesson propounded in the two concluding sentences quoted above.

The scale of the narrative is disappointingly small. The speech of Hermocrates at Gela (4.59–64), which is probably a later addition[8] and seems to have a different object in view, is out of all proportion to its setting.[9] There are many accounts of military episodes in the Archidamian war in which Thucydides confines himself to essentials and evidently chooses to omit much that he knows. It is his practice to select for detailed treatment episodes that seem to him to be especially important or significant. There appears, however, to be no parallel to his statement (3.90.1) that, ignoring operations in Sicily in which the Athenians were not involved, he will record only the most noteworthy of those in which they were.[10] He seems determined to represent the campaign as an unimportant sideline.[11] The almost unrelieved

---

[7] A. W. Gomme, *Historical Commentary on Thucydides* ii (1956), 234–7, discusses this error but does not attempt to account for Thucydides' treatment of it.

[8] Gomme, op. cit., iii. 521. I agree with W. Schmid, *Gesch. der griech. Lit.* i. 5 (1948), 86 n. 8 (cf. Gomme, loc. cit.) that the narrative of the first expedition was written before 415. I have discussed the speech of Hermocrates below, pp. 176–9.

[9] G. P. Landmann, *Eine Rede des Thukydides* (1932), 12.

[10] He does not in fact exclude all military actions in which the Athenians did not take part (cf. 4.25.7–9).

[11] E. A. Freeman, *History of Sicily* iii (1892), 30, observes that 'a general feeling of littleness runs through everything'.

bleakness of his narrative[12] contrasts strangely with references by Aristophanes to Athenian aspirations in the west.[13] Nor is the impression that Thucydides seeks to create altogether consistent with the facts that he records. The fleet sent to Sicily in 427 amounted to only 20 ships (3.86.1), but this expedition was, so far as is known,[14] the first military intervention by the Athenians in the west and must have been considered by many of them to mark a new and significant development in their war policy. When subsequently they decided to send out a reinforcement of 40 ships (3.115.4), the size of their fleet in Sicilian waters was almost equal to that of the fleet originally voted for the expedition of 415 (6.8.2).[15] However insignificant may have been the achievements of this fleet of nearly 60 ships during the months that elapsed between the arrival of the reinforcement towards the end of 425 and the conclusion of peace in the following summer, it is remarkable that Thucydides mentions only that μετὰ τῶν ἐκεῖ ξυμμάχων ἐπολέμουν (4.48.6). His treatment of the whole campaign suggests not merely that it was of little importance but also that it was only remotely connected with the Peloponnesian war, an impression strengthened by his statement referred to above that he will record only its salient events (3.90.1). It is true that it was not a conflict between Athenians and Peloponnesians and that its influence upon the course of the war was slight. Yet some other episodes described much more fully are not less peripheral: an example is the campaign in Lyncestis in which Brasidas found himself compelled to take part in 423 (4.124–8). A further impression created by Thucydides is that, while the Athenians were agreed in sending out the expedition and later in reinforcing it, they were gravely at fault in failing to agree about its purpose, and that this lack of agreement damaged its prospects and handicapped the generals.

[12] Noteworthy exceptions are the brief excursus on the islands of Aeolus (3.88.2–3) and the reference to Homeric Charybdis (4.24.5). The former is largely irrelevant, the latter wholly so (see above, pp. 8–9).

[13] Droysen, op. cit., 9–11, who discusses the references to Carthage in *Knights* 174 and 1303.

[14] The mysterious mission of an Athenian admiral Diotimus to Naples mentioned in a fragment of Timaeus (*F. Gr. Hist.* 566 F 98) did not necessarily involve military operations.

[15] The reinforced fleet in 425 numbered rather less than 60 because the Athenians had sustained some losses since 427 (cf. 4.25.4–5).

The narrative of Thucydides thus seems to have been framed largely with the intention of showing that Pythodorus, Sophocles and Eurymedon were unjustly condemned on the charge ὡς ἐξὸν αὐτοῖς τὰ ἐν Σικελίᾳ καταστρέψασθαι δώροις πεισθέντες ἀποχωρήσειαν (4.65.3); that with the resources available to them and in the conditions in which they found themselves in Sicily, they conducted their mission at least adequately; that the real culprits were the Athenians at home and their leaders, especially the demagogues.[16] There is every reason to accept the validity of his thesis, which, if accepted, is most instructive in helping his readers to understand Athenian policy. He is not falsifying or manipulating the evidence, but his account of the expedition would doubtless have been different, and perhaps more satisfying to modern scholars, if he had been less preoccupied with the establishment of his case. This is a factor that must be borne constantly in mind in examining his narrative.

II. THUCYDIDES ON THE AIMS OF THE EXPEDITION

The decision of the Athenians to send even as many as 20 ships to Sicily in 427 under Laches and Charoeades is somewhat surprising. The Siceliot appeal for help was made under the terms of the alliances with Leontini and Rhegium (3.86.3), which had been renewed in 433/2. The Athenians could, however, hardly have been blamed if they had answered that the situation in Greece absolved them from honouring obligations to distant allies. In 415, when they were in a much happier position and were nominally at peace with Sparta, Nicias maintained that dangers threatening them at home warranted a rejection of the appeal from the Segestans, with whom they were allied.[17] In the late summer of 427 only a few months had elapsed since they had crushed the revolt of Lesbos, and though the plague had tem-

---

[16] Cf. the similar verdict, though the circumstances and the results were totally different, in 2.65.11 on the great Athenian expedition to Sicily. It may be noted that there can be no question of any personal bias on the part of Thucydides in favour of the convicted generals: he is, by implication, severely critical of action taken at Corcyra by Eurymedon in 427 and by Eurymedon and Sophocles together in 425 (Gomme, op. cit., ii. 369, iii. 496, cf. his *Greek Attitude to Poetry and History* (1954), 147–8).

[17] 6.10.1–5, cf. the reply of Alcibiades in 6.17.6–18.1.

porarily abated somewhat,[18] their capacity for offensive action against their enemies at home was still very limited. In these circumstances a proposal to send a fleet to the distant west could scarcely have secured the support of a majority in the Ecclesia unless very cogent arguments could have been advanced in its favour. The motives that led the Athenians to take this step are defined by Thucydides in the following sentence: καὶ ἔπεμψαν οἱ Ἀθηναῖοι τῆς μὲν οἰκειότητος προφάσει, βουλόμενοι δὲ μήτε σῖτον ἐς τὴν Πελοπόννησον ἄγεσθαι αὐτόθεν πρόπειράν τε ποιούμενοι εἰ σφίσι δυνατὰ εἴη τὰ ἐν τῇ Σικελίᾳ πράγματα ὑποχείρια γενέσθαι (3.86.4). The professed reason for intervention was doubtless stated in official documents such as the formal answer to the appeal of the Siceliot allies.[19] It must have been frequently repeated in Sicily in the course of the campaign there and is rejected by Hermocrates in his speech at Gela (4.60.1). Of the two real aims the first is negative and defensive, the second positive and offensive. While there may have been some Athenians to whom it seemed equally desirable and important to stop the flow of supplies to the Peloponnese and to explore the possibility of conquering Sicily, the most natural interpretation of the passage is that the supporters of the proposal to intervene in the west fell into two groups, the members of each group being influenced by different considerations.[20] Summaries of public opinion on important issues are common in Thucydides, and some of them are complex. In a number of instances the views reported by him do not seem to have been all held by the entire community but rather by separate sections of it, though these sections are not specifically differentiated.[21] The passage quoted above surely belongs to this category. The sources upon which he founds his summaries of public opinion doubtless vary considerably, but it is difficult to believe that in any instance he is merely giving his own general impression without possessing any definite evidence to support

[18] The second major outbreak occurred in the winter of 427/6 shortly after the fleet had sailed for Sicily (3.87.1–2).

[19] Cf. the use of προφάσει in 5.53.

[20] I follow F. E. Adcock, *C.A.H.* v (1927), 223–4 on this point; cf. B. H. G. Williams, *C.Q.* xxv (1931), 55–6.

[21] Passages of this kind in which he uses links such as τε, καί, καὶ ἅμα and ἅμα δέ, though he may well be giving the opinions of different factions or bodies, are: 1.44.2–3; 3.92.4; 4.80.1–2; 4.108.3–6; 5.14.1–4 (two examples); 5.28.2; 8.76.3–6.

it.[22] In most instances he must be relying upon his knowledge of public or private debates attended by himself or by some trustworthy informant but not reported in detail in his work. The appeal for assistance made by the envoys of the western allies must have been discussed by the board of generals, by the Boule, and by the Ecclesia. Such discussions are almost certainly the source from which he derives the two real aims attributed to the Athenians.

The desirability of preventing, so far as possible, the shipment of Sicilian grain to the Peloponnese must have been recognised by many Athenians. Whether or not the need to interrupt this traffic was so pressing as to warrant the unprecedented step of sending a fleet to Sicilian waters was doubtless a more debatable question. Athenian weakness since 430 had caused the discontinuance of seaborne raids on a large scale against coastal districts of the Peloponnese which had formed an integral part of Periclean strategy in the first two summers of the war. Only one very modest raid on Laconia had been undertaken (3.7.1–2 and 16.2). The dispatch of 100 ships to districts near the Isthmus in 428, which imposed a severe strain on Athenian manpower weakened by the plague, was a desperate attempt to prevent the Peloponnesians taking steps to relieve the pressure on beleaguered Mytilene, and though its principal aim was achieved, the expedition was little more than a display of force (3.16.1–2).[23] The Periclean raids in 431 and 430 seem to have been designed mainly to create disaffection in the Peloponnese by causing a shortage of food. The Peloponnese was evidently not self-supporting when many of its peasant farmers were absent on active service for part of the summer, so that grain had to be imported from Sicily and elsewhere. Pericles apparently believed that if demand could be so much increased by means of repeated plundering raids that it could no longer be met by imports, some coastal states, where the distress would be most acutely felt, might be impelled to

[22] H. Stein, *Rhein. Mus.* lv (1900) 533, and G. B. Grundy, *Thucydides* i[2] (1948), 360, maintain, wrongly in my view, that 3.86.4 is based only upon personal opinion.

[23] 3.17, in which details are given about the magnitude of the Athenian war-effort, is either spurious or, more probably, misplaced. Adcock, *Camb. Hist. Journ.* i (1925), 319–22, maintains that it refers to 430, not 428, and should follow 2.56.

desert the Spartan cause.[24] In 427 the situation had changed. The Athenians were now forced to consider rather how the shipment of Sicilian grain to the Peloponnese might affect the weight of Peloponnesian attacks on Attica. If Syracuse were to crush the western allies of Athens, who were already hard pressed (3.86.3), and to gain undisputed control of the sea-routes from the west, the volume of this traffic to the Peloponnese could be much increased. The Peloponnesians would then become less dependent upon local production and would be in a position to undertake longer and more devastating invasions of Attica. It had never been practicable to stop imports to the Peloponnese by means of naval blockade,[25] and the Corcyreans were so weakened by recent outbreaks of civil strife that they could no longer be expected to make any effective contribution towards the interception of supplies from the west. To some Athenians the best prospect of countering a dangerous development at home must have seemed to lie in seeking to check the flow of this traffic at its source by sending military aid on a limited scale to their western allies. Regarded in this light, the expedition had a purely defensive aim, and it may well have had the support of some who still clung to the principles of Periclean strategy.

The second of the aims attributed to the Athenians (πρόπειράν τε ποιούμενοι εἰ σφίσι δυνατὰ εἴη τά ἐν τῇ Σικελίᾳ πράγματα ὑποχείρια γενέσθαι) is believed to point forward to the great expedition of 415 and so to have been written when the events of 427 were already long past. To accuse Thucydides of making a somewhat dishonest guess in the light of later developments is

[24] I suggested this explanation in the preceding essay, pp. 84–100 above. Gomme, op. cit. ii. 85, though in general agreement with my views, criticises me for believing that 'Thucydides did not understand Athenian strategy'. Although it was not so much lack of understanding as lack of information about the purpose of seaborne raids that I ascribed to Thucydides, this criticism is fully justified. While Thucydides was not always able to obtain reliable information even about contemporary events (1.22.3), his silences are seldom the outcome of ignorance or doubt. I now believe that his silence on the purpose of seaborne raids, as well as the brevity of his narrative, is due to his preoccupation with a general lesson that he wishes to convey. So eager is he to convince his readers that Periclean defensive strategy was fundamentally sound and could ultimately have brought victory (1.144.1 : 2.65.7–13) that he deals somewhat perfunctorily with the offensive operations of Pericles, which were in any case subsidiary, and does not explain their aim.

[25] See above, pp. 88–9.

surely unwarranted. It is preferable to believe that he has in mind the sending of Sophocles and Eurymedon with the reinforcement of 40 ships;[26] but the phrase does not necessarily presuppose knowledge of later events. It is surely based, as has been suggested above, upon views expressed at Athens when the first Siceliot appeal was being discussed in 427. Even the most optimistic advocates of intervention can hardly have expected a squadron of 20 ships to do more than explore the prospects of western expansion. Yet despite the weakness of Athens at the time there is no reason to doubt that a considerable number of Athenians saw in this appeal an opportunity to test the feasibility of conquering Sicily. The strategy of Pericles had encountered opposition even before the outbreak of the plague (2.21.2–22.1), and during the ensuing period of struggle for survival a widespread reaction against his principles had been developing. Some of his would-be successors, eager to win popular support and to outbid their rivals (2.65.10), looked forward to the adoption of a more offensive strategy at the earliest opportunity, including a revival of attempts to win a decisive advantage over the Peloponnesians by the establishment of Athenian control in more or less distant areas. Although the more enterprising of the military leaders, such as Demosthenes, may have contributed to this reaction against Periclean strategy, its principal sponsors were undoubtedly the demagogues. Secure in the irresponsibility of their unofficial status, they could advocate imperialistic schemes in the knowledge that, if these failed, the generals whose duty it was to carry them out would have to bear the blame.[27] In this instance it was certainly the demagogues and their supporters that welcomed the opportunity to intervene in Sicily as a preliminary step towards the implementation of more ambitious plans when circumstances allowed.[28] To them it was the first move towards a complete break with Periclean strategy. It is most unlikely that a majority in the Ecclesia shared their views at this stage.

The decision to send out a small fleet of 20 ships thus seems to have been the outcome of a situation characteristic of the

[26] Gomme, op. cit., ii. 387–8.
[27] Cf. C. Hignett, *History of the Athenian Constitution* (1952) 262–5. 2.70.4 is an early example of the tendency to blame the generals.
[28] Adcock, *C.A.H.* v. 224.

Athenian democracy at times when strong leadership was lacking. Intervention in Sicily was evidently favoured by most Athenians, who were also probably agreed that because of difficulties at home it must necessarily be on a modest scale.[29] There was, however, no agreement in regard to its aims. This cleavage of opinion between sections of the population whose views on the direction of the war were basically irreconcilable was in this instance conveniently obscured by the official fiction that the object of the expedition was altruistic, namely to protect the western allies of Athens from aggression. Nevertheless, the dangers of such agreements founded on disagreement were obvious.

In the winter of 426/5 the Athenians voted, in response to renewed appeals from their allies, to reinforce their fleet in Sicily by sending out 40 additional ships, a few under Pythodorus at once and the rest under Sophocles and Eurymedon in the spring (3.115.3–5). The progress of their recovery had been such that they could take this action without endangering their security at home. Their motives are stated by Thucydides to have been the following: ἅμα μὲν ἡγούμενοι θᾶσσον τὸν ἐκεῖ πόλεμον καταλυθήσεσθαι, ἅμα δὲ βουλόμενοι μελέτην τοῦ ναυτικοῦ ποιεῖσθαι (3.115.4). It would be a mistake to imagine that he is drawing a distinction between the aims of the first expedition and those of the second. He expects his readers to remember what they have read a few pages earlier and to assume that the Athenians were still actuated by the same motives as before, though clearly more might be expected of a fleet amounting to nearly 60 ships than a mere exploration of the prospects of conquering Sicily. The two new motives supplement and do not supersede those stated earlier, and there is again reason to believe that Thucydides is reproducing the substance of official or unofficial views expressed at the time and not stating his own opinion. It could be, and indeed has been,[30] maintained that the first part of the passage quoted above (ἅμα μέν) represents the view of the demagogues and their supporters, who believed that their ambition to conquer Sicily could be achieved if the fleet

---

[29] Williams, op. cit., 52–6, who sees in the decision a compromise between those who wished to send a larger fleet and those who wished to send none at all, does not seem to me to take sufficient account of Athenian weakness in 427.

[30] G. Busolt, *Gr. Gesch.* iii. 2 (1904), 1082; Adcock, loc. cit.

there were substantially increased; and that the second part represents more moderate opinion. On the other hand, τὸν ἐκεῖ πόλεμον καταλυθήσεσθαι has an official flavour that suggests a different interpretation. καταλύειν, with or without τὸν πόλεμον, as well as κατάλυσις τοῦ πολέμου, occurs not infrequently in official documents quoted verbatim by Thucydides.[31] Hence it is likely that he is here referring to the decree voting the dispatch of the 40 ships, its official language being sufficiently ambiguous to obscure a divergence of view between those who expected their increased expeditionary force to conquer Sicily and those who expected it to deter the Dorian states from further aggression and compel them to agree to a settlement that left the allies of Athens intact.[32]

The second of the two reasons given for the sending of the reinforcement, namely that the Athenians wished to provide practice for their fleet, has puzzled scholars to such an extent that some have refused to take it seriously and have considered it to be intentionally ironical.[33] Irony is not a characteristic of Thucydidean narrative.[34] It might be suggested with greater plausibility that this statement is based upon an ironical or semi-ironical speech or remark which made a deep impression at Athens when the second appeal from Sicily was being discussed. There are, however, good grounds for regarding it as perfectly serious. The crews of triremes needed not only intensive training but also constant practice, preferably on active service, if a fleet were to be really efficient.[35] The plague caused a shortage of

[31] 4.118.6 and 13; 5.23.1 and 2; 5.47.3 and 4; 8.18.2; 8.37.4; 8.58.7.

[32] It seems that καταλύειν τὸν πόλεμον,, or καταλύεσθαι which is normally used without τὸν πόλεμον, almost invariably refers to the termination of a war by negotiation rather than by conquest (1.24.6; 1.81.5; 2.29.5; 2.95.2; 4.18.4; 4.20.2 (καταλύσεως); 4.108.7; 5.15.2; 6.36.4). Thus it could be argued that the views of the less enterprising Athenians are represented more strongly here than those of the extremists.

[33] Busolt, loc. cit.; Marchant, n. ad loc. (quoted by Gomme, op. cit. ii. 431, with qualified approval). Grundy, op. cit. i². 366 finds this statement of Thucydides 'too incomprehensible even for discussion'.

[34] In 2.7.2, where Marchant, n. ad loc., sees irony in the figure of 500 ships that the Peloponnesians are said to have expected to muster, Gomme, op. cit. ii. 7, rightly rejects this interpretation.

[35] This point is emphasised by Pericles (1.142.6–9), cf. 7.14.1 (Nicias), and [Xen.] 'Αθ.πολ. 1.20.

trained oarsmen,[36] and though this shortage seems to have been gradually made good, there had been few opportunities to test new recruits in battle because of the reluctance of Spartan admirals to engage Athenian fleets. In 427 Alcidas had refused to fight first off the Asiatic coast (3.31.1–2) and later off Corcyra (3.81.1). Yet it was as important as ever that the Athenians should maintain their superiority in seamanship: apart from the demands of routine duties arising from Athenian dependence upon seapower, there was always a possibility that the Peloponnesians might find themselves compelled to fight a naval battle on a considerable scale, as indeed happened at Pylos in the summer of 425 (4.13.4–14.4). The expedition under Sophocles and Eurymedon, if it achieved nothing else, was at least likely to provide large numbers of Athenian sailors with valuable experience. This consideration was doubtless in the minds of many Athenians and may well have influenced deeply, perhaps decisively, the reaction of the Ecclesia to the second Siceliot appeal.[37]

It might have been expected that the fleet would have been ordered to sail to Sicily with all speed so that it might throw its weight into the struggle there as early as possible in the summer of 425. Its orders were, however, much more complex (4.2.3–4). In the course of its voyage it was to help the Corcyrean democrats, who had for some time been harried by the exiled oligarchs and were now threatened by the intervention of a large Peloponnesian fleet; and Demosthenes, who was at the time not in office, was at his own request given permission 'to use these ships, if he wished, around the Peloponnese'.[38] These orders reflect continued discord at Athens in regard both to the situation in Sicily

[36] Cf. the expedients adopted to man the fleet sent to the Peloponnese in 428 (3.16.1).

[37] It must also be remembered that expeditions to distant areas were attractive to the masses because they offered the prospect of lucrative employment. Thucydides does not refer to this factor here, but he does when recording the debate that led to the great expedition of 415 (6.24.3). From Aristoph., *Wasps* 925, it seems likely that the western allies (like Segesta in 415) helped to maintain the Athenian fleet by making payments to Laches.

[38] Sophocles and Eurymedon evidently disapproved of this free-lance commission granted to Demosthenes (4.3.3–4). They had doubtless opposed his request without success, and they seem to have had no knowledge of his plans.

and to war strategy generally. Again an unsatisfactory agreement seems to have been reached designed to satisfy widely divergent points of view.[39] It is not surprising that the Athenians gained so little success in Sicily.[40] How different, Thucydides implies, would the handling of this situation have been if Pericles had still controlled Athenian policy.[41]

III. THE PROSPECT OF SICELIOT AID TO THE PELOPONNESIANS

When introducing his account of the first Athenian intervention in Sicily, Thucydides notes that the Dorian group of western cities, now at war with the Chalcidian group and Camarina, πρὸς τὴν τῶν Λακεδαιμονίων τὸ πρῶτον ἀρχομένου τοῦ πολέμου ξυμμαχίαν ἐτάχθησαν, οὐ μέντοι ξυνεπολέμησάν γε (3.86.2).[42] He does not refer again in his narrative of the expedition to this alliance with the Spartans, nor does he mention any anxiety on the part of the Athenians that the western Dorians might eventually be persuaded to intervene in Greece in support of their Peloponnesian kinsmen. It must not, however, be inferred from his silence that the Athenians considered this danger to be negligible and were wholly uninfluenced by it when voting first to send a fleet to Sicily and later to reinforce it. It is not his practice, especially when writing in his most succinct manner, to mention every relevant factor known to him in any situation.[43] In this instance the factor is one to which he has already included a reference and includes several more when writing on the great

[39] From a reference in the *Acharnians* 606 (cf. 76), produced while the expedition was being prepared, it might be inferred that some Athenians disapproved strongly of such ventures; but Aristophanes is intent on his pun and is not necessarily drawing an accurate picture.

[40] Gomme, op. cit. iii. 438.

[41] It may be partly with this thought in mind that Thucydides stresses, and perhaps overstresses, the element of chance in the Athenian victory at Pylos. Gomme, however, op. cit. iii. 488, questions whether the element of chance is so prominent as Cornford and others have suggested.

[42] The demands made by the Spartans at the beginning of the war for ships and money from their western allies are mentioned in 2.7.2.

[43] Cf. Gomme, op. cit. iii. 551, on his omission to explain why Brasidas approached Acanthus first of the cities in Chalcidice. It is difficult to believe that he did not know the reason: elsewhere he is very well informed about the motives and plans of Brasidas.

expedition of 415. From these passages, all of them in speeches,[44] it is clear that, over a period of many years before finally in 412 a Siceliot fleet joined the Peloponnesians off the Asiatic coast (8.26.1), Greeks at home and in Sicily never dismissed from their minds the possibility of naval support being received by the Peloponnesians from their western allies.

These passages are:

(a) Before the outbreak of the war Corcyrean envoys pleading for an alliance with Athens argue that their island is geographically well situated for the interception of a fleet sailing from Italy and Sicily to aid the Peloponnesians (1.36.2, cf. 44.3).

(b) In 416/5 envoys from Segesta seek to convince the Athenians of the danger that, if Syracuse is allowed to dominate Sicily by crushing the Athenian allies there, the Dorians of the west may lend to the Dorians of the Peloponnese the support of formidable resources in a combined effort to destroy Athenian power (6.6.2). Nicias, in urging the rejection of this Segestan appeal, does not deny the possibility of western aid to the Peloponnesians; but he considers it to be more probable if the Athenians make their projected expedition than if they do not (6.10.1 and 11.4). His argument that, if the Syracusans conquer Sicily, they are less likely to help Sparta, because the outcome may be the emergence of a Spartan empire which may overthrow their own (6.11.2–3), smacks of sophistry: it is unrealistic in that it ignores the well-merited reputation of the Spartans for lack of enterprise. It was in fact proved false by events after 404.

(c) Alcibiades supports the Segestan plea by maintaining that the object of Athenian alliances in the west is diversionary, that the role of the western allies is ἵνα τοῖς ἐκεῖ ἐχθροῖς ἡμῶν λυπηροὶ ὄντες δεῦρο κωλύωσιν αὐτοὺς ἐπιέναι (6.18.1).

(d) Hermocrates, speaking in a debate at Syracuse, is inclined to censure his fellowcountrymen for having neglected to help Sparta against Athens (6.34.8).

(e) In the same debate Athenagoras declares that the Athenians are unlikely to attack the Siceliots but rather, in his opinion, are relieved that the Siceliots are not attacking them (6.36.4).[45]

---

[44] One (6.6.2) belongs to a speech summarised in *oratio obliqua*.

[45] This passage is perhaps less significant than the rest, because the speech contains so much ill-founded extravagance.

(f) Euphemus, the Athenian spokesman in a debate at Camarina, makes much the same point as the Segestan envoys make
at Athens. It is, he says, to the advantage of the Athenians for
their western allies to remain strong enough to resist Syracusan
pressure, because in that event Syracuse will be less able to injure
Athens by sending aid to the Peloponnese (6.84.1, cf. 83.2).[46]
There is no necessity to consider the question whether all these
speakers actually used the arguments attributed to them or
whether these arguments are among τὰ δέοντα supplied by
Thucydides. It is sufficient that, as may be inferred from the
volume of the evidence, he believes the possibility of Siceliot
intervention in Greece to have been a real issue that long continued to be taken into account.[47] The danger to Athens was
probably rather remote so long as the Syracusans had to
reckon with the hostility of neighbouring cities allied with the
Athenians,[48] but it would at once become much more pressing,
as the Segestans and Euphemus point out, if these cities lost their
independence and were no longer capable of diverting Syracusan
attention. Even a fleet of modest size might prove of great value
to the Peloponnesians if its quality were higher than that of their
own, as was later shown by the impressive record of the Siceliot
expeditionary force in Asia between 412 and 409.

In the first six years of the Archidamian war the Athenians
could not afford to overlook the possibility of Siceliot aid to the
Peloponnesians, which must have influenced their western policy
in some degree. From 425 to the Peace of Nicias it was doubtless
a factor of much less importance: the Peloponnesians, after losing

[46] It is of little significance that Justin (4.3.5) mentions the danger of
Syracusan aid to Sparta as a possible motive of Athenian intervention in 427.

[47] P. A. Brunt, *C.R.* vii (1957), 245, criticises Wentker, op cit. (cf. 107-8),
for believing that the danger was a real one. The evidence collected above
suggests that Wentker is right, though for the wrong reasons: his views on the
strength of the links between aristocratic families at home and in Sicily
cannot be discussed here.

[48] The events in Sicily leading to the appeal to Athens in 427, which are
summarised in 3.86.2-3, were probably spread over a period of two or three
years. It seems likely that at first the war was confined to Syracuse and
Leontini, that later the allies of both sides in Sicily and Italy were drawn into
it, and that finally the Dorian group of cities proved so much superior that
their enemies had to seek Athenian aid. The assumption of Wentker, op. cit.,
108, that the outbreak of war between Syracuse and Leontini dates only from
the spring of 427 is surely mistaken.

60 ships at Pylos (4.16.3 and 23.1), could no longer hope to challenge the Athenians at sea even if they were to receive substantial assistance from the west.

IV. THE MILITARY NARRATIVE OF THUCYDIDES

If Thucydides had chosen to describe in detail any of the Athenian operations in the west, his account would doubtless have helped to explain the aims that the expedition was intended to achieve. As it is, his brief and scattered notes are not very illuminating in this respect, and it must be borne in mind, as has been suggested above, that his treatment of the episode is influenced by his preoccupation with the general conclusion that he draws from it.

The Athenians used Rhegium as their base throughout the campaign, [49] and much of the fighting in which they were involved took place in or near the straits of Messana, where Messana itself was won in 426 (3.90.4) and lost again in 425 (4.1.1). Although merchantmen could and often did cross the open sea, [50] most of the vessels carrying Sicilian grain to the Peloponnese must have passed through or close to the straits, and it was no doubt partly in order to intercept as many as possible of them that the Athenians devoted so much attention to this area. [51] On the other hand, the Syracusans are stated to have been afraid that the Athenians, when reinforced, might use Messana as a base for an attack on Syracuse (4.1.2). Though Syracusan forecasts of Athenian action were not necessarily correct, the offensive plans sponsored by the demagogues seem to have been kept in mind. The defection of Messana was in several ways a serious blow to the Athenians. Thereafter the Syracusans were able to co-operate more effectively with the Locrians, the most powerful of their allies, and during the summer of 425, while the Athenian reinforcement was delayed at Pylos, they began to regain the initiative. It is interesting that there is little trace of the marked superiority in seamanship that the Athenians expected to enjoy over all other Greeks: the Syracusan and

---

[49] 3.86.5, 88.4 and 115.2; 4.24.4 and 25.11 (also 25.2, if the text is sound).

[50] Gomme, *J.H.S.* liii (1933), 16–17; cf. T. J. Dunbabin, *The Western Greeks* (1948), 194–5, on the routes between Greece and Sicily.

[51] Cf. 4.25.1, where a naval engagement took place in the straits περὶ πλοίου διαπλέοντος, which may well have been bound for the Peloponnese and therefore been deemed by the Syracusans to be worth defending.

Locrian ships must have been at least competently handled and their crews moderately efficient (cf. 4.25.1–6).

A notable feature of the narrative is the prominence of political instability. In the Siceliot and Italiot cities with their mixed populations civil strife was even more prevalent than in the Greek homeland, and the practice of seeking to get the better of local rivals by calling in aid from outside was at least as widespread. In many instances, if the faction in power were ousted, the external policy of the city would be reversed. Before the great expedition of 415 Alcibiades, pointing to the instability of the Siceliots, declared that it impaired their capacity to resist attack (6.17.2–4); and to Athenians who favoured intervention in 427 as a prelude to the eventual conquest of Sicily, this factor doubtless appeared to be a source of weakness that could be exploited in the interests of Athenian imperialism. Such expectations were not fulfilled. It was the allies of the Athenians and not their enemies that were affected by internal discord, which dangerously undermined the loyalty of at least two allied cities. In 425 the Rhegines, weakened by prolonged civil strife, were unable to defend their territory effectively against Locrian attacks (4.1.3), and soon afterwards the Athenians had to withdraw their fleet temporarily from the straits in order to save Camarina from being betrayed to the Syracusans (4.25.7).[52] Siceliot instability thus proved to be a positive handicap to the Athenians.

In general, the strategy of the Athenians seems to have been one of improvisation, their operations being conducted largely with the object of supporting their allies and damaging their enemies wherever opportunity offered.[53] This policy was pursued not without some success by Laches, less happily by Pythodorus. The latter may well have been incompetent, though when he assumed command the Siceliot allies of Athens may already have

[52] Civil strife may have helped the Athenians to win Messana (3.90.4 is not explicit) but also contributed to its defection (4.1.1, αὐτῶν ἐπαγαγομένων).

[53] The attempt of Wentker, op. cit., 113–17, to find a consistent pattern in these operations is unconvincing, being based on conjecture and untenable theories. The observation of Freeman, op. cit. iii. 29–30, is more apposite: 'It is perhaps vain to ask what was the plan of campaign. There was most likely none.' Thucydides gives more information about the strategy of the enemy (4.1.2 and 24.3–4). The Athenians may well have been hampered by the need to consult the selfish interests of the Rhegines, who contributed ten ships (Busolt, op. cit. iii. 2.1056–7).

begun to be affected by war-weariness, as the dissensions at Rhegium and Camarina perhaps indicate.[54] When Sophocles and Eurymedon eventually arrived with the reinforcement, they did not, as might have been expected, at once take advantage of their naval superiority and launch an energetic offensive.[55] Apparently all the Athenian generals interpreted their mission as designed mainly to keep alive the opposition to the Dorian group of cities and to prevent these cities dominating their Siceliot and Italiot neighbours. Such at least is the impression created by the narrative of Thucydides, and it receives some confirmation from another source. The papyrus fragment possibly from Philistus which has been mentioned above[56] presents a similar picture of the Athenians engaged in a series of apparently unrelated operations at a number of scattered points. This fragment contains a little information not included by Thucydides, and there are differences on points of detail, so that it can scarcely be based on his account. Its source may well be the work of Antiochus of Syracuse.[57]

V. THE PUNISHMENT OF THE GENERALS

The conclusion of peace by the Siceliot cities, the withdrawal of the Athenian fleet from Sicily and the condemnation of Pythodorus, Sophocles and Eurymedon are described very briefly (4.65.1-3). After the Congress of Gela the cities allied with Athens informed the generals ὅτι ξυμβήσονται καὶ αἱ σπονδαὶ

[54] The statement in 4.25.12 that the Siceliots continued to fight one another on land ἄνευ τῶν Ἀθηναίων surely does not mean that the Athenians ceased to give their allies any support, but only that their co-operation in land operations mentioned in the preceding sentence was not repeated.

[55] If Timaeus (*F. Gr. Hist.* 566 F 22) is to be believed, Eurymedon found it necessary to stir the allies of Athens to action against Syracuse. War-weary as they were, their reception of the Athenian reinforcement was evidently unenthusiastic and perhaps tinged with suspicion. Thucydides does not mention this point, which might be used to extenuate the apparent inactivity of the Athenian generals.

[56] *F. Gr. Hist.* 577 F 2; see above p. 101 n. 1. This papyrus is edited and discussed by V. Bartoletti, *Pap. Soc. Ital.* xii (1951), 150-7.

[57] Thucydides himself might well have used this work, which was certainly known to him, and K. J. Dover, *Maia* vi (1953), 8-9, maintains that he did. It is, however, more probable that his information about the fighting in Sicily and Italy is derived from Athenians who took part in it (Gomme, op. cit. (*Hist. Comm.*) ii. 389, 392. iii. 521-2), perhaps including the generals.

ἔσονται κἀκείνοις κοιναί (65.2). Although these cities did not
formally make peace until they had consulted the generals, they
had already decided to agree to the settlement negotiated at
Gela,[58] whatever the Athenian attitude might be. They evidently
wished to maintain their ties of friendship with the Athenians,[59]
whose aid they might well need again on some future occasion,
so that, unlike the Spartans at Ithome (1.102.3), they took care
to avoid giving offence in dismissing their allies. They showed,
however, that they were determined to preserve complete freedom of action in their relations with their neighbours. The inclusion of the Athenians in the settlement was presumably effected
by means of a clause whereby the allies of each city represented
at Gela were to be parties to it if they wished. If the settlement
was thought likely to prove unwelcome to the Athenian generals,
this inclusion of Athens in it was a masterly stroke. The generals
had been sent to Sicily τῆς οἰκειότητος προφάσει (3.86.4) and
had no valid grounds for objecting to a peace that was acceptable
to all their allies. It was also impossible for them to delay their
reply until they had received guidance from home. In the circumstances the only course open to them was to give their consent: there was really no alternative if the Athenian alliances in
the west were to be maintained. There is, however, no justification for believing that, as some scholars assume,[60] they agreed
unwillingly to a settlement that was distasteful to them. Thucydides states not that they acquiesced but that they approved
(ἐπαινεσάντων δὲ αὐτῶν, 4.65.2), and his phrase implies at least
satisfaction on their part.[61] The natural interpretation of his
account is that they considered their mission to have been at any
rate adequately discharged and that their reception at Athens
was as unexpected as it was unwelcome. Had they anticipated
prosecution, they could have sent the fleet home and have themselves remained in Sicily or Italy, just as Demosthenes remained

[58] The Congress apparently achieved little more than a general agreement
in principle, see below, pp. 179-80 and n. 15.
[59] Most of the Athenian alliances with western cities apparently remained
in force (cf. 5.4.5; 6.6.2; 6.50.4).
[60] K. J. Beloch, Gr. Gesch. ii. 1 (1914), 336: 'Den Athenern blieb nichts
übrig als gute Miene zum bösen Spiel zu machen'.
[61] ἐπαινεῖν seems always in Thucydides to denote more or less wholehearted
approval and never mere acquiescence, cf. 5.37.5, and 8.86.6 and 8, where,
as here, it is used in connection with diplomatic activities.

in western Greece φοβούμενος τοὺς Ἀθηναίους after the failure
of his Aetolian campaign (3.98.5). Nicias later felt, not
unjustifiably, that for an Athenian general to return home
from an unsuccessful expedition without the sanction of the
Ecclesia was more perilous than to face death in battle
(7.48.3-4).[62]
The attitude of the generals was a perfectly reasonable one if
there is any validity in the conclusions reached above about
Athenian aims. They could claim with some satisfaction that the
war in Sicily had been ended (3.115.4), the *status quo* maintained,
and the danger of Syracusan domination averted. Athenian interests in the west seemed to have been amply safeguarded. Even
if the tide of war in Greece were to change, the Syracusans could
scarcely send naval aid to the Peloponnesians while the western
allies of Athens remained unimpaired. The need to interrupt the
shipment of Sicilian grain to the Peloponnese must have become
much less pressing: Athenian possession of the Spartan prisoners
captured on Sphacteria deterred the Peloponnesians from invading Attica during the remaining years of the Archidamian war
(4.41.1), and it was no longer so vital to divert Peloponnesian
peasant farmers from active service by making it necessary that
as many as possible should be fully occupied in gathering their
own harvests. The generals might also claim that the experience
gained in the course of their operations in the west would prove
valuable in any future attempt by the Athenians to win control
of that area.[63] Their error lay in failing to appreciate how public
opinion at Athens would react to the conclusion of peace in
Sicily.

Few even of their most severe critics can have seriously believed that their approval of the settlement negotiated at Gela was
gained by means of bribes, though possibly they had impru-

[62] Thucydides does not state whether he himself returned to Athens after
the fall of Amphipolis (5.26.5).

[63] Adcock, *C.A.H.* v. 225, followed by G. Glotz, *Histoire grecque* ii (1929),
641, infers from a passage in a speech of Nicias in 415 (οἶσπερ νῦν ὅροις
χρωμένους πρὸς ἡμᾶς, οὐ μεμπτοῖς, τῷ τε Ἰονίῳ κόλπῳ παρὰ γῆν ἤν τις πλέῃ,
καὶ τῷ Σικελικῷ διὰ πελάγους, 6.13.1) that the generals secured an undertaking from the Siceliots not to intervene in the Greek homeland. It is possible
that such an undertaking was given, but this passage is very vaguely worded,
and, as has been pointed out above (pp. 115-16), Siceliot intervention in
Greece was most improbable in the last years of the Archidamian war.

dently accepted presents from their Siceliot allies.[64] Trumped-up charges of this kind were a conventional instrument of the demagogues against officials whose execution of their duties was thought to have been culpable in any way.[65] The condemnation of the generals was certainly the outcome of public disappointment that they had returned home without having made any conquests or even having secured any new allies. It has been maintained above that plans of western expansion had only a very limited influence upon the policy of the Athenians when they decided first to send a small fleet to Sicily and later to reinforce it; but since the spring of 425, when Sophocles and Eurymedon sailed with the reinforcement, their attitude had undergone a fundamental change. The victory at Pylos, which was widely believed to be the achievement of Cleon, and lesser successes gained during the ensuing year caused public feeling to swing very markedly in the direction of greater enterprise in military strategy, which had for some time been advocated by the demagogues. This surge of optimism, which is reflected in the *Knights*, produced in 424, and elsewhere,[66] affected not only the adherents of the demagogues but also many Athenians not normally sympathetic towards them. Temporarily at any rate their demand for a grand offensive must have enjoyed the support of an overwhelming majority in the Ecclesia. It was feelings of this kind that, without a Pericles to curb them, led not only to miscarriages of justice, such as the conviction of Pythodorus, Sophocles and Eurymedon and apparently that of Thucydides himself, but also to grave errors in military strategy (2.65.7 and 11).

It is not at all surprising that the generals failed to foresee the consequences of their action in approving the settlement in Sicily. Pythodorus had been away from Athens since the winter of 426/5

---

[64] Busolt, op. cit. iii. 2.1133, who, ibid., n. 2, rightly rejects the suggestion of Freeman, op. cit. iii. 66, and Stein, op. cit., 533 n. 1, that they were charged with exceeding their powers in approving the conclusion of peace.

[65] Cf. Aristoph., *Knights* 288, διαβαλῶ σ᾽ ἐὰν στρατηγῇς.

[66] Cf. the excellent discussion by Gomme, op. cit. iii. 524–7 (though he perhaps exaggerates the degree of Athenian unity: despite the optimistic tone of the *Knights*, peace is as desirable as ever, cf. 794–6, 1331–2, 1387–95). G. Zuntz, *Political Plays of Euripides* (1955) 88–91, maintains that the *Suppliants* of Euripides was produced in 424, mainly on the ground that the feeling of confidence reflected in the play is appropriate only to that year.

and Sophocles and Eurymedon since the following spring. Although, like Nicias when he was in command in Sicily, they doubtless received official instructions from home from time to time from which some change in Athenian policy must have been apparent, it must have been impossible for them to appreciate the extent to which public feeling had been transformed in their absence. They had left the Athens of the *Acharnians*; they returned to the Athens of the *Knights*. Like Thucydides himself, they were the victims of Athenian success.[67]

---

[67] Eurymedon was perhaps punished less severely than his colleagues in virtue of his efforts, reported by Timaeus (*F. Gr. Hist.* 566 F 22), to rouse the allies to action against the enemy. The inference made by many scholars from passages in the *Wasps* that Laches was prosecuted by Cleon on a charge of having misappropriated public funds while in Sicily and was acquitted has been discussed by Jacoby, *F. Gr. Hist.* iii b, Suppl. i (1954), 500–1, who shows conclusively how weak the evidence is. He suggests that, at the most, Cleon attacked Laches in public speeches and threatened to prosecute him (cf Gomme, op. cit. ii. 430–1). That such an attack was made on Laches not long before the production of the *Wasps* in 422 is indeed very probable. The conviction of his successors in 424 must have lent support to the view that the whole campaign had been mismanaged from the outset, because it had not led to the conquests envisaged by the demagogues. Seeking to incriminate a political opponent who was largely responsible for the One Year's Truce concluded in 423 (4.118.11), Cleon naturally turned to his part in the Sicilian campaign several years earlier. Aristophanes, on the other hand, in the mock trial-scene of the *Wasps*, seems to be suggesting that Laches has battled loyally and vigorously to protect Athenian interests (952, 954–5, 957–9, 968–70).

7

Thucydides and the fall of Amphipolis

The question whether Thucydides culpably neglected his duty as strategos in failing to save Amphipolis from falling into the hands of Brasidas has been debated many times and will not be reconsidered here. This paper will discuss another issue, which is perhaps of greater importance because it involves consideration of Thucydides as a historian rather than as a soldier, namely, how far his own account of this episode (4.102–108) is objective. I shall attempt to show that it is not so objective as it appears to be; that, as in many accounts of other episodes, he is here unobtrusively seeking to guide the judgement of his readers; that his narrative contains, *inter alia*, a very skilful self-justification against the charges which led to his banishment. This issue, and indeed the question of his culpability, would be very much clearer if independent evidence on the fall of Amphipolis were extant. Unfortunately none has survived.[1]

In many respects Thucydides refuses to allow his presentation of the episode to be influenced by its consequences to himself. Its importance is shown to lie primarily in its repercussions on the course of the war. His account is carefully designed to take its place in a wider context, conforming closely to the pattern traceable in the parts of his fourth and fifth books covering the period from the Spartan disaster at Pylos to the end of the Archidamian war. Here the principal and unifying theme is how the decline of Athenian fortunes from the peak of success in 425/4, combined with a partial recovery on the Peloponnesian side for which Brasidas was largely responsible, led first to the One Year's Truce and eventually to the Peace of Nicias. The method of presentation is also to a large extent uniform. Characteristically Thucydides draws attention to the trend of events not by passages of commentary expounding his own views but by inserting at appropriate points in the narrative sketches of public opinion at

---

[1] The brief account of Diodorus (12.68.1–3), who makes no reference to the part played by Thucydides, contributes no information of any value.

Athens, Sparta and elsewhere,[2] which have a function somewhat similar to that of his speeches. By adding to his narrative on the fall of Amphipolis a detailed analysis of public reactions to it at Athens and in the cities of the Athenian empire (4.108) he makes abundantly clear its significance as a link in a historical chain. In drawing the attention of his readers to this factor, which he clearly considers to be the most important aspect of the episode, he writes almost as though he himself played no part in it.

It is also characteristic of him, and very much to his credit, that his account does not differ in scale from his accounts of other episodes. Nor does he include any direct and detailed defence of his own actions.[3] He remains faithful to his historical principles, refusing to permit the intrusion of autobiography, just as elsewhere he refuses to permit the intrusion of biography, into a history of the Peloponnesian war. It is for this reason that his only reference to his banishment μετὰ τὴν ἐς ᾿Αμφίπολιν στρατηγίαν occurs in a different context (5.26.5), where he draws attention to the special advantages which it gave him as a historian by providing him with leisure to study the war and with access to evidence derived from both sides.[4] There are also no grounds for suspecting that his narrative contains any falsehood or distortion of the facts, though its accuracy cannot be effectively tested because no other evidence of any value is available. Nor is there any reason to believe that, while giving a truthful account of the episode, he is trying to mislead his readers by fostering in their minds conclusions known by him to be false. What he states and what he implies is, in his view, the truth, and his honesty in recording events in which he was himself involved is perhaps greater than that of Caesar in the *Commentaries*. Yet it may be doubted whether his record of his own actions is any more objective than that of Caesar.

Many scholars have maintained that he makes no attempt

[2] 4.40; 4.41.3; 4.55; 4.80.1–2; 4.117.1–2; 5.14.1–15, 2. 4.65.4 is rather different because here he expresses his own views more directly, see above, p. 102.

[3] A. W. Gomme, *Historical Commentary on Thucydides*, iii. 1956, 584, cf. his *Greek Attitude to Poetry and History*, 1954, 161–2.

[4] Cf. 2.48.3, where his reference to the fact that he himself suffered from the plague is included only to show how well qualified he was to describe its symptoms (see below p. 132 n. 24, on 4.105.1).

whatever to justify himself.[5] This view is surely based upon inadequate appreciation of his historical technique. Implied judgements on the actions of others frequently underlie his narrative: his treatment of Alcidas, Phormio, Demosthenes, Agis and Astyochus may be cited as examples. Recent studies of his methods have shown how misleading is the belief, once widely accepted, that, except in some passages of discussion and in the speeches, he merely records the facts and leaves his readers to form their own opinions.[6] It is true that in his accounts of some episodes, especially in summaries of minor events, no judgements on the leading characters seem to be implied. In many instances, however, his apparent objectivity is deceptive. Judgements which less discerning readers imagine to be their own are in fact those of Thucydides and have been unobtrusively put into their minds by his selection and arrangement of material, by implied approval and implied criticism, by contrast at one point and emphasis at another. That he uses subtle methods of this kind very extensively to influence the verdict of his readers on the actions of those concerned in the events leading to the loss of Amphipolis will be suggested below when his account is examined. It is, in fact, a thoroughly characteristic narrative and differs from a score of others only in that he is himself among the leading characters whose actions are under review. Much of it suggests that he did everything in his power to save Amphipolis and was not responsible for its fall; not a word points to the conclusion that he was negligent. If this interpretation of his account has any validity, one of his aims, though only a subsidiary aim,[7] is self-justification:

[5] Cf. G. B. Grundy, *Thucydides* i[2]. 1948, 30, 'the impersonal character of his narrative is peculiarly illustrated by his omission of anything resembling a defence of his action', and E. Meyer, *Forschungen* ii, 1899, 343, who is a trifle more guarded. Gomme is slightly inconsistent: he states at one point that Thucydides 'makes no attempt at self-defence' (*Hist. Comm.* iii 584) and at another 'these . . . are almost the only words written by Thucydides in self-defence' (ibid., 578, n. on 4.104.5). F. E. Adcock, *C.A.H.* v, 1927, 244, is, in my view, much nearer to the truth when he refers to 'the apologia which underlies this part of his narrative'.

[6] Cf. Gomme, *Greek Attitude*, 144–8, on Nicostratus and Eurymedon at Corcyra in 427, and 'Ἑλληνικά 13, 1954, 1–10 on Cleon at Amphipolis in 422; and, more generally, J. de Romilly, *Histoire et raison chez Thucydide*, 1956, chs. i–ii.

[7] Its chief aim has been discussed above, pp. 123–4. It might be argued that another aim is to illustrate from his own experience the folly of the Athenians

and, however innocent he may have been of the offences with which he was charged, it cannot be considered to be wholly objective because it presents only the case for the defence. The following examination will perhaps show that a quite considerable proportion of it is indirectly apologetic.

In most Thucydidean narratives of military operations the outcome is seen to turn upon a small number of crucial factors, which are very clearly defined. Prominent among these are the foresight of opposing leaders in framing offensive or defensive strategy and their skill and determination in implementing their own plans and frustrating those of the enemy.[8] At Amphipolis the qualities of Brasidas on the one hand and of the two Athenian generals, Eucles and Thucydides himself, on the other are shown to have profoundly influenced the development of the situation. Another important factor, perhaps the only other one of any consequence, is the reaction of the Amphipolitans to the predicament in which they so suddenly found themselves.

Of these factors the ability of Brasidas as a soldier and diplomatist, though clearly responsible to a very large extent for his success, is less relevant than the others to the question whether the account of Thucydides is objective. It is true that the prominence given to the resourcefulness of Brasidas at each stage of the situation emphasises the difficulty of the task imposed upon the Athenian generals. This assessment of him is, however, one with which readers acquainted with the record of his earlier exploits have already become familiar. There is no reason to believe that Thucydides tends to overrate the qualities shown by Brasidas at Amphipolis because he was himself a victim of them. They were, however, impressive enough. Brasidas paved the way for his attack by conducting secret negotiations with sections of the population disloyal to Athens; he timed it admirably so as to take full advantage of the wintry conditions; his march from

---

in sending out generals with inadequate resources and punishing them if their missions failed. I have tried to show in the preceding essay, pp. 101–5, that in his account of the first expedition to Sicily his main purpose is to criticise the demagogues for encouraging this practice. It does not, however, seem to be a major preoccupation here.

[8] Cf. J. de Romilly, op. cit., 174–9 (who perhaps tends to lay too much emphasis on purely intellectual qualities).

Chalcidice through Argilus was so rapid that he outstripped the news of his approach and achieved complete surprise (4.103.2–4). When after seizing the bridge over the Strymon he found that his supporters inside the town were unable to open the gates to him at once (104.3–4), he used his diplomatic talents so effectively by offering moderate terms that Amphipolis was in his hands before Thucydides, bringing aid from Thasos, was able to intervene (105.2–106.3). One sentence in the account of these events is somewhat puzzling. Thucydides quotes a popular belief current at the time, though he is careful to disclaim any responsibility for its validity (104.2, λέγεται), that if after capturing the bridge Brasidas had proceeded to attack Amphipolis without pausing to plunder the area outside the walls, it would have fallen at once. It is not clear why Thucydides interrupts his narrative to mention a view for which he is not prepared to vouch. Possibly he wishes to indicate that even Brasidas was not infallible in his judgement of military situations. More probably, however, his object is to suggest that, if any plans had been laid to meet a sudden threat of this kind, these broke down completely for the moment; the Amphipolitans were paralysed by the panic and the distrust of one another mentioned in the previous sentence, and Eucles was unable to rally them; only delay by Brasidas, and not any efforts by the defenders, saved Amphipolis from being stormed. Such is the impression conveyed by Thucydides. Another point perhaps suggested here is that, even if he had been at Eion with his seven ships and not at Thasos (104.4), he could not have saved Amphipolis, had Brasidas launched an immediate assault.[9]

The parts played by Eucles and the population of Amphipolis in the narrative of Thucydides are best discussed together because they are interdependent. It is, however, necessary, before examining his evidence on these two factors, to consider a subsidiary factor on which he provides no evidence, namely, the size and composition of the military forces at the disposal of Eucles. It seems to be his normal practice to mention the size of armies and fleets where the figures were known to him, even in bare summaries of unimportant operations, just as he usually gives the names of their commanders, however obscure. In many instances

---

[9] The passage giving the reasons why Brasidas offered moderate terms to the Amphipolitans (105.1) will be considered below (pp. 132–3).

he was doubtless unable to obtain reliable figures, but it is difficult to believe that he did not know approximately how many
men his colleague had at Amphipolis. Yet he gives no figures,
though he mentions that he himself had seven ships at Thasos
(104.5), nor does he supply any information from which even a
rough estimate can be deduced.

The legal status of Amphipolis is perfectly clear. It was an independent state allied with Athens,[10] but the Athenians always
maintained that, because they had founded it, its territory was
legally theirs even after it ceased to be their ally, and this claim
was recognised by others.[11] Accordingly they had every right to
station a military force there if they wished. There is, however,
no evidence that Amphipolis was regularly garrisoned, either in
peace or in war, in spite of its strategic importance. A garrison
was not needed to ensure the loyalty of the Amphipolitans because a majority favoured the cause of Athens (104.4), even
though only a small proportion were of Athenian origin (106.1).
Only in the event of an external threat to Amphipolis or to
its neighbours would the Athenians be likely to station troops
there. When Brasidas reached Chalcidice in the summer of
424, the Athenians took steps to strengthen their defences in the
Thraceward district. The vague phrase with which Thucydides
refers to these measures (82, τῶν ταύτῃ ξυμμάχων φυλακὴν πλέονα
κατεστήσαντο) suggests that they did not amount to much. They
may, however, have included the sending of Thucydides and
Eucles, who do not seem to have taken over their responsibilities
in the area before this time. The former was provided with a
modest squadron of seven ships, but the Athenians were already
preparing for their offensive on land against Boeotia which led
to the battle of Delium and they can have had very few troops
to spare. When at Amphipolis, Eucles is described as φύλαξ τοῦ
χωρίου (104.4), which is not an official title and merely defines
his responsibilities.[12] The only reference to troops under his com-

---

[10] *A.T.L.* iii. 1950, 309 n. 45.

[11] F. Hampl, *Klio*, 32, 1939, 2–5; F. Gschnitzer, *Abhängige Orte im griechi-
schen Altertum*, 1958, 91–2.

[12] The same phrase is used of Demosthenes at Pylos (4.5.2) when, though
left in command of five ships, he held no office (4.2.4). φύλαξ does not seem
to have at any time denoted a garrison commander in the Athenian empire.
From a fragment of Theophrastus quoted by Harpocration s. v. ἐπίσκοπος
(πολλῷ γὰρ κάλλιον κατά γε τὴν τοῦ ὀνόματος θέσιν, ὡς οἱ Λάκωνες ἁρμοστὰς

128

mand is where φυλακή τις βραχεῖα is stated to have been posted at the Strymon bridge (103.5). It is most improbable that Eucles, who was after all a strategos (104.4; 106.2), was sent out entirely alone, but while he must surely have been supplied with a few Athenian or allied hoplites,[13] they can hardly have amounted to more than a handful.[14] To assume, as some scholars have assumed,[15] that he had under his command a military force strong enough to be termed a garrison is unwarranted. It is therefore very likely, though not absolutely certain, that he had to rely almost exclusively upon local levies composed of Athenian settlers and others loyal to Athens; if so, their number can scarcely have been very large, and doubtless many of them were ill-armed and ill-trained.

Brasidas had brought 1,700 hoplites with him from the Peloponnese (78.1), and doubtless most of these accompanied him on his forced march from Chalcidice to Amphipolis. His local allies supplied some further troops (102.1), but their number can hardly have been large: surprise was essential to his strategic plan, and a considerable concentration of troops at his winter base would almost certainly have been reported to the defenders of Amphipolis. The Argilians provided guides for the final stage of his march (103.4), and possibly some troops too. The total force under his command was, in the conditions of Greek warfare, small for an assault on a walled city of considerable size, even when there were good prospects of assistance from traitors. If Eucles had at his disposal a few hundred trained men, the defenders ought, one feels, to have been able to keep disaffection in check and repel attacks on their walls until reinforcements

---

φάσκοντες εἰς τὰς πόλεις πέμπειν, οὐκ ἐπισκόπους οὐδὲ φύλακας ὡς ᾿Αθηναῖοι) it might be inferred that it did (cf. Suda, s. v. ἐπίσκοπος, and G. Busolt and H. Swoboda, *Gr. Staatskunde* ii, 1926, 1355 n. 2), but the terminology of this passage is surely confused (cf. *A.T.L.* iii, 144 n. 17).

[13] G. Grote, *History of Greece* v, 1888, 322 and 331, G. Busolt, *Gr. Gesch.* iii, 2, 1904, 1144 n. 2, and Gomme, op. cit., iii., 577, are inclined to believe that he had no Athenian troops.

[14] The hasty measures taken by the Athenians immediately after the fall of Amphipolis (108.6) suggest that they had very few troops in the area. Thucydides evidently could not even contemplate an effort to recover Amphipolis after he had repelled the attacks on Eion (107.2).

[15] G. E. M. de Ste Croix, *Historia*, 3, 1954–5, 4 with 5 n. 1; D. W. Bradeen, ibid., 9, 1960, 266 with n. 53.

arrived. If, on the other hand, as seems more likely, the forces available were small in number and poor in quality, the rapid collapse of resistance is more excusable. It might also be argued that, if Amphipolis was very weakly held, it was imperative for the fleet of Thucydides to be stationed continuously at Eion and that he, perhaps jointly with Eucles, was neglectful in failing to ensure that it was at hand when Brasidas made his attack. To anyone wishing to determine whether every possible effort was made to save Amphipolis some indication of the resources available to Eucles would have been very helpful. It is significant that Thucydides gives no information whatever.

His account of the steps leading to the acceptance of the terms offered by Brasidas undoubtedly suggests that Eucles was incompetent[16] and the population of Amphipolis irresolute. It can hardly have been the fault of Eucles that the city wall had not been extended to protect the bridge over the Strymon, a weakness later rectified (103.5), perhaps by Brasidas. On the other hand, it is surely implied that Eucles ought to have posted a stronger or more efficient force at the bridge, which Brasidas forced with surprising ease even when allowance is made for the influence of treachery, the wintry conditions and the unexpectedness of the attack (ibid.). Attention has already been drawn to the emphasis laid upon the confusion in the city after the capture of the bridge (104.1–2).[17] This confusion was creditable neither to the Amphipolitans nor to Eucles. Soon, however, the citizens loyal to Athens recovered sufficiently to restrain disloyal elements, who were outnumbered, from opening the gates at once to Brasidas as had been planned (104.3–4). Eucles may have been largely responsible for this recovery, but while he and his supporters sent a message to summon the fleet of Thucydides from Thasos, it seems to be implied that greater determination in trying to suppress disaffection during their brief respite might well have saved Amphipolis.[18]

The proclamation issued by Brasidas offered to the whole

---

[16] Cf. Gomme, op. cit., iii., 579 and 587.

[17] J. de Romilly, op. cit., 168–72, has shown how θόρυβος, the word used here, is often a decisive element in Thucydidean narratives of battles.

[18] During the Theban raid on Plataea shortly before the outbreak of the war the Plataeans showed more resolution in an equally perilous situation (2.3.2–4).

population the choice of remaining in the city with property and civic rights intact or of withdrawing within five days with such possessions as could be moved (105.2). Thucydides gives a masterly sketch of the effect produced by this offer upon a majority of the citizens (106.1–2). He doubtless bases his sketch upon information from some who took advantage of the opportunity to leave the city and joined him at Eion (107.1),[19] and he was presumably able to consult Eucles also. The general tone of the passage, however, in which a note of implied criticism is unmistakable, is entirely his own. In extenuation of the decision to accept the terms offered by Brasidas he mentions that only a small proportion of the citizen body consisted of colonists from Athens[20] and that there was anxiety for the fate of kinsmen captured outside the walls. On the other hand, there is more than a hint that the citizens were lacking in fortitude. Relief that their personal safety was no longer to be endangered influenced their conclusion that the terms were just (τὸ κήρυγμα πρὸς τὸν φόβον δίκαιον εἶναι ὑπελάμβανον). Those of Athenian origin welcomed (ἅσμενοι) the prospect of withdrawing from Amphipolis. That they were in greater danger than the rest of the population because of their Athenian birth and that they did not expect help to arrive promptly are probably two of the excuses offered to Thucydides when they reached Eion.[21] Both suggest that their morale was low, and the second shows a lack of confidence in his speed of action which proved entirely unwarranted. The rest of the population, more pardonably because their ties with Athens were less close, were swayed by equally selfish considerations: they could retain their citizen rights and they were to be unexpectedly freed from danger.[22] Hence a majority favoured acceptance of the terms, which was now openly advocated by the

[19] It may be conjectured that some of these gave evidence at the trial of Thucydides and told a very different story; cf. the fears of Nicias (7.48.4) that most of the soldiers clamouring for withdrawal from Syracuse would slander him and his colleagues on returning to Athens.

[20] Presumably they formed a tribe or more than one tribe, cf. the system at Thurii described by Diodorus (12.11.3), though Amphipolis was not, like Thurii, a Panhellenic colony.

[21] καὶ ἅμα may indicate, as in other passages (see above p. 106 and n. 21), that these sentiments are those of two distinct groups of persons.

[22] The disputed ἐν τῷ ἴσῳ probably means no more than 'at the same time' (Classen) or 'equally', cf. 4.65.4, ἐν ἴσῳ.

supporters of Brasidas (106.2). Eucles was powerless to prevent, or even to delay, this decision, and the phrase used here in referring to him (τοῦ παρόντος ᾿Αθηναίων στρατηγοῦ) is perhaps chosen, in preference to his name, in order to underline his responsibility for safeguarding Athenian interests at Amphipolis. There was little that he could do at this stage to remedy a hopeless position. He cannot have had a force of troops sufficiently large to coerce the citizens and could only try in vain to retain their loyalty by using his personal influence as strategos (οὐκέτι ἀκροώμενον).[23] The account of Thucydides seems somewhat lacking in sympathy towards a colleague who, whatever his faults, was called upon to deal with a situation of very great difficulty.

Thucydides records his own part in the episode with characteristic restraint. As soon as he received the call for assistance from Amphipolis, he sailed from Thasos with all speed (104.5, κατὰ τάχος). His account of his own aims on leaving Thasos (ἐβούλετο φθάσαι μάλιστα μὲν οὖν ᾿Αμφίπολιν, πρίν τι ἐνδοῦναι, εἰ δὲ μὴ τὴν ᾿Ηιόνα προκαταλαβών) is to a large extent superfluous. Its inclusion suggests that even at this stage he had little confidence in the ability of Eucles and his supporters to resist for as long as a single day. It also helps to prepare the reader for the conclusion that he himself made every effort to retrieve an already desperate situation. In a very significant sentence the decision of Brasidas to offer moderate terms to the Amphipolitans is attributed wholly to fears that the approach of Thucydides would stiffen their will to resist; that, because of his influence in the district through his mining interests, most of them would expect him to collect forces from the islands and the Thracian coast and use them for their protection (105.1).[24] There is every reason to believe that this sentence is an authentic report of what Brasidas thought. It is not the practice of Thucydides to give information about the motives and feelings of individuals based upon mere surmise or even upon inference from his knowledge of their characters.[25] He is remarkably well-informed about the

[23] There is no suggestion of military mutiny: the change of feeling in the city (106.1) was wholly that of the civil population.

[24] The reference to his private affairs is included only because they gave him special qualifications for discharging his public duties (cf. above, p. 124 n. 4).

[25] See above, pp. 78–9.

motives and feelings of Brasidas on many occasions,[26] and it has been suggested that when in exile he may have had the opportunity to converse with him.[27] It cannot, however, be assumed that in any instance a complete report is necessarily given of all the motives governing the actions of Brasidas. From the beginning of his mission to the northern Aegean he evidently felt that, because his military resources were so limited, it would be in his interests to build up a reputation for moderation and to pose as a liberator, as is seen from the tone of his speeches at Acanthus (85–7) and later at Torone (114.3–5). The success of this diplomatic offensive is attested by two passages in which Thucydides discusses the reputation which he gained among the allies of Athens.[28] Thus it may be inferred with some confidence that he chose to issue his proclamation to the Amphipolitans, instead of taking military action, partly with the intention of winning the confidence of other cities where revolt might be contemplated. Fear that the prize might be lost through the instrumentality of Thucydides was almost certainly not his only motive. It is noteworthy that the motive mentioned by Thucydides and defined in some detail is one that redounds to his own credit in addition to stressing the respect felt for him by Brasidas. An attack on Amphipolis at this stage supported by traitors inside the walls might well have been successful, and in that event many of its citizens, especially those of Athenian birth, would doubtless have been killed or captured. It is implied that they were much indebted to Thucydides whose influence was largely responsible for the offer of terms whereby they were able to escape unharmed.

In recording his own arrival at Eion with his fleet, Thucydides again draws attention to his speed in bringing assistance (106.3: τῇ ἡμέρᾳ ὀψέ; 106.4: διὰ τάχους). He also points out that, had he not arrived by nightfall, Eion too would have fallen to Brasidas at dawn. His account of his own success in defending Eion (107.1–2) conforms to his normal practice in summarising military operations which were on a small scale or of no great

---

[26] Significant passages are: 4.70.1–2; 4.73.1–3; 4.120.2; 124.4; 5.6.3; 5.8.2–4; 5.16.1.

[27] Adcock, *C.A.H.*, v, 243.

[28] 81.2; 108.2–3 (the chapter of discussion with which Thucydides concludes his account of the episode at Amphipolis).

significance. The passage reads as though Thucydides the historian is determined to represent the actions of Thucydides the general in their proper perspective. Attention is, as usual, concentrated upon the aims of the opposing leaders and upon the result: no details are included about the course of the operations by sea or land. On his arrival at Eion Thucydides took measures, which are not specified, designed to ensure its security against the threat of immediate attack by Brasidas and also against less imminent dangers. Then Brasidas suddenly sailed down the Strymon with the intention of seizing a headland projecting from the walls of Eion from which he could control the mouth of the river. An attack was also made by land,[29] but both were repelled. Here there is surely an implied contrast with the recent course of events at Amphipolis, where lack of vigilance followed by confusion had led to a collapse of resistance which Eucles was unable to prevent. At Amphipolis the Strymon bridge, which was outside the walls, had fallen at once; at Eion the headland, also outside the walls, was successfully defended. It is true that there is no mention of disaffection at Eion, though the defensive measures taken by Thucydides may have included a round up of suspects; and while the attack on Eion was sudden (ἄφνω) and evidently intended to achieve tactical surprise, it was not unexpected (ἦν ἐπίη ὁ Βρασίδας). Nevertheless, despite the brevity of his account Thucydides does convey the impression that he displayed some of the qualities with which he accredits Brasidas and a few other contemporary leaders. There is no reason to question his veracity: the distinction of having thwarted Brasidas was one to which few could lay claim. Yet the prominence given to his success in saving Eion does serve to divert attention from his failure to save Amphipolis.[30] It has undoubtedly had this effect upon many of his readers. Apparently an Athenian jury was less impressed by his achievement.

Finally, there is a second omission, which is more striking than his silence about the military resources available to Eucles. This omission has been endlessly discussed by scholars seeking to determine whether or not he was guilty of negligence. He omits to explain why, when Amphipolis was first threatened, he was at

---

[29] It is not clear whether this attack was directed against Eion itself or, like the attack by sea, against the headland outside the walls.

[30] Busolt, op. cit., iii., 2, 1156 n. 2 (the last sentence).

Thasos with his fleet and not at Eion, whence he could have brought assistance within a very short time.[31] It has been argued that he does not explain why he was at Thasos because he did not consider any explanation to be necessary: that being responsible for protecting the whole northern coastline of the Aegean, he naturally stationed his fleet at Thasos, which was the principal naval base in the area.[32] A decisive objection to this view is that in the passage describing the reaction of the Athenians to the loss of Amphipolis they are specifically stated to have assumed that the line of the Strymon near Eion was being guarded by triremes (108.1). These triremes must be identified with the fleet of Thucydides,[33] whose responsibilities evidently included a share in the defence of the river line. His ships must surely have been based at Eion for a considerable time in the autumn of 424: they probably arrived there while Brasidas was operating in Chalcidice in the late summer. It may well be that, as some scholars maintain,[34] he had left Eion, perhaps very shortly before Brasidas made his attack, to collect as large a force as possible from Thasos and its neighbourhood in order to reinforce the defence of Amphipolis.[35] Such, at any rate, were the expectations of the Amphipolitans as stated in the passage giving the motives of Brasidas in offering them moderate terms (105.1: ἐλπίσαν ἐκ θαλάσσης ξυμμαχικὸν καὶ ἀπὸ τῆς Θρᾴκης ἀγείραντα αὐτὸν περιποιήσειν σφᾶς); they certainly cannot have expected

[31] The distance from Eion to Amphipolis was only 25 stades (102.3).

[32] G. F. Abbott, *Thucydides*, 1925, 114–16, cf. Gomme, op. cit., iii., 586, whose presentation of this argument is much more guarded. There does not seem to be any substance in the view of H. Delbrück, *Die Strategie des Perikles*, 1890, 185–6, that Eion had no harbour and was unusable in winter; cf. the objections of Busolt, loc. cit., and the evidence of its use as a base cited by Gomme, loc. cit. In the previous winter some Athenian ships, doubtless including triremes, sent out to collect tribute had at least called at Eion, where their commander arrested a Persian envoy travelling to Sparta (4.50.1).

[33] Busolt, op. cit., iii., 2, 1154. Steup, i[5]. 1919, *Einleitung* xii–xiii, infers from 108.1 that, when Brasidas was approaching Amphipolis, other triremes were at Eion, perhaps under the command of Eucles. This view is untenable unless Thucydides is guilty of misrepresentation. If there had been other ships at Eion, he could not have claimed that his arrival with his small squadron (106.4–107.2) influenced the situation substantially.

[34] Cf. Busolt, op. cit., iii., 2, 1154–5.

[35] The Athenian general Simonides had in 425 collected troops by similar methods for an attack upon the other Eion in Chalcidice (4.7, ξυλλέξας Ἀθηναίους τε ὀλίγους ἐκ τῶν φρουρίων καὶ τῶν ἐκείνῃ ξυμμάχων πλῆθος).

him to begin collecting reinforcements only after receiving their call for help. Presumably the two Athenian generals envisaged the possibility of an attack on Amphipolis but believed that before it developed Thucydides would have time to complete his mission. Brasidas, having learned from the Argilians or other local supporters that the Athenian squadron had left Eion, doubtless timed his forced march so as to reach Amphipolis before its return.[36] Arrangements had probably been made in advance to recall Thucydides in the event of emergency: he could hardly have reached Eion so rapidly if he had not been ready to sail at very short notice.[37] This reconstruction, though reasonable enough,[38] is based upon a series of conjectures. To put much confidence in it would be highly unwise.

Thucydides has omitted to give his readers any information upon a point of substance. It is not a trivial detail of purely autobiographical interest but a factor which contributed, perhaps decisively, to the loss of a strategically valuable Athenian stronghold. He implies more than once that, had his squadron been close at hand, it might well have saved Amphipolis (104.5; 105.1; 106.1). Even if he had been only an obscure Athenian general with no greater claim to the interest of posterity than Eucles or Simonides (4.7) or Aristeides the son of Archippus (4.50.1 and 75.1), the reason why he was at Thasos would still have been important to anyone wishing to understand why Amphipolis was lost. Remarkable omissions do occur in his *History*, and some of them appear to be capricious.[39] There seems, however, to be nothing capricious in this instance. In his account of another episode at Amphipolis, the battle there in 422 in which Cleon and Brasidas were killed (5.6–11), there are omissions and some lack of clarity. These have, with good reason, been attributed partly to the influence of his prejudice against Cleon, which is unmistakable here.[40] In recording the events at

[36] Busolt, op. cit., iii., 2, 1157.
[37] Gomme, op. cit., iii., 579, suggests that some kind of signalling must have been used to summon Thucydides from Thasos.
[38] One weakness is that Thucydides could surely have divided his small squadron and left part of it at Eion. Triremes were ill-suited for use as troop-carriers, and other more suitable craft could doubtless have been obtained at Thasos.
[39] Gomme, op. cit., iii., 607.
[40] Ibid., iii., 653–4 and Ἑλληνικά 13.4–9.

Amphipolis in 422 he is indirectly damning Cleon; in recording the events of 424 he is indirectly defending himself, if there is any validity in the suggestions made in this paper. He may have had some cogent and entirely creditable reason for not being at Eion which, if known to posterity, would have helped to absolve him from any suspicion of having committed a strategic blunder. It seems, however, at least likely, though very far from certain, that he has omitted to give the reason why he was at Thasos because it would not have strengthened and might have weakened his case for his own defence.

8

Thucydides 4.108.4

καὶ γὰρ καὶ ἄδεια ἐφαίνετο αὐτοῖς, ἐψευσμένοι¹ μὲν τῆς Ἀθηναίων
δυνάμεως ἐπι τοσοῦτον ὅση ὕστερον διεφάνη, τὸ δὲ πλέον βουλήσει
κρίνοντες ἀσαφεῖ ἢ προνοίᾳ ἀσφαλεῖ, εἰωθότες οἱ ἄνθρωποι οὗ μὲν
ἐπιθυμοῦσιν ἐλπίδι ἀπερισκέπτῳ διδόναι, ὃ δὲ μὴ προσίενται λογισμῷ
αὐτοκράτορι διωθεῖσθαι.

This sentence belongs to a passage in which Thucydides discusses the reactions of the Athenians (108.1–2) and of their
subject allies (108.3–6) to the fall of Amphipolis. He describes
very graphically the incautious enthusiasm with which the
allies embarked upon plans for revolt, encouraged by the
Athenian failure to save Amphipolis, which closely followed the
defeat at Delium, and by the tempting propaganda of Brasidas.
The phrase ὅση ὕστερον διεφάνη in the sentence quoted above is
widely interpreted as a reference to the unexpected recovery
of the Athenians in the period after the Sicilian disaster and is
accordingly accepted as evidence that this sentence at least, and
perhaps the whole discussion to which it belongs, cannot have
been written before the closing years of the Peloponnesian war.²
This dating is thought to be confirmed by the fact that a number
of other passages in which Thucydides refers to the surprising
tenacity of the Athenians were all demonstrably written during
the Ionian war or later: these are 2.65.12; 7.28.3; 8.2.2 and 24.5.
Another factor is that when in 4.81.2–3 he discusses, in much the
same terms as in 4.108.3–6, how the achievements of Brasidas
influenced the allies of Athens, he expressly refers to the period
after the Sicilian expedition.³
Gomme makes some interesting comments. He agrees with
other scholars in maintaining that ὅση ὕστερον διεφάνη 'must

---

¹ K. J. Dover, *C.Q.* iv (1954), 81, shows conclusively that ἐψευσμένοι, the
reading of E, is to be preferred to ἐψευσμένοις.
² H. Patzer, *Das Problem der Geschichtsschreibung des Thukydides* (1937), 105;
J. H. Finley, *Harv. Stud.*, Suppl. 1 (1940), 272, cf. 279; J. de Romilly, *Thucydide et l'impérialisme athénien* (1947), 46, cf. 190; W. Schmid, *Gesch. der griech.
Lit.* i. 5 (1948), 132.
³ Cf. Patzer, loc. cit.

refer to the Ionian war',[4] but he believes that, apart from the
single sentence in which this phrase occurs, the discussion in
4.108 'fits in easily with the current narrative'[5] and gives the
impression of having been written at a different time from the
other passage on the reaction of the allies to the success of
Brasidas in 4.81.2–3.[6] Hence he concludes that 4.108.4 'may well
have been *inserted* (his italics) later in an earlier narrative'.[7] He
admits, however, that 'other passages' which are demonstrably
late are partly responsible for his inclination to regard this
sentence as a late insertion.[8] It is the purpose of my note to try
to show that ὅση ὕστερον διεφάνη refers to the period between
the summer of 423 and the summer of 421 and is likely to have
been written, together with the discussion to which it belongs,
before, and not after, the outbreak of the Ionian war.

The similarity in thought between 4.108.4 and other passages
demonstrably late does not provide a reliable basis for dating
this sentence. It is surely very hazardous to assume that passages
in Thucydides in which similar ideas are expressed must have
been composed, or conceived, at much the same time. He was,
one imagines, receptive to new ideas suggested by the progress
of the war, though doubtless much less ready to learn from the
views of others. In some instances, however, he must surely have
found that ideas which he conceived during the early years of the
war, or even before its outbreak, were abundantly confirmed by
later events,[9] and such discoveries doubtless gave him considerable satisfaction. The tendency of other Greeks to underrate the
recuperative powers of the Athenians was a notable feature of

[4] *J.H.S.* lxxi (1951), 73, cf. *Historical Commentary on Thucydides* iii (1956),
582.

[5] *J.H.S.* loc. cit., cf. *Hist. Com.* loc. cit. (note on 108.4).

[6] *Hist. Com.* loc. cit. (n. on 108.2–6).

[7] *Hist. Com.* loc. cit. (n. on 108.4). He finds support for this suggestion by
arguing that 'there is perhaps a slight inconsistency' between ἐπεκηρυκεύοντο
πρὸς αὐτὸν κρύφα (3) and ἄδεια (4). If so, there is surely a more marked
inconsistency between the former phrase and ἐπίστευον μηδένα ἂν ἐπὶ σφᾶς
βοηθῆσαι (5).

[8] *J.H.S.* loc. cit. His 'other passages' are those discussed in his article (ibid.,
70–4), which are all 'comment on the effect of prominent individuals on the
course of the war' (ibid., 70).

[9] His forecast that the war would prove the greatest of all time (1.1.1) is
one of these, unless he is deceiving his readers in claiming that he made this
forecast at the beginning of the war.

the Peloponnesian war. Although most plainly seen during the critical period after the Sicilian disaster, it could have been recognised much earlier by any moderately acute observer. It was prominent during the revolt of Lesbos, as Thucydides makes clear (3.16.1–2), when the effects of the plague were being most severely felt (3.3.1 and 13.3). It was scarcely less prominent in the last years of the Archidamian war after the defeat at Delium (4.108.5, τῶν 'Αθηναίων ἐν τοῖς Βοιωτοῖς νεωστὶ πεπληγμένων) and the loss of Amphipolis and of lesser cities in the same area. That Thucydides may in 4.108.4 be referring to this period, and not to the Ionian war, is surely a possibility to which serious consideration ought to be given.

In examining this suggestion it is first necessary to deal with two points of interpretation. Thucydides begins his discussion of allied reaction to the fall of Amphipolis as though he intends to apply it to the whole Athenian empire (4.108.3, αἱ πόλεις αἱ τῶν 'Αθηναίων ὑπήκοοι).[10] He must, however, be referring only to allied cities in or near Chalcidice, as is clear from the end of this sentence, where he mentions secret negotiations with Brasidas in preparation for revolt.[11] There is no evidence that allies outside this area approached Brasidas, whose military resources were so slender that he could hardly have supported them if they had revolted. Thus, unless 4.108.4 is a remarkably clumsy or careless insertion, ἄδεια ἐφαίνετο αὐτοῖς must apply exclusively to the inhabitants of the same area, and the mistaken estimate of Athenian power must be theirs alone. Secondly, the phrase ἐψευσμένοι μὲν τῆς 'Αθηναίων δυνάμεως ἐπὶ τοσοῦτον ὅση ὕστερον διεφάνη is a strange one. It must mean, as many scholars have maintained,[12] 'their miscalculation of Athenian power was as great as Athenian power was later proved to be great'. The artificial equation between the greatness of a mistake and the greatness of Athenian power, which are conceptions so unlike as to be not easily comparable, is due to a typically Thucydidean compression. Two separate but associated ideas are somewhat

[10] Hude deletes the last four words, perhaps rightly.

[11] The πόλεις in 108.3 are to be identified with the πόλεις in 108.6 (ὧν αἰσθανόμενοι οἱ μὲν 'Αθηναῖοι φυλακὰς . . . διέπεμπον ἐς τὰς πόλεις), which are those immediately threatened by Brasidas, such as Torone (4.110.2). In 4.81.2 ἐς τὰς πόλεις is shown by the context to be limited to the cities of the same area.

[12] Cf. Poppo-Stahl, n. ad loc.; Shilleto quoted by Spratt, n. ad loc.

confusingly blended,[13] namely (a) 'they miscalculated Athenian power to such an extent that they felt that they could revolt with impunity', and (b) 'they failed to realise that Athenian power was as great as it was later proved to be'. The persons to whom this 'later proof' of Athenian power was given are most naturally, though not essentially, to be identified with the persons who had miscalculated its extent. Thus ὅση ὕστερον διεφάνη probably refers, not to an occasion, or occasions, when in the eyes of the Greeks generally Athenian power was most impressively displayed, but rather to a period when the allies now contemplating revolt, whose over-confidence is here described, came to realise how mistaken they had been in their estimate of Athenian power. It is an unjustifiable assumption to maintain that ὕστερον here must be equivalent to ἔς τε τὸν χρόνῳ ὕστερον μετὰ τὰ ἐκ Σικελίας πόλεμον in 4.81.2, the other passage in which allied reaction to the success of Brasidas is discussed.[14]

During the period beginning with the arrival of Nicias and Nicostratus with a strong fleet at Potidaea in the summer of 423 (4.129.2-3) and ending with the recapture of Scione in the summer of 421 (5.32.1) it was indeed made very clear to Athenian allies in or near Chalcidice that they had miscalculated the power of Athens, and many advocates of revolt must have regretted their hasty optimism. Of the cities which revolted during the next few months after the fall of Amphipolis all, with one doubtful exception, had very probably lost their independence by the middle of 421. Several, including the more important, are known to have been recaptured with unenviable consequences to their inhabitants. Thucydides states that the following revolted in this period: Myrcinus, Galepsus and Oesyme (4.107.3), four of the six small towns on the peninsula of Acte (109. 3-5), Torone (110-16), Scione (120.1) and Mende (123.1). Mende fell to Nicias in 423 (130.6-7), Torone (5.3.2-4) and Galepsus (5.6.1) to Cleon in 422, Scione after a long siege in 421 (5.32.1). At Torone and Scione the women and children were enslaved, at Scione the adult males were put to death. The recovery of the other six small places is not recorded by Thucydides, but none

---

[13] Cf. *C.R.* lxii (1948), 2-5 on 7.28.1. This is a feature of Thucydidean style criticised by Dion. Hal. *De Thuc.* 24.51.

[14] For the use of ὕστερον when the interval envisaged is quite brief, cf. 1.64.2; 2.49.6; 3.85.3; 7.26.3 and 85.4.

of them is included in the list of cities in this area to which the Peace of Nicias gave special treatment (5.18.5), presumably because outside Athenian control at the time of its conclusion. Oesyme and the four towns on Acte[15] had almost certainly been recovered by 421, probably by Cleon.[16] Myrcinus was still in revolt when Cleon was defeated at Amphipolis in 422 (5.6.4 and 10.9). The Athenians were doubtless eager to regain it because the neighbourhood was rich in timber for shipbuilding (Hdt. 5.23.2), but its inland situation north of Amphipolis must have made its recovery a difficult task. It perhaps succeeded in maintaining its independence and was ignored in the Peace of Nicias because it was an Edonian city.[17]

The attempt by the Athenians to reimpose their authority in this area by military action is presented by Thucydides as a dismal failure. Nicias and Nicostratus could operate only against Scione and Mende, because the terms of the One Year's Truce protected cities already in revolt when it was concluded (4.118.4 and 122.3–6). The expedition led by Cleon was abandoned after his defeat at Amphipolis had cost 600 Athenian lives including his own (5.11.2–3). The Athenians, according to Thucydides, were so disheartened by successive defeats at Delium and Amphipolis, which, they felt, might encourage further revolts, that they lost confidence in their own strength and were now content to make peace (5.14.1–2). The general accuracy of this picture is beyond doubt; it is confirmed to some extent by the *Peace* of Aristophanes, which reflects the mood of the Athenians at this time. It is, however, undeniable that Thucydides gives insufficient prominence to their progress in suppressing revolts, doubtless because he is unwilling to recognise any merit in the military leadership of Cleon, who was mainly responsible for their successes.[18] Thucydides is perhaps equally reluctant to

[15] Two of these appear in the assessment of 421 (*A.T.L.* ii, A 10) and a third is described by Thucydides as an ally of Athens in the same year (5.35.1).

[16] Gomme, *Hist. Com.* iii. 671. The assessment of 421 (A 10), as well as clauses in the Peace of Nicias, suggests that revolts not mentioned by Thucydides at some other places in this area had been suppressed before the conclusion of the Peace, cf. A. B. West and B. D. Meritt, *A.J.A.* xxix (1925), 59–69, and A. G. Woodhead, *Mnemos.* xiii (1960), 304–6.

[17] Hdt. 5.11.2; Thuc. 4.107.3. It was never a member of Confederacy. Its later history is unknown.

[18] Woodhead, loc. cit.

stress the failure of Brasidas, however excusable, to protect against Athenian reprisals cities which had revolted at his instigation. There were apparently no more revolts after that of Mende either during the One Year's Truce, though Brasidas did not remain inactive (4.135.1), or when it ended. Even the defeat of Cleon at Amphipolis did not produce the further outbreaks expected by the Athenians (5.14.2). While the results of their operations in and around Chalcidice were unsatisfactory to the Athenians themselves,[19] their allies and former allies in this area must have been deeply impressed by their forcefulness and efficiency in transporting overseas and bringing into action large forces of high quality.[20] Although better leadership might have produced greater success,[21] their troops seem to have shown plenty of resolution throughout, even in defeat at Amphipolis (5.10.9). The propaganda of Brasidas, who had sought to encourage disaffection by falsely accusing the Athenians of cowardice during the operations at Nisaea (4.85.7 and 108.5), was effectively belied.

The later events to which Thucydides alludes in 4.108.4 when he states that they proved how mistaken the allies had been in their estimate of Athenian power are surely those of 423–1 and not those of the Ionian war. Thus the only *terminus post quem* for the composition of this sentence is 421, and there is no reason to believe it to be a later addition. On the contrary, it forms an important, almost essential, link in the general discussion of Athenian and allied reactions to the fall of Amphipolis (108.1–6).[22] It would be hazardous to claim that the period in which this discussion was written can be determined with any great confidence, but 4.108.4 provides a valuable clue. Thucydides is not always as precise as his readers could wish; but if he had written

---

[19] Thucydides naturally gives more prominence to Athenian feeling than to allied feeling in a single area because the former had much more influence upon the general trend of events.

[20] Numbers: 4.129.2 (Nicias and Nicostratus); 5.2.1 (Cleon). Quality (recognised even by Brasidas): 5.8.2.

[21] Nicias and Nicostratus both suffered tactical reverses at Mende (4.129.4). The generalship of Cleon is fully discussed by Gomme, Ἑλληνικά, xiii (1954), 1–10, cf. Woodhead, op. cit., 306–10.

[22] In thought and language 108.4 is similar to the rest of the passage (cf. especially διὰ τὸ ἡδονὴν ἔχον ἐν τῷ αὐτίκα, ibid., 6), though such similarities are not wholly reliable criteria.

this sentence during or after the Ionian war, when he was acquainted with further and even more striking illustrations of the extent to which the allies were found to have miscalculated the power of Athens, he would surely have given a more explicit indication of the period to which he is alluding. In 4.81.3, where he has the Ionian war in mind, he makes his meaning perfectly clear by using the phrase ἔς τε τὸν χρόνῳ ὕστερον μετὰ τὰ ἐκ Σικελίας πόλεμον. Thus the events of the Ionian war, far from providing a *terminus post quem* for the composition of 4.108.4, provide a probable *terminus ante quem*. Because this sentence can scarcely have been written earlier than its context, the whole discussion is likely to have been written before the outbreak of the Ionian war.[23] There are, therefore, more solid grounds than mere impression[24] for concluding that the two passages, 4.81.2–3 and 4.108.1–6, in which Thucydides gives his views on the success of Brasidas and its influence upon public opinion were composed at different times.

[23] There are obvious dangers in relying upon the evidence of single sentences to date the composition of long passages (cf. above, pp. 39–40), but here the single sentence would be unintelligible if torn from its context.

[24] Cf. Gomme, cited above, p. 139, n. 6.

9

Sophocles and Nicias as colleagues

τοῦ δὲ Νικίου καὶ διὰ τἆλλα μέγας ἦν καὶ διὰ τὸν πλοῦτον καὶ διὰ τὴν
δόξαν ὁ ὄγκος. λέγεται δ᾿ ἐν τῷ στρατηγίῳ ποτὲ βουλευομένων τι
κοινῇ τῶν συναρχόντων κελευσθεὶς ὑπ᾿ αὐτοῦ πρῶτος εἰπεῖν γνώμην
Σοφοκλῆς ὁ ποιητὴς ὡς πρεσβύτατος ὢν τῶν συστρατήγων ʽἐγώʼ
φάναι ʽπαλαιότατός εἰμι, σὺ δὲ πρεσβύτατοςʼ.
(Plutarch, _Nicias_ 15.2)

This anecdote is inserted in an account of the relations between
Nicias and Lamachus in Sicily after the recall of Alcibiades.
Wishing to focus attention upon the ὄγκος that enabled Nicias to
override his humble colleague, Plutarch gives an illustration of
it evidently belonging to a different context but without any clear
indication of date. There is no other evidence that Sophocles and
Nicias served together on the same board of generals, and it
might be maintained that before Nicias first held office, or at any
rate before he attained the eminence implied in this anecdote,
Sophocles would have been considered too old for election to a
magistracy that was essentially military. Sophocles was undoubtedly general in 441/0, but confused references to his public
life contained in the anonymous _Vita_ do not provide trustworthy
evidence that he served in any other year.[1] Hence, not unnaturally, doubts have been expressed whether the incident described
by Plutarch ever occurred at all.[2]

By introducing his anecdote with λέγεται Plutarch is not suggesting that he suspects its authenticity, though it is not on that
account any more likely to be authentic. In the _Lives_ λέγεται

[1] The statement in _Vita_ 1 that he held office 'with Pericles and Thucydides'
is almost certainly false (V. Ehrenberg, _Sophocles and Pericles_ (1954), 117 n. 1).
G. Perrotta, _Sofocle_ (1935) 42 with n. 1, links the generalship ἐν τῷ πρὸς
᾿Αναίους πολέμῳ (_Vita_ 9) with the story told by Plutarch and assigns it to
428/7. It is, however, difficult to believe that the insignificant operations
mentioned by Thuc. 3.19.2 (cf. 32.2 and 4.75.1) could be described as a 'war
against the Anaeans'. The passage refers to the well-attested
generalship of Sophocles during the Samian revolt, his age being incorrectly
stated.
[2] Recently by Ehrenberg, loc. cit.

commonly marks a change of source: Plutarch uses it where he turns aside from his main authority to tell some story originating from elsewhere which he considers to be for some reason significant.[3] Many stories of this kind are, like the instance quoted above, chronologically unrelated to their setting and may accordingly be difficult to date. Passages introduced by λέγεται are evidently derived from a wide variety of sources, good and bad. In the course of his extensive reading in many branches of literature Plutarch collected a large store of miscellaneous material upon which he drew when writing his *Lives*; he doubtless also used collections compiled by others. Painstaking though he was, much of this material is of somewhat doubtful authenticity, and it cannot be claimed that an anecdote derived from an unnamed source and not recorded elsewhere is by any means above suspicion. Clearly, however, in assessing the value of the surviving evidence for the political career of Sophocles, it would be a mistake to rate the testimony of Plutarch no higher than that of the anonymous *Vita*.

Tradition pictures Sophocles, especially when he was elderly, as an exponent of worldly good sense pithily yet urbanely and modestly expressed. The famous fragment of Ion describing the dinner party at Chios,[4] the story told by Cephalus in the *Republic*,[5] and three passages in Aristotle's *Rhetoric*[6] all present the same picture, which must surely be authentic. One reason for

---

[3] This practice is admirably explained by W. H. Porter in his note on *Dion* 3.4. Other examples in the *Nicias* are 7.7 (a story about Cleon, also told in *Mor.* 799 d), 13.1 (a list of omens), 15.4 (a reference to a courtesan); in each case the preceding narrative is based on good historical evidence ultimately from Thucydides. Among many instances in other *Lives* are *Them.* 17.4 and *Per.* 35.2.

[4] *Fr. Gr. Hist.* 392 F 6. Though the comic poets naturally do not quote his apophthegms, their portrait is similar.

[5] 1.329 b–c.

[6] 1.14.3, 1374 b; 3.15.3, 1416 a; 3.18.6, 1419a (which shows that he was one of the *Probouloi* appointed after the Sicilian disaster, cf. Thuc. 8.1.3, who states that they were elderly men). The strange idea that the Sophocles mentioned in these passages is not the poet must be rejected (cf. P. Foucart, *Rev. Phil.* 17 [1893], 1–10). Eight other passages in the *Rhetoric* refer to the poet (T. B. L. Webster, *An Introduction to Sophocles* [1936], 13), some of them being close to the passages cited above. A less famous Sophocles would surely have been distinguished from the poet by the addition of a patronymic or of a reference to the sphere in which he achieved distinction.

146

SOPHOCLES AND NICIAS AS COLLEAGUES

feeling some measure of confidence in Plutarch's anecdote is that the reply of Sophocles to Nicias strikes exactly the same note as his sayings quoted by writers of the fifth and fourth centuries. There is, however, another consideration that weighs much more heavily in favour of accepting the anecdote. It is beyond doubt that Sophocles and Nicias were members of the same tribe, namely Aegeis.[7] Plutarch was doubtless ignorant of this fact and, even had he been aware of it, would scarcely have appreciated its significance, because he did not fully understand the political institutions of fifth-century Athens. It has been almost wholly neglected by modern scholars.[8] The system whereby two members of a single tribe might serve on the same board of generals is well-attested:[9] it was evidently instituted in the time of Pericles in order that, while he was being re-elected year after year, his fellowtribesmen should not be debarred from holding office. In every case where this system is known to have been adopted one of the generals involved was an outstanding figure in public life, who had already served on the board several times, and he was elected not as the representative of his tribe but ἐξ ἁπάντων. If Sophocles and Nicias were colleagues, it was clearly the latter who must have been elected ἐξ ἁπάντων.[10] Although there is no evidence that a general elected in this way enjoyed legal powers superior to those of his colleagues or acted as chairman of the board throughout his year of office, the distinction of having been singled out for election ἐξ ἁπάντων must have added

---

[7] It is not possible to determine the tribe of Sophocles from his deme because there were apparently three demes named Colonus, each belonging to a different tribe. However in the well-known fragment of Androtion listing the generals of 441/0 (*Fr. Gr. Hist.*, 324 F 38) the names are arranged according to the official order of the tribes, so that Sophocles, whose name is second, must have belonged to Aegeis; cf. *I.G.* ii². 1374-5, where a Sophocles, placed second in a list of ταμίαι of 400/399 is almost certainly the son of Iophon (*I.G.* ii². 1445.13) and grandson of the poet. The deme of Nicias was Cydantidae (cf. *I.G.* i². 302.40), which belonged to Aegeis (cf. *I.G.* ii². 1749.20).

[8] I cannot claim to have been the first to have noticed it. It is mentioned by A. B. West, *A.J.P.* 45, 1924, 156 n. 53, whose views will be discussed below.

[9] It is fully discussed by C. Hignett, *History of the Athenian Constitution* (1952), 347-56.

[10] The ability of Sophocles as a general was, according to himself, rated low by Pericles (*F. Gr. Hist.* 392 F 6 ad fin.), and he was certainly not elected many times, though he probably did not often seek office.

greatly to his prestige,[11] and in practice he was probably often able to exert a preponderant influence upon the decisions of the board. It is surely to precedence of this kind that Sophocles referred when he seized upon the word πρεσβύτατος used by Nicias and neatly repeated it in a different and in fact older sense, which has no relation to old age.[12] Plutarch or perhaps some predecessor, finding the anecdote recorded somewhere without explanation, would naturally assume that Nicias was described as πρεσβύτατος merely because of his wealth and fame, but the reply of Sophocles is more pointed and even more consistent with his reputation for repartee if it be understood to refer to the special position enjoyed by Nicias because of his election ἐξ ἁπάντων.[13] The anecdote must surely have been recorded in the first instance by an author who fully appreciated its point; he may well have been a contemporary.[14] Accordingly it has a much stronger claim to be accepted as authentic than most personal anecdotes recorded in the *Lives* without any indication of their source.

Several scholars have suggested that, while the story may be true, Plutarch has committed, or reproduced, an error of identification; that the colleague of Nicias was not Sophocles the poet but his namesake the son of Sostratides, who with Eurymedon commanded the Athenian fleet sent to Sicily in 425 and was banished when he returned in the following summer.[15] Though

---

[11] Hignett, op. cit., 352–3.

[12] Cf. L. S.[9] s. v. πρέσβυ ad fin., where the oldest sense of the word is stated to be 'going in front of, taking precedence' (cf. Ernst Fraenkel, *Glotta* 32 [1953], 17). In two fragments of lost Sophoclean plays (582 and 605, Pearson) the poetical πρέσβιστος is used without reference to age.

[13] The scene of the incident is laid ἐν τῷ στρατηγίῳ, which was a building at Athens where the generals met (Aeschin. 2.85; [Dem.] 42.14; Plut. *Nic.* 5.1). Hence Nicias cannot have been in command of some expedition with one or more of his colleagues subordinated to him in accordance with a commonly adopted practice. Nor can he have been described as πρεσβύτατος in virtue of his appointment as στρατηγὸς αὐτοκράτωρ of the expedition to Sicily, because Alcibiades and Lamachus were granted powers equal to his.

[14] That this author was Ion is possible but unlikely; he died in the summer of 422 or the following winter (F. Jacoby, *C.Q.* 41 [1947], 1).

[15] G. Busolt, *Gr. Gesch.* iii. 1 (1897), 576 n. 3, and Schmid-Stählin, *Gr. Literaturgesch.* i. 2 (1934), 319 n. 1, offer this explanation very briefly and tentatively. West, op. cit., 156 with n. 53, uses it to support an elaborate reconstruction of the board of generals in 424/3 and their political affinities:

Plutarch himself and many of his authorities were fallible enough, there are several objections to this hypothesis, which appears to be based mainly on the fact that the son of Sostratides is known from other evidence to have been a colleague of Nicias whereas the poet is not. In the first place, the Athenians might well have selected an elderly general (παλαιότατος) to take joint command of a substantial expedition to a distant theatre of war if he had been a well-tried leader with a distinguished record; but the son of Sostratides was certainly not famous and is not known to have held the office of general before.[16] Secondly, he may well be identical with a Sophocles who was one of the Thirty:[17] presumably he returned to Athens at the end of the war, where he may, not unnaturally, have helped to overthrow the democracy which had been responsible for his exile. No member of the Thirty is likely to have been so old that in the middle of the Archidamian war he was already considered elderly and was the oldest general of a board which included Nicias, who was himself older than Socrates.[18] Finally, Nicias was not among the generals of 426/5, the first year in which the son of Sostratides is known to have held office, while for almost all the year 425/4 the latter was absent from Athens; if on his return he attended any meetings of the board before being suspended, Nicias may well have

---

he maintains that Sophocles the son of Sostratides as well as Sophocles the poet belonged to Aegeis and that the former when banished in 424 was replaced by Nicias on the board of generals as the result of a by-election.

[16] The first mention of him is Thuc. 3.115.5 (his appointment to this command).

[17] Xen. *Hell.* 2.3.2. This Sophocles almost certainly belonged to Oeneis (T. Lenschau, *R.E.* vi A 2363-4). West, loc. cit., objects that the son of Sostratides could not have belonged to this tribe because it was represented by Lamachus in 426/5 and 424/3, but the generalships of Lamachus are very uncertain. It is most improbable that he was general when the *Acharnians* was produced early in 425, while, though he served in 424/3 (Thuc. 4.75.1), he may have been appointed to replace the son of Sostratides, who was doubtless re-elected in 424 (Busolt, op. cit. iii. 2 [1904] 1125 n. 1) but because he was put on trial on his return from Sicily (Thuc. 4.65.3), probably never took his place on the board. West's conclusion that the son of Sostratides belonged to Aegeis is reached by eliminating other possibilities: he has already assigned Aristeides to Cecropis (ibid., 145) and Pythodorus to Hippothontis (ibid., 155) largely by the same method, and he is palpably mistaken in assigning Eurymedon to Leontis (cf. S. Accame, *Riv. Fil.* n. s. 13 [1935], 345 n. 4).

[18] Plato, *Laches* 181 d.

been away leading his attack on Cythera[19] and, even if he were at Athens, is unlikely to have shown much regard for the opinions of a colleague who had failed in an important mission and was about to be put on trial for this failure.[20]

Because the anecdote of Plutarch is 'timeless', the year to which it belongs cannot be determined with any certainty. It is, however, possible to define with some degree of confidence the period in which the generalship of Sophocles and Nicias is likely to have fallen. Nicias apparently served on the board before the death of Pericles,[21] but he is not mentioned by Thucydides until the summer of 427, when he led a small force against Minoa.[22] He can scarcely have become a sufficiently outstanding personality to have been elected ἐξ ἁπάντων before the closing years of the Archidamian war. The suggestion has been made that his generalship with Sophocles may belong to the years of uneasy peace between 421 and 415:[23] the sailing of the Sicilian expedition is a certain *terminus ante quem*. Nicias is known to have been a member of the board in most of these years, while not many other names from this period have been preserved. Despite the situation in Chalcidice and the confusion in the Peloponnese there was little likelihood that many of the generals would be required to conduct military operations, and the advanced age of Sophocles might not be regarded as a disqualification.[24] The duties of a general at this time would not necessarily impose a

---

[19] *I.G.* i². 324.21; Thuc. 4.53–4.

[20] Nicias and the son of Sostratides may have been colleagues in 427/6 or some earlier year, but the former had not then established himself as an outstanding figure.

[21] Plut. *Nic.* 2.2, ἦν μὲν ἔν τινι λόγῳ καὶ Περικλέους ζῶντος, ὥστε κἀκείνῳ συστρατηγῆσαι καὶ καθ᾽ αὑτὸν ἄρξαι πολλάκις. The vagueness of this statement suggests a lack of definite evidence: though probably not false, it is surely an exaggeration. In 432/1 and 431/0 Aegeis was represented by Socrates son of Antigenes (G. F. Hill, *Sources for Greek History*² [1951], 402).

[22] Thuc. 3.51.1. There appear to be no references to him by comic poets that can be dated before 424.

[23] Ehrenberg, loc. cit., who, however, as stated above, doubts whether the incident reported by Plutarch happened at all; he points out that 'Sophocles would then have been between seventy-five and eighty'.

[24] There was no upper age-limit for the tenure of Athenian magistracies (U. Kahrstedt, *Untersuchungen zur Magistratur in Athen* [1936], 19). Phocion was general when he was about 80 (Plut. *Phoc.* 24.5, cf. *Mor.* 791 e–f and 819a; Dio Chrys. 73.7).

greater physical strain than those of a *Proboulos* after the Sicilian catastrophe,[25] and there is abundant evidence that the intellectual powers of Sophocles remained unimpaired to the end of his life. On the other hand, there is towards the close of the Archidamian war one year in favour of which somewhat more positive arguments can be advanced, namely 423/2, the year of armistice, when Nicias had already held office at least four times. When the elections for this year took place early in 423, the armistice was about to be signed, and there was general expectation on both sides that before it expired a more permanent agreement would be concluded.[26] At a time when it was anticipated that important and probably difficult negotiations with the Peloponnesians would take place, some generals at least would be required who were believed to possess diplomatic rather than military ability. The conservative Sophocles may well have been one of these:[27] his experience went back to a period in which Athens and Sparta were allies, and his political sympathies lay with Cimon rather than with Pericles.[28] Nicias may perhaps for these reasons have persuaded Sophocles to offer himself as a candidate and later have sought his advice ἐν τῷ στρατηγίῳ when the new board met. Apart from Nicias himself and Nicostratus,[29] its membership is unknown.[30] A mysterious statement in the *Peace*, produced in 421, that Sophocles 'though old and worn out, would set sail on a rush mat to gain money',[31] might refer to some alleged scandal arising from a recent return by the poet to political life and possibly connected with diplomatic activities. The reasons for believing that his candidature might have been especially welcome in 423 do not apply in the same degree to the elections of 421, because negotiations for a permanent peace were then far advanced and not only the Peace of Nicias but also

[25] See above, p. 146 n. 6 on Sophocles' tenure of this office.

[26] This was officially stated in the text of the armistice quoted by Thuc. 4.118.6 and 13–14, cf. ibid., 117.1, 119.3, and 5.15.2.

[27] According to *Vita* 1 he served on embassies.

[28] Webster, op. cit., 10 and 16–17; Ehrenberg, op. cit., 138–9.

[29] The operations conducted by these two generals in Chalcidice (Thuc. 4.129.2) were continued until the late summer of 423 (ibid., 133.4).

[30] Eurymedon may possibly have been a member (H. T. Wade-Gery, *C.Q.* 24 [1930], 33–9), though he had been fined in the previous year (Thuc. 4.65.3).

[31] Aristoph. *Peace* 695–9.

the defensive alliance between Athens and Sparta were concluded before the board of 421/o took office.[32]

This passage, in addition to providing a welcome scrap of information about the political career of Sophocles, also sheds some light on the history of the Athenian *strategia*. The election of two generals from the same tribe seems to have been very exceptional in the period from the death of Pericles to the end of the Peloponnesian war: the only certain instance is that of Alcibiades and Adeimantus, who belonged to the same deme and were both elected to the board of 407/6.[33] Hipponicus the son of Callias was formerly assigned by scholars to the same tribe as Nicias, with whom he served on the board of 427/6, but a new inscription proves he belonged to Antiochis.[34] If the Pythodorus who with two other generals conducted raids on Laconia in 414[35] is to be identified with a Pythodorus from Aegeis mentioned in a choregic inscription of about the same date,[36] Nicias must have been elected ἐξ ἁπάντων for 415/4 or 414/3. This identification, however, is very doubtful: there were many Athenians called Pythodorus,[37] and several were prominent during the Peloponnesian war.[38] The anecdote about Sophocles and Nicias provides a firmer basis for believing that on at least one occasion the latter was, as might have been expected from his almost uninterrupted tenure of office, elected ἐξ ἁπάντων.

---

[32] A possible alternative to 423/2 for the generalship of Sophocles and Nicias is 418/7, when Nicias and several other conservatives are known to have been members of the board while Alcibiades was not elected.

[33] Hignett, op. cit., 349.

[34] B. D. Meritt, *Hesperia* 5, 1936, 410. The attribution of Hipponicus to Aegeis has encouraged erroneous views about the rise of Nicias; Thucydides certainly supplies no ground for believing that in 427/6 he was sufficiently well-established to have been elected ἐξ ἁπάντων.

[35] Thuc. 6.105.2.

[36] *I.G.* i². 770a.

[37] *Prosop. Att.* s. v. lists nearly 50 of them.

[38] Cf. Busolt, op. cit. iii. 2 (1904), 1351 n. 1.

10

ʽΩΣ Εἰκός in Thucydides

The use of the neuter participle εἰκός, with ἐστι or ἦν sometimes expressed but more often understood and usually with a dependent infinitive,[1] becomes very common in the second half of the fifth century. It occurs most frequently in early oratory,[2] in which so many of the arguments are based on probability, but it is commonly found in other branches of prose literature[3] and is by no means uncommon in tragedy and comedy. It is a word of very wide range: it means 'reasonable', 'appropriate', 'natural', 'to be expected' and so 'likely', 'probable', but it may also convey an idea of moral duty and mean 'fitting', 'right', 'equitable', which seems to be its most common meaning in tragedy.

Thucydides uses εἰκός freely, especially in speeches,[4] and most commonly with a dependent infinitive. With this construction it may bear any of the senses listed above: for example, it may mean 'reasonable' (6.80.1, οὐχ ἀθρόους γε ὄντας εἰκὸς ἀθυμεῖν, cf. 5.26.2), 'natural' (6.72.3, οὐ μέντοι τοσοῦτόν γε λειφθῆναι ὅσον εἰκὸς εἶναι, cf. 4.128.4), 'probable' (referring to the past, 8.94.2, εἰκὸς δ᾽ αὐτὸν καὶ πρὸς τὸν παρόντα στασιασμὸν τῶν Ἀθηναίων, δι᾽ ἐλπίδος ὡς κἂν ἐς δέον παραγένοιτο, ταύτῃ ἀνέχειν, cf. 1.10.4, or to the future, 6.17.4, οὐκ εἰκὸς τὸν τοιοῦτον ὅμιλον οὔτε λόγου μιᾷ γνώμῃ ἀκροᾶσθαι οὔτε ἐς τὰ ἔργα κοινῶς τρέπεσθαι, cf. 7.74.2) or 'right' (5.9.9, αὐτός τε ἀνὴρ ἀγαθός γίγνου, ὥσπερ

---

[1] The construction is explained by J. M. Stahl, *Kritisch-historische Syntax des gr. Verbums* (1907), 197.

[2] Cf. W. Süss, *Ethos* (1910), 3–10 and 228–30; F. Solmsen, *Antiphonstudien* (*Neue Philolog. Untersuchungen* 8 [1931]), 53; E. Mikkola, *Isokrates* (1954), 101. In early speeches εἰκός occasionally occurs several times within a few sentences; for example, seven times (including ἀπεικός, τὰ εἰκότα and εἰκότερον) in Antiphon 2 β 5–8 and four times in Lys. 12.27–8. εἰκός is discussed in later works on rhetoric and is defined by Aristotle in *Rhet. A* 2.1357 a 34 and *Anal. Pr.* 2.70 a 3.

[3] Including scientific works. For example, it occurs approximately twenty times in the not very long treatise *Airs, Waters and Places*, which is believed to be among the earliest works of the Hippocratic corpus.

[4] Cf. O. Danniger, *Wien. Stud.* 49, 1931, 12–31 (though his conclusions are unconvincing).

L

σε εἰκὸς ὄντα Σπαρτιάτην, cf. 2.41.5). Although there is a tendency for the boundaries of these meanings to overlap, in almost every instance the context clearly indicates which of them εἰκός bears.

A point of importance so far as this note on ὡς εἰκός is concerned is that εἰκός with the infinitive may mean 'it is probable that', where Thucydides himself or one of his speakers is in doubt whether the statement that follows is true, but that he also uses it frequently in other senses.

Phrases made from εἰκος include κατὰ τὸ εἰκός, παρὰ τὸ εἰκός, ἐκ τοῦ εἰκότος, τῷ εἰκότι, τὰ εἰκότα, ὡς εἰκός and ὥσπερ εἰκός (the last two being used both with and without ἐστι or ἦν). All these phrases, except ὥσπερ εἰκός, occur in Thucydides. There seems no reason why all should not be used in all the senses of εἰκός with the infinitive, but in practice their range tends to be limited, and this limitation cannot be wholly explained by the fact that they occur less commonly than the infinitive construction. κατὰ τὸ εἰκός occurs ten times in Thucydides (1.121.4; 2.54.3; 3.30.2; 4.8.8; 5.9.7 and 86; 6.72.4; 8.68.3, 71.1 and 87.4). In every passage it can, and in almost all unquestionably does, mean 'probably', and the verb is future or virtually future. Other authors who wrote before the middle of the fourth century seem to use κατὰ τὸ εἰκός similarly (cf. Antiphon 5.63; Xen. Hell. 7.1.2; Plato Tim. 56c), and though there may well be passages written before this date in which the phrase means 'naturally' or 'equitably', I have yet to find one.[5]

A parallel limitation operating in the opposite direction may be traced in the use of the parenthetical ὡς εἰκός and ὥσπερ εἰκός, which seem to be interchangeable. In Herodotus the Ionic ὡς οἰκός and ὥσπερ οἰκός with or without ἐστι or ἦν invariably mean 'as is natural', 'as was natural'. The list of passages is: 1.45.3 Κροῖσος μέν νυν ἔθαψε, ὡς οἰκὸς ἦν, τὸν ἑωυτοῦ παῖδα; 3.50.2 τούτους ὁ μητροπάτωρ Προκλέης . . . ἐφιλοφρονέετο, ὡς οἰκὸς ἦν θυγατρὸς ἐόντας τῆς ἑωυτοῦ παῖδας; 3.108.2 καί κως τοῦ θείου ἡ προνοίη, ὥσπερ καὶ οἰκός ἐστι, ἐοῦσα σοφή; 3.139.1 ἄλλοι τε συχνοὶ ἐς τὴν Αἴγυπτον ἀπίκοντο Ἑλλήνων, οἱ μέν, ὡς οἰκός, κατ᾽ ἐμπορίην; 4.31.1 τὰ κατύπερθε ταύτης τῆς χώρης αἰεὶ νίφεται, ἐλάσσονι δὲ τοῦ θέρεος ἢ τοῦ χειμῶνος, ὥσπερ καὶ οἰκός; 7.218.1

[5] τὸ εἰκός means 'probability', cf. Hdt. 7.239.2 (οἰκός), Antiphon 5.43 and 49, and four times in Plato Phaedr. 272 e–273 d—also later in Aristotle very frequently, cf. Poet. 1451, a 38. Its meaning in Thuc. 5.96 is uncertain.

ψόφου δὲ γινομένου πολλοῦ ὡς οἰκὸς ἦν φύλλων ὑποκεχυμένων ὑπὸ τοῖσι ποσί.[6] Where other writers contemporary or nearly contemporary with Thucydides use this phrase, the meaning of εἰκός is 'natural' or, less commonly, 'right', 'proper'. I have found the following: Soph. *El.* 1140 (ὡς εἰκός), *Phil.* 361 (ὡς εἰκὸς ἦν) and 498 (ὡς εἰκός); Eur. *Med.* 1386 (ὥσπερ εἰκός); Crates fr. 23, Kock (ὥσπερ εἰκός); Aristoph. *Thesm.* 722,974,1144 (ὥσπερ εἰκος), *Plut.* 662 and fr. 621, Oxford (ὥσπερ εἰκὸς ἦν); Andoc. 2.10 (ὥσπερ εἰκός); Lys. 1.6 (ὥσπερ εἰκὸς ἦν), and 13.40 (ὡς εἰκὸς ἦν). In none of these passages does εἰκός mean 'likely', 'probable': the writer is not indicating that he feels doubtful whether his statement is accurate.[7] A little later Xenophon uses ὡς εἰκός and ὥσπερ εἰκός frequently and in the same way as his predecessors.[8] In Plato, however, there seems to be less consistency: ὡς τὸ εἰκός, which he apparently uses more freely than ὡς εἰκός, often, though not always, means 'probably' (cf. *Laches* 190 d, *Protag.* 311 a, *Crito* 45 d, *Gorg.* 520 c, *Symp.* 200 a, where the following sentence confirms that it must bear this sense, *Phaedo* 67 a, *Rep.* 407 d and 610 e); but, as has already been noted, he and other writers use τὸ εἰκός for 'probability', and it is not a necessary assumption that ὡς τὸ εἰκός and ὡς εἰκός are interchangeable.[9] In *Laches* 187 c and *Laws* 780 b the meaning of ὡς εἰκὸς may be 'probably', but 'as was natural' is admissible and, in my opinion, preferable in both passages.[10]

There is therefore good reason to believe that, at any rate to Greeks of the generation to which Thucydides belonged, ὡς εἰκός, as well as ὥσπερ εἰκός which he does not use, normally meant 'as is natural', 'as was natural' (or, less commonly, 'right', 'proper'). Where neither ἐστι nor ἦν is expressed, the verb to be

[6] I have excluded 2.56.2 where ὥσπερ ἦν οἰκός, though it has the same meaning as in the above passages, is followed by a dependent infinitive.

[7] The statement of L. S.⁹ s. v. ἔοικα iv. 3, that ʽὡς εἰκός Ion. ὡς οἰκός = ὡς ἔοικεʼ is, in my view, invalid; it is not substantiated by passages in which the phrases occur.

[8] *Anab.* 3.4.24; *Hell.* 2.3.55; 3.4.24; 5.2.24; 3.20 and 4.29; 7.2.15 and 5.21; *Cyrop.* 2.1.1–2, 2.10 and 3.20; 4.1.7 and 2.27; 6.1.28, 2.12 and 3.15; 8.7.1; *Symp.* 1.7 and 8. This list is not exhaustive. Isaeus uses ὥσπερ εἰκός similarly in 8.16; cf. 6.41 (οἷον εἰκός) and 8.15 (οἷα εἰκός).

[9] Xen. *Anab.* 3.1.21, where ὡς τὸ εἰκός surely means 'probably', may be contrasted with the passages from Xenophon listed in the previous note in which ὡς εἰκός or ὥσπερ εἰκός means 'naturally'.

[10] Similarly in Aen. Tact. 4.11.

supplied in the parenthesis is normally in the same tense as the verb of the clause to which the parenthesis is attached: there does not seem to be any evidence to show that contemporaries of Thucydides when referring to past events ever used ὡς εἰκός to convey the meaning 'as *is* probable', 'probably', understanding ἐστι in the parenthesis. Hence, although the language of Thucydides is boldly original, there is a strong presumption that where he uses ὡς εἰκός, as he does in six passages, the phrase may be expected to mean 'naturally' rather than 'probably'. In four of these six passages most modern editors and translators believe the phrase to mean 'probably', but the normal meaning 'naturally' is not palpably inadmissible in any of them and should, I maintain, be accepted in each instance. The early translators Valla (1452) and Hobbes (1628) apparently assumed that where ὡς εἰκός occurs in Thucydides it invariably means 'probably',[11] and their influence has been unfortunate. The question is of some importance to historians because it affects the historical interpretation of passages in which the phrase is found. 'Probably' denotes lack of confidence in the veracity of a statement, or part of it, whereas 'naturally' may be used to confirm its veracity on logical grounds. Thucydides is at least as critical as any ancient historian in his treatment of sources and, when he lacks confidence in them, he feels himself under an obligation to express his doubts. He has a number of phrases, such as ὡς λέγεται, which he uses for this purpose, but ὡς εἰκός is not one of them.

The six Thucydidean passages in which ὡς εἰκός occurs are the following:[12]

(a) 1.4 τό τε ληστικόν, ὡς εἰκός, καθῄρει (sc. ὁ Μίνως) ἐκ τῆς θαλάσσης ἐφ᾽ ὅσον ἐδύνατο, τοῦ τὰς προσόδους μᾶλλον ἰέναι αὐτῷ. There seems to be almost universal agreement among editors and translators, during the past century at least, that ὡς εἰκός here means 'as was natural' and not 'as is probable'. It was natural that Minos should make every effort to suppress piracy because its suppression would benefit him financially.[13] Thucy-

---

[11] Stephanus, *Thesaurus Linguae Graecae* (1572) s. v. εἴκω, is not at all accurate in dealing with ὡς εἰκός but does mention meanings other than 'ut verisimile est'. The scholia do not contribute anything of value on this point.

[12] I do not include 7.44.2 ὡς ἐν σελήνῃ εἰκός (though εἰκός undoubtedly means 'natural') because the words are not parenthetical.

[13] Cf. the notes of Croiset, Steup and Maddalena.

dides does not claim that the details which he records about this thalassocracy are beyond dispute, but his uncertainty is expressed by ὧν ἀκοῇ ἴσμεν at the beginning of the chapter.

(b) 2.21.2 αὐτοῖς, ὡς εἰκός, γῆς τεμνομένης ἐν τῷ ἐμφανεῖ, ὃ οὔπω ἑωράκεσαν οἵ γε νεώτεροι, οὐδ᾽ οἱ πρεσβύτεροι πλὴν τὰ Μηδικά, δεινὸν ἐφαίνετο. Here again ὡς εἰκος, which is to be taken with αὐτοῖς ... δεινὸν ἐφαίνετο, undoubtedly means 'as was natural': the distress felt by the Athenians was natural in view of the facts in the recorded genitive absolute. Thucydides is surely basing his picture upon personal observation and certainly does not doubt its accuracy.

(c) 3.104.6 τὰ δὲ περὶ τοὺς ἀγῶνας καὶ τὰ πλεῖστα κατελύθη ὑπὸ ξυμφορῶν, ὡς εἰκός. The interpretation favoured by most scholars is 'were discontinued, probably because of disasters': they evidently believe that Thucydides, lacking trustworthy information and feeling uncertain why most parts of this Delian festival were discontinued, suggests that disasters (presumably the barbarian conquests of Ionia[14]) were probably responsible rather than any other possible cause such as a decline of enthusiasm for the festival. Jowett, however, translates 'the games and the greater part of the ceremonies naturally fell into disuse, owing to the misfortunes of Ionia': when the Ionians of the Asiatic mainland had suffered ξυμφοραί, it was only to be expected that the festival should be held on a reduced scale. This interpretation is surely to be preferred. Thucydides shows in this chapter that, in addition to the *Homeric Hymn* which he quotes, he possesses excellent sources of information on Delian history. He is not suggesting a plausible reason for an unexplained occurrence; on the contrary, he is pointing out that the traditional reason is supported by common sense.

(d) 6.2.4 Σικελοὶ δ᾽ ἐξ Ἰταλίας (ἐνταῦθα γὰρ ᾤκουν) διέβησαν ἐς Σικελίαν, φεύγοντες Ὀπικούς, ὡς μὲν εἰκὸς καὶ λέγεται, ἐπὶ σχεδιῶν, τηρήσαντες τὸν πορθμὸν κατιόντος τοῦ ἀνέμου, τάχα ἂν δὲ καὶ ἄλλως πως ἐσπλεύσαντες. The generally accepted view is that ὡς εἰκός here means 'as is likely':[15] the Sicels probably used rafts, and there is a tradition that they did. It is, however, perfectly legitimate to supply ἦν and not ἐστι and to translate 'as

[14] Gomme n. ad loc. For ὑπὸ ξυμφορῶν cf. 2.68.5.
[15] Cf. the recent translation by L. Bodin and J. de Romilly (1955), 'il est vraisemblable et la tradition le veut, qu'ils avaient passé sur des radeaux'.

was natural': the use of rafts rather than ships was natural when it was reasonably safe to cross on rafts κατιόντος τοῦ ἀνέμου. It would have been a waste of labour for the Sicels, who were not a seafaring people, to have built large numbers of ships for a single short though dangerous crossing. Undeniably Thucydides is in some doubt whether they adopted only the rather primitive method of crossing on rafts and for this reason suggests that they may perhaps have used other means as well, but his uncertainty is expressed not by εἰκός but by λέγεται, which occurs frequently elsewhere in passages where he is distrustful of his source.[16] Here εἰκός gives the reason why he is inclined to accept a somewhat ill-attested tradition. He is dealing with a point of detail which is by no means essential to his brief narrative and is perhaps mentioned only because there has been some discussion about it.[17]

(e) 8.2.3 ἡ δὲ τῶν Λακεδαιμονίων πόλις πᾶσί τε τούτοις ἐθάρσει καὶ μάλιστα ὅτι οἱ ἐκ τῆς Σικελίας αὐτοῖς ξύμμαχοι πολλῇ δυνάμει, κατ' ἀνάγκην ἤδη τοῦ ναυτικοῦ προσγεγενημένου, ἅμα τῷ ἦρι ὡς εἰκὸς παρέσεσθαι ἔμελλον. The end of this sentence is usually rendered 'would in all probability arrive at the beginning of spring'. According to this interpretation Thucydides is suggesting that the Spartans felt somewhat uncertain whether their Sicilian allies would really come to their aid.[18] Such uncertainty is hardly consistent with the confidence attributed to the Spartans in this chapter, nor does there seem to be any parallel for the use of εἰκός in close association with μέλλω, meaning 'probably would'. It is surely preferable to translate ὡς εἰκός 'as was natural'.[19] The

[16] A long but by no means complete list is given by G. Busolt, *Gr. Gesch.* iii. 2 (1904), 653 n. 3.

[17] The difficult problem of the sources used by Thucydides in his account of the movements of population into Sicily (6.2–5) cannot be discussed here. F. Jacoby, *F. Gr. Hist.* iii b (1955), 609–11 is now very cautious in his treatment of this problem and has modified the views expressed ibid., i (1923), 456–7, cf. L. Pearson, *Early Ionian Historians* (1939), 228–30, and K. J. Dover, *Maia* n. s. 6, 1953, 1–20.

[18] ὡς εἰκός might be taken with ἅμα τῷ ἦρι alone, i.e. the Sicilian fleet would arrive probably neither earlier nor later than the beginning of spring. There seems, however, no reason why so much emphasis should be laid upon the time of its arrival.

[19] B has ἦν after ὡς εἰκός, but the reading is rejected by almost all editors because in all the other cases in Thucydides where the phrase occurs the verb is understood.

genitive absolute gives the principal reason why it was natural: because the Sicilians had been forced by circumstances to acquire sea power,[20] they would naturally send a strong fleet in the spring to aid their allies in Greece. During the Archidamian war Spartan hopes of naval aid from the west had been disappointed (2.7.2; 3.86.2; 6.34.8), but the Athenian expedition to Sicily had fundamentally changed the situation.

(f) 8.88 Ἀλκιβιάδης δὲ ἐπειδὴ καὶ τόν Τισσαφέρνην ἤσθετο παριόντα ἐπὶ τῆς Ἀσπένδου, ἔπλει καὶ αὐτὸς λαβὼν τρεῖς καὶ δέκα ναῦς, ὑποσχόμενος τοῖς ἐν τῇ Σάμῳ ἀσφαλῆ καὶ μεγάλην χάριν (ἢ γὰρ αὐτὸς ἄξειν Ἀθηναίοις τὰς Φοινίσσας ναῦς ἢ Πελοποννησίοις γε κωλύσειν ἐλθεῖν), εἰδώς, ὡς εἰκός, ἐκ πλέονος τὴν Τισσαφέρνους γνώμην ὅτι οὐκ ἄξειν ἔμελλε, καὶ βουλόμενος . . . If the words εἰδώς . . . γνώμην mean, as most scholars believe, 'probably because he had long known the intention of Tissaphernes', Thucydides is expressing some uncertainty about the motives of Alcibiades.[21] It would be hazardous to maintain that he cannot have lacked reliable information on this point: Alcibiades did not disclose his motives to the Athenians at Samos, and they cannot have been widely known. There are, however, many passages in Book 8 in which Thucydides records fully and confidently the motives and secret plans of Alcibiades (17.2; 47.1; 56.2–4; 81.2; 82.3) and none in which he confesses ignorance or doubt, whereas he is much less certain about those of Tissaphernes (cf. 46.5; 56.3). Again ὡς εἰκός surely means 'as was natural'. Whereas other Greeks were baffled by the policy of Tissaphernes and had no means of knowing what action he intended to take in regard to the Phoenician fleet, it was natural that Alcibiades, who had been in close contact with him for a considerable time, had accurate knowledge of his intentions.[22]

It may be added that where Thucydides uses οἶον or οἶα

[20] τοῦ ναυτικοῦ is certainly the Sicilian fleet (Steup, n. ad loc.) and not the Peloponnesian (Classen n. ad loc.).

[21] It would be possible to take ὡς εἰκός with the temporal ἐκ πλέονος only (cf. p. 158 n. 18 above). The meaning would then be that Alcibiades knew and had probably long known the intention of Tissaphernes. Clearly, however, the length of time that Alcibiades had possessed this knowledge is a factor of limited importance.

[22] Classen n. ad loc., explains this passage better than any other editor: 'weil er, wie das (bei seinem vertrauten Verkehr mit ihm) leicht zu erklären war, schon lange seine wahre Absicht kannte'.

adverbially with εἰκός and the phrase seems to be equivalent to ὡς εἰκός, the meaning undoubtedly is 'as was natural' (2.54.2 ἐν δὲ τῷ 'κακῷ οἷα εἰκὸς ἀνεμνήσθησαν καὶ τοῦδε τοῦ ἔπους; 6.103.4; 7.25.8).[23] On the other hand, in 1.141.5 ὅπερ εἰκός, which refers to the future, means 'as is likely'.

[23] In 4.26.2 οἷον, is not adverbial, while in 6.69.2 most editors prefer οἵας the reading of C, to οἷα.

11

Thucydides 2.65.11

ἐξ ὧν ἄλλα τε πολλά, ὡς ἐν μεγάλῃ πόλει καὶ ἀρχὴν ἐχούσῃ, ἡμαρτήθη καὶ ὁ ἐς Σικελίαν πλοῦς, ὃς οὐ τοσοῦτον γνώμης ἁμάρτημα ἦν πρὸς οὓς ἐπῇσαν, ὅσον οἱ ἐκπέμψαντες οὐ τὰ πρόσφορα τοῖς οἰχομένοις ἐπιγιγνώσκοντες ἀλλὰ κατὰ τὰς ἰδίας διαβολὰς περὶ τῆς τοῦ δήμου προστασίας τά τε ἐν τῷ στρατοπέδῳ ἀμβλύτερα ἐποιουν καὶ τὰ περὶ τὴν πόλιν πρῶτον ἐν ἀλλήλοις ἐταράχθησαν.

In this celebrated sentence Thucydides gives his opinion more specifically than anywhere in the narrative of Books 6 and 7 on the reasons for the failure of the Sicilian expedition. Unfortunately, however, he expresses his views with some lack of clarity, and this has led to disagreement among modern scholars who have sought to determine precisely what he means. It is also unfortunate that he does not state the evidence upon which he bases his conclusion that the expedition failed because of struggles for political leadership at Athens. The main purpose of this paper is to consider the meaning and implications of this sentence, which can, I believe, be clarified by reference to other passages in which Thucydides uses οὐ τοσοῦτον when debating the causes of past actions. A closely allied problem, that of the relationship between this sentence and the narrative of Books 6 and 7, will also be discussed. A. W. Gomme has maintained that this relationship throws some light upon the date of composition of Books 6 and 7.[1] There is no doubt whatever that the sentence was written at or after the end of the Peloponnesian war (ibid. 12), and if there are differences of outlook, even inconsistencies, between it and the narrative which show that Thucydides cannot have written, or at any rate conceived, both at the same time, he almost certainly wrote the narrative before the end of the

[1] *J.H.S.* lxxi (1951), 72. Although I do not agree with his conclusions on some points, it will be seen that the latter part of my paper owes much to his brief but admirable discussion. See also the notes on this sentence in the second volume of his *Historical Commentary on Thucydides* ii (1956), 195–6, which was published after the first draft of my essay had been completed.

war.[2] In my opinion there is inconsistency on one point only, but
here the inconsistency is sufficiently marked to suggest not only
that Books 6 and 7 were written considerably earlier than 2.65.11,
but that they were written within the next few years after the
conclusion of the Sicilian campaign.

1. οὐ τοσοῦτον γνώμης ἁμάρτημα ἦν πρὸς οὓς ἐπῇσαν

When Thucydides expresses the view that the Athenians blun-
dered in embarking on the Sicilian expedition (. . . ἡμαρτήθη καὶ
ὁ ἐς Σικελίαν πλοῦς), he is giving an illustration of his earlier
statement that they neglected the advice of Pericles (2.65.7).[3] In
his opinion they committed a fundamental error of principle in
contravening the doctrines of Periclean strategy.[4] He then proceeds to discuss more specifically the reasons why the expedition
failed. In the phrase quoted at the head of this section the words
πρὸς οὓς ἐπῇσαν[5] show that he is here considering the decision of
the Athenians from an exclusively military standpoint.[6] They
made the mistake of failing to exercise the caution advocated by
Pericles: did they also make the mistake of attacking an enemy
whose strength was such that the expedition could not have
succeeded? It is widely believed that Thucydides is here giving
an unequivocally negative answer to the question whether they
were or were not guilty of a military blunder. Scholars who take
this view evidently assume that οὐ τοσοῦτον . . . ὅσον here means
little more than οὐ . . . ἀλλά,[7] but this interpretation seems to me

---

[2] Gomme, loc. cit. (*J.H.S.*), concludes: 'judgement and narrative were not
written at the same time, in the same breath as it were, both in the mind of
the writer all the time. The judgement is late; and the narrative presumably
earlier'.

[3] Steup, n. ad loc., rightly points out that this section refers principally to
the Sicilian expedition, cf. Gomme, op. cit. (*J.H.S.*), 71, and *Commentary* n.
ad loc., who debates which other actions on the part of the Athenians Thucydides has in mind.

[4] These are summarized at the beginning of 65.7. To Thucydides the
Athenians were virtually at war throughout the twenty-seven years from 431
to 404 (5.26.1–2), so that not even during the ὕποπτος ἀνοκωχή was neglect of
Periclean doctrines justifiable.

[5] Croiset, n. ad loc., points out that περὶ τούτων must be supplied as the
antecedent.

[6] Gomme, n. ad loc.

[7] J. de Romilly, *Thucydide et l'impérialisme athénien* (1947), 179 n. 4, states
(rightly in my opinion) that οὐ τοσοῦτον . . . ὅσον does not normally bear

162

to be invalid, as I shall endeavour to show by examining a group of passages in which Thucydides uses οὐ τοσοῦτον, normally followed by ὅσον, in discussing the possible causes of a past action. The list is as follows:

(a) 1.9.1, Ἀγαμέμνων τέ μοι δοκεῖ τῶν τότε δυνάμει προύχων καὶ οὐ τοσοῦτον τοῖς Τυνδάρεω ὅρκοις κατειλημμένους τοὺς Ἑλένης μνηστῆρας ἄγων τὸν στόλον ἀγεῖραι. Here the usual order is inverted, but the sentence is nevertheless closely parallel to the other passages in this list. Thucydides does not commit himself to a definite rejection of the traditional view that it was because of the oaths sworn by the suitors that Agamemnon was able to assemble the expeditionary force. He seems to have thought that this factor may have had some influence, but he presses the claims of a second, and in his opinion more cogent, explanation based upon his own rationalizing and strikingly modern interpretation of epic tradition.[8]

(b) 1.11.1 αἴτιον δ᾽ ἦν οὐχ ἡ ὀλιγανθρωπία τοσοῦτον ὅσον ἡ ἀχρηματία. In seeking to determine from the evidence of the Homeric Catalogue the strength of the expedition against Troy, Thucydides has concluded that οὐ πολλοὶ φαίνονται ἐλθόντες, ὡς ἀπὸ πάσης τῆς Ἑλλάδος κοινῇ πεμπόμενοι (10.5). Its modest scale, he suggests, might be ascribed to shortage of man-power in Greece at this time, but he prefers his own explanation, namely, that poverty was the chief factor in limiting its size, and he proceeds to argue that the operations conducted by the Greeks at Troy provide evidence of ἀχρηματία (11.1–2). He does not choose to discuss the question whether at this time Greece suffered from ὀλιγανθρωπία, which might have affected the scale of the expedition.

(c) 1.88, ἐψηφίσαντο δὲ οἱ Λακεδαιμόνιοι τὰς σπονδὰς λελύσθαι καὶ πολεμητέα εἶναι οὐ τοσοῦτον τῶν ξυμμάχων πεισθέντες τοῖς λόγοις ὅσον φοβούμενοι τοὺς Ἀθηναίους μὴ ἐπὶ μεῖζον δυνηθῶσιν, ὁρῶντες αὐτοῖς τὰ πολλὰ τῆς Ἑλλάδος ὑποχείρια ἤδη ὄντα. Attention has often been drawn to the similarities between this passage and 1.23.6, where Thucydides expounds his view on the causes of the Peloponnesian war: οὐ τοσοῦτον τῶν ξυμμάχων

---

this meaning in Thucydides. She regards 1.9.1 as an exception; I do not (see below), and Steup's note on this passage seems to me to be misleading.

[8] Cf. 1.9.3, οὐ χάριτι τὸ πλέον ἢ φόβῳ, where the influence of χάρις is not wholly discounted.

πεισθέντες τοῖς λόγοις corresponds to αἱ δ᾽ ἐς τὸ φανερὸν λεγόμεναι αἰτίαι in 1.23.6, and ὅσον φοβούμενοι τοὺς Ἀθηναίους κτλ. to τὴν μὲν γὰρ ἀληθεστάτην πρόφασιν (cf. 1.118.1–2). He is insistent on the validity of his ἀληθεστάτη πρόφασις, but he certainly does not deny the importance of the αἰτίαι, to which he devotes almost half his first book. His conviction that the αἰτίαι caused the war to break out when it did (1.23.6) scarcely suggests that he considered the Spartans to have been wholly unmoved by the complaints of their allies, which were based largely upon the αἰτίαι.

(d) 1.127.2, οὐ μέντοι τοσοῦτον ἤλπιζον παθεῖν ἂν αὐτὸν τοῦτο ὅσον διαβολὴν οἴσειν αὐτῷ πρὸς τὴν πόλιν ὡς καὶ διὰ τὴν ἐκείνου ξυμφορὰν τὸ μέρος ἔσται ὁ πόλεμος. Thucydides here states the motives of the Spartans in demanding that the Athenians should 'drive out the curse' and so banish Pericles. He maintains that their primary motive was to bring discredit upon Pericles, but the last words of the preceding sentence, νομίζοντες ἐκπεσόντος αὐτοῦ ῥᾷον ἄν σφίσι προχωρεῖν τὰ ἀπὸ τῶν Ἀθηναίων (127.1), show conclusively that, in his view, the Spartans were not without some hope of bringing about the banishment of Pericles by this manœuvre.[9] This passage, like the others listed here, mentions two possible reasons for a past action, but it differs from them in one respect. In the other cases both factors, the one attached to οὐ τοσοῦτον and the other to ὅσον, might have contributed to bring about the action to which Thucydides refers, whereas in this instance the demand of the Spartans was designed to cause Pericles either to be banished or to lose popular support: if he were banished, war would presumably be averted, and the possibility that he might be held responsible for it could not arise.

(e) 8.45.2, λέγειν κελεύων (sc. ὁ Ἀλκιβιάδης) τὸν Τισσαφέρνην πρὸς αὐτοὺς ὡς Ἀθηναῖοι ἐκ πλέονος χρόνου ἐπιστήμονες ὄντες τοῦ ναυτικοῦ τριώβολον τοῖς ἑαυτῶν διδόασιν, οὐ τοσοῦτον πενίᾳ ὅσον ἵνα αὐτῶν μὴ οἱ ναῦται ἐκ περιουσίας ὑβρίζοντες οἱ μὲν τὰ σώματα χείρω ἔχωσι δαπανῶντες ἐς τοιαῦτα ἀφ᾽ ὧν ἡ ἀσθένεια ξυμβαίνει κτλ.[10] It was natural to assume, and must have been assumed by many, that at the end of 412 the Athenians were paying their

---

[9] Subsequent events proved that the position of Pericles was not impregnable (2.65.3).

[10] There is general agreement that after διδόασιν some words have been lost referring to irregularity of payment (Steup, *Anhang* 286–7).

sailors only three obols a day because of lack of funds. Alcibiades, however, maintained, or rather urged Tissaphernes to maintain in negotiating with the Peloponnesians, that a stronger reason was their desire to prevent indiscipline and demoralization. In his conversations with Tissaphernes his aim was to produce cogent arguments, and he doubtless cared little whether they were founded on fact or on fiction, but even he can scarcely have denied that poverty played some part in determining Athenian financial policy at this time. The rate of pay for sailors had been a drachma a day at the beginning of the Sicilian expedition (6.31.3, cf. 6.8.1), and there is every reason to believe that it had been reduced because of financial embarrassment, [11] which had become acute since the occupation of Decelea. Though Thucydides tends to neglect Athenian finance, he refers several times to the difficulties of this period (7.28.4; 8.1.2 and 15.1). [12]

These five passages have much in common with one another and differ from others in which Thucydides uses οὐ τοσοῦτον . . . ὅσον. [13] They are concerned wholly with opinions which might or might not be deemed valid and not with acknowledged facts. In each case Thucydides sets side by side two explanations of a past action. The one is a widely accepted, conventional, or seemingly obvious reason which has been, or might have been, deduced from a knowledge of the essential facts. The other is a latent reason which has apparently not hitherto occurred to anyone and is now advanced by Thucydides himself (or in 8.45.2 by Alcibiades as reported by Thucydides) by virtue of a deeper study and more penetrating understanding of the situation. In each passage the second explanation is claimed to be more cogent

[11] A. H. M. Jones, *Past and Present* i (1952), 16 n. 33 (on p. 28).

[12] The phrase ἐκ πλέονος χρόνου ἐπιστήμονες ὄντες τοῦ ναυτικοῦ in the above passage means only that the Athenians had learned from their past experience, which was greater than that of the Peloponnesians. It does not imply that the Athenian rate of pay for sailors had always been three obols. 3.17.4 suggests that the normal rate during the Archidamian war was a drachma. Thus the question whether or not the Athenians had in the past suffered from poverty does not arise, though there is evidence that they had in 428 (3.13.3 and 19.1).

[13] 2.87.4 (ὑμῶν δὲ οὐδ᾽ ἡ ἀπειρία τοσοῦτον λείπεται ὅσον τόλμῃ προύχετε), 5.95 (οὐ γὰρ τοσοῦτον ἡμᾶς βλάπτει ἡ ἔχθρα ὑμῶν ὅσον ἡ φιλία), and 6.72.3 (οὐ μέντοι τοσοῦτόν γε λειφθῆναι ὅσον εἰκὸς εἶναι) are fundamentally different from the passages listed above; *inter alia*, in each instance the first of the two considerations weighed against one another is an acknowledged fact.

than the first, but the validity of the first is not expressly denied: it is merely not discussed. It is a mistake to imagine that a true cause is contrasted with a false one. Together these passages constitute a Thucydidean formula employed in discussing the causes of past actions, and his use of it was evidently an idiosyncrasy: there are remarkably few parallels in the prose literature of the fifth and fourth centuries,[14] though their paucity may be partly attributable to the fact that few authors shared his interest in causation.

2.65.11 is another instance of this formula and should be interpreted accordingly. As has already been pointed out, many scholars have regarded this sentence as evidence that Thucydides did not consider the Athenian action in embarking upon the Sicilian expedition to have been in itself an error of judgement.[15] Eduard Schwartz takes the opposite view and interprets the sentence as meaning that in the opinion of Thucydides the expedition was a grave error but became an irreparable error only when the Athenians recalled Alcibiades.[16] Comparison with the passages examined above suggests that, while the second of these interpretations is to be preferred, neither is wholly correct. In the phrase γνώμης ἁμάρτημα ἦν πρὸς οὓς ἐπῇσαν Thucydides states the orthodox view without expressly committing himself to a verdict as to its validity, while in the words that follow ὅσον he expounds the personal, and apparently novel, judgement which a careful study of all the relevant facts has led him to prefer. That the Athenians immediately after the failure of the expedition regarded it as a military blunder is implied by Thucydides himself (8.1.1), and evidence from the fourth century shows that many Athenians of later generations concurred.[17]

If my interpretation of οὐ τοσοῦτον γνώμης ἁμάρτημα ἦν πρὸς οὓς ἐπῇσαν is correct, the phrase is entirely consistent with the

---

[14] Cf. Hdt. 7.16 a 2 (which is not, however, closely parallel), and (much better) Dem. 4.11, οὐδὲ γὰρ οὗτος (Philip) παρὰ τὴν ῥώμην αὐτοῦ τοσοῦτον ἐπηύξηται ὅσον παρὰ τὴν ἡμετέραν ἀμέλειαν.

[15] Examples are: K. J. Beloch, *Gr. Gesch.* ii². 1 (1914), 356 n. 1; J. H. Finley, *Thucydides* (1942), 152 (but cf. *Harv. Stud.*, Suppl. vol. i (1940), 286–7, where he expresses a different view); Schmid-Stählin, *Gr. Literaturgesch.* i. 5 (1948), 97. I interpreted the passage in the same way in *C.Q.* xxxv (1941), 61.

[16] *Das Geschichtswerk des Thukydides²* (1929), 241 n. 3.

[17] Andoc. 3.30; Isocr. 8.84; Aeschin. 2.76. It is immaterial that all these passages contain gross inaccuracies.

guarded attitude adopted by Thucydides towards the same military problem in the narrative of Books 6 and 7, where he seems to have regarded the arguments for and against the generally accepted view as nicely balanced. While he states that the Athenians through ignorance of Sicily underestimated the magnitude of the enterprise (6.1.1), this statement does not prove that their decision to embark upon it was in his opinion necessarily a blunder. He leaves his readers in no doubt that he considers the arguments of Nicias against the expedition to have been more cogent than those of Alcibiades in favour of it, and he makes the point more than once that Syracuse was better equipped for resisting the Athenian attack because the two states were similar in character and organisation.[18] On the other hand, he states as an acknowledged fact that the Athenians were superior to the enemy (6.31.6),[19] but this passage is not decisive, because a soldier of his experience cannot have failed to appreciate that an expeditionary force operating so far from home must enjoy a very marked superiority, in numbers or quality or both, if any real confidence was to be felt in its prospect of success.[20] More important is his insistence that Syracuse was at one moment in almost desperate straits (7.2.4, παρὰ τοσοῦτον μὲν αἱ Συράκουσαι ἦλθον κινδύνου), though even after the attainment of this major objective the expedition might ultimately have proved harmful to Athenian interests. It is perhaps fair to conclude from Books 6 and 7 as well as from 2.65.11 that, if Thucydides had been asked whether in his opinion the expedition was an error of judgement from the military standpoint, he would have answered that on balance he was inclined to consider that it was; but in both cases he seems somewhat reluctant to commit himself.[21]

---

[18] 6.20.3 (speech of Nicias); 7.55.2, cf. 8.96.5.

[19] The views ascribed to Demosthenes in 7.42.3, though Thucydides certainly shared them, apply only to a particular situation which could hardly have been foreseen.

[20] Arnold in his note on 2.65.11 cites 6.31.6 and 7.42.3 (wrongly in my opinion) as evidence that Thucydides did not condemn the expedition on military grounds. Gomme, n. ad loc., takes the same view.

[21] He may possibly have agreed with the view attributed to both Nicias (6.11.1) and Euphemus (6.86.3) that, even if the expedition were to achieve military victory, Sicily would be difficult to govern because of its remoteness from Athens and its large population.

II. THUCYDIDES' OWN EXPLANATION

The words οἱ ἐκπέμψαντες οὐ τὰ πρόσφορα τοῖς οἰχομένοις ἐπιγιγνώσκοντες appear at first sight to mean that the Athenians at home failed to give military and financial support on a sufficiently generous scale to their forces operating in Sicily. Scholars who have interpreted the phrase in this way have with good reason felt it to be inconsistent with the narrative of Books 6 and 7, which contains no hint that the Athenians at home neglected their responsibilities.[22] The response to a request for cavalry and money was prompt and adequate (6.74.2, 93.4, 94.4), while the reinforcement under Demosthenes and Eurymedon, though not, as Nicias had recommended, as large as the original expeditionary force (7.15.1), was nevertheless a very powerful armament.[23] It is not impossible that Thucydides changed his mind; that when he wrote Books 6 and 7, which must be based largely upon reports of Athenians who had served in Sicily (cf. 7.44.1), he believed the expedition to have been at least adequately supported from home but that later, perhaps after his return from exile, he obtained further information that caused him to revise his judgement.[24] There is, however, another way of interpreting this part of the sentence which is in my opinion very much more satisfactory. It has been suggested that ἐπιγιγνώσκοντες should be taken not only with the preceding words but also with ἀλλὰ κατὰ τὰς ἰδίας διαβολὰς περὶ τῆς τοῦ δήμου προστασίας:[25] thus οὐ goes closely with τὰ πρόσφορα,[26] and the whole phrase means that the Athenians at home 'later made decisions that were not in the best interests of the expeditionary force but (were made) because of their private enmities in competition for the

[22] Cf. Jowett, n. ad loc., 'these words seem to imply a neglect of the expedition which is scarcely indicated in Thucydides' own narrative', and Gomme, n. ad loc.

[23] Only the order given to Demosthenes to raid Laconia in the course of his voyage (7.20.2) appears to merit criticism.

[24] Plato, Menex. 243a, attributes the failure of the expedition to the difficulty of supporting it from home (εἰς ἀπορίαν τῆς πόλεως καταστάσης καὶ οὐ δυναμένης αὐτοῖς ὑπηρετεῖν), but the value of this passage as historical evidence is almost negligible.

[25] So Poppo-Stahl, n. ad loc., 'mente repete ἐπιγιγνώσκοντες'.

[26] For the position of the negative cf. 3.57.1, εἰ δὲ περὶ ἡμῶν γνώσεσθε μὴ τὰ εἰκότα, and 3.67.2, οὐκ ἐκ προσηκόντων ἁμαρτάνουσιν.

leadership of the democracy'.[27] Interpreted in this way, the passage does not conflict with the impression created in Books 6 and 7 that the Athenians at home discharged most zealously their obligations to their forces in Sicily. It was, in the opinion of Thucydides, lack of wisdom on their part rather than lack of energy that ruined the prospects of the expedition; their sins were not sins of omission but of commission.

To Thucydides their gravest disservice to the expeditionary force was evidently the recall of Alcibiades. It has often been stated, and is undoubtedly true, that he had this decision in mind when he wrote 2.65.11.[28] The phrase κατὰ τὰς ἰδίας διαβολὰς περὶ τῆς τοῦ δήμου προστασίας is echoed in passages in Book 6 in which the attacks on Alcibiades are described, namely 28.2, οἱ μάλιστα τῷ Ἀλκιβιάδῃ ἀχθόμενοι ἐμποδὼν ὄντι σφίσι μὴ αὐτοῖς τοῦ δήμου βεβαίως προεστάναι, and 29.3, βουλόμενοι ἐκ μείζονος διαβολῆς, ἣν ἔμελλον ῥᾷον αὐτοῦ ἀπόντος ποριεῖν, μετάπεμπτον κομισθέντα αὐτὸν ἀγωνίσασθαι (cf. 61.1 and 89.5).[29] In Book 6 Thucydides does not name the personal enemies of Alcibiades who incited popular feeling against him with the object of clearing their own path to political leadership, but from 8.65.2 the demagogue Androcles is known to have been principally responsible for his exile.[30] That Thucydides in 2.65.11 should lay the blame for the failure of the Sicilian expedition largely upon Androcles and other ambitious politicians who were jealous of Alcibiades is entirely consistent not only with the view expressed in his preceding sentence (ibid. 10) condemning the political successors of Pericles but also with his general disapprobation of demagogues.

The narrative of Books 6 and 7 certainly does not provide obvious corroboration of the thesis that the Sicilian expedition failed because Alcibiades was recalled. It is true that the decision to recall him is represented as an important event: had Thucydides regarded it otherwise, he would scarcely have described so fully the successive steps in the development of the accusations against him. This decision is subsequently shown to have had

[27] Possibly τὰ πρόσφορα may be adverbial and not the object of ἐπιγιγνώσκοντες. For ἐπιγιγνώσκω cf. 1.70.2 and 3.57.1.
[28] Recently noted by J. de Romilly in the Budé Thucydides, vol. iv (1955), Notice xiii–xiv.
[29] Cf. also Xen., Hell. 1.4.13 ἐπιβουλευθεὶς δὲ ὑπὸ τῶν ἔλαττον ἐκείνου δυναμένων μοχθηρότερά τε λεγόντων καὶ πρὸς τὸ αὐτῶν ἴδιον κέρδος πολιτευόντων.
[30] Cf. Plut., Alcib. 19.1–3.

M

far-reaching consequences, for not only did it leave first Nicias and Lamachus and later Nicias alone in command of the expedition but it also led to the highly successful efforts of Alcibiades to damage Athenian interests after his arrival at Sparta. On the other hand, the narrative of Books 6 and 7 contains no evidence that Thucydides rated the military leadership of Alcibiades at all highly[31] and at least some indication that he did not. The achievements of Alcibiades during the brief period of his service in Sicily were unimpressive.[32] Although it was his strategic plan that was adopted at the conference with his colleagues at Rhegium (6.50.1), it achieved very little, and even the Athenian success at Catana was largely the result of a lucky accident (6.51.1–2).[33] It is indeed arguable that Athenian prospects were improved by his removal from command because the inevitable friction between him and Nicias might well have had damaging consequences. When Thucydides wrote Books 6 and 7, he can scarcely have believed that the military qualities of Alcibiades would have proved a decisive factor in the Sicilian campaign.[34] Hence, so far as his estimate of these qualities is concerned, there is a good case for concluding that 2.65.11 is not altogether consistent with the narrative of Books 6 and 7.

What can have caused him to be much more favourably impressed by the military qualities of Alcibiades when he wrote 2.65.11 than when he wrote Books 6 and 7? A very probable answer to this question is that, writing in or after 404, he had evidence of these qualities from which he formed the conviction that the recall of Alcibiades from Sicily was a decisive blunder fatal to the prospects of the expedition; and that this evidence consisted of information, which Thucydides must have collected in detail, about the series of successes achieved by Alcibiades despite inadequate support from Athens during the years 411 to

---

[31] 6.15.4 will be considered below (n. 36).

[32] His experience of military leadership before the Sicilian campaign seems to have been slight (5.52.2, 55.4, 84.1).

[33] The plot to bring about the betrayal of Messana, which Alcibiades disclosed to the enemies of Athens just before he left Sicily (6.74.1), would, if it had been successful, have provided the Athenians with a strategically valuable base (6.48, cf. 4.1.1–2), but its success was not assured.

[34] Gomme, n. ad loc.: 'at the most we can surmise that Alkibiades' diplomacy might have won some successes and that when he found he could delay the attack no longer he would have attacked with more vigour than Nikias'.

407 when virtually in control of Athenian operations in the Hellespont, Propontis and Bosporus.[35] That Thucydides had a high opinion of his leadership in this period is confirmed by a well-known passage in which his influence upon Athenian history is discussed,[36] and if there is any truth in a somewhat rhetorical description by Plutarch of his return to Athens in 407, the Athenians then felt that the Sicilian expedition would not have failed had he remained in command of it.[37] Because his military leadership is rated much more highly in 2.65.11, when his exploits between 411 and 407 were undoubtedly known to Thucydides, than in the narrative of Books 6 and 7, it is at least very probable that the narrative was written when these exploits were not yet known, or not fully known, to Thucydides. This conclusion, if valid, lends support to the view of Schwartz and others that he wrote Books 6 and 7 during the years immediately after the conclusion of the Sicilian expedition.[38]

Does Thucydides mean that, apart from the recall of Alcibiades, other ill-advised decisions by the Athenians at home arising from political rivalries contributed to the failure of the

---

[35] A. Andrewes, *J.H.S.* lxxiii (1953), 2–9 shows how the military situation there was adversely affected by political friction between the fleet and the restored democracy. J. Hatzfeld, *Alcibiade* (1940), 288–9, contrasts the successes of Alcibiades with the failures of Athens elsewhere during this period.

[36] 6.15.4, κράτιστα διαθέντι τὰ τοῦ πολέμου. These words refer to the actions of Alcibiades between 411 and 407, as Gomme, op. cit. (*J.H.S.*), 74, maintains, and not to those of 415. The passage to which the words belong is almost certainly a late insertion in Book 6.

[37] *Alcib.* 32.4, cf. Nepos, *Alcib.* 6.2, which is doubtless derived ultimately from the same source.

[38] Schwartz, op. cit., 212–13; Schmid-Stählin, op. cit. i. 5.96–7. I cannot agree with the conclusion of Gomme, op. cit. (*J.H.S.*), 72, from καὶ δοκεῖ Ἀλκιβιάδης πρῶτον τότε καὶ οὐδενὸς ἔλασσον τὴν πόλιν ὠφελῆσαι (8.86.4) that 'Thucydides himself could not have thought much of his strategy in 415', when he wrote Book 8. If πρῶτον is the right reading, as seems likely, and the words mean that this was the first occasion on which Alcibiades had benefited Athens, Thucydides is being somewhat careless, as not infrequently in this book. He has omitted to insert some phrase limiting the application of this judgement to the immediate past: he is not giving a verdict on the whole previous career of Alcibiades but only on events of the last few months. He means that all the recent intrigues of Alcibiades had scarcely benefited his country but that here at least he was doing it a real service in successfully opposing the proposal to sail against the Four Hundred. Book 8 is remarkably self-contained, and references to earlier events are few.

expedition? One decision that he may have had in mind is the dispatch of thirty Athenian ships in the summer of 414 to raid the coast of Laconia (6.105.1-2). He expresses the view that this open violation of the Peace of Nicias encouraged the Spartans to invade Attica and fortify Decelea because they could now do so without incurring the taint of war-guilt by which their consciences had been troubled during the Archidamian war (7.18.2-3). Androcles and other demagogues now in control of Athenian policy probably sponsored the attack on Laconia,[39] and Thucydides evidently disapproved of it. There is, however, no reason to believe either that it was caused by struggles between rival politicians or that it had any direct influence upon the fate of the Sicilian expedition. The retention of Nicias in command at Syracuse (7.16.1), which Thucydides certainly regarded as a blunder, may possibly have been the outcome of political intrigues or political bargaining, but there is no evidence that it was, and the decision seems to have been reached on purely military grounds. If Thucydides eventually came to regard the sending of the reinforcement under Demosthenes and Eurymedon to have been an act of folly instigated by demagogues, which seems unlikely,[40] it could not be maintained that the Athenians thereby τὰ ἐν τῷ στρατοπέδῳ ἀμβλύτερα ἐποίουν.[41] Unfortunately, little is known about domestic politics at Athens at this time, and there may have been important issues of which no record has been preserved. On the whole, however, it seems likely that Thucydides was thinking almost exclusively of the decision to recall Alcibiades when he wrote his condemnation of οἱ ἐκπέμψαντες. It may seem strange that he did not choose to refer expressly to this decision, but 2.65.6-12 is a passage of general discussion which he seems to have written in deliberately general terms.

[39] Cf. E. Meyer, *G. d. A.* iv². 2 (1956), 232-5. Laispodias, one of the commanders of the Athenian fleet, was accused of being a warmonger and seems to have held radical views before he joined the Four Hundred (U. Kahrstedt, *R.E.* xii [1924], 517).

[40] He can hardly have held this view when he wrote 7.28.3, and the same note of admiration for Athenian perseverance is struck in 2.65.12, though here he is writing of the period after the disaster in Sicily.

[41] The absurd story of Plutarch (*Nic.* 20.1) that the dispatch of a second armament to Sicily was delayed by leaders jealous of the success achieved by Nicias is palpably false.

172

Finally, the last words of the sentence, τὰ περὶ τὴν πόλιν πρῶτον ἐν ἀλλήλοις ἐταράχθησαν, introduce a new point unconnected with the expedition. Mention of the ἴδιαι διαβολαί leads him to put forward not another reason why the expedition failed but another reason, apart from the failure of the expedition, why the Athenians lost the Peloponnesian war. He is thus anticipating κατὰ τὴν πόλιν ἤδη ἐν στάσει ὄντες in the next sentence (65.12). It is characteristic of his style that he introduces this new point into a sentence of which the main theme is the Sicilian expedition and into a clause of which the subject is οἱ ἐκπέμψαντες.[42]

[42] I am grateful to Dr G. E. F. Chilver and Dr B. R. Rees, whose criticisms have been most valuable to me.

12

Hermocrates the Syracusan

A noteworthy feature of Greek overseas expansion to which attention is frequently drawn is that in some cases a new city
established abroad outstripped its mother-city at home. It is perhaps more remarkable that these colonies, which were founded
on sites chosen for their agricultural or commercial advantages
and enjoyed political independence from the outset, did not soon
become the chief centres of power in the Greek world and that
old Greece did not become a political backwater long before the
Hellenistic Age. Many reasons might be suggested to explain why
this development did not take place, but the most influential
single factor was probably the political instability of the overseas
settlements, where strife between rival factions, often combined
with strife between neighbouring cities, was even more prevalent
and intense than in the Greek homeland. Although Greeks
settled abroad felt pride in their membership of the Greek race
and reached a high standard of literary and artistic achievement,
they were less firmly rooted in their homes, because their cities,
being comparatively new, had not accumulated a store of local
traditions. Most of them lived in close contact with non-Greek
peoples with whom they probably intermarried more than was
generally admitted. A sharp division often developed between
the leading families responsible for founding the colony, who
owned most of the land, and the mixed mass of the population
usually eager for any revolutionary change. In Sicily all these
influences were at work, and in addition the tyrants sowed the
seeds of future unrest by forcibly transplanting whole populations
from one city to another and by enfranchising their discharged
mercenaries. Both these practices led almost inevitably to conflict
between the new citizens and the old. The Sicilian Greeks often
proved strangely reluctant to submit to discipline or to make any
sustained effort in their own defence until their liberty and pros-

perity were almost lost. They produced few great leaders who were not tyrants, because they were seldom willing to accept unpalatable advice. That these defects imposed a severe handicap upon even the most enlightened of those who sought to lead them is seen in the career of Hermocrates.

It is not surprising that Greek Sicily seemed in the fifth century to be a tempting prey to two great powers, Athens and Carthage. As soon as Athens became a naval power, some Athenians began to show an interest in the west, Themistocles being apparently one of these. There seems to have been much talk of western expansion at Athens during the Pentecontaetia, but it is a mistaken assumption from later events to imagine that many Athenians seriously contemplated an attempt to conquer Sicily.[1] Pericles is said to have disapproved of Athenian imperialism in the west.[2] He did, however, favour the establishment of Athenian influence there, as elsewhere, provided that military action was not involved: he played a leading part in the foundation of Thurii and was probably responsible for the alliances with Leontini and Rhegium concluded perhaps about 445.[3] These cities and others of Chalcidian origin had begun to feel their security threatened by the Syracusans, who since the expulsion of the tyrants had won for themselves a dominating position in eastern Sicily and were suspected of imperialist ambitions.[4] The Athenians evidently welcomed the opportunities afforded by these alliances to establish their influence firmly in Sicily and to curb the increasing power of the Syracusans, who, it was believed, might well send naval and financial aid to the Dorians of the Peloponnese.[5]

When the outbreak of the Peloponnesian war was imminent,

---

[1] Cf. Plut. *Per.* 20.3–4, where the general picture of Athenian ambitions is extravagantly rhetorical and the reference to Sicily looks forward to the schemes of Alcibiades.

[2] Plut. *Per.* 20.4–21.1, cf. *Alcib.* 17.1.

[3] M. N. Tod, *Greek Historical Inscriptions* i² (1946), 57 and 58. They were renewed in 433; the year in which they were originally made is uncertain. In 458/7 the Athenians had concluded an alliance with Elymian Segesta.

[4] Cf. Diod. 12.30.1, where the military preparations of the Syracusans and the extent of their ambitions seem to be exaggerated. H. Wentker, *Sizilien und Athen* (1956), 78–81, overrates the significance of this passage.

[5] 1.36.2, cf. 44.3; 2.7.2; 6.6.2; 6.18.1. (These and all subsequent references in which the name of the author is not stated are to Thucydides.)

the Spartans instructed their western allies to provide ships for service against the Athenians (2.7.2). The number of ships which they demanded from the west is not certain but was probably two hundred; if so, the figure was outrageously optimistic.[6] No ships were sent, or apparently even built, and by 427 the cities allied with Athens were at war with the Syracusans and their allies (3.86.2). The antecedents of this war are unknown, but it may be that the Syracusans were the aggressors, feeling that the Athenians, weakened by the plague, would be unable to intervene. The Chalcidian states proved no match for their enemies and appealed to Athens for naval support. Twenty ships were sent, which, arriving in Sicilian waters in the autumn of 427, could do no more than keep the war alive by engaging in operations of limited scope. A further appeal to Athens at the end of 426 led to the dispatch of a larger fleet of forty ships. It sailed in the following spring but, because it became involved in the fighting at Pylos, did not reach Sicily until the campaigning season of 425 had ended. The scale of Athenian intervention now evidently alarmed the smaller cities on both sides, and in 424 they began to negotiate with the object of terminating an exhausting war conducted in the selfish interests of the great powers. The initiative came from Gela, a Dorian ally of Syracuse.[7] The Geloans concluded an armistice with their neighbours and kinsmen the Camarineans, who, though Dorians, were fighting on the Athenian side, and subsequently a general peace conference was held at Gela. Its opening stages were contentious and unpromising, each delegate pressing the grievances of his own city (4.58).

It is at this point that Hermocrates makes his first appearance in the *History* of Thucydides, introduced merely as 'Hermocrates, the son of Hermon, whose speech also proved to be the most convincing' (4.58). Thucydides gives no details of his career hitherto[8] and includes at this stage no estimate of his ability. The

[6] In 2.7.2, where the text is disputed, this figure, which appears in Diod. 12.41.1, has been supplied by emendation. Even if the Siceliots and Italiots could have built two hundred ships, the training of skilled crews to man them would have been a long and laborious task.

[7] This detail, which seems to be authentic, is supplied by Timaeus, *F. Gr. Hist.* 566 F 22.

[8] He must already have been a political figure of some standing when appointed as a delegate to this Congress. There is, however, no foundation

quality of the man is at once apparent from the quality of his speech (4.59–64).[9]

His plea is for Siceliot unity. The Greeks of Sicily, having a common name and a common heritage, should settle their differences by negotiation and should unite in resisting intervention by outsiders such as the Athenians, who sought to exploit these differences in the pursuit of their own imperialist ambitions. It would be hazardous to claim that this doctrine had never been preached before or was never preached again; but there was perhaps only one leading figure in Siceliot history whose policy was based on similar principles, namely Timoleon, who was not a Siceliot by birth. Apart from the primary loyalty of a Greek to his own city, there was the somewhat artificial bond between Dorian and Dorian, Ionian and Ionian, and also the broader feeling of kinship between all Greeks, varying considerably in intensity from time to time, which divided them from 'barbarians'. That the Greeks of Sicily were united by living in one island and were thereby isolated from the inhabitants of all other lands, Greek and barbarian, was an idea that did not develop naturally and was not easily fostered; it ignored the fact that Sicily was shared with four other races. To Hermocrates, however, the Siceliot cities were so closely linked with one another that in a striking phrase he describes feuds between them as *stasis*, as though they were rival factions in a single community.[10]

There was not much difficulty in making out a convincing case for the view that the aims of the Athenians were selfish and that the presence of their forces could harm all Siceliots, including the

---

for the view of Wentker, op. cit., 81 with n. 366, that he had been the prime mover of an imperialist policy since before 440.

[9] The vexed question of Thucydidean speeches cannot be discussed here, but it is surely beyond doubt that Thucydides was well-informed about the content of this speech and of the later speeches of Hermocrates at Syracuse and Camarina. They strike an individual note, and none reads as though Thucydides has merely improvised τὰ δέοντα. On the other hand, Steup in an appendix on 4.58 (Anhang, 287–8) goes too far when he claims to find in certain unusual turns of phrase in these speeches authentic traces of the style of Hermocrates. The version of the speech at Gela produced by Timaeus (*F. Gr. Hist.* 566 F 22) was evidently no more than a frigid rhetorical exercise bearing no relation to what was actually said, though it is known only from the criticisms of it by Polybius.

[10] 4.61.1, cf. 64.5, οἰκείου πολέμου, and the somewhat similar view of Plato, *Rep.* 5.470 b–d.

Chalcidians in whose interests they had ostensibly intervened. It is, however, significant that Hermocrates does not attempt to stir up moral indignation against Athens: imperialism, he says, is natural and excusable, and his criticism is rather of those who make insufficient efforts to avoid becoming its victims (4.61.5–6). Whatever his personal views may have been, it was politic to adopt this attitude towards imperialism because his own city could not claim a blameless record in the decades since the expulsion of the Deinomenids. As spokesman of the most powerful city, he was confronted with a delicate situation demanding skilful handling. Had an Athenian taken part in the debate, as at Camarina nine years later, it would have been easy for him to have argued that the motive of the Syracusans in supporting the proposed settlement was to give themselves a free hand to coerce their Chalcidian neighbours when the Athenians had withdrawn. Hermocrates fully appreciated the suspicion with which his city was regarded: he maintains that the Syracusans despite the strength of their position are prepared to sacrifice the opportunity of damaging their enemies and to make concessions for the common benefit of the Siceliots because they realise the impossibility of controlling destiny (4.59.1; 64.1).[11] This argument, which cannot have been at all reassuring, suggests that he is trying to evade an embarrassing practical issue; and most modern scholars consider the whole speech to be insincere.[12] They believe that Hermocrates, while professing to promote the interests of all Greek Sicily, in fact cared only for those of Syracuse; and Syracusan relations with Leontini after the Athenian withdrawal may be thought to confirm this interpretation. It must, however, be remembered that he was never in a position to direct the policy of Syracuse as Pericles had directed that of Athens. He was sent to Gela with instructions to negotiate a settlement if he could, and evidently he was himself convinced that peace was desirable. It may well be that some Syracusans favoured its conclusion because they hoped to exploit the situation created thereby in the interests of Syracusan imperialism, but his speech does not prove that he was one of them, and it cannot be assumed that he prompted, or indeed approved of, subsequent action taken by Syracuse. There is no evidence that at any time in his

[11] He uses a similar argument in his speech at Camarina, 6.78.2.
[12] From A. Holm, *Gesch. Siciliens* ii (1874), 8, to Wentker, op. cit., 125–6.

career he encouraged aggression by the Syracusans against other Siceliots, and on one occasion, which will be noted below, he was the prime mover of a decision that involved renouncing an opportunity for aggression.[13] His speeches and actions suggest rather that he strove to prevent local wars because they led to intervention from abroad, and it was for this reason that he tried to create his new kind of patriotism. Thucydides, who cannot be considered gullible, seems to have been convinced of his sincerity, especially as he draws a distinction between the opinions of Hermocrates and those of the other delegates to the Congress, who were concerned only with the interests of their own cities (4.58).

This speech contains only one definite recommendation, which is of a general character and largely negative: that the Siceliots should stop fighting one another, thereby depriving the Athenians of their excuse for intervention. It may be that Thucydides has chosen to omit some details from his version of the speech, but Hermocrates probably considered that it would be unwise to make specific proposals, at any rate at this stage, because the delegates from other cities must not be allowed to feel that Syracuse was dictating to them. They must be left free to conclude with one another whatever agreements they wished, founded on the general principles established by his speech.

The Congress agreed to end the war on a *status quo* basis, and after the cities allied with Athens had informed the Athenian generals and obtained their consent, peace was concluded (4.65.1–2). Had this agreement been made half a century later, it would probably have included a clause guaranteeing the autonomy of all the signatories, and much uncertainty would have been avoided. At this time, however, the type of general pacification known as κοινὴ εἰρήνη had not yet been developed in Greece: the doctrines of Hermocrates may possibly have contributed to its birth. Thucydides adds that Syracuse ceded Morgantina to Camarina in return for an agreed sum of money. Morgantina was an insignificant place, and his inclusion of this detail is somewhat surprising. He probably mentions it in order to show that the Syracusans made a gesture designed to prove their acceptance of the principles established at the Congress by making a concession to a weaker neighbour. No other agreements

[13] See below, pp. 191–2.

are mentioned, and it seems unlikely that any were made.[14] There is evidence that the Athenian alliances with Siceliot cities were not formally abrogated.[15] Thus, while Hermocrates gained his first objective in removing for the moment the pretext of Athenian intervention, he made scarcely any progress towards the creation of a union of all Greek Sicily.

Not long afterwards there occurred at Leontini a character-istically Siceliot outbreak of civil strife, which led to intervention by Syracuse. The upshot was that Leontini virtually lost its identity as an independent state and that while some Leontines were content to migrate to Syracuse, most of them established themselves at two forts in Leontine territory, whence they con-ducted hostilities against the Syracusans (5.4.2–4). The opinions of Hermocrates on this Syracusan intervention are not recorded; but he can hardly have approved of it.[16] Nothing was more likely to revive Athenian interest in Sicily, and indeed in 422 a diplo-matic mission led by Phaeax was sent from Athens with orders to persuade as many Siceliot cities as possible to take up arms against Syracuse in support of the Leontines. Camarina and Acragas agreed to take action, but Phaeax failed at Gela, where-upon he abandoned his mission realising that he would not con-vince the rest (5.4.1 and 5–6). He must have felt that without military aid from Athens only an alliance including almost all Siceliot cities could successfully challenge Syracuse. Yet the series of events at Leontini, together with a similar episode at Messana (5.5.1), and the success of Phaeax at Camarina and Acragas, left the Athenians in no doubt that the Siceliots were as divided as ever and that excuses for intervention could be found at will.[17]

Hermocrates is next mentioned when Thucydides gives an

[14] A. W. Gomme, *Historical Commentary on Thucydides* iii (1956), 523, who believes that agreements were reached between other cities but have been omitted by Thucydides (op. cit., iii., 522), classes the reference to the agree-ment between Syracuse and Camarina among 'relics of notes made at the time' by Thucydides on unimportant details. One possible reason for its in-clusion has been given above, but subsequent events also suggest that no other detailed agreements are mentioned because none was made, and that the Congress achieved no more than a general agreement in principle.

[15] 5.4.5; 6.6.2; 6.50.4. The alliance with Camarina may have been an exception (6.82.1); Thucydides is not altogether consistent on this point (6.88.2, cf. 75.3, 79.1).

[16] E. A. Freeman, *History of Sicily* iii (1892), 69.

[17] Cf. the highly coloured picture drawn by Alcibiades in 6.17.2–4.

account of a debate in the Syracusan assembly in the summer of
415, after the great Athenian expeditionary force had already
sailed for Sicily. Most of this report consists of speeches by two
leading figures, Hermocrates and the demagogue Athenagoras
(6.32.3–41). The former seeks to convince his audience that the
Athenians are really on their way and intend to conquer Sicily
(33.1–2), that prospects of defeating them are good (33.3–6), that
energetic measures for defence must be put into operation without delay (34.1–9). More than half of the speech is devoted to the
last of these, so that, in contrast to his speech at Gela, it consists
largely of positive recommendations. Missions must be sent to the
Sicels, to the rest of Sicily, to Italy and even to Carthage, and the
Spartans and Corinthians must be urged to send help at once and
to resume the war in Greece. Much more surprising is the proposal that the Syracusans together with their Siceliot allies should
send every available ship to Taras and the Iapygian promontory
to intercept the Athenian fleet before it could reach the Italian
coast. Hermocrates points out the difficulties that this move
would cause to the Athenians, who in his view would not even
leave Corcyra if they knew that the crossing was to be contested.
He also claims that unexpected resistance at this stage would
damage Athenian morale. His plan is indeed a bold one, and
modern scholars have with good reason doubted not only its
wisdom but also its feasibility.[18] At a time when navigation and
communications had reached only a primitive stage of development, there were palpable dangers to the Siceliots in trying to
intercept so far from their own bases an enemy whose seamanship
they could not hope to match. One factor that surely rendered
the plan impracticable was lack of time. The fleet of the
Athenians and their allies was already assembling at Corcyra
when Hermocrates made his speech (6.42.1, cf. 32.3), and in his
closing words he declares emphatically that the enemy 'has
almost arrived' (6.34.9). It would surely have been impossible to
muster a fleet including contingents from other Siceliot states
(6.34.4) and then to make the long voyage to the heel of Italy
before the Athenians left Corcyra. It is also clear that at this time
the number of ships fit for immediate service and the number of
trained crews available to man them cannot have been sufficient
to enable the Syracusans to undertake an operation on a large

[18] Notably G. Busolt, *Gr. Gesch.* iii. 2 (1904), 1300–1.

scale in distant waters. In the war ended by the Congress of Gela the highest recorded number of ships that they and their allies succeeded in mustering was a little over thirty (4.25.1). In the war now about to begin they at first made no attempt to use their fleet (cf. 6.52.1), and it was only in its closing months that, after long preparation and practice and with assistance from their Peloponnesian allies, they were eventually able to challenge the Athenian fleet in conditions that gave them a considerable advantage.

Why then did Hermocrates put forward his ambitious plan? It may be that he completely misjudged the strategic situation,[19] but a man of his sagacity and experience (6.72.2) can hardly have been blind to the difficulties of putting his plan into operation.[20] It might be argued that Thucydides has incorporated in a single speech the substance of several speeches made by Hermocrates on the defence of Sicily and that this proposal was made at an earlier meeting of the assembly. This explanation would, however, meet only the objection that it could not be put into operation in time to be effective. A more convincing explanation is suggested by two passages in the speech. In the first he declares that he will state his plan although the Syracusans are not likely to adopt it promptly because of their habitual inertia (6.34.4); in the second that his plan is the best course of action but that if the Syracusans reject it they must 'make every other preparation for the war with all possible speed' (6.34.9). From these passages it appears that, confronted with the difficult task of persuading the Syracusans to take energetic measures to meet the danger that was almost upon them, he adopted the debating manœuvre of proposing action demanding of them efforts far greater than any that they were willing to make; he calculated that, as the supporters of Athenagoras were hostile towards him, the assembly would not accept the whole of any defence programme proposed by him but, if given the opportunity to reject his plan to intercept the Athenians in Italy, would be more likely to adopt at least some of the measures recommended in the earlier part of his

[19] Cf. Busolt, loc. cit.
[20] A. W. Gomme, *Gnomon*, xxx (1958), 17, rightly criticises J. de Romilly, *Histoire et raison chez Thucydide* (1956), 61 and 195, n. 1, for subscribing to the view that the plan of Hermocrates 'is stated in order to make clear the folly of the Athenian expedition'.

speech. Nicias had, with an entirely different object in view, used somewhat similar tactics some months earlier when he tried to deter the Athenians from embarking upon their expedition by insisting that it required military resources on a very large scale (6.19.2; 24.1).

While Hermocrates deals mainly with the needs of the situation by which the Syracusan assembly was confronted on the day of the debate, the speech contains echoes of his views on wider issues. He naturally begins by emphasising the danger to his own city (6.33.1–2), but the defence measures that he proposes are designed to safeguard all Greek Sicily and not Syracuse alone. One passage implies censure of the Siceliots for having failed to respond to the Spartan demand for aid in the Archidamian war (6.34.8); it thus suggests that in his view the destruction of Athenian power, which would automatically have ended Athenian intervention in Sicily, was more important than the establishment of a Syracusan hegemony while the Athenians were diverted from the west by their preoccupations in Greece. Hence his idea of a united Sicily, though much less prominent here than in his speeches at Gela and Camarina, is not forgotten.

Hermocrates failed to convince many of the Syracusans, and some treated the subject of the debate with contempt and ridicule (6.35.1). Folly of an even more dangerous kind is seen in the speech of Athenagoras (6.36–40), whom Thucydides pictures as a typical demagogue, introducing him in terms very similar to those in which he introduces Cleon.[21] The speech is almost a caricature, in which the ignorance, over-confidence and violent prejudice of the speaker are mercilessly exposed.[22] His main contention is that the rumours of impending attack have been fabricated by the oligarchs with the intention of creating panic and thus overthrowing the democracy and enslaving the populace. He does not attack Hermocrates directly but makes his charges against the young oligarchs, whom he addresses as ὦ νεώτεροι (6.38.5) and blames for the prevalence of civil strife. His preoccupation with party issues helps to explain why the Syracusans often rejected the advice of enlightened leaders such

[21] Athenagoras, 6.35.2; Cleon, 3.36.6.
[22] There is no antilogy in which Thucydides enlists the sympathy of his readers more plainly on behalf of one of the two speakers.

as Hermocrates. To unite Greek Sicily was indeed a formidable task when the population of Syracuse was so deeply divided.

An unnamed general, who apparently presided over the assembly, then closed the debate without permitting any further speeches (6.41.1). He claimed that he and his colleagues had the situation in hand and would make preparations to repel the enemy, even though these preparations might prove to be unnecessary. The proposal to send a fleet to Italy is not mentioned (6.41.2–4). Hermocrates had at least secured an official assurance that the threat of invasion would not be ignored, but scarcely any action seems to have been taken until the Athenian fleet was known to have arrived at Rhegium (6.45; 73.2).

Because the speech of Athenagoras throws some light on rivalries between factions at Syracuse, it is appropriate to discuss briefly at this point the position of Hermocrates in local politics. There is no doubt that the Syracusan constitution was at this time a democracy:[23] Thucydides expressly states that it was (7.55.2), and all issues of major importance were referred to the popular assembly. Nevertheless a programme of far-reaching reforms, based on the principles of extreme democracy, was introduced in 412 by the demagogue Diocles, who, like Athenagoras, was an opponent of Hermocrates. Thereafter most of the magistrates were chosen by lot, and archons instead of generals presided at meetings of the assembly.[24] It is clear, therefore, that before and during the Athenian invasion the Syracusan democracy was less extreme than that of Athens and might even be described as moderate.[25] There is no reason to believe that Hermocrates disapproved of the constitution as it was before the reforms of Diocles and would have welcomed its overthrow. If a tradition of somewhat doubtful authenticity be accepted, he was a member of an aristocratic family;[26] but so were almost all the

[23] The evidence is conveniently summarised by P. A. Brunt, *C.R.* vii (1957), 244–5, in a review of Wentker, op. cit.

[24] W. Huttl, *Verfassungsgeschichte von Syrakus* (1929), 86.

[25] A. Andrewes, *The Greek Tyrants* (1956), 136–7, believes that Diocles restored full democracy, which had been in operation before the Syracusans, on the advice of Hermocrates, reduced the number of generals from fifteen to three (6.72.4–73.1). There is, however, no evidence that this measure, which was certainly desirable on military grounds, had any political significance, or that the work of Diocles consisted merely of restoration.

[26] The evidence consists of a fragment of Timaeus (*F. Gr. Hist.* 566 F 102a),

184

leaders of the Athenian democracy before the Peloponnesian war. The widely accepted view that he favoured oligarchy is based partly on the fact that among his opponents were the two demagogues Athanagoras and Diocles and partly on the speech of the former. Athenagoras associates him by implication with the young oligarchs who are accused of plotting to overthrow the democracy but, as has already been pointed out, does not attack him directly.[27] This absence of direct attack in a speech full of unrestrained violence is significant: Athenagoras would surely have denounced him personally as a would-be subverter of the democracy if this charge would have carried any conviction. It was the practice of demagogues to brand as enemies of the people all who did not share their own extreme views. The political sympathies of Hermocrates were probably no more oligarchical than those of Nicias and other Athenians who, while accepting the principles of democracy, disapproved of demagogues such as Cleon and Hyperbolus. One reason for the dearth of information about his position in local politics may be that he stood aloof from feuds between factions, and the absence of party support may have proved a handicap to him when trying to secure the adoption of his proposals.

During the two years of conflict that ended with the destruction of the Athenian forces he served Syracuse and Sicily more effectively in the assembly than on the field of battle. Knowing the weaknesses of his fellow-countrymen, he was always at hand to give wise counsel and to fortify their morale in times of adversity by encouragement and example. The first occasion on which he is known to have performed this service was in the autumn of 415, when over-confidence and lack of discipline caused the Syracusans to be defeated in their first major battle (6.63–71). After the Athenians had withdrawn, he made a speech in the assembly of which Thucydides gives a summary in

who, regarding the Athenian disaster in Sicily as a punishment for the impious mutilation of the Hermae, declares that the man chiefly responsible for the disaster was Hermocrates the son of Hermon, ὃς ἀπό τοῦ παρανομηθέντος διὰ πατέρων ἦν. Timaeus was addicted to antiquarian flights of fancy and may have inferred the alleged descent of the family from Hermes only from the names of Hermocrates and his father.

[27] By no stretch of the imagination could Hermocrates, who had represented Syracuse at Gela nine years earlier, be included among νεώτεροι whose age disqualified them from being legally appointed to any office (6.38.5).

oratio obliqua (6.72.2–5). Instead of reproaching the Syracusans for their neglect of his advice, he consoled them by arguing that they had not lacked courage and that their inferiority to a far more experienced enemy had not proved so great as might have been expected. He urged the enlargement of their hoplite force and the introduction of compulsory training: it appears that few had undergone training voluntarily. He also proposed that the board of fifteen generals should be replaced by a smaller board with discretionary powers. The reasons given for this proposal show that hitherto the generals had had to consult the assembly on military matters to an extent harmful both to security and to efficiency. The assembly adopted all these recommendations, electing three generals with full powers including Hermocrates himself (6.73.1). Nevertheless the Syracusans did not yet fully appreciate the urgency of the situation: the fifteen generals were not superseded by Hermocrates and his two colleagues until the following summer when their term of office expired (6.96.3).

Meanwhile Hermocrates was called upon to exercise his powers of persuasion at Camarina. The Camarineans were suspect because they alone of the Dorians in Sicily had been allied with Athens during the Archidamian war. In 415 they had refused to receive the Athenians (6.52.1) and had sent a token force of cavalry and archers to Syracuse, which took part in the battle fought there in the autumn (6.67.2); but the insignificance of this force intensified the suspicions of the Syracusans, who feared that the Athenian victory might encourage Camarina to desert them. They heard that the Athenians were making a fresh approach to the Camarineans, and a counter embassy was accordingly sent under the leadership of Hermocrates (6.75.3–4). Both embassies attended a meeting of the assembly, and the occasion is marked by another Thucydidean antilogy, the first speech being delivered by Hermocrates and the second by the Athenian spokesman Euphemus (6.76–87).

The speech of Hermocrates resembles his speech at Gela in that the keynote of both is the need for Siceliot unity. To argue convincingly that the Athenian aim is purely selfish, namely the enslavement of Sicily, is now even easier, but it is as difficult as ever for him to dispel fears of Syracusan imperialism. He admits that some Siceliots may, through envy or apprehension, wish

186

Syracuse to be weakened, but he maintains that destiny cannot be so conveniently controlled (6.78.2). Siceliots fighting on the Syracusan side will be fighting for their own survival and not for that of Syracuse, and their prospects of success will be much brighter while Syracusan power remains unbroken. Camarina will be the next victim and will not be saved by electing to remain neutral now (6.78.3–4). The end of the speech contains a threat of reprisals if the Camarineans refuse to listen and Syracuse is victorious (6.80.4). He claims that such reprisals would not constitute aggression but punishment for treachery.

The speech of Euphemus is mainly an attempt to convince the Camarineans that Syracusan imperialism is much more dangerous to them than Athenian because Syracuse is their neighbour whereas Athens is far away. He also defends Athenian policy in Sicily and elsewhere against the charges of Hermocrates. The speech is an interesting example of Thucydidean method, for in no other antilogy does the second speaker concentrate to such an extent on seeking to refute the first.[28]

Almost all the arguments of Hermocrates and Euphemus are applicable to Siceliots other than the Camarineans. The issue that both speakers have most at heart is whether the Siceliot cities generally will support Syracuse or Athens or neither.[29] Upon the decisions of these cities much depended. It is tempting to envisage the struggle at Syracuse as one between the Athenians on the one side and the Syracusans with Peloponnesian support on the other, but Thucydides frequently emphasises the influence of other Siceliots.[30] Here he is following his practice of foreshadowing through the medium of speeches a factor that is to be prominent in the subsequent narrative.

The Camarineans eventually decided to support neither side at present (6.88.2), adopting one course of action from which Hermocrates had tried to deter them (6.80.1–2). Thus his mission was unsuccessful. Yet the analysis of their feelings given by

[28] Cf. the able discussion by J. de Romilly, op. cit., 186–94.
[29] Both refer to the attitude of 'the others', cf. 78.4 and 80.3 (Hermocrates), 87.1 and 5 (Euphemus).
[30] Cf. 7.1.5; 7.2; 25.9; 32.1–2; 33.1–2; and his statement in 58.4, which might seem superfluous, that the Syracusans supplied more troops than the other Siceliots.

Thucydides suggests that they favoured the Athenians rather than the Syracusans (6.88.1), so that, though failing to win their co-operation, Hermocrates at least performed a valuable service in securing that they chose neutrality.

The period of a few months in 414 during which he held the office of general was the unhappiest phase of his career. Epipolae, the strategic key to Syracuse, was at once lost. While the retiring generals were evidently guilty of having neglected to prepare for defence of this plateau, Hermocrates and his colleagues allowed themselves to be surprised and outmanœuvred by the enemy (6.96–7). The situation continued to deteriorate rapidly. The Syracusan hoplites proved so much inferior to the Athenians in discipline and skill that the generals first decided not to commit their forces to any further engagements on a large scale and later, when they had twice failed to cut the Athenian wall now being built across Epipolae, had to withdraw their entire army within the city defences. There seemed to be no hope, with the forces at present available, of preventing the completion of the Athenian wall (6.98–102). Already consultations about surrender were being held among the Syracusans themselves and also with Nicias.[31] In an age when the technique of siege operations was so undeveloped that the defenders of small towns such as Potidaea and Plataea were reduced to surrender only by hunger, it was highly discreditable to the Syracusans that they so soon found themselves in a situation that appeared to be desperate. It is not surprising that in the prevailing atmosphere of depression and suspicion their generals were made scapegoats. Hermocrates and his colleagues were dismissed on the ground that the present crisis was the outcome of 'either their ill luck or their treachery' (6.103.4). Of their three successors two appear again as generals when the demagogue Diocles was at the height of his power.[32] Hence it is likely that popular agitation, led perhaps by Athenagoras, caused the dismissal of Hermocrates and his two colleagues. Charges of treachery were in the demagogic tradition. If an impeachment followed, the defendants must have been acquitted: the influence of Hermocrates continued to be considerable, while

[31] 6.103.3–4, cf. 7.2.1; Plut. *Nic.* 18.11–12.
[32] Xen. *Hell.* 1.2.8, Eucles and Heracleides (the son of Aristogenes, who is to be distinguished from Heracleides, the son of Lysimachus, who was a colleague of Hermocrates, 6.73.1).

Sicanus, who was dismissed with him, apparently served on the board of generals in the following year.[33]

When Hermocrates makes his next appearance in the narrative of Thucydides, only a few months have passed, but meanwhile the situation has been transformed. The blockade has been broken, and on land the Syracusans have gained the initiative. While various factors contributed to this change, the most important was undoubtedly the success of the Spartan Gylippus in organising the defence. Thucydides nowhere suggests that Gylippus possessed the inspiring personality of Brasidas, and according to Timaeus the Syracusans found him uncongenial (*F. Gr. Hist.* 566 F 100). Nevertheless he quickly succeeded where Hermocrates and others had failed: discipline was greatly improved and substantial aid was obtained from other parts of Sicily. It was not the only occasion in their history that the Siceliots showed a surprising willingness to obey a leader from the Greek homeland. In the spring 413 Gylippus and Hermocrates together urged the Syracusans to undertake the formidable task of challenging the Athenians at sea. From the summaries of their speeches given by Thucydides in *oratio obliqua* it appears that Gylippus spoke with characteristically Laconic brevity, leaving to Hermocrates the responsibility of producing convincing arguments (7.21.2–4). The latter pointed out that the Athenians had not always possessed their skill in seamanship but had acquired it compulsorily in consequence of the Persian invasion. He also argued that the very unexpectedness of their resistance at sea would give the Syracusans an advantage that would discount their lack of experience.[34] The combined pressure of Gylippus, Hermocrates and others overcame any misgiving that may still have been felt, and at long last the Syracusans prepared to use their fleet (7.21.5).

This collaboration between Gylippus and Hermocrates, which must have benefited the Syracusan cause in other ways during the last months of the campaign, throws light upon the character of the latter. Inevitably, and perhaps justifiably, he must have

---

[33] 7.46; 50.1; 70.1; Diod. 13.13.2 and 6. An achievement accredited by Polyaenus (1.43.1) to Hermocrates during his generalship is the suppression of a slave revolt by means of trickery. This sensational story has been justifiably suspected (Freeman, op. cit., iii. 673–4), but it may well have some foundation.

[34] Cf. 6.34.6–8, where he uses a similar argument.

felt that the failures of the Syracusans during his generalship were due to their own shortcomings and not to faulty leadership on his part. Nevertheless he was prepared to use all his energy and influence in support of Gylippus, who had in effect supplanted him. He gave his services unsparingly wherever they seemed likely to further the cause of Greek Sicily, and, unlike Alcibiades, he did not allow personal considerations to blunt his patriotism. He is not known to have played any part in the work of preparing the fleet for action, which was largely a Corinthian achievement, or to have fought in the sea battles in the Great Harbour. The only record of his participation in military operations at Syracuse after his dismissal from the generalship is a statement by Diodorus (13.11.4) that he commanded a detachment of picked troops in the night battle on Epipolae. This body after a spirited resistance was put to flight (7.43.4–5), and the Athenian advance was first stemmed by the Boeotians.

The last of his services during this campaign was one that substantially influenced the course of history. Had he not acted as he did, the defeat of the Athenians would have been grievous enough, involving the loss of the entire fleet operating in Sicily; as it was, they lost almost the whole of their army as well and suffered an overwhelming disaster. The story, which is a very famous one, illustrates both his resourcefulness and his persistency in refusing to abandon his aims despite seemingly insuperable obstacles. The Athenians had planned to withdraw from Syracuse to Catana by land if they failed in their final attempt to break out of the Great Harbour (7.60.2), and as soon as the sea battle was lost, they made preparations to put this plan into operation during the ensuing night. Hermocrates, appreciating that the Athenians could still be formidable if allowed to escape to some other part of Sicily, urged the generals to have the principal roads blocked and guarded before nightfall. The generals agreed with his views but were convinced that their orders would not be obeyed by troops already beginning to celebrate the victory together with a feast of Heracles which happened to fall on that day. Accordingly he sent some of his friends at dusk to the Athenian camp, where they shouted a warning to delay the withdrawal and make it in daylight after due preparation because the roads were already guarded. As he intended, these messengers were mistaken for traitors who had long been in touch with Nicias, and their false message was believed to be authentic. The Athenians postponed their evacuation, and from that moment their fate was sealed.[35]

Thucydides does not record the views of Hermocrates on the proposal that Nicias and Demosthenes should be executed (7.86.2–4). According to Diodorus and Plutarch he was howled down in the assembly when he tried to dissuade the Syracusans from treating the generals and other prisoners inhumanely, declaring that the honourable use of victory was superior to victory itself.[36] Although this story is almost certainly derived from a Sicilian source which might tend to exaggerate the magnanimity of Hermocrates, there is no adequate reason to reject it. His principal aim was now achieved in that Greek Sicily was safe from the menace of Athenian intervention, at any rate for some years. Savage reprisals against helpless prisoners would contribute nothing towards the permanent removal of Athenian imperialism.

Although the Syracusans were weakened by their efforts of the last two years, their self-confidence and their prestige must have been enormously enhanced. It might have been expected that they would now proceed to exploit their victory by attempting to establish a hegemony over eastern Sicily and that, if the plea of Hermocrates for Siceliot unity had been designed to pave the way for Syracusan expansion, he would have been active in encouraging the pursuit of these ambitions. Syracuse, however, does not appear to have made a determined effort even to punish those Siceliots who had sided with the Athenians. Hostilities against the Chalcidian cities dragged on for several years, but Catana maintained its independence, apparently without much difficulty, aided by Athenians who had evaded their pursuers during the withdrawal from Syracuse or had later escaped from captivity.[37] This absence of vigorous action by the Syracusans against their local enemies cannot be attributed wholly to exhaustion or to their tendency to relaxation of effort when not

[35] 7.73.1–74.1. The versions of the story by Diodorus (13.18.3–5), Plutarch (*Nic.* 26.1–2) and Polyaenus (1.43.2) add nothing of any substance.

[36] Diod. 13.19.5–6; Plut. *Nic.* 28.3. The story quoted by Plutarch (*Nic.* 28.5) from Timaeus (*F. Gr. Hist.* 566 F 101) that Hermocrates contrived to give the Athenian generals the opportunity to commit suicide in prison is certainly false.

[37] 7.85.4; Lys. 20.24–26; Paus. 7.16.5; Diod. 13.56.2.

directly threatened, for they sent a fleet to co-operate with the Peloponnesians in the Aegean. Thucydides expressly states that Hermocrates was the principal instigator of this decision, urging the Siceliots to 'join in completing the destruction of Athens' (8.26.1). The Peloponnesians expected naval assistance from Sicily (8.2.3), and indeed the Syracusans could have been charged with ingratitude if they had not attempted to repay their allies for the substantial aid received during the Athenian invasion. To Hermocrates, however, the fleet surely did not sail only to discharge a debt of honour, nor was the enterprise merely an act of retaliation. Athenian intervention had always constituted the greatest obstacle to his plan for Siceliot unity, and here was an opportunity to remove this danger for ever. He was himself chosen to command the expeditionary force, an appointment perhaps supported by his political opponents, who may already have been planning to take advantage of his absence. The size of this force, which consisted of twenty Syracusan and two Selinuntine ships together with a body of hoplites, may seem modest, even niggardly, but because its members were veterans of the battles in the Great Harbour, it was an asset of great value to the inexperienced Peloponnesians. Even its size is not unimpressive when it is remembered that no Greek state other than Athens sent a larger expedition to a distant theatre of war throughout the fifth century.

The Syracusans distinguished themselves in their first engagement in Asia (8.28.2) and continued to show fighting qualities superior to those of other contingents. Their effectiveness was undoubtedly due in some degree to the leadership of Hermocrates. Yet while he overshadowed his colleagues on the Peloponnesian side both in ability to win the loyalty of his troops and in strength of character, his influence upon the course of the campaign was limited by his subordination to a succession of Spartan admirals. The principal reason why so little progress was made against the weakened and disunited Athenians was that relations became increasingly strained between the Peloponnesians and the satrap Tissaphernes, who had become their paymaster but soon began to withhold part of the agreed subsidy with the object of prolonging the war and weakening both sides. Hermocrates, speaking on behalf of the whole fleet, protested more vigorously than any of the other commanders against this humiliating and dishonest treatment, and his protests caused Tissaphernes to make some concessions. Unlike most of his colleagues, he refused Persian bribes, and his forthright attitude gained him the lasting enmity of the satrap (8.29.2; 45.3; 85.3). Feeling against Astyochus, the Spartan admiral, and Tissaphernes subsequently became so embittered that mutinous disturbances occurred at Miletus, in which the Syracusans played a leading part (8.78; 83-4). The malcontents blamed Astyochus because he did not engage the Athenian fleet in a major battle and had not secured the payment of the Persian subsidy; they were even more enraged against Tissaphernes for failing either to pay his Greek allies or to produce the Phoenician fleet which was to have aided them. Some officers supported the action of their men, but the attitude of Hermocrates towards these disturbances is not recorded. He doubtless approved of attempts to bring pressure upon Tissaphernes, but it seems unlikely that he encouraged insubordination against the supreme commander of the Peloponnesian forces, though the weakness and incompetence of Astyochus evidently exasperated him.

When Astyochus soon afterwards sailed for home having completed his term of office, he took with him an agent representing Tissaphernes, who was anxious to exculpate himself in the eyes of the Spartans (8.85.1-2). At the same time a second mission left for Sparta consisting of a Milesian embassy and Hermocrates. The Milesians were sent to denounce the satrap, while Hermocrates 'intended to show that Tissaphernes was ruining the Peloponnesian cause in association with Alcibiades and was playing a double game'.[38] Thucydides does not record how these

[38] 8.85.2. Thucydides refers at this point to the dismissal and banishment of Hermocrates (8.85.3), and Wilamowitz, *Hermes* xliii (1908), 608-12, and Steup in an appendix on this passage (Anhang, 295-6) maintain that he was already an exile when he accompanied the Milesian envoys to Sparta (summer, 411). They reject the evidence of Xenophon (*Hell.* 1.1.27-31), who dates his banishment much later (autumn, 410), and of Diodorus (13.39.4), who states that he fought at Cynossema. The problem is a complicated one, but it seems preferable to accept the view of many scholars (cf. T. Lenschau, *R.E.* viii (1912), col. 886) that Thucydides is here referring to a later event out of its chronological context. A similar anticipation occurs in the preceding chapter, where he mentions the death of the Spartan Lichas which occurred some time afterwards (8.84.5, cf. 87.1, where Lichas accompanies Tissaphernes to Aspendus). It is true that τὰ τελευταῖα in 8.85.3 means not 'subsequently' but 'finally': the phrase marks the culmination of the quarrel

missions fared: in any book other than the eighth he might well have included speeches summarising the debate at Sparta. According to Xenophon, however, the charges made by Hermocrates against Tissaphernes were supported by Astyochus and were accepted by the Spartans as proven (*Hell.* 1.1.31). If, as is probable, these denunciations of Tissaphernes contributed to the Spartan decision to transfer the fleet from his satrapy to that of Pharnabazus, Hermocrates helped to terminate a situation which might well have led to the disintegration of the Peloponnesian forces in Asia.[39]

After Mindarus had moved from Ionia to the Hellespont, he had to face an Athenian fleet much better handled than his own and accordingly suffered a series of defeats. In the major battles at Cynossema and Cyzicus the Syracusans seem to have fought with more skill or more determination than their allies. At Cynossema they pressed the enemy hard at first but were later forced back and took to flight when they saw the rest of the fleet routed; only one of their ships fell into enemy hands, whereas the losses sustained by most other contingents were proportionately much higher.[40] At Cyzicus, where the Peloponnesians were overwhelmed, only the Syracusan ships were burned by their crews before the Athenians could seize them; all the rest of the fleet was captured by the enemy (Xen. *Hell.* 1.1.18).

Xenophon provides one last glimpse of Hermocrates with the Syracusan fleet in Asia, and it is an illuminating one (*Hell.* 1.1.27–31). The passage is characteristic of its author, commonplace in thought and expression, probably inaccurate in detail, and yet portraying most graphically the relations between troops on active service and their leaders, a subject of which he had much personal experience. While the Syracusans were at Antan-

between Hermocrates and Tissaphernes, and Thucydides perhaps completes his account of this quarrel here because he does not intend to mention it again. The accusation of Tissaphernes that Hermocrates had asked him for money is doubtless a malicious distortion of the protests which Hermocrates had made when pressing for the payment of the Persian subsidy (8.29.2; 45.3).

[39] Cf. 8.99. Presumably Mindarus, the successor of Astyochus, had orders to sail for the Hellespont if Tissaphernes did not at once give the Peloponnesians wholehearted support.

[40] 8.104–6. At Abydos, where the Peloponnesians were again defeated, the Syracusans fought on the left wing (Diod. 13.45.7); nothing further is known of their part in the battle.

drus building ships to replace those lost at Cyzicus, news arrived that their generals had been banished by popular vote. There is every reason to believe both that this action was taken on political grounds at the instigation of Diocles, who had recently introduced his programme of constitutional reform, and that the loss of the Syracusan ships at Cyzicus afforded a pretext for the impeachment. Hermocrates, acting as spokesman for his colleagues at a mass meeting of the Syracusans, protested that they had been banished unjustly and illegally, but rejected the clamorous demand that they should continue in office and defy the decision of the home government.[41] This refusal by the generals to consider only their own interests is highly creditable: had they consented, a state of civil war would have been created similar to that between the Athenian forces at Samos and the Four Hundred at Athens, and the consequences might have proved harmful to the Peloponnesian cause. The generals did, however, agree to remain in command until the arrival of their successors, and most of the trierarchs undertook to secure that the sentences of banishment should be revoked when the fleet returned home. Xenophon draws a lively picture, which must surely be authentic, of the devotion to Hermocrates felt by his officers and men and of their regret that he would no longer lead them: he had made himself immensely popular by his care for their interests and by his practice of taking them into his confidence and welcoming their advice. When the new generals arrived, he visited Pharnabazus with whom he had evidently established friendly relations, for the satrap provided him unasked with money for effecting his return to Syracuse.[42] Later he joined an embassy sponsored by Pharnabazus which was on

[41] The sentence in which Xenophon describes the reactions of this military assembly (*Hell.* 1.1.28, οἱ δ’ ἀναβοήσαντες ἐκέλευον ἐκείνους ἄρχειν, καὶ μάλιστα οἱ τριήραρχοι καὶ οἱ ἐπιβάται καὶ οἱ κυβερνῆται) has been given a political interpretation by some scholars (Freeman, op. cit., iii., 430–1; Busolt, op. cit., iii., 2.1549 with n. 1) which is surely unwarranted. Xenophon, who had himself attended many meetings of this kind, is only pointing out that the generals were most enthusiastically supported by the more responsible members of the audience whose military status gave them the greatest influence. He is not suggesting that the crews of the ships were even lukewarm, much less that they were eager to be rid of their generals for political reasons. The whole passage implies solidarity in support of Hermocrates and his colleagues (cf. 29, οὐδενὸς δὲ οὐδὲν ἐπαιτιωμένου).

[42] Xen. *Hell.* 1.1.31; Diod. 13.63.2.

its way to the Persian court,[43] but he cannot have accompanied it far, for shortly afterwards he was back in Sicily.

It is regrettable that the closing stages of his career are known only from the account of Diodorus (13.63; 75.2-9), who seldom provides a coherent picture of important characters. His actions after his return to Sicily seem to be reported accurately enough, but the motives underlying them are not at all clear. The recent Carthaginian invasion, in which Selinus and Himera were destroyed, had exposed once more the weakness and disunity of Greek Sicily, and the efforts of the Syracusans under Diocles to save their Siceliot kinsmen had lacked determination and military skill. Hermocrates seems to have felt himself called upon to serve his fellow-countrymen against Carthage as he had served them against Athens.[44] With money supplied by his friend Pharnabazus he built five ships at Messana and hired 1,000 mercenaries.[45] Then after a vain attempt to secure his recall through the influence of his friends at Syracuse, he proceeded to pillage the Carthaginian province with a force now swollen to 6,000. Though he was not strong enough to besiege the fortified towns of Motya and Panormus, his raids were very successful and inflicted severe damage. He must have appreciated the danger of provoking another Carthaginian offensive. For the present, however, his success created a favourable impression at Syracuse, where the populace was now willing to restore him, though opposition was to be expected from his enemies; for the future he may have believed that his old dream of a united Greek Sicily could best be realised by launching a crusade against Carthage.[46] The booty gained during these raids must have been very welcome, for apart from the funds provided by Pharnabazus his

[43] Xen. *Hell.* 1.3.13. Xenophon gives a confused account of this embassy, and it is not clear why Hermocrates was invited to join it or why he left it.

[44] E. Meyer, *G. d. A.* v (1902), 70. There was even a possibility of co-operation between Carthage and Athens: they were in diplomatic contact in 406 (cf. K. F. Stroheker, *Historia*, iii (1954-5), 163-71).

[45] Lenschau, op. cit., col. 885, maintains that the ships were built in Messenia and are to be identified with the Sicilian ships which took part in the recovery of Pylos (Diod. 13.64.5 with Wesseling's emendation). It is, however, difficult to believe that the phrase αἱ μὲν ἀπὸ Σικελίας refers to ships built in the Peloponnese. On other occasions ships from Sicily assisted the Peloponnesians in operations off the coast of Greece (8.91.2).

[46] A similar policy was later adopted by the elder Dionysius, though his motives were almost certainly more selfish.

financial resources can hardly have been substantial and must have been strained by the growth of his army.

He then took a further step designed to win support at Syracuse, and also to discredit his opponents there, by recovering the bones of the Syracusans killed at Himera and having them conveyed to their homes. This action caused an outbreak of popular anger against Diocles, who, when in command of the force sent to relieve Himera, had left the Syracusan dead unburied. Diocles was now banished, but Hermocrates was not recalled and withdrew to western Sicily: according to Diodorus (13.75.5) the Syracusans were afraid that, if given a position of authority, he would establish a tyranny.[47] Soon afterwards he returned to the vicinity of Syracuse at the instigation of his partisans in the city, who seem to have misjudged the feelings of the populace. Being apparently led to believe that if once he showed himself inside the walls he would be acclaimed by a great majority of the Syracusans, he pressed forward by night with a few men and arrived at the gate of Achradina, which his partisans had already occupied. While he was awaiting the rest of his army, large numbers of armed Syracusans gathered in the market-place and fighting broke out in which he and most of his followers were killed. The survivors were tried and banished except some of the most seriously wounded who escaped impeachment because their relations alleged that they were dead. Among these was the future tyrant Dionysius.

Diodorus reports the suspicion that Hermocrates intended to make himself a tyrant without stating whether or not it had any foundation and without providing his readers with adequate evidence to enable them to judge the issue for themselves. Presumably the authority upon which his narrative is based was equally non-committal. Greek statesmen who displayed marked ability and individuality tended to incur charges of plotting to establish a tyranny, the stock example being that of Alcibiades. It was almost inevitable that the actions of Hermocrates since his return to Sicily gave rise to such accusations by his fellow-citizens, who had had long experience of his initiative and determination. There is no justification for assuming that, because hitherto he had subordinated personal ambition to patriotic zeal—a view that this essay has sought to establish—the

[47] The validity of these suspicions is discussed below.

suspicion that he now intended to make himself tyrant should necessarily be dismissed as groundless. It would doubtless have suited him best to have occupied a position similar to that of Pericles and to have been in effective control of Syracusan policy without being invested with dictatorial powers. The Syracusan democracy, however, was far less developed than that of Athens, and his intimate knowledge of its defects must surely have convinced him that he could accomplish little if his authority were limited and insecure. He might have been content with the status of στρατηγὸς αὐτοκράτωρ, but apparently no one who was not a tyrant held this office before the time of Dion.[48] Syracuse had proved dangerously vulnerable in the earlier stages of the Athenian siege before the Peloponnesians intervened, and the more recent Carthaginian invasion suggested that these weaknesses might even have been intensified by the reforms of Diocles. Another Carthaginian invasion might shatter the prosperity of Greek Sicily or even drive the Greeks from the island. Conscious of all this, Hermocrates may well have concluded that only by becoming tyrant would he enjoy sufficient authority to enable him to put into effect the drastic and unpopular measures which the situation demanded. The benevolent tyranny of Gelon, who was for generations remembered with affection by the Syracusans,[49] afforded a precedent.

Hermocrates is one of Thucydides' few heroes. That he is a member of this select company may seem surprising, because his personal successes are far outweighed by his failures, at any rate during the phases of his career about which any information has been preserved. At Gela his plea for Siceliot unity was virtually ignored. When nine years later he urged the Syracusans to prepare energetically for defence before the arrival of the Athenian expedition, his advice was to a large extent unheeded. His speech at Camarina proved only partly successful, and the brief period of his generalship was one of almost uninterrupted

[48] E. Pais, *Storia dell' Italia antica e della Sicilia*, i² (1933), 431 expresses the reasonable view that because Hermocrates would have had to assume a dictatorship of some kind, the question of his status is not one of much consequence. It is, however, very doubtful whether at Syracuse in this period any position other than that of tyrant could have been devised which would have satisfied his needs.

[49] Cf. Plut. *Timol.* 23.7; [Dio Chrys.] 37.21.

failure for the Syracusans. Although Sicilian tradition, unwilling to admit that Syracuse survived mainly through the intervention of Gylippus and the Peloponnesians, pictures Hermocrates as its saviour,[50] the more objective account of Thucydides shows that, valuable as his contribution was, it was only one of several influential factors. In Asia his uncompromising opposition to Tissaphernes and his inspiring leadership of the Siceliot contingent were highly creditable, but in all three major engagements at sea he was on the losing side, and in the third the whole Siceliot fleet was lost. Finally, after his return to Sicily his attempt to secure reinstatement at Syracuse ended in a somewhat inglorious debacle.

Why then among contemporary leaders does he occupy a place of honour in the *History* of Thucydides next only to Pericles and perhaps to Brasidas? It is hardly necessary to point out that Thucydides does not measure greatness solely by the criterion of success;[51] but while Pericles and Brasidas had their failures, they were far more consistently successful than Hermocrates. It might be argued that Thucydides has based his estimate of Hermocrates largely upon knowledge of achievements in Sicily not mentioned in his work because they were not relevant to the history of the Peloponnesian war. He was doubtless in possession of information about Hermocrates which he has for this reason not chosen to record, though leading figures in whom he was particularly interested tend to receive rather fuller treatment than would seem strictly necessary, as may be seen in the case of Themistocles. Yet Hermocrates is pictured to so large an extent as the embodiment of the qualities in a leader most valued by Thucydides[52] that his high estimate of him seems to be founded mainly upon the evidence included in the *History*.

Hermocrates is presented as a man of complete integrity and high principles which he refused to abandon or compromise, preferring to accept the handicaps which they imposed. Because

---

[50] This was undoubtedly the standpoint of Timaeus, cf. especially *F. Gr. Hist.* 566 F 102, with Jacoby's commentary on F 99–102, and Polyb. 12.25k2 and 11 (where Polybius, though severely critical of Timaeus, evidently accepts his estimate of Hermocrates).

[51] His admiration for Antiphon (8.68.1–2) affords a striking illustration of this.

[52] G. F. Bender, *Der Begriff des Staatsmannes bei Thukydides* (1938), 82–103, shows that Hermocrates has all the hallmarks of statesmanship as defined in 2.60.5.

Syracuse was politically immature, it was far more difficult for him than for Pericles to win for himself a position of personal authority which would have enabled him to put his enlightened ideas into practice. Unlike the successors of Pericles whose methods Thucydides condemns (2.65.10), he refused to seek personal advancement by gratifying the mob. On the contrary, like Pericles himself, he was prepared to endanger his own popularity and prospects by advocating measures which he knew to be unwelcome but believed to be desirable. His attitude towards what may be termed political morality contrasts with that of Timoleon, who later for a short time achieved in Sicily much that Hermocrates had attempted in vain. Timoleon, though enjoying the advantages of a dictatorship, was willing in the public interest to adopt unscrupulous methods when dealing with unscrupulous opponents;[53] Hermocrates evidently was not. It was only at the end of his life that the shortsightedness and ingratitude of the Syracusans led him to resort to force in an attempt to win personal ascendancy, and even then, if the interpretation given above has any validity, he was actuated by patriotism rather than by ambition.

He was indeed a true patriot; and true patriotism was rare enough among politicians during the Peloponnesian war. It was a quality seen rather in military leaders who played little or no part in politics such as Phormio, Demosthenes and Lamachus. Hermocrates, however, was a patriot of an unorthodox kind in that his patriotism was not limited by the boundaries of his own city-state but embraced all Greek Sicily, foreshadowing in some degree the panhellenism of the fourth century. It was perhaps this conception more than anything else that won for him the admiration of Thucydides; for to Thucydides the intellectual quality of a statesman was crucial,[54] while of the intellectually gifted only the greatest, such as Pericles, possessed the spark of genius, a combination of idealism with imaginative vision, capable of creating original and illuminating ideas. Hermocrates' dream of a united Sicily, abortive though it was, is scarcely less noble, and certainly less conventional in Greek eyes, than the ideals of the Funeral Speech.

[53] Cf. my *Timoleon and his relations with tyrants* (1952), *passim*.
[54] Bender, op. cit., 95, n. 261, draws attention to the prominence of ξύνεσις in Thucydidean judgements on great leaders.

In addition to moral and intellectual qualities Thucydides demands of his great men practical ability and a capacity for leadership. As a strategist and tactician Hermocrates appears from the extant record of his career to have been undistinguished, and the judgement of Thucydides on his military qualities (6.72.2, κατὰ τὸν πόλεμον ἐμπειρίᾳ τε ἱκανὸς γενόμενος) does not credit him with any natural aptitude in this sphere and seems a trifle lukewarm. On the other hand, there can be no doubt of his personal bravery, to which Thucydides refers in much stronger terms in the same passage (ἀνδρείᾳ ἐπιφανής). Not only was he courageous himself in difficult situations but also indefatigable in his efforts to sustain the morale of others, as he showed during the Athenian siege and while commanding the Siceliot contingent in Asia. The impact of his personality is perhaps most clearly discernible from the passage of Xenophon, to which reference has already been made, describing the scene when the news of his banishment was received. In his contacts with others he seems to have shown the genial warmth of Brasidas rather than the cold austerity of Pericles.

Should Thucydides' picture of Hermocrates be accepted as a true one? Unfortunately its authenticity cannot be tested by examining the evidence of other contemporary authorities. As might have been expected, Hermocrates apparently made much less impression upon public opinion in Greece than Brasidas, who became a sort of bogy in Attic comedy,[55] and it is perhaps not wholly fortuitous that in no extant work written at the end of the fifth century or at the beginning of the fourth is Hermocrates even mentioned, apart from that of Thucydides. Later writers from Xenophon onwards could have been, and most doubtless were, influenced by Thucydides' estimate of him or by that of the Sicilian tradition, which, as already noted, was led by local patriotism to exaggerate his achievements.[56] It might be argued that Thucydides has treated him too sympathetically because the Syracusan assembly banished him. Several other

[55] Aristoph. *Wasps*, 475, cf. 288; *Peace*, 281–3 and 640.
[56] Plato, who during his visits to Syracuse must have heard much about Hermocrates and may well have discussed him with the historian Philistus, introduces him as a character in the *Timaeus* and *Critias* and was to have made him the principal speaker in the third dialogue of the trilogy, which was never written.

characters whose ability is rated most highly in the *History* were, like Thucydides himself, the victims of an unappreciative mob: Themistocles, Alcibiades, Pericles at the end of his life, perhaps Phormio. It is, however, possible, and in my opinion very probable,[57] that the parts of the *History* in which Hermocrates is most prominent were composed before 410, the year of his banishment. Although Thucydides should not be assumed to be infallible, his general reputation for impartiality does afford some grounds for accepting his picture of Hermocrates as authentic and unprejudiced. A more specific indication of impartiality is his rejection of the temptation, to which the Sicilian tradition succumbed, to represent Hermocrates as the saviour of Syracuse despite his own admiration for him and despite the fact that some at least of his information about him was doubtless derived from Siceliots whose reports can hardly have been entirely free from bias. As in other cases, he has refused to allow his judgement to be warped either by his own predilections or by those of his informants.

[57] See above, pp. 170–1.

13

Individuals in Xenophon, *Hellenica*

Few Greeks can have been so well qualified as Xenophon to write a historical work on the last decade of the fifth century and the first four decades of the fourth century, which is the period covered by the *Hellenica*. The life that he led provided him with exceptional advantages for writing contemporary history. He was personally acquainted with many leading figures of his time; with a few of them he was on intimate terms. In dealing with a period of almost continuous warfare it was a potential asset to him to have had wide experience of active service and some of military command. He also had personal knowledge of civil war: when he was a young man, he certainly witnessed, and probably played a part in, the series of bitter struggles at Athens when the democracy was overthrown by the Thirty and was later restored. After leaving Athens when still in his twenties, he was, it appears, never again actively involved in political life, and he was less interested in politics than in war. He was, however, thoroughly familiar with the methods whereby Greek cities conducted their internal government and their external relations with one another. He also enjoyed the misfortune, so valuable to a historian, of having been exiled.[1] Banishment, as Plutarch points out,[2] was the lot of many Greek historians; it was almost a professional qualification.[3] Xenophon was absent from his native city for at least thirty-five years and lived for most of this period in the Peloponnese. Although he might have made better use of the opportunities for historical research afforded by his long exile, it did confer some obvious advantages, one of them being that the *Hellenica* is not written wholly from the viewpoint of a single city.

Evidence that Xenophon was well endowed with literary qualities is as abundant in the *Hellenica* as it is in his other works.

[1] Thucydides, in a famous passage (5.26.5), claims that his exile gave him special qualifications to write his *History*.

[2] *Mor.* (*De exilio*), 605 c, where he lists Thucydides, Xenophon, Philistus, Timaeus and Androtion as historians who wrote in exile. Herodotus, Theopompus and Polybius also suffered banishment.

[3] T. S. Brown, *Amer. Hist. Rev.* lix (1954), 841-3.

His narrative is almost everywhere lucid and graphic, and he has a flair for dramatic presentation of violent action, based upon acute observation of the distinctive features in any episode. He is adept at recreating the atmosphere of a tense situation.[4] He is also capable of writing good speeches and even better dialogue. His love of *oratio recta*, which is a distinctive feature of all his major works, contributes to the literary attractiveness of the *Hellenica*. So strong is its influence that in a very large number of passages reporting what was said by someone or in a conversation between two persons, though he begins his report in *oratio obliqua*, he promptly switches into *oratio recta*, usually inserting ἔφη.[5] This habit helps to produce an impression of directness analogous to that of Herodotus.

Plentiful and varied experience of warfare, an adequate knowledge of politics, and a talent for writing clear and attractive prose provide an excellent foundation upon which to build a historical work. In antiquity the *Hellenica* was much admired, and critics tended to rank Xenophon as a historian beside Herodotus and Thucydides.[6] This high assessment is, however, based very largely upon literary merits;[7] it is undeserved, indeed almost ludicrous, if other qualities desirable in a historian, such as accuracy, impartiality, methodical arrangement and an understanding of causation, are taken into account. There is widespread agreement among modern scholars that the *Hellenica* is, on balance at least, a failure.[8] It is not my intention to attempt a

---

[4] In addition to famous scenes such as 2.2.3–4 (news of the disaster at Aegospotami is received at Athens), 4.5.11–17 (the destruction of a Spartan *mora* by Iphicrates) and 6.4.35–7 (the murder of Alexander of Pherae), there are many admirably vivid accounts of minor events. Examples are 4.8.32–9 (the defeat and death of Anaxibius), 5.1.7–9 and 19–23 (naval attacks on the Athenians from the Spartan base at Aegina).

[5] There are instances throughout the *Hellenica* from the beginning (1.1.14) to the end (7.4.40, cf. 5.1–2). It is noteworthy that negotiations conducted by Tissaphernes (3.4.5) and later by Tithraustes (ibid., 25–6) with Agesilaus are reported in dialogue form, although in both cases the principal negotiators remained many miles apart.

[6] Lucian, *Quomodo historia conscribenda sit*, 4; Marcellinus, *Vit. Thuc.* 38–40, cf. Diod. 1.37.4.

[7] Dion. Hal., *De compositione verborum*, 10 and *Epist. ad Pomp.* 4; Diog. Laert. 2.6.57.

[8] M. I. Finley, *Greek Historians* (1959), 14, refuses to include any passages from the *Hellenica* in his selection of extracts on the grounds that 'it is very

comprehensive survey of its merits and defects but to examine a single element of the work, its treatment of leading individuals. This element is an important one, especially as Xenophon is intensely interested in personality and is fond of introducing personal touches better suited to biography than to history.[9] He has often been criticised for allowing his own feelings to colour his presentation of individuals, particularly those with whom he had personal contacts; and he is undoubtedly guilty of bias in some instances. My purpose here is to try to show that there is an even graver defect in his treatment of individuals, namely that in assessing their importance and their qualities his criteria are basically unsound.

Among the uses to which the practice of including speeches in historical works might be put by ancient historians one was to throw light upon the speaker. It will be convenient first to examine briefly how in the *Hellenica* Xenophon uses speeches for this purpose. In his report of a peace conference held at Sparta in 371 he includes a speech by Callias, one of the Athenian envoys, who is introduced as 'the kind of man who derives as much pleasure from being praised by himself as by others' (6.3.3). In this speech (ibid., 4–6) Callias glorifies himself and his family, and he pleads for peace between Athens and Sparta on the grounds, which must have seemed somewhat absurd even to a Greek audience, that the mythical ancestors of both sides had been on friendly terms. Only one sentence makes any explicit reference to the contemporary situation which gave rise to the conference (ibid., 5). The speech provides a delightfully malicious exposure of a pompous and conceited man, and it is skilfully and wittily written. Its historical value, however, is almost negligible. Although Callias belonged to a prominent and wealthy family, his own political and military career was humble and undistinguished; he makes only two fleeting appearances elsewhere in the *Hellenica* (4.5.13–14; 5.4.22).

Xenophon occasionally shows a capacity for using speeches for the serious portrayal of important individuals. His account of the Thirty at Athens includes long speeches by Critias (2.3.24–34)

---

unreliable, tendentious, dishonest, dreary to read, and rarely illuminating on broader issues'. This harsh verdict, if somewhat exaggerated, is not altogether unmerited.

[9] I. Bruns, *Literarisches Porträt* (1896, reprinted 1961), 39–45.

and Theramenes (ibid., 35–49) when the former impeached the latter before the Boule. These speeches, which form an effective antilogy, focus attention on the cynicism of Critias, who coldly argues that bloodshed is inevitable when governments are changed, and on the self-possession of Theramenes, who calmly defends his own adoption of a middle course in politics, though conscious that nothing can save him from execution. The attacks made by each speaker upon the other are also instructive in spite of their palpable bias. Unfortunately Xenophon seldom chooses to adopt this method of throwing light upon leading figures;[10] it is more normally his practice to use speeches attributed to nonentities as the vehicle of his personal opinions. Examples are a speech by Euryptolemus, an obscure cousin of Alcibiades, at the trial of the Athenian generals in command at Arginusae (1.7.16–33) and two speeches by Procles of Phlius, an even more shadowy figure, on relations between Athens and Sparta after Leuctra (6.5.38–48; 7.1.2–11).[11] Among the most interesting speeches in the *Hellenica* is one presenting a picture not so much of the speaker but of someone else. It is the report to the Spartans by Polydamas of Pharsalus on his negotiations with Jason of Pherae, who was subjecting him to a sort of political blackmail (6.1.4–16). The portrayal of Jason by Xenophon will be discussed below (pp. 209–10), but here attention may be drawn to the fact that he makes the speech of Polydamas contribute substantially to it.

Much more distinctive and instructive than his use of speeches is a feature of his attitude towards leading individuals which is prominent throughout the *Hellenica*. He evidently built up in his mind an image of an ideal military commander endowed with certain qualities which seemed to him to be particularly desirable and admirable. He tends to apply this image as a yardstick in presenting military leaders about whom he wrote. The extent of its influence was not appreciated by modern scholars until a few years ago when an excellent study of the evidence was published which has established its importance beyond dispute.[12] It is my

[10] An effectively revealing speech of a totally different kind is that of the Spartan Teleutias to his sailors at Aegina (5.1.14–17).

[11] Cf. E. Delebecque, *Essai sur la vie de Xénophon* (1957), 17, 210, 313–15, 457.

[12] H. R. Breitenbach, *Historiographische Anschauungsformen Xenophons* (1950), especially 60–101. Most of the evidence is derived from the *Hellenica*, though

206

belief that from this evidence some conclusions may be drawn which may be deemed to throw light upon the historical value of the *Hellenica*.

The characteristics envisaged by Xenophon in his ideal military commander may be outlined as follows. He must win and maintain the loyalty of his men by devoting himself to their welfare. He must make every effort to ensure that they are well paid, well fed and well cared for. If there is a shortage of food, he must himself be content with a ration as small as theirs or even smaller. He must seek to alleviate their hardships, and where hardship is inevitable, he must share it with them. Similarly, he must share all the dangers to which they are exposed. He must be affable and approachable, always ready to lend a sympathetic ear to their complaints and petitions. He must set an example to them by his own self-control and physical fitness. He must see that they are well trained so that they may prove as effective in battle as they can be made to be. The best method of achieving this aim is to hold exercises designed to harden their physique and to improve their discipline and proficiency; prizes should be offered as incentives in these training exercises. He must also be a sufficiently persuasive speaker to be capable of bolstering their morale in dangerous situations and of conducting delicate negotiations in their interests. Finally, he must be a skilful tactician, ingenious enough to devise stratagems whereby he may outwit the enemy on the field of battle.

Leading figures in the *Hellenica* to whom Xenophon attributes several or many characteristics of his ideal commander are Hermocrates, Agesilaus, Teleutias, Iphicrates and Jason. A case could be made out for adding Thrasybulus and Dercylidas to the list. It will suffice to consider briefly how Xenophon presents Hermocrates, Teleutias and Jason: these three are chosen because their careers and personalities were widely different and because his treatment of each seems especially instructive.

He describes most vividly (1.1.27–31) the scene when news reached the Syracusan squadron in Asia that its commanders, who included Hermocrates, had been banished by popular vote. At a mass meeting he and his colleagues protested that their banishment was unjust and illegal; but they urged their officers

he also deals with other works. In the following pages I am much indebted to his survey, but I disagree with him on some points, as will be seen below.

and men, who clamoured that they should remain in command, not to defy the orders of the Syracusan state but to serve it as loyally as in the past. The generals did, however, consent to continue in office until their successors arrived. Xenophon lays emphasis upon the regret felt by the subordinates of Hermocrates when his devoted and sympathetic leadership was lost to them. He also mentions that it was the practice of Hermocrates to call the ablest of these associates together twice each day to meetings at which he informed them of his intentions and gave them instruction. These gatherings must have been valuable, and Xenophon is doubtless justified in declaring that the reputation of Hermocrates was enhanced by this paternal attitude towards those serving under his command.[13] Nevertheless, while it must be remembered that most of his career falls outside the period covered by the *Hellenica*, the presentation of him is surely one-sided: it dwells in rather extravagant terms upon a single element, and perhaps not even a vital element, in his qualities as a statesman and soldier.

Teleutias, who was the brother of Agesilaus, was evidently a dashing leader with an attractive personality, a combination most unusual in a Spartan. He conducted a bold and spectacular raid on the Piraeus, admirably described by Xenophon, which caused a panic at Athens and won large quantities of booty (5.1.19–24). Apart from this exploit his achievements while commanding small Peloponnesian fleets in the Aegean were almost negligible. He has little claim to be ranked as a man of outstanding distinction, but he is highly praised by Xenophon in two passages portraying his relations with the troops under his command. The first describes the manifestations of loyalty and affection when he leaves Aegina after his term of office has expired. Here Xenophon comments that such displays of devotion are better evidence of merit than exploits involving heavy expenditure and exposure to dangers (5.1.3–4). The second passage creates a similar impression by a different method (5.1.13–18). When Teleutias is sent to resume command of the same force at Aegina, he greets his men with a speech of encour-

---

[13] 1.1.31 (first sentence) seems to make this claim but is not altogether logical. It is not made clear why his private consultations with his friends should have influenced his reputation in the council of allied commanders (ἐν τῷ συνεδρίῳ). On this scene see above, pp. 194–5.

agement:[14] he offers to undergo privations even worse than theirs, he promises to be as approachable as he has been in the past, and he urges them to provide their own subsistence by plunder won from the enemy. They respond enthusiastically to his words, and he orders them to man their ships for the attack on the Piraeus mentioned above. Teleutias must have been personally known to Xenophon, who might be expected to be prejudiced in favour of a brother of Agesilaus. Personal considerations may have influenced in some degree his eulogistic treatment of a secondary figure,[15] but another factor, which is perhaps more important, is that the most conspicuous characteristics of Teleutias coincide with those of his ideal commander. He saw in him a man after his own heart.[16] When reporting how Teleutias lost his life at the siege of Olynthus Xenophon does at last become critical of him (5.2.37–3.7). The tone of admiration so prominent in the passage on his naval commands is again found in the narrative describing the earlier stages of his mission to Olynthus, though in fact he does not seem to have made much progress towards the completion of his task. Eventually he became enraged by the success of the Olynthian cavalry and rashly committed his forces to an engagement in which they were handicapped through having to operate too close to the city walls. He was himself killed and his army routed. Xenophon makes the sensible comment that it was a fatal error when attacking an enemy to be guided by ὀργή and not γνώμη. This passage shows that he did not consider even his ideal commanders to be beyond reproach; he displays an equally creditable absence of bias towards another of them, Iphicrates, whom he charges with mishandling an expedition to the Peloponnese (6.5.49–52).

Jason stands somewhat apart from the rest of the leaders listed above. To Xenophon, who is most unlikely to have had any personal contact with him, he is an absorbing but mysterious figure. He is also presented to a large extent in an abnormal way, as has already been noted,[17] namely through the speech of

[14] See above, p. 206, n. 10.
[15] Delebecque, op. cit., 283–4, believes that Xenophon wrote this part of the *Hellenica* soon after the death of Teleutias whose virtues he stressed in order to console Agesilaus for the loss of his brother. This ingenious suggestion does not appear to be supported by any evidence.
[16] J. Luccioni, *Les idées politiques et sociales de Xénophon* (1948), 184.
[17] See above, p. 206.

Polydamas at Sparta.[18] He is, however, credited in this speech, and to a lesser degree in the narrative, with many characteristics of an ideal commander as conceived by Xenophon. He was conspicuous for his physical energy and toughness, and he was constantly training his mercenaries so that they should become hardened troops of the highest quality; he was also generous in rewarding them for good service and in caring for their welfare (6.1.5–6, 15; 6.4.28). The circumstances of his assassination suggest that he was more approachable than most tyrants (6.4.31); and he showed a capacity to resist the temptations of the flesh (6.1.16), a quality rare among Thessalians who were notoriously self-indulgent. That he possessed diplomatic gifts is illustrated by the accounts both of his interview with Polydamas and of his negotiations with the Thebans and the Spartans immediately after the battle of Leuctra (6.4.22–5). It may indeed be felt that, because Xenophon dwells on his intelligent use of bluff and propaganda and on his imaginative schemes for the realisation of far-reaching ambitions, the treatment of him is altogether more penetrating, and shows more awareness of what qualities go to make up a great leader, than that of others to whom the characteristics of an ideal commander are attributed. There is, however, every reason to include him in the list.

A few leaders are represented by Xenophon as conspicuously lacking in the characteristics of his ideal commander. A flagrant case is that of Mnasippus, a Spartan admiral sent with an expeditionary force to attack Corcyra (6.2.4–8, 15–26). When the Corcyreans were on the point of surrender, he discharged some of his mercenaries and withheld the pay of others, though he was said to have suffered from no shortage of funds. The discipline of his troops soon deteriorated, and when some of his officers protested, he lost his temper and struck them. The outcome of his misguided leadership was that he was defeated and killed and that the expedition failed ignominiously. Another Spartan, overwhelmed by disaster because, it is suggested, he scandalously neglected his duties while holding a military command, is Thibron (4.8.17–19); but Xenophon seems to have had a grudge

[18] Xenophon may well have met and questioned Polydamas, cf. M. Sordi, *La lega tessala* (1958), 162–3, who discusses the question of the sources from which his account of Jason may have been derived. On the personality of Jason see Westlake, *Thessaly in the Fourth Century B.C.* (1935), 122–5.

against him and may have presented him unfavourably (cf. 3.1.4–8; 4.8.22) for that reason.[19]

Because this image of an ideal commander evidently had a deep and lasting influence upon Xenophon, the problem of its origin is of considerable importance. At first glance he might seem to have taken Agesilaus, or rather his own conception of Agesilaus, as his model and to have sought in other leaders the characteristics which he admired in Agesilaus. It is, however, at least arguable that the image of an ideal commander was already crystallised in his mind before he wrote about Agesilaus and that it helped to determine his presentation of him. Indeed it is not always easy to reconcile the admirable qualities attributed to Agesilaus with the crude and unimaginative policy of represssion which he undoubtedly pursued, though this question cannot be discussed here. It is preferable, in seeking the prototype of the ideal commander, to look further back to a portrait which Xenophon certainly formed in his own mind before he first came into contact with Agesilaus—the portrait of himself as drawn in the *Anabasis*.[20] He is in fact his own ideal commander. The qualities of this ideal figure are precisely the qualities which he claims in the *Anabasis* to have displayed while holding a military command, as a selection of relevant passages will show. It will also be seen how the limitations of his own experience as a military leader unfitted him to assess the leadership of others.

His care for the wellbeing of his troops and his willingness to share their hardships and dangers are themes mentioned frequently in the *Anabasis*. When the Greeks were struggling to forestall the enemy in occupying the summit of a steep hill, a hoplite complained of having to carry a heavy shield while Xenophon was riding on horseback. Xenophon promptly dismounted and took over the shield, though he was also burdened by the weight of a cavalry breastplate (3.4.47–9). In Armenia he set a salutary example to his troops by his toughness when there had been a heavy fall of snow (4.4.11–12); and he made every effort to help those suffering from exhaustion (4.5.7–9). He claims to have been accessible at all times: all his soldiers

---

[19] Delebecque, op. cit., 134.
[20] Whether he actually wrote the *Anabasis* before or after the parts of the *Hellenica* dealing with Agesilaus is a disputed question which is not relevant here.

knew, he declares, that they need have no hesitation in approaching him, even when he was eating or sleeping, if they had anything of value to tell him (4.3.10). He quotes a remark made about him by a Thracian prince that he was φιλοστρατιώτης to such an extent as to damage his own interests (7.6.4 and 39). The *Anabasis* contains many speeches, most of them by Xenophon. In one of the last of these, when he has become unpopular and is even in danger of being put to death, he dwells upon his unselfish devotion to his troops in the past and argues that it entitles him to better treatment now: 'you used to call me father and promise that you would always remember me as a benefactor' (7.6.35–8). Speeches delivered in the early stages of his command were designed mainly to bolster the morale of the Greeks.[21] He also claims to have shown diplomatic skill, after the worst dangers were past, in conducting negotiations on their behalf.[22] Finally, he credits himself with an inexhaustible capacity for devising military stratagems whereby he extricated them from difficult situations. For example, in two consecutive episodes, shortly before they sighted the Euxine, serious obstacles are shown to have been overcome by means of tactical plans proposed by himself (4.6.7–27 and 7.1–14).

While he undoubtedly exaggerates his own contribution to the achievement of the Ten Thousand, he had good reason to look back with satisfaction to the period during which he found himself so unexpectedly undertaking the responsibilities of military command. It is, however, evident that the leadership demanded of him by the circumstances of his command was of an exceptional kind. The problems confronting the leaders of the Ten Thousand were abnormal, indeed unique; they differed fundamentally from those of conventional Greek warfare. Although there was plenty of hard fighting, it was mainly of an unusual sort against outlandish tribesmen, who in many instances tried to bar the passage of the army at defensible points on mountain passes or river crossings. Often difficult country, severe weather and shortages of food and other commodities were hazards more formidable than enemy attacks. Because the Ten Thousand were a variegated force of mercenaries drawn from a large number of

[21] Cf. 3.2.8–39, where he combines encouragement with practical advice. 6.3.12–14 (17), which belongs to a much later stage, is similar.
[22] Cf. 5.5.13–23, which is a mixture of conciliation and threats.

cities[23] and served together for nearly two years in areas remote from their homes, it was exceptionally important for their officers to win their confidence and loyalty.

It may be that Xenophon and his colleagues, being forced to improvise, showed tactical inventiveness from which valuable lessons could and should have been learned.[24] They were, however, to a very large extent denied the opportunity to prove themselves as strategists; it was impossible for them to show whether they possessed qualities of generalship and statesmanship such as are associated with leaders of the highest class. It was surely to a large degree because the personal experience of Xenophon in military command suffered from these limitations that his criteria in assessing the qualities of others, as seen in the *Hellenica*, are misconceived; that he admires the wrong leaders or admires the right leaders for the wrong reasons. Gifts of intellect and imagination carry little weight; a capacity for strategic planning on a large scale, for creating and directing the military policy of a powerful state, is hardly considered at all. There were a few major figures in the period covered by the *Hellenica* who had some conception of high-level strategy, but they receive scarcely any credit for it, as will be seen below. Xenophon tends to envisage military history from the viewpoint of a battalion commander, and he assesses military leaders by this standard. Gibbon in a celebrated sentence of his *Autobiography* remarks that 'the captain of the Hampshire Grenadiers (the reader may smile) has not been useless to the historian of the Roman empire'. To Xenophon experience of military command was to a large extent a positive handicap.

Two leaders to whom Xenophon does not attribute the characteristics of his ideal commander have very strong claims to be considered the greatest figures in the half century covered by the *Hellenica*. They are Lysander and Epaminondas.[25] The presentation of these two leaders by Xenophon, who does less than justice

[23] H. W. Parke, *Greek Mercenary Soldiers* (1933), 28–9, collects information about the origin of named individuals.

[24] G. T. Griffith, *Mercenaries of the Hellenistic World* (1935), 5.

[25] Breitenbach, op. cit., 89–91, includes in a section entitled 'die richtige strategische Planung' an examination of the measures and motives attributed to Epaminondas during the campaign leading to the battle of Mantinea (cf. op. cit., 120–1). He thus seems to rank Epaminondas as one of the ideal commanders. I disagree with this view because, as pointed out below, the

to the achievements of either, throws further light upon his assessment of individuals and serves to confirm the conclusions drawn from his preoccupation with his image of an ideal commander. His treatment of Epaminondas, which will be examined first, is astonishing and illustrates how unpredictable he can be.

Epaminondas is mentioned for the first time in the *Hellenica* as the leader of an unimportant expedition to Achaea in 366 (7.1.41), when he already had far greater accomplishments to his credit. He had made an outstanding contribution to the rise of Thebes; he had won his crushing victory over the Spartans at Leuctra; he had liberated Messenia and destroyed the long-established Spartan domination of the Peloponnese. These events, except for the liberation of Messenia, are fully described by Xenophon but without any reference to the part played in them by Epaminondas. The reason for this strange suppression of the protagonist is abundantly clear. The successes of Thebes against Sparta were unwelcome to Xenophon, who must have found the evident superiority of Epaminondas to Agesilaus especially painful. There is, however, no evidence whatever that Xenophon was influenced by personal animosity: he treats Pelopidas in a similar way, mentioning him only as the leader of an embassy to the Persian court (7.1.33–40).

His attitude towards Epaminondas undergoes a sudden and remarkable change in the closing pages of the *Hellenica* where he records the fourth and last of the Theban expeditions to the Peloponnese culminating in the battle of Mantinea (7.5.4–25). His narrative gives the impression that his sense of justice has belatedly impelled him to make amends for his refusal hitherto to acknowledge the military genius of Epaminondas. It includes a careful and skilled analysis of the motives underlying the decisions of Epaminondas at each stage of the campaign. This analysis explains why he delayed at Nemea (7.5.6); why he encamped inside the fortifications of Tegea and remained for a time on the defensive (8); why he eventually attempted a surprise attack on Sparta (9);[26] why he chose to deliver this attack at one

Mantinea campaign was on a totally different plane, and demanded different qualities of leadership, from such operations as the raid by Teleutias on the Piraeus (op. cit., 92).

[26] According to Xenophon it was due only $\theta\varepsilon\dot{\iota}\alpha$ $\tau\iota\nu\dot{\iota}$ $\mu o\dot{\iota}\varrho\alpha$ (10) that he did not find the city totally undefended (cf. $\tau\dot{o}$ $\theta\varepsilon\tilde{\iota}o\nu$ in 12).

particular point (11); why he withdrew from Sparta (14); why he decided to fight a pitched battle before leading his army home (18); why at Mantinea he gave the enemy the impression that he had no intention of committing his forces to action immediately (21–2); why in the battle itself he launched a spearhead assault with the strongest part of his army (23); why he massed cavalry and infantry together in a single formation and posted a force on high ground on one wing (24). It is important to observe, because it is unusual in the *Hellenica*, that he is here presented as a leader whose decisions were dependent upon logical reasoning, upon the intelligent use of all available information. The verbs λογίζομαι and νομίζω occur frequently,[27] and he is praised for his πρόνοια (8). In no other passage of the *Hellenica* is so much insight shown into the essence of military leadership at the highest level. Some of the decisions taken by Epaminondas are purely tactical, but Xenophon is not here drawing attention to minor stratagems used to outwit an enemy in unimportant operations, as he often does when writing of Agesilaus (cf. 4.5.3) and other ideal commanders.[28] He is helping his readers to understand the planning and direction of a campaign which, judged by Greek standards, was on a very large scale indeed. Nor is he merely reporting what he has learned from someone closely associated with Epaminondas, since it is most unlikely that he consulted any Thebans about this campaign.[29] He is using his own knowledge of warfare to reconstruct the intellectual processes on which the strategy of Epaminondas was based. It is regrettable that he did not choose to adopt this technique elsewhere.

The presentation of Epaminondas in the *Hellenica* has, apart from the suppression of his earlier achievements, another serious defect. Xenophon nowhere credits him with any qualities other than those of a military leader. He fails to appreciate, or refuses to appreciate, that Epaminondas was also a statesman with enlightened views which were by no means confined to the

[27] Breitenbach, op. cit., 90–1; H. Montgomery, *Gedanke und Tat* (1965), 110–12.

[28] At only one point in the narrative of the Mantinea campaign has the image of the ideal commander left a clear mark, namely where the troops of Epaminondas are stated to have been eager for battle because he had trained them so well (7.5.19–20).

[29] Much of his information may have been derived from his son Diodorus who was serving with the Athenian cavalry (Delebecque, op. cit., 441).

advancement of Theban imperialism and were at times in conflict with it.[30] There are, it is true, modern scholars to whom Epaminondas was a soldier and only a soldier.[31] To this assessment, which I believe to be basically mistaken,[32] the treatment of him in the *Hellenica* has doubtless contributed.

The presentation of Lysander is more characteristic of Xenophon, and therefore even more instructive, than that of Epaminondas. Another reason for examining it is that it belongs to the first three books of the *Hellenica*, where Xenophon is widely believed to be at his best and where the influence of his prejudices is undoubtedly less marked than in other parts of the work. His treatment of Lysander sheds a considerable amount of light upon his qualities as a historian.

It was under the leadership of Lysander that the Spartans achieved the total victory which, contrary to the expectation of most Greeks immediately after the Athenian disaster in Sicily,[33] had eluded them for years. One important reason for their repeated failures to take advantage of Athenian weakness was that their admirals commanding the allied forces in Asia had to undertake responsibilities for which very few Spartan leaders were adequately equipped. Because these *nauarchoi* served only for one year, they had no opportunity to acquire the experience necessary to enable them to discharge their duties competently. They had to direct naval operations on a large scale; they had to organise a coalition of allies; above all, they had to negotiate with the Persians, from whom financial subsidies must be secured if the Peloponnesian fleet was to be maintained in an efficient condition for any length of time. In all these spheres, Lysander, when actually or virtually in command in Asia, was far more successful than any of the other Spartan leaders. Xenophon, though nowhere disparaging his achievements, is evidently reluctant to acknowledge that his outstanding ability turned the scale.

It is true that Lysander was fortunate in his first contacts with the Persians. When he took up his command in Asia, Cyrus, who was genuinely eager to help the Peloponnesians, had arrived at

[30] Cf. N. G. L. Hammond, *History of Greece* (1959), 510.
[31] M. Fortina, *Epaminonda* (1958), 108–13.
[32] Cf. my review of Fortina, op. cit., in *C.R.* x (1960), 160–1.
[33] Thuc. 8.2.1–2; 24.5; cf. 2.65.12.

Sardis and taken over responsibility for relations with them from Tissaphernes, who had pursued a policy of trying to weaken both sides. Xenophon records an anecdote which illustrates the diplomatic skill whereby Lysander obtained from Cyrus an increase in the daily wage of the Peloponnesian crews (1.5.6–7). This anecdote, however, seems to be included mainly because of its dramatic qualities, which are fully exploited. Lysander won and retained the confidence of Cyrus, with whom he established a close friendship (2.1.13–15) with the result that, while he was in Asia, the flow of Persian subsidies was uninterrupted and not ungenerous. For this achievement, which was of immense value to the Peloponnesians, he receives hardly any credit from Xenophon, who devotes far more attention to his antagonistic attitude towards Callicratidas, his successor as *nauarchos* (1.6.1–11). His efforts to create difficulties for Callicratidas may have been wholly the outcome of personal animosity, as Xenophon assumes, but he may well have felt that the boldness of his successor, combined as it was with inexperience in naval leadership and in diplomacy, might prove disastrous to Spartan interests and must be curbed as much as possible.[34] If he held this view, the Peloponnesian defeat at Arginusae abundantly confirmed his misgivings. Xenophon shows warm admiration for Callicratidas, whose forthrightness, chivalry and impatience of subservience to Persia he found far more attractive than the shrewd realism of Lysander. He does, however, acknowledge that the allied cities in Asia requested the Spartans to send out Lysander to take command there because of the high reputation which he had won during his previous term of office (2.1.6). Though debarred by law from serving again as *nauarchos*, he was appointed *epistoleus* and this appointment gave him in practice the powers of supreme commander because the new *nauarchos*, in theory his superior, was a nonentity.

Spartan commanders in Asia were confronted with difficult problems of organisation. They had to try to weld into an effective fighting force a navy composed of contingents drawn from many states and differing widely from one another in technical efficiency. Another problem was to make the best possible

---

[34] D. Lotze, *Lysander und der peloponnesische Krieg* (1964), 24, 26 and 70, who finds some support for this conclusion in the views attributed to the friends of Lysander in 1.6.4.

use of the many Asiatic Greek cities now on the Peloponnesian side, which were often in need of protection and could well prove a liability. It was essential to ensure that as much assistance as possible should be extracted from them in the war against the Athenians.[35] The success of Lysander in these tasks, while actually or virtually responsible for conducting the war in Asia, receives no recognition in the *Hellenica*. Nor is he given much credit for his two major victories in battle, at Notium and Aegospotami, which are to a large extent attributed to the errors of his opponents. At Notium the engagement was precipitated by the foolish bravado of Antiochus, who disobeyed the orders of Alcibiades to take no offensive action; but Lysander evidently took full advantage of the opportunity offered to him (1.5.11–14). Similarly at Aegospotami the Athenian generals were at fault in refusing to recognise the danger of their exposed position despite the warning by Alcibiades. On the other hand, the plan of Lysander, namely to decline battle on four successive days and then to make a surprise attack when many of the Athenian ships were unmanned, was cleverly conceived and effectively executed. It was a stratagem of a kind that appealed to Xenophon, who shows some admiration for it, but his narrative gives the impression that the decisive factor was Athenian incompetence (2.1.20–29). When describing how the Peloponnesians massacred their prisoners after the battle, he does not expressly vindicate or condemn Lysander. He explains that this mass execution was a reprisal for atrocities committed or threatened by the Athenians and that Lysander referred the decision to a meeting of allies; but he also makes clear that Lysander initiated the discussion on the fate of the prisoners and that he personally cross-examined and put to death one of the Athenian generals who had had some captives drowned (2.1.31–2). While the account of this episode may be entirely accurate, its tone is unsympathetic towards Lysander.

During the final months of the war, when Lysander had established a blockade of the Piraeus and was apparently at

---

[35] Plutarch (*Lys.*, 5.5–8) and Diodorus (13.70.4) provide evidence that soon after his arrival in Asia Lysander altered the political structure of many Ionian cities with the object of bringing them under the effective control of his own supporters (cf. H. Schaefer, *Würzb. Jahrb.* iv (1949–50), 301–3). Xenophon does not mention these measures.

Samos,[36] Theramenes came to consult him about peace terms and remained with him for over three months (2.2.16–18). Why this visit lasted so long is not satisfactorily explained by Xenophon or any other authority. Theramenes wished to waste time while starvation made the Athenians more amenable to harsh terms (ibid., 16), but he could not have prolonged his visit without the consent of Lysander. On his return to Athens he reported that Lysander had detained him till then and had eventually told him to go to Sparta because only the ephors had the authority to give him an answer (ibid., 17). Lysander could undoubtedly have made up his mind at once on this constitutional point if he had wished. He must have acted in collusion with his visitor, believing that his own interests would best be served by causing Theramenes to stay away from Athens for a considerable time;[37] both must have wished to give the Athenian oligarchs the opportunity to strengthen their position while the suffering caused by the blockade, for which the democrats were held responsible, became more and more intense. Xenophon, though perhaps handicapped by lack of information from the Spartan side, fails to give Lysander credit for what was surely an astute move.

After the surrender of Athens and later of Samos, Lysander returned home to Sparta with all his spoils and the unspent balance from the funds assigned to him by Cyrus, which amounted to a very large sum. Xenophon mentions that he handed all this treasure over to the state but makes no comment (2.3.8–9). Although he is stated to have established a decarchy at Samos (2.3.7), there is no reference to his policy of imposing this system of government on many cities[38] or to the immense personal authority that it brought him. Readers of the *Hellenica* would not suspect that at this moment he enjoyed a reputation at least as high as that of any other figure in Spartan history or that, as is attested from other sources,[39] many states granted him official honours of a kind never before paid to a living Greek.

The remainder of his career is to some extent an anti-climax.

[36] Lotze, op. cit., 41, who accepts the account of Plutarch (*Lys.*, 14.2).

[37] Lotze, op. cit., 44, is probably right in thinking that Lysander did not disclose to the ephors the presence of Theramenes at his headquarters.

[38] In a much later passage of the *Hellenica* (3.4.2) there is a reference back to the establishment of decarchies by Lysander (cf. 3.5.13).

[39] Lotze, op. cit., 52–8, has collected the evidence.

A widely accepted belief that his power was suddenly overthrown in 403 is not supported by any cogent evidence, and his system of decarchies seems to have been maintained until 397.[40] It was, however, impossible for him, in spite of his immense prestige throughout the Greek world, to maintain the influence on Spartan policy which he had exerted while victory over the Athenians was an overriding consideration. His authority was undermined by the difficulty of winning support from successive boards of ephors and by the jealousy habitually evoked at Sparta by triumphs abroad. During the decade after the fall of Athens there were three episodes, described in the *Hellenica*, in which he played an important part; in two of these, and perhaps also in the third, he was unable to achieve his object as a result of rivalry with one of the Spartan kings. Because his attainments in this period were relatively modest, there is perhaps less reason to criticise Xenophon for failing to do justice to his talents. The tone is largely unchanged: it is the tone of Xenophon when writing about persons or subjects of little interest to him or of little importance in his estimation.

The part played by Lysander in the establishment of the Thirty at Athens, which is known to have been considerable, is virtually ignored in the *Hellenica* (2.3.2–3). Later, when they asked Sparta for a harmost and a mercenary garrison in order to intimidate their opponents, they made their request through Lysander, who secured that it was granted (2.3.13–14). After the democratic rising under Thrasybulus the oligarchs again turned to Lysander for aid; he supported their appeal with enthusiasm and arranged to have himself sent to Athens as harmost with his brother as admiral. Xenophon attributes to him the belief, which proved unfounded, that the democrats at the Piraeus could quickly be reduced by blockade (2.4.28). The prospect that 'he would win glory and also make Athens his personal possession' then aroused the jealousy of his enemy, the king Pausanias, who, supported by a majority of the ephors, was appointed commander of an army sent to Attica. Pausanias took over the direction of operations there and eventually negotiated a settlement whereby the civil war was ended (2.4.29–39). This policy of reconciling opposing factions evidently commended itself to Xenophon, whereas that of Lysander, who wished to keep the oligarchs in

[40] R. E. Smith, *C.P.* xliii (1948), 145–56.

power by crushing the democratic movement, was abhorrent to him and its failure gave him considerable satisfaction.

Some years later Lysander again found his plans thwarted in consequence of a conflict with a Spartan king. After supporting the disputed claims of Agesilaus to the kingship (3.3.3), he persuaded him to offer to lead an expeditionary force to Asia, where the Persians were reported to be making military preparations on a large scale. He believed, according to Xenophon, that the Greeks would prove much superior at sea and was confident about prospects on land because of the safe return of the Ten Thousand from the heart of Asia (3.4.1–2). The first of these predictions was belied by the defeat off Cnidus two years later, but at least he is given the credit of having based his sponsorship of the expedition upon an assessment of strategic factors. Xenophon adds, however, another reason, which is more personal and less creditable, why Lysander was eager to accompany Agesilaus: he wished to secure the re-establishment of his decarchies in Asiatic cities, which the ephors had recently abolished (3.4.2). The intention of directing the campaign in Asia himself and using Agesilaus as a puppet is not expressly ascribed to him, but the narrative at least suggests the possibility that such was his aim. He can hardly have failed to foresee what happened when the expeditionary force was at Ephesus, namely that the Asiatic Greeks, to whom he was well known, paid court to him to such an extent that he appeared to be king and Agesilaus a private individual (3.4.7). While the Spartiates accompanying the expedition loudly denounced what they held to be an illegal act of usurpation, Agesilaus made no comment but rejected all petitions submitted to him by protégés of Lysander. Though protesting at this humiliation, Lysander chose to express the view that the conduct of Agesilaus was more reasonable than his own. He asked to be entrusted with duties elsewhere and was sent to the Hellespont (3.4.8–10).

This clash between leading personalities offers opportunities for dramatic presentation of which Xenophon takes full advantage, and his account illustrates his skill in writing dialogue. He does not, however, give any clear indication of his own views on the behaviour of the two leaders, and the reason may be that he felt some embarrassment because Agesilaus exposed himself to charges of ingratitude towards a friend to whom he was deeply indebted.[41] On the other hand, there is some implied admiration for the astuteness and firmness with which Agesilaus frustrated a threat to his legitimate authority while avoiding an open conflict. Less interest is shown in the part played by Lysander. He seems to have behaved with dignity and restraint, but he had no alternative; he must have realised that he had misjudged Agesilaus and that he had no constitutional means of challenging the authority of a king. Xenophon fails entirely to appreciate one aspect of the episode: if Lysander had become virtually commander-in-chief, the planning and direction of the campaign in Asia would undoubtedly have been more imaginative and probably more effective.[42]

Xenophon gives a perfunctory and unusually colourless account of the episode in which Lysander lost his life. His narrative describing the similar circumstances leading to the death of Teleutias at Olynthus some years later is much livelier, and he adds a comment of his own, as has already been noted.[43] At the outbreak of the Corinthian war the Spartans planned to crush the Thebans by a two-pronged invasion of Boeotia. Lysander was sent to mobilise contingents from Phocis and other northern allies and to march them to Haliartus, where Pausanias, advancing from the south with a Peloponnesian army, was to arrive on the same day (3.5.6). On reaching the vicinity of Haliartus Lysander was not content to wait inactive for the Peloponnesians under Pausanias, who had not yet appeared; he approached the walls and tried to persuade the Haliartians to revolt from Thebes. When this move was foiled, he launched an assault upon the fortifications, but his troops were attacked by a Theban force hastening to the rescue, and he was himself among the killed (3.5.17–19).

In his account of this engagement Xenophon expresses uncer-

[41] Breitenbach, op. cit., 40, points out that Xenophon omits the episode in his encomiastic *Agesilaus*.

[42] Plutarch, who seems to be mainly dependent on the *Hellenica* for his knowledge of this episode, judges it, as is his custom, from the viewpoint of a moralist. In the *Lysander* (23.7) he censures Agesilaus for having treated a benefactor so harshly, though acknowledging that he was justified in refusing to be virtually ousted from the position of supreme commander; in the *Agesilaus* (8.5–7, cf. 7.4) he attributes the breach between the two leaders to excessive ambition on the part of both.

[43] See above, p. 209.

tainty whether Lysander was taken by surprise by the Theban attack or whether he expected it but stood his ground believing that he could resist it successfully (3.5.19). It is made clear that in either case his judgement was at fault. There are, however, two other questions of greater importance to which Xenophon makes no specific reference. In the first place, why did Lysander not await the arrival of the Peloponnesian army, which would undoubtedly have improved Spartan prospects of winning Haliartus either by intimidation or by force? The narrative seems to suggest that he was eager to restore his somewhat tarnished reputation by gaining a striking personal success and to prevent any credit going to his enemy Pausanias,[44] who was to assume command of both invading armies after they met at Haliartus (3.5.6). The second question is whether Lysander arrived too early or Pausanias too late. According to Xenophon one of the charges against Pausanias when later impeached *in absentia* was that 'he arrived at Haliartus later than Lysander after having agreed to arrive on the same day' (3.5.25). This accusation presupposes that Lysander arrived on the agreed day, but Xenophon seems to imply that Pausanias, whom he presents favourably elsewhere, may have been unjustly condemned. At all events, Lysander is not expressly exonerated from the charge of having arrived too early, though Xenophon very probably possessed enough evidence to have absolved him if he had so wished.[45] This omission is typical of his attitude towards Lysander.

There is abundant evidence that the personality of Lysander was unattractive, even for a Spartan. In this respect he had more in common with Gylippus than with Brasidas. Nor was he

[44] E. Meyer, *G.d.A.* v⁴ (1958), 227, is surely right in concluding that such was his motive. S. Accame, *Ricerche intorno alla guerra corinzia* (1951), 34–6, suggests a totally different interpretation, namely that the account of Xenophon is prejudiced in favour of Lysander and shields him against charges of rashness at Haliartus. This view seems to me to be mistaken; that it could be held at all indicates negligence on the part of Xenophon in failing to give his readers adequate guidance.

[45] Plutarch states that a message from Lysander to Pausanias was intercepted by the enemy (*Lys.*, 28.3–4) and that Lysander at first decided to wait for Pausanias before approaching Haliartus but later changed his mind (ibid., 6). These statements, neither of them palpably untrustworthy, suggest that, according to the version followed by Plutarch, it would be unfair to Lysander to accuse him of a rash attempt to win credit for himself before his rival appeared.

conspicuous for the simple honesty and dedicated loyalty to the state which the Spartan way of life was designed to engender. Although Theopompus praises him for having resisted the snares of self-indulgence to which so many powerful men became victims,[46] he acquired a reputation for arrogance, oppressiveness, unscrupulousness, and duplicity. He was also believed to have on several occasions pursued his own interests in preference to those of Sparta. Plutarch liked to find more virtues than vices in the great men whose biographies he wrote, especially if they were Greeks; but his *Lysander*, which is based on a wide variety of sources, is unusually critical and gives a largely unfavourable picture. Although Lysander is preferred to Sulla (they are paired in the *Parallel Lives*), some very disparaging phrases are used of him.[47] Nevertheless, if he lacked personal charm and if his policy of oppressive imperialism may have proved short-sighted and ill-advised, there is no shadow of doubt that he was a man of outstanding ability. He was the Spartan counterpart of Themistocles; but, while Themistocles was exposed to the fickleness of the Athenian populace, he had to contend with the far greater obstacles confronting any Spartan leader—especially if he were not a king—who was sufficiently enterprising and original to reject the inhibiting, parochial outlook fostered by Spartan institutions. Although he never entirely overcame these obstacles, he was certainly more successful in this respect than Pausanias (the victor of Plataea), whose character and ambitions have some affinities with his, and probably more successful than any other leader throughout Spartan history. Why then does the *Hellenica* fail to convey a more positive impression of his quality?

The personal prejudices of Xenophon, which are so marked in the middle and latter parts of the *Hellenica*, have also had some influence upon the opening books. They have doubtless contributed to some extent to his presentation of Lysander. He could not bring himself to take an entirely objective view of a man who had lent wholehearted support to the Thirty at Athens, who had

[46] *F. Gr. Hist.* 115 F 20 (cf. F 333). It would, however, be hazardous to infer from this fragment, which is mainly concerned with qualities shown in private life, that Theopompus must have drawn a wholly favourable picture of Lysander.

[47] Among the most striking are: πανοῦργος καὶ σοφιστής (7.5), ὑπεροψία καὶ βαρύτης (19.2), τῷ λόγῳ θρασὺς καὶ καταπληκτικός (22.1), χαλεπὸς ὢν ὀργήν (28.1).

tried to undermine the authority of the Spartan dual kingship,[48] and who, most important of all, had become estranged from Agesilaus. It is not, however, primarily his prejudices that cause his portrait of Lysander to be so inadequate; indeed he makes some effort to curb them. Its inadequacy is due in a far greater degree to a defect to which much attention has already been given: he fails to draw a distinction between the competent, popular, mediocre leader and the great man capable of making a deep impact upon the course of history, because his own sympathies lie with the former. His treatment of Alcibiades, against whom he had no reason whatever to be prejudiced, is very similar. Except for one passage looking back to earlier stages in the career of Alcibiades outside the period covered in the *Hellenica* (1.4.13–17), it betrays the same failure to recognise ability of outstanding quality. It is relevant to recall the familiar phrases used by Thucydides of some leading figures in his *History*: κράτιστος δὴ αὐτοσχεδιάζειν τὰ δέοντα of Themistocles (1.138.3); ἐγνώσθη ἡ πρόνοια αὐτοῦ ἡ ἐς τὸν πόλεμον of Pericles (2.65.6); ἐς τἆλλα ξύνεσιν οὐδενὸς λειπόμενος of Hermocrates (6.72.2); ἀρετῇ τε οὐδενὸς ὕστερος καὶ κράτιστος ἐνθυμηθῆναι γενόμενος καὶ ἃ γνοίη εἰπεῖν of Antiphon (8.68.1). Although Thucydides perhaps overrated the importance of intellectual qualities in statesmen and generals, he fully understood the essence of greatness. Xenophon did not.[49]

[48] Xenophon does not refer to this, but he must have been aware of it.

[49] I am much indebted to Mr D. M. Leahy for help and advice while I have been preparing this paper for publication.

14

The Sicilian books of
Theopompus' *Philippica*

Although acknowledged in antiquity to be the most important
work on the history of Greece and Macedonia during the reign
of Philip, the *Philippica* of Theopompus seems to have had less
influence upon the literary tradition than it deserved. Its vast
length evidently daunted all but the most painstaking of re-
searchers: Diodorus, for example, though the *Philippica* was
known to him, certainly did not base upon it the chapters of his
Book 16 dealing with Greece and Macedonia. Its many digressions, however, being of more manageable dimensions, were
extensively used by historians, biographers, moralists and all
manner of learned compilers, especially those whose interests lay
mainly in personalities. The digression on Athenian politicians
included in Book 10 of the *Philippica* was more widely studied
than any other, but the account of Sicilian history under the
Dionysii seems also to have received some attention despite strong
competition from the Platonic tradition and the well-known
work of Timaeus. The aim of this essay is to investigate the scope
of the Sicilian digression, its central theme, its attitude towards
the principal characters of the period, and its influence upon the
surviving records of Sicilian history. The difficulties involved in
trying to reconstruct this part of the *Philippica* are considerable,
the greatest obstacle being the loss of all major authorities for
Sicilian history written before the first century B.C. with the
exception of the Platonic *Epistles*.

I. CONTENT OF THE SICILIAN BOOKS

The limits and subject-matter of the Sicilian digression are defined by Diodorus in the following bibliographical note:

τῶν δὲ συγγραφέων Θεόπομπος ὁ Χῖος ἐν τῇ τῶν Φιλιππικῶν ἱστορίᾳ
κατέταξε τρεῖς βύβλους περιεχούσας Σικελικὰς πράξεις. ἀρξάμενος δὲ
ἀπὸ τῆς Διονυσίου τοῦ πρεσβυτέρου τυραννίδος διῆλθε χρόνον ἐτῶν
πεντήκοντα καὶ κατέστρεψεν εἰς τὴν ἔκπτωσιν Διονυσίου τοῦ νεωτέρου.

226

THE SICILIAN BOOKS OF THEOPOMPUS' 'PHILIPPICA'

εἰσὶ δὲ αἱ βύβλοι τρεῖς, ἀπὸ τῆς μιᾶς τεσσαρακοστῆς ἄχρι τῆς τρίτης καὶ τεσσαρακοστῆς.[1]

Every numeral in this passage has been suspected, and one at least (τῆς μιᾶς τεσσαρακοστῆς) is demonstrably false. The digression began at Book 39 and not at Book 41, for no less than eight fragments dealing with Sicilian history are expressly stated to have been derived from Books 39 and 40,[2] and while book-numbers are often suspect, textual corruption can scarcely have occurred in all eight instances, or even in a majority of them. Beloch seeks to absolve Diodorus from error by inserting δεούσης between μιᾶς and τεσσαρακοστῆς and reading πέντε for τρεῖς at the beginning and end of the note.[3] He thus postulates a Sicilian digression of five books, namely 39 to 43. It is, however, most improbable that all these five books were devoted to Sicilian history. Whereas most of the fragments certainly derived from Book 43 are concerned with the western Mediterranean (F 199–204), none refers to Sicily, so that in this book, and perhaps in the preceding one also, Theopompus has evidently turned to a survey of other western lands.[4] The difficulties normally encountered in

[1] 16.71.3. Schwartz, R.E. v. coll. 669 and 687, and Beloch, Gr. Gesch. iii[2]. 2.22, believe that Diodorus derived it from his chronological source, but Hammond, C.Q. xxxii (1938), 142, is probably right in maintaining that, because it differs from other bibliographical notes in defining only part of a historical work and not the whole, Diodorus composed it himself from his own knowledge of the Philippica. His chronographical source is thoroughly reliable (Jacoby, F. Gr. Hist. ii. C., 28), but in undertaking a task normally performed for him he may well have made mistakes.
[2] F 185, 188–90, 192–4, 196 (from Athenaeus or Steph. Byz.). Fragments (F) and testimonia (T) are throughout this paper cited from Jacoby, F. Gr. Hist. 115 (ii B, 526–617).
[3] Gr. Gesch. loc. cit.
[4] Jacoby, ii D, 383. The content of Book 42 is virtually unknown, though there is a possibility that it contained material on Sicily. The only two fragments assigned to it are brief notes by Steph. Byz. (F 197–8). In the former the book-number is probably corrupt: the words ἔστι καὶ πόλις Σικελίας are a supplement not derived from Theopompus and are rightly excluded by Grenfell and Hunt (Hellenica Oxyrhynchia cum Theopompi et Cratippi fragmentis) fr. 191. F 198 refers to a Sican town: the Sicans were politically almost negligible in the fourth century, and the reference to this town (as well as F 371) may have occurred in an ethnographical description of Spain (cf. F 199–201), whence the Sicans were alleged to have migrated to Sicily (Thuc. 6.2.2). F 234, a note on a place situated on the Adriatic, may possibly belong to Book 42 (cf. crit. not.). As will be shown below, Theopompus reached the first

227

attempting to reconstruct a lost work are here aggravated by the fact that the *Philippica* was not at all systematically arranged. Theopompus was apparently guided by the dictates of his own whim in passing from one topic to another. Unlike Ephorus, he did not attempt to forge each book into an independent unit,[5] and the *Philippica* would seem, so far as can be judged from the fragments, to have been cut up into books by some mechanical process bearing little relation to the natural divisions of the subject-matter. The opening of Book 39 apparently dealt with Macedonian operations in Epirus (F 183); Theopompus then interrupted his account of this campaign in order to write about Sicily and the west and returned to it at the end of Book 43 (F 206–7). Thus the entire digression on the western Greeks must have occupied rather less than five books and was probably arranged as follows: most of 39 together with the whole of 40 and 41 and some part of 42 were concerned with Sicily, the remainder of 42 and most of 43 with other western lands. If this reconstruction be accepted, Diodorus is not necessarily mistaken, indeed he is substantially right, in stating that three books were devoted to Sicilian history. He is, however, wrong in assigning Books 41–43 to Sicily, and his error may well have arisen from having confused the whole digression, which ended in Book 43, with the Sicilian section of it, which consisted of three books.[6]

A further problem is created by the statement in the bibliographical note that Theopompus 'after beginning from the tyranny of the elder Dionysius, covered a period of fifty years and ended with the expulsion of the younger Dionysius'. Since Dionysius I established his tyranny not later than 405/4, the period between his accession and the expulsion of his son by Timoleon,[7] which took place in 343/2,[8] amounts to more than

---

expulsion of the younger Dionysius before the end of Book 40, and it is not very probable that he devoted more than two books to the period between the first expulsion and the second.

[5] Jacoby ii D, 358–9.

[6] The elaborate explanation of Laqueur, *R.E.* v A col. 2217, is based upon very insecure foundations.

[7] Jacoby ii D, 383 points out that Diodorus cannot be referring to the expulsion of Dionysius II by Dion. At least two fragments almost certainly belonging to the Sicilian digression (F 186–7) are concerned with the period that followed the death of Dion.

[8] Diod. 16.70.1.

sixty years. Hence it is necessary to conclude either that Theopompus began his digression at a point later than the accession of Dionysius I or that Diodorus is mistaken in believing the digression to have covered a period of fifty years.[9] Beloch defends the accuracy of Diodorus by maintaining that Theopompus had included Sicilian history in his *Hellenica,* which ended with the battle of Cnidus (394), and therefore began his Sicilian narrative in the *Philippica* at the year 393; the digression thus covered a period of fifty years from 393 to 343.[10] This ingenious explanation is not at all convincing. It is impossible to prove that the *Hellenica* did not include Sicilian history; very few fragments survive, and the absence of any references to events in Sicily could be fortuitous. The term *Hellenica* is a wide one,[11] and indeed it would be more natural to find Sicilian history included in a work entitled *Hellenica* than in a work entitled *Philippica,* though in practice histories covering Sicily as well as the Greek homeland seem normally to have borne the title ἱστορίαι.[12] On the other hand, there is absolutely no evidence that Theopompus devoted any part of the *Hellenica* to events in Sicily. Thucydides, whose work Theopompus was continuing in his *Hellenica,* dealt with the history of Sicily only where it impinged upon that of Greece, while the *Hellenica* of Xenophon, an earlier continuation of Thucydides, excludes Sicilian affairs, apart from a few notes which are undoubtedly spurious. Theopompus did not necessarily limit the scope of his subject-matter in conformity with the practice of his predecessors, but it is quite illegitimate to infer, as Beloch does,[13] that the greater scale of his work in comparison with those of Thucydides and Xenophon is due to the inclusion of Sicilian history. The difference of scale undoubtedly owes its origin to the

[9] It is conceivable that the numeral may be corrupt, but no easy emendation suggests itself.

[10] Op. cit. iii. 2, 11 and 21–2.

[11] It is discussed by Jacoby, *Atthis,* 129 with n. 4 (on p. 321).

[12] Cf. the list of titles in Jacoby, *F. Gr. Hist.* ii A, 1–2 (though ἱστορίαι did not necessarily include Sicilian history). Of the better known historians Ephorus, Diyllus and probably Duris wrote ἱστορίαι of which a substantial proportion was devoted to Sicily, while Callisthenes and Anaximenes wrote *Hellenica* from which Sicilian affairs were apparently excluded.

[13] Op cit., 3.2.11, where he points out that Theopompus covered on average only one-and-a-half years in each book of the *Hellenica,* whereas the corresponding figures for Thucydides and Xenophon are three and seven respectively.

tendency of Theopompus to embark upon lengthy discussions on all manner of subjects normally excluded by Thucydides.[14] The history of Greece and the Aegean from 411 to 394 was so packed with important events and interesting personalities that a writer so prolix as Theopompus could well have devoted twelve books to it without dealing with the scarcely less crowded history of Sicily in this period.[15] It may also be observed that the explanation proposed by Beloch in fact produces a digression of more than fifty years, namely from 394/3, the year after the battle of Cnidus, to 343/2, when Dionysius II fell.[16] Finally, the most natural interpretation of the phrase ἀπὸ τῆς Διονυσίου τοῦ πρεσβυτέρου τυραννίδος is surely 'from the *beginning* of the tyranny of the elder Dionysius'; if any other meaning had been intended, further definition would have been essential.

The figure of fifty years assigned by Diodorus to the Sicilian digression could be the result of an error in arithmetic. It is, however, more likely to have originated from a confusion between the first expulsion of Dionysius II by Dion and the second expulsion by Timoleon. In his account of the former event Diodorus notes that the tyranny of the Dionysii had lasted for fifty years,[17] a figure that is consistent with his own date (406/5)[18]

[14] Of this feature there is abundant evidence in the fragments as well as in Dion. Hal. *ad Pomp.* 6 (= T 20). The best known example is afforded by the penetrating scrutiny to which Theopompus subjected his leading characters (aptly compared by Dion. Hal. to the examination undergone by the souls of the dead before the judges of the underworld).

[15] The main theme of the *Hellenica* was evidently the attempt made by the Spartans, whom Theopompus greatly admired, to dominate the Greek world (Meyer, *Theopomps Hellenika*, 143; Momigliano, *Riv. Fil.*, 9 (1931), 236–42).

[16] Hammond, op. cit., 142–3, who also believes that the *Hellenica* included material about Sicily, is here more accurate than Beloch, though I do not find his arguments convincing. He maintains that the account of Sicilian history in the *Philippica* began with the year 392/1 (namely, from the conclusion of peace with Carthage, which marks a new phase in the tyranny of Dionysius I) and thus covered a period of exactly fifty years. This view presupposes that if Theopompus linked his two accounts of Sicily he must have continued his Sicilian narrative in the *Hellenica* beyond the point (395/4) at which he terminated his account of Greece, but an overlap of this kind is not impossible, for the *Hellenica* certainly did not conform to the Thucydidean system of διαίρεσις (Bloch, *Harv. Stud.*, *Suppl. Vol.* i (1940), 312–13; Jacoby, *C.Q.* xliv (1950), 3 with n. 4).

[17] Diod. 16.11.2, cf. Plut. *Dion* 28.4.

[18] Jacoby ii D, 383.

for the accession of Dionysius I. Diodorus may have had this figure in mind when he wrote his bibliographical note and have forgotten that it refers to uninterrupted tyranny only and not to the entire period from the accession of Dionysius I to the final abdication of Dionysius II.

While Theopompus probably included in his Sicilian narrative the whole period of the Syracusan tyranny from its foundation, there are strong reasons for believing that he devoted a far smaller proportion of his digression to the career of Dionysius I than to that of Dionysius II. None of the fragments quoted by ancient authors from Books 39 to 42 of the *Philippica* and none of those assigned to these books with some degree of confidence by modern scholars[19] contains any reference to Dionysius I, except as the father of Hipparinus and Nysaeus, or to the events of his tyranny. It is true that only about twenty fragments certainly or probably belonging to the books dealing with Sicily have been preserved, and some are brief and uninformative notes on place-names bearing no indication of date. Nevertheless, the fortunes of Dionysius II and other descendants of Dionysius I are well represented, and while the preservation of these fragments may be attributable in some degree to the zest of Athenaeus for passages in which Theopompus castigated disreputable characters, not all are concerned with licentiousness. Dionysius I did not share the grosser vices of his family,[20] but he had other unpleasant qualities that might, and indeed did in another book of the *Philippica*,[21] evoke the strictures of Theopompus, who abhorred most tyrants and all upstarts.[22] The tyranny of Dionysius I, which lasted some thirty-eight years, occupied more than three-fifths of the period probably covered by the Sicilian digression, and if Theopompus had written a detailed account of it, the absence of any reference by ancient authors to this account, though it could be a coincidence, would at least be somewhat surprising.[23]

[19] Jacoby ii B, 575 gives a list of these, adding a question mark where there is any doubt.

[20] McKinlay, *T.A.P.A.* lxx (1939), 51–61, shows that there is no reliable evidence of intemperance on the part of Dionysius I, except perhaps in the last days of his life, whereas evidence of his temperance is abundant.

[21] F 134, which is discussed below.

[22] v. Fritz, *Amer. Hist. Rev.* xlvi (1941), 776–7 (cf. 781); Murray, *Greek Studies*, 160–1.

[23] Diodorus himself might well have used it. In his long accounts of Sicilian

GREEK HISTORIANS AND GREEK HISTORY

More positive evidence that the Sicilian digression was mainly concerned with the period after the death of Dionysius I is provided by fragments of Books 39 and 40. Theopompus seems to have reached the accession of Dionysius II and the opening years of his tyranny in Book 39, for the intemperance of Apollocrates, the eldest son of Dionysius II, and his estrangement from his father were mentioned in this book (F 185). Dionysius II was born not earlier than 398,[24] so that his son cannot have been of an age to indulge in drunkenness and family quarrels until several years after the death of Dionysius I. Hipparinus and Nysaeus, who were considerably younger than their half-brother Dionysius II, may also have been mentioned in Book 39 (F 186–187),[25] while events that took place after the withdrawal of Dionysius to Locri were described in Book 40 (F 192, 194). This evidence shows that the period of rather more than ten years from the accession of Dionysius II to his first expulsion from Syracuse was covered partly in Book 39 and partly in Book 40.

Further light is thrown upon the content of the Sicilian digression by the only fragment in which Theopompus expresses his opinion of Dionysius I, who is censured for encouraging vice in others (F 134). The significance of this fragment lies in the fact that it is derived from Book 21 and not from the Sicilian books. The numeral is above suspicion, because Book 21 contained an ethnographical account of the countries on both sides of the Adriatic (F 128–32), where Dionysius founded colonies (F 128 c); mention of these colonies gave Theopompus the opportunity to criticise Dionysius and apparently even to indulge in moral reflections on other tyrants, including Peisistratus.[26] That Theopompus

affairs contained in Books 13 and 14 he cites Ephorus and Timaeus several times, but Theopompus never. He was undoubtedly acquainted with the Sicilian digression in the *Philippica* and, though capricious in his selection of sources, *could* at least have referred to it on points where he notes a disagreement between Ephorus and Timaeus (cf. 13.80.5; 14.54.5–6) if it had contained a detailed account of the career of Dionysius I.

[24] Diod. 14.44.6–7.
[25] F 185 on Apollocrates is quoted by Athenaeus from Book 39, but F 186–7 on Hipparinus and Nysaeus, though they occur in the same passage of Athenaeus, may belong to a later book: the tyranny of Nysaeus (F 187) can hardly have been reached in Book 39. Nysaeus and Apollocrates (the latter incorrectly described as the son of Dionysius I) were also mentioned in Books 40 and 41 (F 188).
[26] F 135–6, cf. Jacoby ii D, 378–9.

should have described the Adriatic enterprises of Dionysius, apparently in some detail, in Book 21, and even commented on his character, is indeed remarkable if a full account of his tyranny was to be included in the Sicilian digression. Some alteration in the plan of the *Philippica* may have taken place after Book 21 was completed and before Book 39 was begun, but it is noteworthy that Athenaeus, the source of F 134, quotes an attack on Dionysius I from Book 21 and none from the Sicilian books, though he, or the author of the anthology from which he may have drawn his excerpts,[27] was well-acquainted with Books 39–41, as is proved by a number of fragments (F 185–8, 192–3).

It would be idle to maintain that Theopompus cannot have dealt fully with the tyranny of Dionysius I because it lay wholly outside the reign of Philip, which was the central theme of the *Philippica*. Theopompus was inclined to stray beyond the limits of his subject and his period, and he began the first of his two digressions on eastern lands as far back as the reign of Evagoras (F 103–124). On the other hand, the position of the digression on Sicily and the western Mediterranean in the structure of the *Philippica* is significant. As has already been stated, it interrupts an account of Macedonian operations in Epirus, which belong to 343/2,[28] and this is the year in which Dionysius II was finally expelled from Sicily and sent to live in exile at Corinth. The chronological setting of the Sicilian digression suggests that it was written principally to explain the fall of the Syracusan tyrant-house.

All these considerations point to the conclusion that, while Book 39 contained a few pages dealing with Dionysius I, perhaps designed to illustrate the magnitude of the inheritance bequeathed to his son, it can scarcely have included a detailed treatment of his long and eventful career; these pages were only an introductory sketch prefixed to a much fuller narrative of the period beginning with the accession of Dionysius II.[29] If this

[27] The passage in Athenaeus 10.435 d–436 b, which includes F 185–8 and 283 a, is apparently derived from a learned catalogue of φιλόποται used also by Aelian *V.H.* 2.41.

[28] Beloch, op. cit. iii. 2, 291–2, correcting Diod. 16.72.1 (cf. Jacoby ii D, 385).

[29] Some further support for this conclusion may be found in the treatment of Dionysius I by Justin in epitomising the *Historiae Philippicae* of Trogus, whose sources very probably included the *Philippica* of Theopompus. Although

view be accepted, the phrase ἀπὸ τῆς Διονυσίου τοῦ πρεσβυτέρου τυραννίδος in the biographical note of Diodorus, while it creates a misleading impression,[30] is not actually erroneous.

II. RIVAL TRADITIONS ON DIONYSIUS II, DION AND TIMOLEON

To modern scholars the history of Sicily in the middle of the fourth century is dominated by the liberators, Dion and Timoleon, rather than by the tyrant Dionysius II. This conception of Sicilian history is attributable in some degree to the influence of Plutarch, whose *Dion* and *Timoleon* are among the most brilliant of his *Lives,* but its origin may be traced much further back in the works of contemporary writers who were partisans or admirers of both liberators. Although Plato tries to be fair to Dionysius II and is not blind to the faults of Dion,[31] his deep affection for the latter has undoubtedly coloured his tributes to him in the *Seventh* and *Eighth Epistles.* The Academy, which lent its wholehearted support to the attempt to expel Dionysius, naturally set Dion in the centre of the stage, and one of its members, Timonides of Leucas, who took part in the expedition, wrote an account of his experiences in which personal feelings almost certainly influenced his judgement.[32] The career of Dion, the practical Platonist, evoked the sympathetic interest of many philosophers and historians. Timaeus, whose work, though severely criticised by many ancient writers, established itself as the standard history of Sicily, must have included

---

it would be hazardous to assume that Justin has epitomised the work of Trogus faithfully or intelligently, the career of Dionysius in its earlier stages seems to have been treated as subordinate to Carthaginian history (Justin 19, cf. Trogus *Prol.* 19), in its later stages as subordinate to Italian history (Justin 20, which may owe much to the account of the Adriatic in Book 21 of the *Philippica*; Trogus *Prol.* 20, however, lays rather more emphasis on Dionysius). Far more interest is shown by Justin in the character and private life of Dionysius II (cf. below, p. 240).

[30] There is an equally misleading statement in the bibliographical note on Herodotus (Diod. 11.37.6), who is said to have begun his history at a point before the Trojan war. This statement is true (Hdt. 1.1–2), but if the work had not survived, readers of the bibliographical note would have been justified in assuming that he gave a full account of the Trojan war and the Dark Ages.

[31] Cf. *Ep.* 4.321 b–c.

[32] This account undoubtedly underlies the *Dion* of Plutarch, though he is unlikely to have used it directly.

a long account of the first liberation of Syracuse and its sequel, but his opinion of Dion is not determinable,[33] and the extent of his influence on the *Dion* of Plutarch and the *Dion* of Nepos is problematical. On the other hand, his attitude towards Timoleon is well-attested: his extravagant eulogy drew upon him the violent, and perhaps somewhat unfair, censure of Polybius.[34] The *Timoleon* of Plutarch and the *Timoleon* of Nepos are ultimately based upon the work of Timaeus and to a large extent reproduce his point of view.[35]

There are, however, unmistakable traces of a rival tradition in which the achievements of the two liberators were subordinated to the fortunes of the tyrant-house. The earliest representative of this tradition is Theopompus, who must have been its creator. This conclusion is supported by the fragments of the *Philippica* dealing with Sicily and by the fact that he chose to end his Sicilian digression with the final eclipse of Dionysius II, thereby excluding the later and greater achievements of Timoleon. It is also consistent with such indications of his political prejudices, his general outlook and his conception of historiography as may be assembled by examining all the fragments of his works.[36] In his eyes the decline and fall of the Syracusan tyrant-house through the moral degeneracy of its members seems to have been the central and most interesting theme of Sicilian history in the middle of the fourth century. He was provided with an opportunity for minute dissection of character[37] and for development of a favourite motif by illustrating the disastrous consequences of

---

[33] Clasen, *Timaios von Tauromenion*, 70–1, believes that Timaeus treated Dion with judicious impartiality, and Morrow, *Studies in the Platonic Epistles*, 40, maintains that 'the rapid conversion of Dion from the hero to the villain of the tale' in the *Dion* of Nepos reflects a similar change in the work of Timaeus. There is, however, no clear evidence on this question.

[34] This subject is discussed in my *Timoleon and his relations with tyrants*, 5–7.

[35] Westlake, *C.Q.* 32 (1938), 65–74. No fragments survive from the works of Arrian on Dion and Timoleon. It is not certain that these were biographies, but they must have belonged to the tradition dominated by the careers of the two liberators (*F. Gr. Hist.* 156 T 4 a, ii B, 838).

[36] A careful and discerning study of the evidence has been made by v. Fritz, op. cit., 765–87, who gives reasons for modifying the conclusions of Momigliano, op. cit., 230–42 and 335–53. Cf. also Laqueur, *R. E.* vA. coll. 2176–2223, and Murray, op. cit., 149–70. Theopompus seems to have resembled Tacitus, though his methods were much less subtle.

[37] Cf. Dion. Hal. *ad Pomp.* 6 (= T 20.7–8).

luxury and licentiousness. The descendants of Dionysius I possessed none of the qualities that he admired and most of the qualities that he detested.[38] They were neither aristocrats nor conservatives; they based their power upon violence and the support of the masses; they were incapable of preserving order; most important of all, they were notorious for the practice of vices traditionally associated with tyranny. The weakness of their characters and its influence upon their exercise of power are also likely to have been underlined; unlike Philip and his Macedonians, they were unable to prevent their self-indulgence from impairing their effectiveness as rulers.[39]

Neither Dion nor Timoleon is mentioned by name in any fragment of Theopompus, and there is no direct evidence to show how fully or how sympathetically he dealt with either liberator.[40] At first sight it might appear that the achievements and character of Dion were such as might well have won the approval of Theopompus:[41] he overthrew a tyranny, favoured an oligarchical system of government,[42] and was a bitter opponent, both in theory and practice, of extreme democracy, while his private life was austere and free from the vices characteristic of tyrant-houses. In the last year of his life, however, Dion acted so arbitrarily that he alienated even his own oligarchical supporters,

---

[38] These are discussed by v. Fritz, op. cit., 774-6.

[39] Theopompus is doubtless guilty of exaggeration. The rival tradition took a more indulgent view at least of Dionysius II. Plato never wholly lost confidence in him (cf. *Ep.* 8.356 a–b), and some trace of sympathy for him may be observed in the *Dion* of Plutarch (cf. 9.2).

[40] F 331, where Plutarch (*Dion* 24) gives a long list of portents said to have occurred when Dion sailed to attack Dionysius, ends with the words ταῦτα μὲν οὖν Θεόπομπος ἱστόρηκε. Plutarch does not state how much of this catalogue is derived from Theopompus. Jacoby (ii D, 396) is content to express uncertainty on this point, but the implied view of Grenfell and Hunt (fr. 302), who print only the latter half of the chapter, and Ziegler (in the Teubner text), who begins a new paragraph at 24.5, is surely correct: only the portents observed in Sicily, which foretold the fall of Dionysius, and not those appearing to Dion on his voyage, were derived from Theopompus. The opening words of 24.5 (λέγεται δὲ καί) suggest a change of source, and the references in 24.2–4 to Miltas the seer, who was a member of the Academy (22.6), may well originate from the Platonist Timonides. Hence this passage gives no indication of the scale on which Theopompus treated the expedition of Dion. (See now Porter's note on Plut. *Dion* 3.4).

[41] Cf. v. Fritz, op. cit., 774-5.

[42] Plut. *Dion* 53.3-4.

and he is pictured in the biography of Nepos as almost a tyrant.[43] It is probable that this hostile account originates from the work of Athanis, the contemporary Syracusan historian, who was a partisan of Heracleides, the democratic opponent of Dion. It is, however, in a fragment of Theopompus that the political associations of Athanis are recorded,[44] and if, as seems likely, this information is derived from Athanis himself, Theopompus was acquainted with his account of the struggle at Syracuse and may well have followed him in condemning the despotism of Dion. The corrupting influence of absolute power is a subject on which Theopompus is likely to have dealt with considerable relish.[45]

A more cogent reason for believing that Theopompus felt little sympathy for Dion may be found in one of the best-attested of his antipathies. There is abundant evidence that Theopompus detested Plato and Platonism,[46] and none that may legitimately be interpreted as indicating approval.[47] If Dion had been a friend

---

[43] Nepos *Dion*, 6–10, cf. below, pp. 250–64. The brevity and vagueness of Plutarch at the end of his *Dion* may be due to the suppression of unpalatable facts.

[44] F 194. Nepos may have drawn the material for his *Dion* from the history of Timaeus (cf. the view of Morrow mentioned p. 235 n. 35, above), who may have used the work of Athanis. Theopompus also, however, probably consulted the latter work, and it is even possible that the unflattering picture of Dion contained in it reached Timaeus not directly but through the Sicilian digression of Theopompus, with which he was certainly acquainted (F 341 = Timaeus F 117 in *F. Gr. Hist.* iii B, 634).

[45] A passage in Athenaeus (11.508 e–f) lends some support to the view that Theopompus may have treated Dion unsympathetically. While the main point is that Callippus, the murderer of Dion, was among the many disciples of Plato whose subsequent careers were dishonourable, the reference to Dion as ἐξιδιοποιούμενον τὴν μοναρχίαν imputes most discreditable motives to him. Athenaeus does not name his source, but most of his excerpts dealing with Sicilian history in the middle of the fourth century are derived from Theopompus. He has just quoted the treatise of Theopompus against Plato (F 259), and his information on the treachery of Callippus is likely to have been drawn either from this work, in which Theopompus presumably expressed the same views on Callippus and Dion as in the *Philippica*, or from the *Philippica* itself.

[46] T 7, F 275, 294–5, 359, as well as the quotation (mentioned in the previous note) from the treatise against Plato (F 259; possibly T 48 may contain a reference to the same treatise, but the text is uncertain).

[47] v. Fritz, op. cit., 769–71, maintains that Platonism was one of the subjects upon which Theopompus was guilty of inconsistency, expressing both favourable and unfavourable opinions. The only evidence of approval that he adduces is F 250, which deals with Hermias of Atarneus and his connection

and disciple of Plato in the same sense as Alcibiades was a friend and disciple of Socrates, Theopompus might have overlooked his enthusiasm for Platonism and taken a favourable view of his military and political achievements. These achievements, however, were inseparable from his association with the Academy, as is abundantly clear from the Platonic *Epistles* and the *Dion* of Plutarch. His expedition might not even have been attempted if Speusippus had not encouraged him to take action and members of the Academy had not volunteered to serve under his command, several of them being among his principal officers.[48] In his plans for constitutional reform at Syracuse, which he did not live to execute, he was guided largely by Platonic doctrine,[49] and even Diodorus, who does not expressly mention the Academy, refers to his training in philosophy and its effect upon his statesmanship.[50] To most Greeks his achievement in liberating Syracuse, as well as his subsequent failure to restore political stability, were intimately linked with Plato and the Academy.[51]

In narrating the series of conflicts precipitated by the expedition of Dion Theopompus must have found himself in a somewhat embarrassing situation. All the contestants for control of Syracuse—Dionysius II, Dion with his band of volunteers from the Academy, and the democratic opponents of Dion led by

---

with the Academy, but this fragment surely neither expresses nor implies any judgement on the merits or demerits of Platonism. The question whether Hermias is receiving praise (Laqueur op. cit., col. 2185; v. Fritz, op. cit., 769) or blame (Jaeger, *Aristotle*[2], 112 with n. 2; Wormell, *Yale Class. Stud.*, v (1935), 66) lies outside the scope of the present investigation, though the latter interpretation seems preferable. The best that the phrase βάρβαρος μὲν ὢν μετὰ τῶν Πλατωνείων φιλοσοφεῖ can imply is that Hermias, though a barbarian, was an educated man capable of appreciating philosophy: whether the philosophy that he studied was good or bad is an issue with which Theopompus is not here concerned.

[48] Cf. Plut. *Dion* 22.7 and Diod. 16.10.5 on the discouraging attitude of most Syracusan exiles, though their unresponsiveness may have been exaggerated by the Academy.

[49] Plut. *Dion* 53.4, cf. below, pp. 260–1.

[50] Diod., 16.6.3 and 20.2.

[51] It is arguable that Theopompus, who is believed to have been inconsistent in his judgements (cf. T 19), may have praised Dion as a liberator and condemned him as a Platonist. His inconsistency, however, seems to have taken the form of castigating the private lives of characters—Philip is the best example—whose statesmanship he admired, and the private life of Dion was above reproach.

Heracleides—represented ideals that seem to have been abhorrent to him. How he met this difficulty is uncertain. He probably depreciated the achievement of Dion in liberating Syracuse, which was the central theme of the rival tradition, on the ground that it led only to prolonged anarchy, and much of his attention was certainly concentrated upon the thesis that the vices of Dionysius and his relatives brought about the downfall of the tyranny.

The fragments of Theopompus throw scarcely any light upon his account, which must surely have been detailed, of the events leading to the liberation of Syracuse by Timoleon and the banishment of Dionysius to Corinth.[52] One fragment deals with the circumstances in which Timoleon overthrew the tyranny of his own brother Timophanes at Corinth many years before he was sent to Sicily (F 334); it shows that the account of his mission must have been preceded by an introductory sketch of his antecedents, which was doubtless intended to illustrate his deeprooted hatred of tyrants.[53] If, as seems very probable,[54] the chapters in which Diodorus describes the liberation of Syracuse by Timoleon are based upon the account contained in the *Philippica*, Theopompus must have praised Timoleon highly, though not extravagantly. There is certainly no reason for believing his attitude to have been unsympathetic. Timoleon was entirely free from the taint of Platonism; he was an enemy of tyrants and expelled many; he restored order throughout Greek Sicily, and though the constitution that he established at Syracuse was democratic, it was a democracy of the most moderate type, which developed some years later into a narrow oligarchy.[55] If, however, Theopompus had heroised him, as Timaeus subsequently did, the Sicilian narrative in the *Philippica* could not have ended at a point that excludes his greatest triumphs as a general and statesman. The attention of Theopompus was focused rather upon the fall of the tyrant-house.

[52] F 341 is of little value except for the evidence that it provides on the relation between Timaeus and Theopompus.

[53] This fragment is almost certainly derived from the Sicilian books of the *Philippica*, though it could conceivably belong to some other digression. The overthrow of Timophanes took place several years before the accession of Philip, the point at which Theopompus began his account of Greek history.

[54] Hammond, op. cit., 141–4, whose conclusions will be discussed below.

[55] See below, pp. 293–305.

This conception of Sicilian history in the middle of the fourth century was less widely accepted in antiquity than that of the rival tradition, but its influence was by no means negligible. The private life of Dionysius II interested Peripatetic writers,[56] whose works were extensively used by later moralists, anecdote-hunters and biographers. A certain amount of this material is favourable to Dionysius and is not likely to have been derived from Theopompus,[57] but the *Philippica* was evidently a rich quarry for collectors of scandals about the members of the tyrant-house, as is shown by the catalogue of them preserved by Athenaeus, who cites Theopompus as his principal authority.[58] The influence of the same tradition may be traced in the works of Justin and Aelian.[59] Both wrote some five centuries later than Theopompus, whose account was not used directly by Justin, and very probably not by Aelian either. To Justin the ignominious career of Dionysius II was the only noteworthy feature of Sicilian history in the middle of the fourth century,[60] and he includes the story that drunkenness affected his eyesight which is quoted by Athenaeus and Aelian from Theopompus (F 283); neither Dion nor Timoleon is mentioned, both expulsions of Dionysius being apparently attributed to purely local risings.[61] Justin is an inaccurate epitomator with a taste for scandal and little understanding of military or political history, and Trogus, his sole authority, gave at least some account of Dion and Timoleon.[62] Nevertheless, the epitome of Justin suggests that Trogus devoted at least half of a book to the career of Dionysius, whose most discreditable actions must have been described in some detail and apparently with considerable relish. Very little is known about the sources from which the *Historiae Philippicae* of Trogus were drawn,[63] but the title and scope of the work indicates that the

[56] Clearchus fr. 10 (Müller, *F.H.G.* ii. 307); Satyrus fr. 2 (ibid., iii. 160). This material could, however, have been derived from Aristotle or Theophrastus, who are quoted by Athenaeus 10.435 d–e on the private habits of Dionysius.

[57] Cf. Plut. *Timol.* 15.1–7; Aelian *V.H.* 12.60.

[58] 10.435 d–436 b = F 185–8 and 283 a.

[59] Its influence on Diodorus will be discussed in the next section.

[60] 21.1–3 and 5.   [61] 21.2.4–8 and 5.1.

[62] *Prol.* 21, where the emendation *per Dionem* is convincing. The treatment of Dionysius I by Trogus and Justin has been discussed above, p. 233 n. 29.

[63] The question of the relationship between Trogus and Timagenes

Philippica of Theopompus was probably among the most important of them. A passage of Aelian presents a similar picture.[64] He describes how Dionysius II inherited the tyranny of his father with all its vast resources and lost it through his own viciousness, ending his life in poverty and disgrace. Dion is dismissed in a genitive absolute and Timoleon not even mentioned; the aim of the extract is to point the moral that the character of Dionysius was responsible for the transformation of his fortunes. The effect of drunkenness upon his eyesight is quoted from Theopompus (F 283b), and the ultimate source of the whole passage, as well as of the account by Justin, may very well be the *Philippica*.[65]

III. THEOPOMPUS AND DIODORUS

Diodorus is a historian of so little originality that his indebtedness to his sources is by no means confined to the facts with which they supply him. He also derives from them to a large extent the general colouring of his narrative, including his presentation of the leading characters and conception of the central theme. Where his principal authority may be identified with some degree of confidence, he provides a mirror in which a picture of this authority is reflected, though the outline may be somewhat blurred. Much, for example, may be learned about Timaeus from the Sicilian chapters of Books 13 and 14, and still more about Hieronymus from Books 18–20. Unfortunately, however, in the many cases where it was open to Diodorus to have based a major section of his narrative upon one, or more than one,[66] of several authorities known to have covered the period, and

---

(Jacoby ii C, 220–1; Laqueur, *R.E.*, vi. A, coll. 1065–6) is not relevant here, for Timagenes must have been acquainted with the *Philippica* of Theopompus. Schanz-Hosius, *Gesch. d. röm. Lit.* ii. 323–4, believes that Trogus derived even the title of his work from Timagenes.

[64] *V.H.*, 6.12, cf. Val. Max. 6.9 ext. 6.

[65] Jacoby ii. D, 392 tentatively suggests this conclusion. The passage of Aelian seems to me to summarise very aptly the central theme of the Sicilian books of the *Philippica*. There is a further reason to believe that Justin and Aelian are following the same tradition: both state that Dionysius killed his brothers (Justin, 21.1.6–7, cf. Trogus *Prol.*, 21; Aelian, loc. cit.), a charge that does not occur elsewhere and may well be false.

[66] From an examination of Book 17 Tarn, *Alexander the Great* ii. 63–91, concludes that its material was derived from a large number of sources. He points out, however, that Diodorus did not necessarily compose each book in the same way (p. 63). It is also possible that in cases where Diodorus appears

where there is little or no evidence to show which of these he may have chosen, his personal contribution to his own work is sufficently great to render the task of identification a very difficult one. To this latter category belongs his Sicilian narrative in Book 16, and in attempting to identify its source, or sources, modern scholars have reached widely differing conclusions.[67] If it were possible to produce indisputable proof that Diodorus drew from Theopompus the substance of all, or even some, of these chapters, his account could legitimately have been used as a basis for reconstructing this part of the *Philippica*. In the circumstances it is possible only to adopt the opposite course of seeking to determine which parts, if any, of the Sicilian narrative in Book 16 of Diodorus may have been derived from the *Philippica*, using *inter alia* such conclusions as have been reached in the foregoing sections of this paper.

The most recent investigation of the chapters in Book 16 of Diodorus dealing with Sicilian history is that of Hammond, who has made a new approach to the problem by 'regarding the narrative from the general angles of fullness, accuracy, military and political detail, and the conception of the central theme' instead of relying largely upon citations and other minutiae.[68] He concludes that Diodorus used Theopompus continuously until the end of the Sicilian digression and then turned to

---

to have used many authorities concurrently the work of conflating these authorities may have been done for him by some almost or wholly unknown predecessor.

[67] The extent of this divergence may be illustrated by the following list, which is by no means exhaustive, of works in which the chapters of Diodorus on the career of Dion are stated (in some cases with qualifications or exclusions) to have been derived from Timaeus, Ephorus or Theopompus. For Timaeus, Meyer, *G.d.A.* v. 512–14 (cf. iv². 270), and Barber, *The Historian Ephorus*, 169; for Ephorus, Clasen, op. cit., 66, Schwartz, *R.E.* v. col. 681 and *Hermes*, 44 (1909), 486, Walker, *Hellenica Oxyrhynchia*, 91–2, and Morrow, op. cit., 35; for Theopompus, Reuss, *Jahrb. f. class. Phil.*, 42 (1896), 325, and Hammond, op. cit., 141–4. Laqueur, *R.E.*, vi. A, coll. 1150–6, maintains that Diodorus conflated Ephorus and Timaeus; his claim to be able to split up the text of Diodorus into sections derived from each authority does not increase confidence in his general conclusions.

[68] *C.Q.* 31 (1937), 81. This statement of principles is made in the first part of his paper, which deals with the Greek and Macedonian chapters of Book 16. Reference has already been made to the second part of his paper dealing with the Sicilian chapters (*C.Q.* 32 (1938), 137–51). Both parts of this paper are packed with original and ingenious ideas.

Timaeus for the later achievements of Timoleon. Much of his argument seems to me to be thoroughly convincing. A change of source after the banishment of Dionysius II to Corinth, the point at which the Sicilian digression ended, is highly probable. It is also likely that the chapters describing the mission of Timoleon down to the liberation of Syracuse (65–70) are derived from a single source, and that this source is the *Philippica*: the agreements and discrepancies between this account and that of Plutarch in the *Timoleon*[69] are most easily explained by believing that, whereas Diodorus followed Theopompus, Plutarch followed Timaeus, who, as shown above,[70] was familiar with the work of Theopompus but certainly drew much of his material from other sources.[71] Although Timoleon is the central figure of this narrative, Dionysius is also prominent, and parts of it deal with events in which Timoleon was not involved.[72]

It is much more difficult to accept the view of Hammond that the chapters of Diodorus on the liberation of Syracuse by Dion[73] are based upon the *Philippica*. The conception of Dion is one that, if my conclusions in the previous section of this paper are valid, Theopompus can scarcely have held. Not only is the narrative a panegyric of Dion, who is pictured as solely responsible for the liberation of Syracuse,[74] but his philosophical training is twice mentioned with the warmest approval.[75] It is true that Diodorus, unlike Plutarch, does not adopt the device of emphasising the virtues of Dion by blackening his adversaries, but the impartiality of his narrative, to which Hammond draws attention,[76] is incompatible with the violent partisanship of Theopompus, who is

[69] Hammond, op. cit., 145–8 compares the accounts of Diodorus and Plutarch. The melodramatic picture of Timoleon killing his brother with his own hand in the marketplace (65.4) and the bias shown against the proletariat (65.3) and in favour of the upper classes (65.6) lend a little support to the view that Diodorus is here following Theopompus.

[70] Cf. p. 237 n. 44, above.

[71] His own father Andromachus, who had been an ally of Timoleon, must have provided him orally with valuable information, though it can scarcely have been unprejudiced.

[72] Cf. 67.1–68.3.

[73] Chapters 6, 9–13 and 16–20. Chapter 5, in which Dion is not mentioned, will be discussed below.

[74] 11.2, διʼ ἑνὸς ἀνδρὸς ἀρετήν. Other passages in which Dion is highly praised are 6.1; 9.3; 12.4; 17.5; 20.6.

[75] 6.3 and 20.2.   [76] Op. cit., 137.

unlikely to have praised Philistus and Nypsius, the officers of the tyrant, or Heracleides, the champion of the Syracusan proletariat. The two criticisms of Dion mentioned by Hammond, namely that he was suspected of aiming at a tyranny and that he sided with the mercenaries against the Syracusans,[77] are not very damaging. The former was a current belief mentioned even by Plato,[78] and Diodorus only refers to it indirectly without expressing any opinion on its validity. The second passage is more creditable than discreditable: Dion assumed command of the disaffected mercenaries with the greatest reluctance, and instead of agreeing to their demand to be led against the Syracusans he tried to prevent bloodshed by setting out for Leontini.

The considerations leading to the conclusion that the chapters in which Diodorus narrates the career of Dion can scarcely have been derived from Theopompus do not apply to the first chapter of Book 16 dealing with Sicilian history (5). This chapter is concerned wholly with Dionysius and introduces the story of his decline and fall: it contains no reference to Dion. As Hammond points out,[79] there is the closest affinity between the content of this chapter and the final comments of Diodorus on the banishment of Dionysius to Corinth by Timoleon.[80] The same circumstances evoke the same sentiments expressed in very similar language, and these sentiments are consistent with the picture of Dionysius that was probably presented in the Sicilian books of the *Philippica*, though emphasis is laid rather upon his ineptitude as a ruler than upon the licentiousness of his private life. Very similar sentiments are expressed in a passage of Aelian discussed above which contains a quotation from Theopompus and very probably echoes his views.[81] There is a further link with Theopompus in the statement of Diodorus that Dionysius was sent to

[77] 17.3 and 4, cited by Hammond, op. cit., 137.

[78] *Ep.* 7.333 b–c, 334 a.

[79] Op. cit., 140. I cannot agree with Hammond, op. cit., 137, that Dionysius 'is treated with impartial moderation'. Every point made by Diodorus in Chapter 5 is to the discredit of Dionysius except the foundation of the Adriatic colonies (5.3), and these soon required his presence with substantial forces (10.2). [80] 70.2–3.

[81] *V.H.* 6.12, cf. above, pp. 240–1. The last sentence of this passage contains verbal parallels with Diod. 70.2. The occurrence of the striking phrase 'bonds of steel' in both passages of Diodorus (5.4 and 70.2) and in Aelian is less significant than it might seem to be at first sight: the phrase appears twice in the

Corinth in a small merchant-ship:[82] this detail is known to have been similarly recorded by Theopompus, though differently by Timaeus.[83]

The close connection between the two passages in which Diodorus introduces[84] and dismisses Dionysius do not prove that all the intervening account of Sicilian history is derived from the same source. Apart from the difficulty of reconciling the eulogistic treatment of Dion with the probability that the picture of Dionysius originates from Theopompus, there are strong reasons for believing that Diodorus did not in this instance follow a single authority continuously. The first three chapters of his Sicilian narrative, which belong to three consecutive archon-years, are unusually disjointed and lacking in cohesion.[85] Chapter 5, as already stated, is devoted exclusively to Dionysius and makes no reference to Dion. In Chapter 6 Diodorus introduces Dion, mentioning his connection by marriage with the tyrant-house,[86] his outstanding qualities, his flight from Sicily when Dionysius tried to kill him, his preparations to overthrow the tyranny by force, and the departure of his expedition from Zacynthus.[87] Chapter 9 begins with a second and more general introduction to the expulsion of Dionysius by Dion:[88] while the resources of the

---

Dion of Plutarch (7.6; 10.4), which belongs to the rival tradition. It is attributed by Diodorus and Plutarch to Dionysius I and could have been quoted by any of the historians writing on this period of Sicilian history. Its ultimate origin is Aesch. *P.V.* 6. [82] 70.3.

[83] F 341 (cf. above) surely indicates that Diodorus is here following Theopompus and not Timaeus (Laqueur, op. cit., col. 1156). Volquardsen, *Untersuchungen ü. Diod. xi bis xvi*, 101, maintains that Diodorus, reading the criticism of Theopompus by Timaeus, was free to choose either version and chose that of Theopompus because it afforded a more striking contrast. This perverse argument attributes to Diodorus a mental process of which he was scarcely capable; it forms part of a desperate attempt to establish an untenable theory. If Theopompus was wrong, as Timaeus believed, he was characteristically sacrificing accuracy to rhetorical antithesis.

[84] The brief note on the accession of Dionysius in 15.74.5, which pictures him as a dutiful son, is a mere postscript to the account of his father's death.

[85] Chapter 5 belongs to 359/8, chapter 6 to 358/7 and chapter 9 to 357/6.

[86] The same facts are similarly recorded by Nepos *Dion* 1.1, though his subsequent narrative differs somewhat from that of Diodorus (Morrow, op. cit., 32–4).

[87] The two transports mentioned in 6.5 (cf. 9.2 and 4) also appear in Nepos *Dion* 5.3, and with additional details in Plutarch *Dion* 25.1.

[88] 9.1–3, cf. Hammond, op. cit., 140.

former, which are fully described, were overwhelmingly superior, the personal qualities of Dion, combined with the enthusiastic support of the Syracusans, unexpectedly gave him a decisive advantage. Diodorus then resumes his narrative from the point at which he left it at the end of Chapter 6. The insertion of this second introduction at a point where Diodorus has already begun to describe the expedition of Dion is somewhat surprising: he may well have put it together himself[89] from material drawn from subsidiary sources.[90] There is, however, no reason to believe that he has changed his principal authority at this point: the central theme remains the glorious achievement of Dion in overthrowing the tyranny and liberating Syracuse, and there are several links between passages in Chapter 6 and passages in the narrative resumed after the second introduction on the enterprise of Dion.[91] On the other hand, Chapter 5 presents a totally different outlook towards Sicilian history in this period and has no strong links with the chapters dealing with Dion.[92] There is every reason to believe that it is derived from a different source.

Examination of the Sicilian narrative in Book 16 has led to the conclusion that Diodorus composed it in the following way. He began by using the *Philippica* for his first chapter on Sicilian history; he then turned to another source and followed it throughout his account of Dion, which breaks off abruptly in 356/5 after the defeat of Nypsius;[93] when he resumed his Sicilian

[89] There is an even more striking case of a discussion being introduced at an inappropriate point in 18.53.1–5, where consideration of the changes of fortune experienced by Eumenes of Cardia involves a recapitulation of his career (cf. ibid., 59.5–6 for the end of this discussion).

[90] The substance of this second introduction is found in Nepos *Dion* 5.3, and Plutarch *Dion* 14.3 and 50.4. It cannot therefore be a wholly original creation by Diodorus.

[91] Hammond, op. cit., 137–8.

[92] Hammond, op. cit., 138, points out that the Adriatic colonies mentioned in 5.3 reappear in 10.2, but all historians who wrote at all fully about this period of Sicilian history must have referred to them; they constituted almost the only positive achievement of Dionysius II.

[93] On Sicilian history between 356/5 and 346/5 Diodorus gives only three short notes derived from his chronographical source (31.7; 36.5; 45.9). If he used the *Philippica* continuously for Sicilian affairs, it is difficult to account for this strange gap in the middle of a book: Theopompus dealt fully with the period, as several fragments show (F 187–8, 192). Hammond, op. cit., 140 n. 4, seems to me to underrate the significance of this gap.

narrative with a description of the events leading to the mission of Timoleon (65), he again used the *Philippica* until the termination of its Sicilian digression with the banishment of Dionysius II in 343/2 compelled him to make another change of source. The temporary abandonment of a work from which he had derived only a single chapter is somewhat surprising and perhaps inconsistent with his normal practice; for his changes of source seem usually to occur where he completed one of his own books and began another or where he reached the end of a work, or part of a work, upon which he was basing his narrative. In this instance, however, he may have been influenced by personal feelings on one of the few subjects about which he betrays any marked prejudice. He was proud of his native Sicily and, though writing a universal history, could not resist the temptation to devote to it an unwarrantably large proportion of his work. Occasionally he even makes original contributions from his knowledge of Roman Sicily in his own times.[94] When he found that Theopompus was more interested in Dionysius than in Dion, he may well have felt that the achievement of a Sicilian in liberating the greatest of Sicilian cities merited more eulogistic treatment than it received in the *Philippica*. The indifferent, perhaps even contemptuous, attitude of Theopompus towards the philosophical training of Dion may also have shocked him. Accordingly he seems to have sought an author who made Dion the central figure of Sicilian history in this period and gave greater prominence to the virtues of the liberator than to the shortcomings of the tyrant. His failure to ensure the consistency of his narrative by turning back and revising the chapter already derived from Theopompus has many parallels in other parts of his work.

To identify the author followed by Diodorus in his chapters on Dion is by no means easy, and a full discussion of the problem would involve treatment of controversial topics outside the scope of a paper on Theopompus, such as the attitude of Timaeus and Ephorus towards Dion and Heracleides and the sources of Nepos' *Dion* and Plutarch's *Dion*. It may, however, be stated with every confidence that the author is not Timaeus. In recording the circumstances in which Dion became an exile from Sicily Plutarch cites Timaeus, and his version of this episode is fundamentally

[94] Cf. 13.90.5; 16.7.1, 70.6, 83.2–3.

different from that of Diodorus.[95] Among the sources used by Timaeus for the career of Dion were almost certainly the Platonic *Epistles*, especially as not only the *Dion* of Plutarch, who may have used the *Epistles* independently, but also the *Dion* of Nepos, who clearly did not, show unmistakable traces of their influence; on the other hand, the chapters of Diodorus on Dion do not appear to owe anything to the *Epistles*.[96] Lastly, Timaeus is known to have slandered Philistus in violent terms, whereas Diodorus praises him warmly.[97]

Of the standard historians known to have written on the career of Dion Ephorus has the strongest claims to be identified with the author followed by Diodorus. Like Theopompus, Ephorus was fond of passing moral judgements on historical characters,[98] but, unlike Theopompus, he had no reason to be prejudiced against Dion as a Platonist in spite of his own ties with Isocrates. The admiration shown for Dion as a man, the absence of influence by the Platonic *Epistles* and of any specific statement that the liberation of Syracuse was sponsored by the Academy,[99] and the generous treatment both of Heracleides and of Philistus and Nypsius, the officers of Dionysius,[100] are all compatible with the probable outlook of Ephorus. More significant, however, is the fact that, as Schwartz has pointed out,[101] Ephorus is known to have ended his account of Sicilian history at approximately the point where Diodorus so strangely breaks off his narrative before reaching the final stage of the struggle for Syracuse.[102] It has

[95] Plut. *Dion*, 14.4–7 (= Timaeus F 113 in *F. Gr. Hist.* iii. B, 633); Diod. 16.6.4. Nepos *Dion*, 4.1–2 agrees closely with Plutarch. Cf. Morrow, op. cit., 35.

[96] Morrow, op. cit., 31–6.

[97] Plut. *Dion* 36. 1–2 (= Timaeus F 154 in *F. Gr. Hist.* iii B. 644); Diod. 16. 16.3–4.

[98] Jacoby ii C, 38 (note on T 23); Barber, op. cit., 89–90 and 102–4.

[99] As has already been noted (above, p. 243 with n. 5) Diodorus twice refers to the advantages derived by Dion from his philosophical training, but he lays far more emphasis than Plutarch upon the extent to which Dion was indebted to local support (Diod. 16.9.6 and 10.5; Plut. *Dion* 27.1 and 5.).

[100] Cf. Plut. *Dion* 36.3 on the treatment of Philistus by Ephorus.

[101] He seems to have been the first to explain the break in the narrative of Diodorus by reference to the limits of Ephorus' work (*R.E.*, v col. 681, and, rather more fully, *Hermes* 44 (1909), 486–7). He is followed by Walker, op. cit., 91, and Cavaignac, *Mélanges Glotz*, i. 154.

[102] Some scholars maintain that Ephorus continued his Sicilian narrative

already been noted that Diodorus tends to be capricious in selecting material for inclusion in his work, and in this instance he may
have been unwilling to dwell upon the failure and death of Dion.
Nevertheless, it is astonishing that he did not continue his account
as far as the surrender of Ortygia by Apollocrates,[103] which took
place only a few months after the defeat of Nypsius. The most
convincing explanation is that Diodorus was using the work of
Ephorus, which here failed him. Finally, while there remains a
possibility that Diodorus may have relied upon some author
whose account has perished without leaving any trace, he seems
normally to have confined himself to the works of a few standard
historians mentioned in his bibliographical notes, and if Theopompus and Timaeus are excluded,[104] there is a strong presumption in favour of Ephorus.[105]

The foregoing investigation has led to the following conclusions. The Sicilian digression in the *Philippica* covered about three
books; it began with a brief introduction on the tyranny of
Dionysius I, but the bulk of it was devoted to the period from the
accession of Dionysius II to his final expulsion by Timoleon, the
central theme being the decay and collapse of the tyranny

---

beyond this point, but Hammond, op. cit., 141, has conclusively shown that,
because Diyllus began his first *Syntaxis*, dealing with Greek and Sicilian
affairs, in 357/6 (Diod. 16.14.5), Ephorus must have ended here. It is true
that Diodorus carries his Sicilian narrative into 356/5 (ibid., 16–20); there is,
however, no reason to believe that Ephorus ended his Books 27 (on Greek
affairs) and 29 (on Sicilian affairs) at precisely the same point. The writer
from whom Diodorus derived his bibliographical notes (ibid., 14.3–5) had in
mind Greek rather than Sicilian history. On reaching the mission of Timoleon
Diodorus could not use Ephorus, and the reasons that had led him to desert
Theopompus were no longer valid.

[103] Plut. *Dion* 50.2.

[104] Of less famous writers Athanis and Timonides may both be excluded;
as already stated, the former was a partisan of Heracleides and can scarcely
have treated Dion with any sympathy, while Timonides, being a member of
the Academy, is likely to have stressed the part played by its members in the
liberation of Syracuse. A further reason for excluding Timonides is that his
account of the death of Philistus, which is quoted by Plutarch (*Dion* 35.4–5),
differs fundamentally from that of Diodorus (16.16.3).

[105] The arguments of Hammond, op. cit., 141–2, against Ephorus being
the authority followed by Diodorus are mainly dependent upon his view that
his Groups 1 (on Dion) and 2 (on Timoleon as far as his liberation of Syracuse)
form a unity derived from a single source. I have tried to show that his
Group 1 is composed of two separate sections.

through the self-indulgence of Dionysius II and his relatives. The achievement of Dion in liberating Syracuse is likely to have been depreciated because he was a disciple and friend of Plato, while Timoleon, though much more sympathetically treated, was probably not allowed to dominate the latter parts of the digression. Theopompus had very little influence on the tradition contributing most to the surviving records of Sicilian history in the middle of the fourth century and represented primarily by the relevant biographies of Plutarch and Nepos, who focused the attention of posterity upon the two liberators. Timaeus, whose work was very widely read, was mainly responsible for this tradition, though for the career of Dion the Academy made a substantial contribution to it. On the other hand, Book 21 of Justin and a passage of Aelian, together with several quotations from the *Philippica* by Athenaeus, show that some authors followed Theopompus in concentrating upon the tyrant-house. Some of the chapters dealing with Sicilian history in Book 16 of Diodorus, which reflect the same point of view, are probably based on the *Philippica*. Diodorus seems to have at first followed Theopompus but soon to have turned to another historian, probably Ephorus, for his account of the expedition of Dion, finding that the attitude of Theopompus towards Dion was distasteful to him. On reaching the mission of Timoleon, he seems again to have used the *Philippica* until its Sicilian digression ended with the banishment of Dionysius to Corinth.[106]

[106] The valuable edition of Plutarch's *Dion* by W. H. Porter was published after this article had been completed.

15

Dion: a study in liberation

In 357 B.C. Dion returned to Sicily from exile at the head of a small mercenary army with the avowed intention of expelling his relative, the younger Dionysius, from Syracuse and overthrowing a tyranny which had lasted for nearly half a century. He was welcomed everywhere as a liberator, and the greater part of the city fell into his hands without resistance, only the fortified island of Ortygia remaining in possession of the tyrant. Three years later he was murdered by his own mercenaries at the instigation of a close friend, and Sicily was plunged into anarchy which continued for a decade. He did not fail because he was murdered: it might rather be contended that he was murdered because he had already failed. Although Plato never lost faith in him, he seems to have lost faith in himself, and he died as isolated and distrusted as any tyrant. His failure to restore stability and confidence is in striking contrast to the achievement of Timoleon some years later, even if the political reconstruction effected by the latter was eventually swept away by the tyrant Agathocles. Most of the attention devoted to the career of Dion in the past forty years has been incidental: it has been studied for the light which it throws on the attitude of Plato towards the practical needs of the Syracusan state, and especially for its relation to the dispute on the authenticity of the Platonic *Epistles*.[1] The obstacles encountered by Dion during three stormy years have a certain interest for their own sake, which is perhaps increased by contemporary parallels. History provides many examples of the diseases to which states newly liberated from internal or external tyranny are subject, but the problems of fourth-century Syracuse may perhaps be more readily appreciated when those of several European countries in the period since the fall of Mussolini are fresh in the memory.

[1] Opinion on this problem has gradually changed since the beginning of the present century, when the *Epistles*, as well as some of the later Dialogues including the *Laws*, were widely believed to be spurious. Today almost all Platonists accept the more important *Epistles*, though a few, which could in any case have little value as historical evidence, are still suspected.

The easiest way of explaining the failure of Dion to establish a stable republican régime is to believe that he did not intend to succeed. It has been suggested that, while posing as a liberator, his aim was to supplant the tyrant whom he expelled, that he used his association with Plato and the Academy to cloak his selfish ambitions, and that his status in the last year of his life was virtually that of a tyrant.[2] Stated in its crudest form, this theory is clearly untenable and has won little approval. As Dion was conspicuously deficient in diplomatic skill, it is inconceivable that he should for years have hoodwinked not only Plato, who continued to defend his integrity after his death, but also the many members of the Academy who participated in his expedition. Nor, if his object had been to emulate the elder Dionysius, would he have hesitated to adopt the violent methods of dealing with political opponents traditionally associated with the establishment of a tyranny.[3] Nevertheless this view contains a germ of truth in that he certainly intended from the outset to use the authority invested in him as a liberator to impose upon Syracuse the form of government which he considered to be best. His uncompromising pursuit of this aim was responsible for the determined opposition of the democratic party, led by his former friend and fellow-exile Heracleides. The conflict between them lies at the root of the tragedy, and the complex story of their quarrels must be critically examined.

Unfortunately the extant records of this period are tinged with bias mainly in favour of Dion but also in some degree against him, since contemporary accounts, which have not survived, were written both by his supporters and by his opponents. In the *Dion* of Plutarch, one of the most attractive of the *Lives*, Heracleides is a melodramatic villain, who turned demagogue to frustrate the plans of his enemy and to promote his own aspirations. His services as admiral are obscured by omission, and no opportunity is lost of underlining his failures and attributing his actions to the basest motives. Here the partisan influence of Timonides of Leucas, a prominent subordinate of Dion, who wrote an account of his experiences for the benefit of Speusippus, may be detected. On the other hand, the Syracusan historian

---

[2] This view was originally put forward by Beloch, *Gr. Gesch.*, iii.1.131 and 260–1, and has been revived by Glotz, *Histoire grecque*, iii. 410–12.

[3] Meyer, *Geschichte des Altertums*, v. 521.

Athanis was among the colleagues of Heracleides elected during the temporary eclipse of Dion and was presumably a democrat. Hence he might reasonably be held responsible for any glorification of Heracleides or depreciation of Dion found in surviving accounts. It happens that, though a favourable picture of Heracleides is drawn by Diodorus, he is nowhere extravagantly praised, but the highly unflattering account of Dion's later actions found in the second half of the brief *Dion* of Nepos may be ultimately due to the partisanship of Athanis. The attitude of Plato towards Heracleides is instructive. Most of his references belong to the events leading to the banishment of Heracleides by the younger Dionysius,[4] but he condemns this decision as unjust, and the only passage in which he refers to the party struggles at Syracuse in this period seems to imply that the character of Dion was largely responsible for their disagreements.[5] His treatment of Heracleides contrasts with his indirect references to Callippus, the murderer of Dion, whose name he cannot bring himself even to mention. It is a reasonable inference that, as Heracleides is not unsympathetically treated by Plato and other authors, his character has been somewhat too luridly painted by Plutarch either through the influence of partisanship or to provide an ethical contrast to the virtues of Dion.[6]

The two leaders had been associates before they were successively banished,[7] and Heracleides, though far less prominent than Dion, had held military commands of some importance. While in exile in Greece, they collaborated at first in organising an expedition against the tyrant, but before their preparations were complete they quarrelled with the result that Heracleides did not sail with Dion and appeared at Syracuse with a second force some months after its partial liberation. The cause of their

---

[4] *Ep.*, 3.318 c–319 a; 7.348 b–349 e.

[5] *Ep.*, 4.320 e–321 c (see footnote 17). In *Ep.* 7.351 c there is a hint that Plato disapproved of the murder of Heracleides.

[6] In fairness to Plutarch it should be stated that, while intensely interested in Dion as a philosopher-statesman, he is critical of him in his *Comparison between Dion and Brutus* and elsewhere. Hence his bias in favour of Dion and against Heracleides in the central section of his biography seems to be largely due to the influence of the tradition which he followed.

[7] *Ep.*, 3.318 c. According to Plutarch, *Dion* 12, they had already agreed that, if Dionysius could not be induced to rule less despotically, the tyranny should be overthrown and a republican régime substituted.

quarrel is unspecified,[8] but it may be explained by reference to another passage where Plutarch states that out of at least one thousand persons exiled by the tyrant no more than 25 returned to Sicily with Dion.[9] Cowardice is said to have deterred the rest, but their reluctance has been ascribed by several scholars to a feeling that, though led by a Syracusan, the expedition was not so much a 'freedom movement' on the part of the Syracusans as a crusade undertaken by the Academy, from which many of its leaders were drawn, the remainder being professional *condottieri*. Heracleides, who had no associations with the Academy, may well have shared the distrust felt by his fellow-exiles, and many of those who had refused to sail with Dion perhaps accepted his leadership and accompanied him to Syracuse. If so, the two expeditions represented irreconcilable ideals.

Friction between Dion and the Syracusan populace had already become acute before the arrival of Heracleides. In the first enthusiasm of their liberation the Syracusans voted that Dion and his brother Megacles should be 'generals with full powers', a dictatorial office which might legitimately be filled to deal with a critical situation. So long as the troops of the tyrant occupied Ortygia, an appointment to this office was clearly desirable, but it had gained an unsavoury reputation through its use by the two Dionysii to lend a semblance of legality to their tyranny. For this reason Dion and Megacles prudently insisted upon the election of twenty officials described as 'colleagues', half being chosen from the exiles who had returned with them; but neither Megacles nor the 'colleagues' receive any further mention, and for some nine months Dion was virtually military governor of the city. When Dionysius, who had been absent during the entry of the liberators, returned to Ortygia, he at once showed how well he understood the character both of Dion and of the Syracusan populace: he professed his willingness to come to terms but addressed all his proposals to Dion personally as one dictator to another. Though a sortie launched by his troops during these negotiations was repelled only by the determination of Dion and

---

[8] *Dion* 32.4. The word used is normally associated with party strife and is later applied by Plutarch to the party struggles at Syracuse. Hence their differences may have been political rather than personal.

[9] *Dion* 22.7. Diodorus (16.10.5), whose figures are consistently less creditable to Dion, gives the number as 30.

his mercenaries, many Syracusans began to fear that the city now had two tyrants instead of one. Accordingly, when Heracleides arrived, the populace gladly turned to him, and he became the leader of the democratic faction. If he had served under the tyrants, he had no ties of relationship with them, and his easy manner compared favourably with the unapproachable austerity of Dion.

The verdict of the principal authorities in condemning the Syracusan populace for its instability, turbulence and cowardice in this period is perhaps not wholly merited and may be influenced by Plato's dislike of democratic government. Distinctions of class and wealth were doubtless more marked than in most Greek states, for tyranny tended to eliminate the middle class which Aristotle believed to be the best safeguard against faction. The policy of the tyrants in encouraging Italic and Gallic mercenaries to settle in Sicily after their discharge had brought a new infusion of barbarian blood to a stock already somewhat mixed, but its influence was not necessarily harmful. The Syracusans had often shown, and were to show again, most steadfast courage in the face of Carthaginian invasions, and their chief weakness lay in their inability in most periods to produce capable leaders. The so-called 'Sicilian way of life', severely criticised by Plato (*Ep.* 7. 326b) and others, can have been practised in its most luxurious form by the rich only, though its notoriety possibly reflects the envy felt by Greeks of the barren homeland for their fellow-countrymen enjoying somewhat easier economic conditions. The behaviour of the Syracusans at this time was often unwise but scarcely unnatural in a newly liberated people, of whom only a fraction had any experience of political freedom. Their over-eagerness to control their own fortunes before military victory was complete, their impatience of any restraint or discipline, and their excessive distrustfulness and sensitiveness all have modern parallels. Their reluctance to be the object of a Platonic experiment in statecraft is neither surprising nor discreditable. What they wanted was freedom to follow their own tastes and express their own opinions.

The first clash between Dion and Heracleides took place when the popular assembly elected the latter to the office of admiral. This election was contrary to established practice, since a 'general with full powers' had the right to appoint an admiral of his own choosing. Dion forced the assembly to rescind its decree and then proceeded to nominate Heracleides himself. His motive was presumably to show that his authority must be obeyed, but his choice of an example was ill-advised and only increased his unpopularity. Soon the Syracusans began to resent the presence of his mercenary troops, whose maintenance must have been costly. The demand that they should be dismissed was reinforced when Heracleides defeated a substantial fleet brought from Italy by the historian Philistus, who was captured and put to death. To this victory neither Dion nor his mercenary army contributed, and the Syracusans now became confident that they were strong enough to dispense with both, especially as Dionysius offered to surrender Ortygia if granted a safe conduct to Italy. This offer was made to Dion, who acted correctly in referring it to the assembly and against his personal interests in recommending its acceptance, since the withdrawal of the tyrant would have weakened his claim to retain his dictatorial powers. The Syracusans, however, elated by their success, were eager to capture Dionysius alive and were furious when he escaped to Italy leaving his son Apollocrates to continue the struggle. Although the topography of Syracuse is such that to maintain a strict blockade of Ortygia was almost impossible in antiquity, Heracleides forfeited his popularity for a time and might have been prosecuted for neglecting his duty as admiral. At this moment a democratic leader proposed a redistribution of land, a drastic measure which might have been desirable after the complete liberation of the city but was certainly premature at this stage.[10] The scheme can scarcely have been laid before the assembly without some preliminary planning, so that the statement of Plutarch (*Dion* 37.5) that Heracleides had it put forward to divert attention from his own negligence is not very convincing. Its introduction, however, enabled him to deliver a successful attack upon the whole foundation of Dion's authority. Despite opposition he carried proposals in the assembly to proceed with the redistribution of land, to discontinue the pay of the mercenaries and, since the annual election of magistrates was due (summer, 356 B.C.), to elect a board of twenty-five generals without special powers,

[10] A redistribution of land was among the reforms later carried out by Timoleon, but he did not introduce it until he had liberated the city from tyranny and Carthage. I have tried to elucidate his political, social and economic reconstruction on pp. 276–312, below.

which did not include Dion. Among those elected were Heracleides himself and the historian Athanis. The Syracusans then
tried to seduce the discharged mercenaries from their loyalty to
Dion by promises of citizenship. Acceptance of this offer would
have removed a potentially dangerous private army and provided the already dwindling population with a welcome supplement, but a large majority of the mercenaries urged Dion to lead
them away to Leontini, which remained faithful to him.[11] He was
somewhat reluctant to assume command, anticipating clashes with
the Syracusans, and indeed his men were twice attacked on the road
to Leontini, but they repelled the citizen troops without difficulty.

Heracleides and the democratic party now seemed likely to
win a decisive advantage by securing the reduction of Ortygia.
The garrison had exhausted its stocks of food and was on the
point of surrender[12] when a relieving squadron arrived bringing
reinforcements and stores. The Syracusans won a sea-battle, but
while they were celebrating their victory with ill-timed potations,
the enemy broke into the city and the situation became so
desperate that they had to beg Dion to come to their aid. His
compliance with their request is ascribed to his magnanimity and
patriotism, but clearly it gave him an opportunity of regaining
his lost prestige and authority. His mercenaries consented to
follow him, but while they were marching to Syracuse, the troops
of the tyrant retired to Ortygia, and democratic elements in the
city, successively defined as 'the demagogues', 'the generals' and
'the enemies of Dion', sent to inform him that his assistance was
not now required. Heracleides is not mentioned at this point, but
when a second attack developed and much of the city was in
flames, he sent his brother and then his uncle with personal
messages to Dion. Subsequently, while the rest of the democratic
leaders fled, he and his uncle gave themselves up to Dion, an
indication that they did not participate in the worst follies of
their colleagues. The battle fought in the blazing ruins is bril-
liantly described by Plutarch. The troops of the tyrant resisted
desperately, but they were eventually forced to withdraw behind
their fortifications.

[11] A fragment of Theopompus (*F. Gr. Hist.*, 115 F 194) proves that some
mercenaries remained in Syracuse, apparently in state service.
[12] This fact is known only from Diodorus (16.18.2), being among the points
favourable to the opponents of Dion omitted by Plutarch.

Dion was deservedly the hero of the hour. His supporters urged him to rid himself of Heracleides while his prestige stood so high, and his refusal to seize this opportunity is among the factors which acquit him of Machiavellian aims. There was, however, no specific charge on which Heracleides could be brought to trial.[13] He could plead that he had tried to serve the interests of Syracuse as he interpreted them, and he had taken an active part in the fighting and been wounded. At the next meeting of the assembly he moved that Dion should again be appointed 'general with full powers'; the Syracusans accepted his proposal but clamoured that he should be restored to his command as admiral, and Dion granted their request. This second dictatorship differed from the first, being precisely parallel to that of the two Dionysii: it does not seem to have been subject to any time-limit, and Dion had now no co-dictator and no 'colleagues'. The popular favour which he had gained through his victory and strengthened by his nomination of Heracleides as admiral was soon lost when he vetoed decrees relating to the redistribution of land and houses, which had evidently not been implemented during his absence. There is no evidence that a 'general with full powers' had the right to revoke decrees already approved by the assembly, and this action, besides being arbitrary, appears to have been actually illegal. At the same time Heracleides was removed from the political scene by being sent to Messana with the fleet, presumably with orders to operate against Dionysius, who was living at Locri.

Information on the second dictatorship of Dion, which he probably held for rather more than a year (from the spring of 355 until his death in June, 354), is both scanty and confused. Diodorus ignores Sicilian affairs except for one brief note, while the narrative of Plutarch, though continuing to be detailed on personal matters, becomes much less adequate in its presentation of the political and military situation. The biography of Nepos, hitherto as eulogistic as that of Plutarch, now changes its tone completely, as has already been noted, and includes material of a most discreditable character not recorded elsewhere. The brevity and vagueness of Plutarch, believed by some scholars to indicate that the contemporary account of Timonides ended

---

[13] The friends of Dion evidently appreciated this. They advocated handing him over to the soldiers, a euphemism for execution without trial.

before the death of Dion, has also been attributed to the suppression of facts damaging to his reputation.

An obscure feature of the period is the somewhat half-hearted intervention of Sparta in Sicilian affairs. A Spartan officer named Pharax arrived in Sicily declaring that he had been sent to restore freedom and to overthrow the dictators.[14] His mission, together with that of his successor Gaesylus, may have been the result of appeals by Heracleides, who is known from a casual reference by Plato (*Ep.* 4.321b) to have addressed official letters to Sparta. Heracleides negotiated with Pharax from Messana, evidently hoping to use Spartan influence to secure the expulsion of Dion, but Pharax could not ignore the interests of Dionysius, who had granted naval support to Sparta some years earlier, and his aim appears to have been to form a coalition of elements hostile to Dion. The Syracusan democrats, feeling that they had exchanged a drunken tyrant for a sober one, now regarded Dionysius in a more favourable light, but the mysterious negotiations which Heracleides conducted with him through Pharax must have seemed treasonable to Dion if he had any knowledge of them. Pharax somehow collected an army and inflicted a slight defeat upon the troops of Dion near Acragas, which is attributed to internal discord among the Syracusans. Heracleides took advantage of this setback to sail to Syracuse with the object of restoring the democrats to power, but Dion hastened back by land and forestalled him. Pharax now disappears from the scene, his troops being apparently disbanded; his efforts had neither ended Sicilian dissensions nor furthered Spartan interests, and he was replaced by the almost more enigmatic Gaesylus, who believed himself to be invested with dictatorial powers to effect a settlement. Though Heracleides welcomed him, Dion naturally refused to accept his own interpretation of his mission, and his only achievement was to bring about a temporary reconciliation between the rival leaders, who resumed their uneasy partnership.

The troops of Dionysius on Ortygia were now in desperate straits, and their insubordination compelled Apollocrates to surrender the island on condition that he should be allowed to sail

[14] Plut., *Timol.* 11.6 and *Comp. Timol. et Aemil.* 2.5. He is coupled in both passages with Callippus and accused of acting treacherously and illegally in the interests of personal ambition.

away with his relatives and associates. Syracuse was completely liberated at last, and the prestige of Dion rose once more. His next move was to reduce Heracleides to the status of a private citizen by disbanding the fleet on the ground that it was expensive and no longer required, but he neither dismissed his mercenaries nor resigned his dictatorial powers. He probably claimed that his retention of office was justified by the urgent need of constitutional and social reform. His subsequent acts, however, were far from reassuring: he rewarded his personal friends and his mercenaries so lavishly that financial embarrassment was caused, and if Nepos is to be believed, he confiscated the property not only of his opponents but also of some Syracusan aristocrats with the result that he alienated members of the party which supported him.[15] Even more damning was his refusal to demolish the fortifications on Ortygia, which encouraged the suspicion that he intended to occupy the castle of the tyrants himself. Heracleides condemned this decision in the assembly and also attacked him for sending to Corinth for advisers to help him in his political reconstruction, an action held to be insulting to the Syracusans. Legal experts would be required, especially as a corresponding revision of the legal code would also be necessary, as in the time of Timoleon, and men with experience of this work were unlikely to be many in a city which had been deprived of constitutional government for half a century. The opposition of the democrats probably sprang less from wounded pride than from a conviction that the form of government drafted by Corinthians would be distasteful to them. As Plutarch points out, Dion expected that advisers from Corinth, which was governed by an oligarchy at this time, would share his political views and help him to curb the powers of the assembly.

Unfortunately the constitutional aims of Dion are known only in the broadest outline, though it is legitimate to infer that they conformed to the principles of the roughly sketched constitution which some years later Plato recommended for Syracuse in the *Eighth Epistle*. Plato advised the appointment of three kings,

[15] Nepos *Dion* 7.1–2. From the *Seventh* and *Eighth Epistles* and from the situation when Timoleon began his mission it is clear that the aristocratic party as a whole remained faithful to Dion. An earlier statement of Nepos (ibid., 6.3) that Heracleides had no less influence with the aristocrats than Dion, while certainly exaggerated, perhaps refers to this incident.

whose functions were to be mainly formal, while control of the state was to rest largely in the hands of 35 'guardians of the laws'. This system is obviously modelled on the *Laws* and has affinities with that of Sparta, which he greatly admired. The bare references by Plutarch to constitutional reform in the *Dion* seem to be based solely upon a knowledge of the *Eighth Epistle* and the *Laws*, apart from the mention of the Corinthian advisers. As Dion made so little progress before his death, it may be doubted whether any further information would have been available to a contemporary: he had apparently determined the framework of the constitution and the legal code no more precisely than that they should be consistent with Platonic principles. This lack of preparation is remarkable in view of his close association with the Academy in the years which had passed since he first contemplated the liberation of Syracuse.

Whatever the details of this reform might have been, it would certainly be abhorrent to the democratic party, which was in a strong position because the radical system introduced by Diocles in 412 had theoretically remained in operation throughout the tyranny. Consequently Dion would have to abrogate a system favoured by the democrats before establishing one favoured by himself. A 'general with full powers' could doubtless ensure that his proposals were not rejected by the assembly, but to imitate too closely the methods of the elder Dionysius had obvious disadvantages. So long as Heracleides remained to lead the opposition, the passage of this reform would be stormy and difficult, and yielding to the insistent pressure of his partisans, Dion at last had him murdered. The democrats bitterly resented the removal of their champion, and although Dion is said to have convinced them that order could never be restored while Heracleides lived, this statement, coming from a prejudiced source, perhaps means only that they took no action to show their displeasure and acquiesced in a *fait accompli*. As political assassination was traditionally associated with tyranny, their suspicions now seemed to be confirmed.

Heracleides was far from being an enlightened statesman, and his methods were often those of the typical demagogue. Yet his opposition to Dion seems to have been actuated rather by a desire to bring back the reality of democratic freedom than by personal ambition. While he aspired to the leadership of a

261

restored democracy, he must have appreciated that he could maintain this position only by observing the wishes of the assembly. The swing of popular feeling against him after the escape of Dionysius illustrated the precariousness of any authority granted to him. He is nowhere accused of trying to persuade the mercenaries, of whom many had sailed from the Peloponnese under his command, to lend their armed support to his ambitions, and the statement of Diodorus (16.17.3) that no one regarded him as a potential tyrant is entirely convincing. His negotiations with Dionysius while he was serving as admiral under Dion were certainly treasonable, but his probable aim was to use one dictator against another in the interests of the democrats: Plato retained a surprising faith in Dionysius, who seems to have been weak rather than vicious, and advocated his appointment as one of the three kings in the constitution of the *Eighth Epistle*. The willingness of Heracleides to accept the grave risks which his struggle against Dion entailed, when the personal advantages to be gained by success were so limited, suggests that he was sincere in championing democratic government. Whether or not he believed his own assertions that Dion intended to make himself tyrant cannot be determined with certainty; perhaps he was more afraid that his native city might be dominated by a clique of doctrinaire idealists.

Within a few months Dion too was dead, the victim of a conspiracy by the Athenian Callippus, who had been among his most trusted associates. The story of the murder, dramatically told by Plutarch, has little historical importance. The motives of Callippus were entirely selfish, but the unpopularity of Dion enabled him to pose as a liberator until he could establish a tyranny.[16] Several details, on which Nepos and Plutarch agree, are significant: the number of conspirators was large, the assassins were Zacynthian mercenaries who had served under Dion from the outset, and his guards could have saved him if they had shown any resolution. He had evidently forfeited the loyalty even of the mercenary soldiers, who had hitherto remained faithful, and only the Syracusan aristocrats now supported him. He

[16] Apart from the astonishing conclusion of Aristotle that Callippus was almost innocent because he had had some disagreement with his victim (*Rhet.* 1.1373 a), ancient writers are unanimous in condemning him as an unprincipled adventurer.

received many warnings that his life was in danger, but remorse for the murder of Heracleides led him to neglect his safety, and the brooding depression of his last days suggests that he had at last realised the futility of pursuing ideals which were unacceptable to an overwhelming majority of the Syracusans. He died almost willingly, reluctant to survive the frustration of his hopes.

The failure of Dion is largely attributable to his own character and upbringing. In the *Fourth Epistle*, which was written when the struggle with Heracleides and the democrats had already begun, Plato reminds him that a statesman cannot hope to achieve success unless he tries to please others, quoting the proverb 'haughtiness has isolation for his fellow'.[17] This outspoken criticism is substantiated even by the evidence of biographers and historians whose inclination is to be too indulgent towards a philosopher-statesman. Dion was deficient in the qualities of leadership required to secure the devotion of subordinates and to win and retain the favour of the populace; indeed he seems at times to have deliberately courted unpopularity. Doubly connected by marriage with the tyrant-house, he had never before felt the need of these qualities, and when he returned to Syracuse he was too old, and perhaps too unadaptable, to develop them. His arbitrary exercise of authority, combined with his austere earnestness and obstinate pursuit of his ideals, encouraged the suspicion which his record as a collaborator of the Dionysii naturally evoked. His experience of administration was a handicap rather than an advantage, since it had been gained under the tyrants, and despite his study of Platonic doctrine he seems to have been unable to understand the practical operation of constitutional government in a free city. His task was perhaps neither more nor less formidable than that of Timoleon in the following decade. The latter had to contend with Carthaginian invaders as well as with tyrants, but this additional danger, together with the social and economic decay of the intervening years, served to unite the Sicilian Greeks and render them somewhat more tractable. The far greater measure of success which Timoleon achieved

[17] 321 b–c, which is quoted no less than four times by Plutarch (*Dion* 8.4 and 52.5; *Coriol.* 15.4; *Mor.* 69f). The *Fourth Epistle* is the only one addressed to Dion himself; it is natural that in the *Seventh* and *Eighth*, written to his supporters after his death, Plato should omit any reference to his faults.

must be ascribed not to fortuitous circumstances but rather to his undoubted superiority in securing the loyal co-operation of all parties and in dealing realistically with practical problems.[18]

[18] The third volume of Jaeger's *Paideia* (1945) was published after this essay was written. Though not much concerned with the problem which I have discussed, Jaeger believes in the integrity of Dion on the ground that Plato 'cannot have been entirely wrong about one of his closest friends' (211). On the other hand, he describes the idealism of Dion as 'bold and adventurous but shallow and credulous', thus dissociating himself from the tendency of Platonists to be over-indulgent towards Dion merely because he was a friend of Plato.

16

The purpose of Timoleon's mission

What Timoleon accomplished in Sicily is, in broad outline, undisputed; what he was sent to accomplish is much less clear. His achievement is admirably summarised in the Syracusan decree read at his funeral and reproduced by Diodorus and Plutarch in which reasons are given for the honours paid to him.[1] On the other hand, the substance of the Siceliot appeal to Corinth and of the orders issued to him by the Corinthian government, which must have been closely parallel, is not recorded with a similar precision and unanimity. He was evidently entrusted with the task of protecting the Syracusans and other Siceliots against oppressors or potential oppressors, but the question whether it was against the Carthaginians or the Sicilian tyrants or both simultaneously that Corinthian aid was sought and granted is one of some complexity, and all three interpretations of the somewhat indefinite and even contradictory evidence have received a measure of support from modern scholars.[2]

The earliest reference to the mission of Timoleon, which occurs in the pseudo-Aristotelian *Rhetorica ad Alexandrum* (8. 1429b), appears at first glance to support the first of these views. Despite its brevity the passage is of some interest because it was almost

---

[1] Diodorus, 16.90.1 (ὅτι τοὺς τυράννους καταλύσας καὶ τοὺς βαρβάρους καταπολεμήσας καὶ τὰς μεγίστας τῶν Ἑλληνίδων πόλεων ἀνοικίσας αἴτιος ἐγενήθη τᾶς ἐλευθερίας τοῖς Σικελιώταις); Plutarch, *Timol.* 39.5. In spite of their divergences, which are the result of inaccurate transmission, these passages amount virtually to documentary evidence. Some Sicilian writer, probably Athanis or Timaeus, must have copied the decree.

[2] For the first (Carthage): Arnoldt, *Timoleon*, 73; Holm, *Gesch. Siciliens*, ii. 193; Lenschau, *R.-E.*, viii. col. 1594; Stier, *R.-E.*, vi A, coll. 1277–8. For the second (tyranny): Meltzer, *Gesch. der Karthager*, i. 319; Clasen, *Jahrb. f. cl. Phil.*, xxxii (1886), 316; Beloch, *Gr. Gesch.*, iii. 1, 581; Glotz, *Hist. grecque*, iii. 413. For the third (both): Freeman, *History of Sicily*, iv. 292–3; Hackforth, *C.A.H.*, vi. 285–8 (though he is inclined to believe that 'it was fear of an attack by the Carthaginians that occasioned this appeal'); Pais, *Storia dell' Italia antica e della Sicilia*, ii[2]. 572–3 (apparently). Wickert, *R.-E.*, iv A, col. 1515, believes the problem to be insoluble. Contrast Thucydides, 6.8.2 on the orders issued to the commanders of the Athenian expedition to Sicily.

certainly written too early to have been derived from Timaeus, whose work has, for good or ill, so deeply influenced the surviving records of Sicilian history.[3] The author mentions, among other instances of unexpected success against overwhelming odds, the achievement of the Corinthians who Συρακοσίοις ἐννέα τριήρεσι βοηθήσαντες Καρχηδονίους ἑκατὸν καὶ πεντήκοντα ναυσὶν ἐπὶ τοῖς λιμέσι τῶν Συρακοσίων ἐφορμοῦντας τὴν δὲ πόλιν ἅπασαν πλὴν τῆς ἀκροπόλεως ἔχοντας οὐδὲν ἧττον κατεπολέμησαν. He is, however, interested only in the result of the Corinthian enterprise and not in its motives, and the purpose of his work is to give advice to orators, from whom meticulous accuracy in their illustrations from history does not seem to have been expected. In one respect the passage is palpably misleading: a reader unfamiliar with Sicilian history in this period would naturally conclude that the nine Corinthian triremes engaged the large Carthaginian fleet in battle, and this inference is in fact made by Aelian.[4] The implication, and it is only an implication, that assistance was given to the Syracusans because they were being attacked or threatened by Carthage may be equally fallacious.

It will be convenient to consider next the *Timoleon* of Plutarch, who supplies a greater volume of evidence on this question than any other author, though he seems never to have asked himself why his hero went to Sicily. Preoccupied with personal issues and moral lessons, he is never tired of speculating on the part played by τύχη and ἀρετή in the successes of Timoleon,[5] but the purely historical question here under discussion is one to which, even if the answer was readily available to him,[6] he was probably indifferent. In this instance, as so often in his *Lives*, the value of his work to the historian lies in what he preserves incidentally and almost accidentally. Several passages in the *Timoleon* throw light upon the aims of the Corinthian mission, but before they are examined it is necessary to point out that some of the

[3] It is noteworthy that the author refers only to 'Corinthians' and does not mention Timoleon, although in his preceding example he attributes to Dion the achievement of having expelled Dionysius II.

[4] *V.H.* 4.8, which seems to have been derived directly from this passage.

[5] Ziegler, *Rh. Mus.*, lxxxii (1933), 54–8.

[6] If, as I have suggested in *C.Q.*, xxxii (1938), 65–74, much of the *Timoleon* is dependent upon a Peripatetic biography and not directly on Timaeus, the author of this work may well have omitted to define the purpose of the Corinthian mission.

THE PURPOSE OF TIMOLEON'S MISSION

evidence applied to this problem and ostensibly relevant to it is inadmissible.

In the most recent biographical sketch of Timoleon it has been maintained that, because the Syracusans honoured him by resolving to employ a Corinthian in any subsequent war against barbarians (Plut., 38. 4, ὁσάκις συμπέσοι πόλεμος αὐτοῖς πρὸς ἀλλοφύλους), his mission must have been directed against Carthage and not against tyranny.[7] A parallel, though equally unconvincing, argument might be advanced in support of the opposite conclusion, namely, that Timoleon must have been charged with the suppression of tyranny rather than with the defence of Greek Sicily against Carthaginian aggression because he did not resign his command immediately after the conclusion of peace with Carthage but retained it until he had overthrown Mamercus and Hippo. Arguments of this kind are based upon a confusion between intentions and results. A number of passages in the *Timoleon* stress the magnitude of the successes gained against the Carthaginians or the tyrants or both,[8] but they are totally irrelevant to the present discussion. Just as Timoleon was led by circumstances to launch a programme of political and social reconstruction which he can scarcely have envisaged at the outset, so his military operations undertaken in defence of Siceliot liberties were largely dependent upon the aggressive moves of his opponents. The attainments of his mission must have far exceeded, and probably tended to obscure, its aim, and it is essential to discriminate carefully between them.

In one passage Plutarch states unequivocally that the Siceliot appeal to Corinth was prompted by fear of the Carthaginians, who had recently landed large forces in Sicily (2.1, ἐν τούτῳ δὲ Καρχηδονίων στόλῳ μεγάλῳ παραγενομένων εἰς Σικελίαν καὶ τοῖς πράγμασιν ἐπαιωρουμένων, φοβηθέντες οἱ Σικελιῶται πρεσβείαν ἐβουλεύοντο πέμπειν εἰς τὴν Ἑλλάδα, καὶ παρὰ Κορινθίων βοήθειαν αἰτεῖν). This statement, however, stands entirely alone, and he proceeds to stultify it before the end of the same sentence by

---

[7] Stier, *R.-E.*, loc. cit.

[8] Apart from 39.5, cited in n. 1 above, the most important are: 23.2 and 4 (though there may be some significance in the fact that the official proclamation in 23.2 mentions only the suppression of tyranny, whereas the unofficial comment in 23.4 includes also successes against Carthage); 29.6; 35.1; 37.5. Diodorus, 16.65.9 also deals exclusively with results.

using language from which the reader must infer that Corinthian assistance was sought against the tyrants (2.2, τὴν πόλιν ὁρῶντες φιλελεύθερον καὶ μισοτύραννον οὖσαν ἀεί).[9] This latter view is presupposed elsewhere by Plutarch and underlies his entire narrative, as may be seen from the following:

(a) 7.6. In the dispatch in which Hicetas tried to deter the Corinthians from intervening in Sicily he explained that their tardiness in answering the appeal had forced him to form an alliance with the Carthaginians against Dionysius. He was acting in bad faith and sought only to anticipate charges of treachery for having first associated himself with the appeal and then intrigued with Carthage (cf. 7.3, μηνύοντα τὴν μεταβολὴν αὐτοῦ καὶ προδοσίαν). His argument indicates, however, that Dionysius and not Carthage was the enemy against whom protection was solicited. To justify collaboration with a third party on the ground that he required immediate help against the enemy was at least a plausible defence: to justify collaboration with the enemy on the ground that he required immediate help against a third party would have been somewhat ridiculous.

(b) 9.6. The envoys of Hicetas informed Timoleon at Rhegium that he must dismiss his fleet and army ὡς τοῦ πολέμου μικρὸν ἀπολείποντος συνῃρῆσθαι. The war to which Plutarch here refers is certainly the war against Dionysius,[10] whom Hicetas had a few days earlier defeated and deprived of all Syracuse except Ortygia, as is recorded in the same chapter (9.3). The envoys evidently assumed that it was in this war that Timoleon had been sent to intervene.[11]

(c) 10.7–8. Andromachus of Tauromenium is described as one who πρὸς τοὺς τυράννους φανερὸς ἦν ἀεὶ διακείμενος ἀπεχθῶς καὶ ἀλλοτρίως and accordingly (διό) co-operated with the Corinthians in their attempt to liberate Sicily. This explanation of his policy is incompatible with the view that they had come to protect the Siceliots against Carthage. It probably originates from Timaeus, who was the son of Andromachus, and is not merely an inference by Plutarch from his knowledge of the general situation.

[9] Cf. the use of μισοτύραννος in 3.4 discussed below, p. 274.
[10] Cf. 1.6, where, before any mention has been made of Carthaginian aggression, the Syracusan aristocrats appoint Hicetas to be στρατηγὸν τοῦ πολεμοῦ (also Nepos, *Timol.*, 2.1, quoted below, p. 270).
[11] Clasen, *Timaios von Tauromenion*, 75, n. 3.

(d) 11.6. Timoleon was at first distrusted by the Siceliots because Callippus and Pharax ἀμφότεροι φάσκοντες ὑπὲρ τῆς ἐλευθερίας ἥκειν καὶ τοῦ καταλύειν τοὺς μονάρχους had proved even more oppressive than the tyrants. The passage implies that Timoleon, like his ill-famed predecessors, was sent to Sicily to eradicate tyranny and declared this to be the aim of his mission in a diplomatic offensive begun as soon as he landed (12.1). The Siceliots suspected that they were being cajoled by specious promises εἰς μεταβολὴν δεσπότου καινοῦ (12.1). Hence they must have believed his first objective to be the expulsion of their present masters.[12]

From the cumulative evidence of these passages the conclusion may be drawn with some confidence that to Timaeus, whose work undoubtedly supplied Plutarch, directly or indirectly, with the foundation of his *Timoleon*, the Siceliots appealed for help against tyranny and the orders issued to the Corinthian expeditionary force were to answer this appeal. This evidence surely outweighs the single unambiguous statement quoted above that the Siceliots appealed to Corinth through fear of Carthage (2.1). Plutarch is occasionally guilty of a palpable blunder, and in this instance he, or more probably the Peripatetic biographer upon whom he may have relied at this stage, may well have erred through somewhat careless condensation of a much longer narrative. As the sentence stands, what the Siceliots feared may be assumed to have been the Carthaginian activities described in the genitive absolute. This genitive absolute, however, probably summarises a substantial excursus (ἐν τούτῳ) by Timaeus on Carthaginian plans to take advantage of Siceliot dissensions, ending with an account of the landing by Carthaginian forces in Sicily and the repressive measures undertaken by them in their own province, of which some details are preserved by Diodorus.[13] To a biographer of

[12] 16.2–3 is also noteworthy. The Corinthians were encouraged to send reinforcements to Timoleon because within fifty days after landing in Sicily he had gained possession of Ortygia and expelled Dionysius. While this passage is valuable for its indication that the mission of Timoleon was not directed against Dionysius alone, it also implies that the reinforcements were sent to enable him to complete the task so auspiciously begun, namely the suppression of tyranny throughout Greek Sicily. Nevertheless, it is not entirely certain that the object of the second expedition was the same as that of the first.

[13] 16.67, which is, however, probably derived from Theopompus and not from Timaeus (see n. 18). If the views on the chronology of Diodorus expressed

Timoleon these events would be of little interest and could be almost entirely ignored. After completing the excursus Timaeus must have returned to his main theme, the struggle for possession of Syracuse, and have proceeded to describe the fears of the Siceliots which led them to appeal to Corinth. Hence it may be only through compression that the aggressive attitude of the Carthaginians and the fears of the Siceliots have become connected in the narrative of Plutarch.

If Polybius is to be believed, Timaeus was abnormally fallible because he was abnormally prejudiced (cf. 12.7.1), and it would be hazardous to assume that if he held the view on the aim of the Corinthian mission ascribed to him above he was necessarily right. Here, however, his attitude cannot have been influenced by his admiration for Timoleon, which Polybius and others believed to have been excessive:[14] whatever the task assigned to the Corinthian expeditionary force, the credit due to its leader was unaffected. Moreover, Timaeus had every reason to be well-informed on this point. His father was the first Siceliot ally with whom Timoleon conferred, and their consultations began before the development of the situation at Syracuse suggested that Carthaginian intervention might prove more dangerous than the tyranny of Dionysius.

The evidence of Nepos, though relatively insignificant both in quantity and in quality, points to the same conclusion as that of Plutarch. In his *Timoleon*, which is certainly dependent upon the tradition established by Timaeus,[15] he refers to the reoccupation of Syracuse by Dionysius, *cuius adversarii opem a Corinthiis petierunt ducemque quo in bello uterentur postularunt* (2.1). This statement confirms the view that to Timaeus Corinthian aid was sought and granted against the tyrants rather than against the Carthaginians, whom Nepos does not even mention until he records their defeat at the Crimisus (2.4). His assumption that the Siceliot appeal was

---

below (p. 273) are accepted, the Carthaginian landing took place after the Corinthians had made preparations to answer the Siceliot appeal, but Timaeus was not an annalist and perhaps chose to record in the same passage all the activities of the Carthaginians anterior to the arrival of Timoleon.

[14] Polybius, 12.23.4–7; Cicero, *Ad Fam.*, 5.12.7; Marcellinus, *Vit. Thuc.*, 27.

[15] I have analysed this wretched compilation and discussed its relation to the *Timoleon* of Plutarch in *C.Q.* xxxii (1938), 65–7.

for assistance against Dionysius alone is probably mistaken,[16] but there is no reason to doubt the general accuracy of his brief statement.

The contribution of Diodorus is of considerably greater value. The appeal to Corinth was, he states, for a general τὸν ἐπιμελησόμενον τῆς πόλεως καὶ καταλύσοντα τὴν τῶν τυραννεῖν ἐπιβαλομένων πλεονεξίαν (16.65.1). This phrase is deplorably vague, but it has been too lightly rejected by those who believe that the Siceliots appealed for help against Carthage. It implies that the embassy was sent to Corinth before Dionysius had firmly re-established his tyranny at Syracuse,[17] and here Diodorus, who at this stage was probably following Theopompus,[18] may well have been better informed than Plutarch. The absence of any explicit reference to Dionysius may be deliberate:[19] it gives a further indication that aid was sought against the widespread recrudescence of tyranny throughout Greek Sicily (cf. τυραννίσι πολλαῖς καὶ ποικίλαις δουλεύειν ἀναγκαζόμενοι in the same sentence), but it may also reflect a reluctance to urge open conflict between the Corinthians and Dionysius, who had maintained the friendship with Peloponnesian states initiated by his father.[20] The activities of the Carthaginians before the fleet and army of Mago appeared at Syracuse to co-operate with Hicetas are described far more fully by Diodorus than by Plutarch, but his account is somewhat confused. He explains that shortly before the arrival of Timoleon the Carthaginians πυθόμενοι τὸ μέγεθος τοῦ κατὰ Σικελίαν ἐσομένου πολέμου had made overtures to the tyrants, especially Hicetas, and landed a large expeditionary force under Hanno, which proceeded to besiege the Campanians of Entella, a town in their own

---

[16] Cf. Plutarch, *Timol.* 16.2–3, discussed in n. 12 above, and Diodorus, 16.65.1, discussed in the next paragraph.

[17] Probably the aristocratic refugees at Leontini claimed to act on behalf of the Syracusan πόλις (hence the description of Hicetas as τὸν τῶν Συρακοσίων δυναστεύοντα in 67.1, unless this is an error), but ἐπιβάλλεσθαι, which must mean 'attempt' here, indicates that some part of Syracuse was still free at the time of the appeal.

[18] Hammond, *C.Q.*, xxxii (1938), 141–4, whose arguments, so far as his Group 2 is concerned, seem to me to be conclusive.

[19] Diodorus fails to mention the return of Dionysius, who reappears abruptly in the narrative in 68.1, where the attempt of Hicetas to besiege Syracuse is recorded.

[20] He sent a fleet to aid the Spartans soon after his accession (Xenophon, *Hell.* 7.4.12). Corinthian support for Dion had been almost negligible.

province (67.1–3). The narrative of Diodorus has been adduced as evidence that the Carthaginian decision to intervene was prompted by the mission of Timoleon.[21] This interpretation seems to be an arbitrary one: the 'impending war' is surely the struggle between Dionysius and his adversaries led by Hicetas, which was only beginning when the Carthaginians assembled their armament,[22] combined probably with outbreaks of violence elsewhere precipitated by the ambitions of military adventurers.[23] It is difficult to believe that the Carthaginians felt their interests to be seriously endangered by the dispatch of an obscure Corinthian at the head of a few hundred mercenaries. Their motive in sending a large force to Sicily was partly to suppress an insurgent movement in their own province and partly to exploit the weakness and dissensions of the Siceliots. They appear to have already pushed their frontier eastwards as the empire of Syracuse disintegrated;[24] they may now have hoped to dominate the straits of Messana[25] and thereby to gain access to the markets of South Italy and the Adriatic formerly controlled by the Syracusans. In one respect the mission of Timoleon seemed likely to facilitate the attainment of their ambitions: it compelled Hicetas to accept their advances and to invite their collaboration in his conflict with Dionysius.[26]

[21] Beloch, *Gr. Gesch.* iii. 1. 581–2; Hackforth, *C.A.H.*, vi. 286.

[22] It is in fact the same war as is referred to by Plutarch, 1.6 and Nepos 2.1 (see above, p. 268 with n. 10), though in each passage this war is at a different stage of development. Diodorus, 66.6, where the Carthaginian envoys at Metapontum ἐντυχόντες τῷ Τιμολέοντι διεμαρτύραντο μὴ κατάρχειν πολέμου is somewhat different, though nevertheless relevant to the present discussion. If Timoleon were sailing with orders to fight against the Carthaginians, mere protests on their part would have been entirely inappropriate; if he were sailing with orders to fight against the tyrants, a warning that they would use their formidable resources to prevent Corinthian intervention might have caused a less determined leader to dismiss his troops.

[23] Pais, op. cit., ii. 576, makes the acute suggestion that Mamercus and Hicetas were probably rivals at this time. Both may have aspired to dominate the whole plain of Leontini, one of the most productive areas in Sicily.

[24] On the south coast, Beloch, *Gr. Gesch.* iii. 1.581, n. 4 (the objections of Scheliha, *Dion*, 153–4, n. 7, to this view are unconvincing); on the north coast, Diodorus, 19.2.2 (Thermae under Carthaginian control before the birth of Agathocles about 361).

[25] Carthaginian influence was strong at Messana (Diodorus, 69.6).

[26] From Diodorus, 67.1, it is clear that the Carthaginians initiated these negotiations. Plutarch, who blackens the character of Hicetas for dramatic

The chronological arrangement of his material by Diodorus suggests that the Corinthians and the Carthaginians decided almost simultaneously to intervene in Sicily, neither side being actuated by a desire to frustrate the other. He assigns to 346/5 the Syracusan appeal to Corinth and the appointment of Timoleon; to 345/4 the assembly and departure of the Corinthian expedition, its arrival at Metapontum and Rhegium, the Carthaginian decision to send a force to Sicily, and the first operations of this force in the west. His account of Carthaginian activities is prefixed by the words βραχὺ πρὸ τούτων τῶν καιρῶν (67.1), which are tantalisingly inexact, but they surely mean that the Carthaginian intervention in Sicily described in chapter 67 took place shortly before the events recorded at the end of chapter 66, namely the voyage of Timoleon and his arrival off the Italian coast. Hence, unless the annalistic system of Diodorus has broken down, the embassy to Corinth was apparently sent in the first half of 345, and both expeditions were organised during the following winter, the Carthaginians landing in the spring of 344 and the Corinthians reaching Italy in the early summer of the same year.[27] If chronological evidence alone were taken into consideration, Carthaginian intervention might have been the result of the appeal to Corinth, though there are good reasons for believing that it was not; on the other hand, the appeal to Corinth cannot have been the result of Carthaginian intervention.

Two rather more general considerations lend support to the view that Corinthian aid was sought and granted against tyranny and not against Carthage. The prime movers of the Siceliot appeal were evidently the Syracusan aristocrats who had found refuge at Leontini after the return of Dionysius.[28] This aristocratic faction must have been recruited largely from the survivors

contrast with that of Timoleon, implies the opposite (2.3; 7.4–6), but his narrative shows that Hicetas was reluctant to incur obligations which might have proved embarrassing if he had succeeded in supplanting Dionysius as tyrant of Syracuse: he called in Carthaginian aid on a large scale only when the success of Timoleon had begun to endanger his own prospects.

[27] Beloch, *Gr. Gesch.* iii. 2. 380–2, who does not, however, attempt in this discussion of the chronology to date the appeal to Corinth or the landing of the Carthaginian force in western Sicily.

[28] Diodorus defines the petitioners as 'the Syracusans' (65.1), Plutarch first as 'the Siceliots' and later as 'the Syracusans' (2.1 and 3), Nepos as 'the

of the friends of Dion to whom Plato had addressed his *Seventh* and *Eighth Epistles*. The scheme advocated in the *Eighth Epistle* to end the deadlock between rival factions and individuals, if it had ever offered a workable compromise, had become obsolete, and no peaceful reconciliation of this kind could now be contemplated.[29] In these circumstances the appeal of the aristocrats to Corinth is more likely to have been designed to secure by force the liberation of their fellow-citizens and their own return to power at Syracuse than to obtain protection for the whole of Greek Sicily against an undeveloped threat of Carthaginian aggression. Secondly, Timoleon appears to have had only one qualification, apart from personal courage, for his appointment as leader of the Corinthian expedition,[30] namely, that he was μισοτύραννος (Plutarch, 3.4) and had rescued Corinth from tyranny by causing the death of his own brother Timophanes.[31] The selection of Timoleon, which enabled the Corinthian government to avoid both the sacrifice of a more valuable leader and the odium of having rejected the appeal,[32] is more appropriate if the task entrusted to him was the eradication of tyranny.

There is some superficial attractiveness in the view that a dual menace from tyrants and Carthaginians alike was responsible for the appeal to Corinth and the expedition of Timoleon. The originators of the appeal, perhaps suspecting that the Carthaginians were trying to entice Hicetas and might soon embark

---

enemies of Dionysius' (2.1). It is clear from the narrative of Plutarch that the Syracusan aristocrats were largely, if not wholly, responsible for the appeal: they had put themselves under the leadership of Hicetas (1.6), who shared in sending the embassy to the Peloponnese (2.3; 7.4). On their claim to represent Syracuse see above, n. 17.

[29] Of the three 'constitutional monarchs' (*Ep.* 8.355e–356b) the son of Dion and the Hipparinus who expelled Callippus were now dead, while Dionysius was disqualified by having regained his tyranny.

[30] Plutarch (3.2) ascribes his appointment to divine agency operating through an obscure citizen who nominated him.

[31] The description of him by Diodorus (65.2) as πρωτεύοντα τῶν πολιτῶν ἀνδρείᾳ τε καὶ συνέσει στρατηγικῇ seems to be an exaggeration based on his subsequent exploits in Sicily. According to Plutarch he was serving in the ranks as a hoplite in a battle fought not long before he retired for twenty years from public life, while his more spectacular brother, who evidently overshadowed him, led the cavalry (4.1) and was later put in command of 400 mercenaries (4.4).

[32] Westlake, *C.Q.* xxxiv (1940), 45.

upon an aggressive policy, may have instructed their envoys to invite the Corinthians to liberate Greek Sicily without defining explicitly the adversaries likely to be encountered. On the other hand, the Corinthians, who normally kept in close touch with Syracuse, cannot have been ignorant of the general situation in Sicily, and almost all the evidence examined above points to the conclusion that their aid was sought and given against tyranny. If they had anticipated Carthaginian intervention on a large scale, they would surely have sent with Timoleon a much stronger force or none at all.[33] It is true that the Syracusans, as in other crises of their history, stood less in need of military resources than of a disinterested leader unaffected by local jealousies, and Gylippus had arrived in Sicily with a fleet even smaller than that of Timoleon.[34] Gylippus, however, could count upon an almost wholehearted response by the Syracusans against the common enemy, together with substantial support from other cities; Timoleon could not.

[33] Clasen, *Jahrb. f. cl. Phil.* xxxii. 316, emphasises that the Corinthian force was too small to have much prospect of success against the Carthaginians.

[34] The fleet assembled by Gylippus at Leucas numbered 17 ships, but he left 13 of these to follow later, and they might well have been intercepted (Thuc. 6.104.1; 7.2.1, 4.7, 7.1).

17

Timoleon and the
reconstruction of Syracuse

The achievement of Timoleon in the field of reconstructive statesmanship received far less attention from ancient writers than the exploits of his crusade which liberated Greek Sicily from tyranny and from Carthage. Timaeus, who was largely responsible for the literary tradition, had no experience of practical politics and was therefore considered by Polybius to be unqualified to deal with political issues.[1] The *Timoleon* of Plutarch is a brilliant work, in which some aspects of his career receive detailed treatment, but except in two digressions it is wholly dependent on the tradition established by Timaeus.[2] Moreover, to a biographer who was primarily a moralist constitutional and social reform could scarcely be an attractive theme, and it is not surprising that he sketches the reconstructive accomplishments of his hero in terms of vague eulogy without fully appreciating their significance. Diodorus, on the other hand, was profoundly interested in the political and economic development of Syracuse. The parts of Book 16 devoted to the career of Timoleon reproduce his customary faults: the narrative is ill-arranged and highly compressed, degenerating here and there into a string of disconnected notes, and in its later chapters it depends upon the tradition of Timaeus.[3] Yet it constitutes the chief source of information on the reforms of Timoleon.[4] The contribution of a third-rate historian is in this sphere more valuable than that of a first-rate biographer.

[1] Polyb., 12.25 g 1, h 5.

[2] Westlake, *C.Q.* 1938, 65–74.

[3] According to Hammond, *C.Q.* 1938, 137–45, Diodorus followed Theopompus when recording the earlier stages of Timoleon's career and turned to Timaeus only when the excursus of Theopompus on Sicilian affairs ended. Unfortunately the references to political and social reform are more numerous in the chapters derived from Timaeus.

[4] The lost work of Arrian on Timoleon (*F. Gr. Hist.* 156 T 4) may have contained valuable material, but he too was probably influenced by the Timaeus tradition, as is Nepos in his very brief *Timoleon*.

The evidence of Diodorus and Plutarch cannot be supplemented from other authorities, since references to Timoleon in literature are strangely few. It is remarkable that Demosthenes at the end of his struggle for freedom ignores a mission which united Greek city-states in successful resistance to the challenge of barbarism and tyranny, that Aristotle does not refer in the *Politics* to the recent and ambitious reform of the Syracusan state. In general, the orators and political philosophers of the fourth century, with the exception of Plato, show little interest in Sicily —perhaps because the cities of the Greek homeland could no longer attempt to exploit its material resources, which had once tempted them. Documentary evidence too is disappointingly meagre. Though Sicilian coinages are many and illuminating, no contemporary inscriptions from Sicily are available, and few from other districts or of other periods are relevant to the Sicily of Timoleon. Finally, owing to the lacuna in Sicilian history which extends from his death to the rise of Agathocles the immediate consequences of his work are obscure, and a view of it in retrospect, which might have been revealing, is unobtainable.

I. TIMOLEON'S DICTATORSHIP

It is unnecessary to show that Timoleon must have enjoyed very wide powers at Syracuse, and the almost universal verdict of modern scholars that he held the office of στρατηγὸς αὐτοκράτωρ[5] requires little substantiation. Yet his appointment to a dictatorship is nowhere recorded, nor is the title of his office precisely defined. Diodorus and Plutarch do not reproduce official terminology, and their use of στρατηγός, στρατηγεῖν or στρατηγία is indefinite and even ambiguous. When at the outset the Syracusan exiles at Leontini appealed to Corinth, their request was for a στρατηγός (D. 65.1);[6] it was as στρατηγός that Timoleon was sent to Sicily (D. 65.2, 66.1; P. 3.2, 7.5); at the end of his career he

[5] Kahrstedt, *Griechisches Staatsrecht*, i. 367–8; Hüttl, *Verfassungsgeschichte von Syrakus*, 127; Schwahn, Pauly-Wissowa-Kroll, *Real-Encyclopädie der classischen Altertumswissenschaft*, Suppl. vi, 1130–1; Stier, *R.-E.*, vi A, 1287. Scheele, *Strategos Autokrator*, 48–9, has some doubts, which seem unwarranted.

[6] Throughout this essay Diodorus 16 is referred to as D., and Plutarch's *Timoleon* as P.; where reference is made to books of Diodorus other than 16 or to *Lives* of Plutarch other than the *Timoleon* the normal abbreviations are used, as Diod. 19 or Plut. *Dion*.

had 'held the office of στρατηγός for eight years' (D. 90.1). His position is once described as μοναρχία (P. 37.10), and the use of this word is the more striking in that it occurs in a quotation from Athanis, a contemporary historian.[7] The term αὐτοκράτωρ is once used by Plutarch, where Timoleon is 'sent to be αὐτοκράτωρ over the Syracusans', but this passage belongs to the *Comparison of Timoleon and Aemilius Paullus* (2.7) and has little value; for in these *Comparisons* he naturally follows his authorities far less closely than in the *Lives* themselves, and his choice of this word is perhaps influenced by its use in his own day as a translation of *imperator*. It is rather from the scope of Timoleon's activities than from the vague phraseology of the authorities that his tenure of a dictatorial office may be inferred. He was manifestly neither a mere mercenary captain employed by the Syracusans so long as they required his services nor a member, for a number of successive years, of a college of Syracusan στρατηγοί. His military achievements and, still more, the drastic measures of reform to be discussed below, of which most were evidently executed on his own authority, leave no room for doubt that he held the office of στρατηγὸς αὐτοκράτωρ in the Syracusan state. But this dictatorship raises several problems with which it is necessary to deal before examining his reforms.

The formal relationship between Timoleon and Corinth is left obscure by the authorities. What official status, if any, did he enjoy in the Corinthian state? With this question is closely allied another, which depends largely upon it, namely, how far his mission is to be regarded as a Corinthian enterprise. It has been argued that he was στρατηγὸς αὐτοκράτωρ of Corinth as well as of Syracuse,[8] but this view is unsupported by any cogent evidence or by any parallel case in Corinthian history, and it seems incompatible with the attitude of the Corinthians towards his mission. Whereas at Syracuse the office of στρατηγὸς αὐτοκράτωρ, though extra-constitutional, was more or less legitimised by traditional practice, at Corinth there was no precedent, so far as is known,

---

[7] The fragment was probably transmitted to Plutarch indirectly through Timaeus and a Hellenistic biographer (Westlake, *C.Q.* 1938, 70 n. 8), but there is no reason why this word should have been altered in the course of transmission. In recording the appointment of Agathocles as σ. α. Diodorus (19.9.4) uses the verb μοναρχεῖν. Another passage of Diodorus (19.70.3) implies that Timoleon conducted τὴν τῶν ὅλων ἐπιμέλειαν.

[8] Kahrstedt, *Gr. Staatsrecht*, 366–7.

for such an appointment.[9] More important, the Corinthians were apathetic towards the Syracusan appeal: they sent a man who was unlikely to be of any service to themselves, they supplied him with a meagre armament, and it was only when he had gained unexpected successes that they began to co-operate with any enthusiasm.[10] In these circumstances it is hard to believe that they invested him with unrestricted powers over their own city. Plutarch, it is true, usually describes the army of Timoleon as 'the Corinthians' and pictures the whole enterprise as Corinthian,[11] but this attitude is probably influenced by Timoleon's own policy and reflects his loyalty to Corinth rather than Corinthian loyalty to him. Corinth had sunk very low in the fourth century, and he was naturally eager to raise the prestige of his native city by associating it with him in his success.[12] To re-establish an intimate connection between Corinth and Syracuse would be advantageous to both cities, and for this reason he remained a Corinthian citizen till his death (D. 90.1; P. 39.5). This point of view and its implications must have been communicated to Andromachus of Tauromenium, the ally of Timoleon and father of the historian Timaeus, whose work is the ultimate source of Plutarch's narrative.[13] Diodorus, on the other hand, who does not seem to have relied wholly on Timaeus,[14] lays no emphasis on the part played by the Corinthians. Though prone to excessive loyalty to his native Sicily, he cannot be accused of prejudice in this instance, since achievements are

[9] Timophanes, the brother of Timoleon, could have smoothed his path to tyrannical power if he had first secured from the populace, which supported him (D, 65.3), the office of σ. α. But he was forced to adopt more violent methods.

[10] Westlake, *C.Q.* 1940, 45.

[11] Kahrstedt, *Gr. Staatsrecht*, 366–7, collects the relevant passages. The most important of these, being virtually documentary evidence, is the inscription quoted in 29.6, in which Κορίνθιοι καὶ Τιμολέων ὁ στρατηγός dedicate in Corinthian temples a part of the spoils captured at the Crimisus. The dedication is not, however, that of the whole army but only of those soldiers who were citizens of Corinth.

[12] The plea of the envoys whom he sent to Corinth to ask for support for his programme of colonisation confirms this view (P. 23.1; cp. 29.5, βουλόμενος αὐτοῦ τὴν πατρίδα πᾶσιν ἀνθρώποις ζηλωτὴν εἶναι).

[13] Hence Plutarch often credits the Corinthians with a nobility of sentiment which the facts belie (2.2, 3.1, 7.7).

[14] See above, n. 3.

accredited to Timoleon rather than to the Syracusans. If the liberation and reconstruction of Syracuse had been primarily a Corinthian accomplishment, the Corinthians would surely have tried to reap the fruits of their success by maintaining close contact with Syracuse after the death of Timoleon. But, apart from the mission of Acestoridas, who was apparently sent at the request of the Syracusans in accordance with a law passed in Timoleon's lifetime (Diod. 19.5.1; P. 38.4), there is no evidence of any subsequent contact between the two cities.

Timoleon held no Corinthian magistracy, nor can he have been nominated by Corinth to be στρατηγὸς αὐτοκράτωρ at Syracuse.[15] A στρατηγὸς αὐτοκράτωρ could be elected only by the vote of the Syracusan people,[16] and even if the exiles at Leontini claimed to constitute the Syracusan state, it was scarcely within their power to delegate to the government of another city the right of nominating a dictator. When Timoleon sailed for Sicily, he was no more than a commander of mercenaries dispatched with the not very enthusiastic blessing of the Corinthians. An obvious parallel is the case of Gylippus, who was sent from Sparta with the vague commission to be ἄρχοντα τοῖς Συρακοσίοις (Thuc. 6.93.2, cp. 91.4). Whether Gylippus ever held any official position at Syracuse is extremely doubtful,[17] and, if he did, his office was exclusively military.[18] He certainly cannot have been nominated by Sparta to hold a Syracusan dictatorship.[19]

At what stage in his career was Timoleon appointed στρατηγὸς αὐτοκράτωρ? The landing of his force in Sicily almost certainly belongs to the summer of 344,[20] and this is the point from which his dictatorship is believed to date. But he remained at Catana

[15] Kahrstedt, *Gr. Staatsrecht*, 367, believes that this was the case, but he relies upon the passage in the *Comparison* (2.7) cited above, which, as has been pointed out, cannot be accepted as trustworthy evidence. In Diodorus (66.1) Timoleon is appointed by the Corinthians ἐπὶ τὴν ἐν Συρακούσσαις στρατηγίαν, but this does not necessarily imply a dictatorship.

[16] Diod. 19.9.4; Polyaen. 5.3.7 (Schwahn, *R.E.* Suppl. vi. 1130).

[17] Scheele, *Strat. Autokr.*, 35–6. Hüttl, *Verf. v. Syrakus*, 79 n. 88, is surely mistaken in believing that he was a member of the college of Syracusan *strategi*.

[18] He was unable to save Nicias and Demosthenes from execution (Thuc., 7.86.2).

[19] Kahrstedt, *Gr. Staatsrecht*, 30 n. 2 and 365 n. 3. The anecdote of Polyaen., 1.42.1 is a palpable fabrication, but it at least suggests that Gylippus was not αὐτοκράτωρ when he arrived.

[20] Beloch, *Gr. Gesch.* iii. 2. 380–1.

with most of his army throughout the following winter and until the summer of 343. In the meantime Ortygia was occupied almost exclusively by the mercenaries and followers of Dionysius,[21] while the rest of the city was in the hands of Hicetas and the Carthaginians. Hence no representative meeting of the assembly, and consequently no legitimate election of a dictator, can have taken place before the liberation of the whole city by Timoleon and the withdrawal of Hicetas. Moreover, it is highly unlikely that the Syracusans elected to an office so liable to be abused a citizen of another city about whom they knew nothing except that he was a hater of tyrants.[22] This consideration is another obstacle to the conventional assumption that Timoleon became στρατηγὸς αὐτοκράτωρ of Syracuse as soon as, or even before, he landed in Sicily. It was not to liberate the city from Dionysius, Hicetas and the Carthaginians that he was elected dictator, and his appointment must be posterior to this liberation, when he had already afforded clear evidence of his disinterested intentions and his talent for leadership. A dictator was required owing to the menace of tyrants, who still held other Sicilian cities, and owing to the need of reconstruction within the Syracusan state. This view raises a chronological difficulty, but it is not serious. According to Diodorus (90.1) Timoleon died in the archonship of Phrynichus (337/6) στρατηγήσας ἔτη ὀκτώ, and if, as is likely, this refers to his dictatorship, his election would appear to have preceded the liberation of Syracuse (70.1), which was completed at the beginning of the archonship of Pythodotus (343/2). But in Plutarch (37.6) his entire career in Sicily is said to have lasted rather less than eight years. Diodorus has mistakenly assumed that his dictatorship dated from the moment of his arrival, just as in the same sentence his death is confused with his abdication.[23]

The powers with which he was invested by his election to the office of στρατηγὸς αὐτοκράτωρ can be inferred only from his own

[21] Diodorus and Plutarch disagree concerning the abdication of the tyrant, and its date is disputed. My own view is that Dionysius came to terms with Timoleon towards the end of 344, but was not sent to Corinth until the late summer of 343.
[22] As Plutarch points out (11.6), the Siceliots had bitter memories of so-called liberators from Greece.
[23] Beloch, Gr. Gesch. iii. 2. 384; Kahrstedt, Gr. Staatsrecht, 368 n. 3.

activities[24] and from those of other dictators at Syracuse. There is, however, some discrepancy between the dictatorships on which evidence survives. An office of this nature, often combined with a tyranny, was liable to arbitrary interpretation, and the character of each dictatorship was to some extent determined by the circumstances under which the dictator was appointed. Dion was twice στρατηγὸς αὐτοκράτωρ, but between his first dictatorship and his second there were fundamental differences. In the first he had a co-dictator, whose competence equalled his own,[25] though in fact Megacles appears to have been a nonenity. On their own request the dictators were assisted by a board of twenty συνάρχοντες, and apparently their term of office was limited to the period prior to the next annual election of normal *strategi*; for, when this period had elapsed, they were not re-elected owing to a change of popular feeling. Nevertheless, their office was a genuine dictatorship while it lasted, since they enjoyed the right of convening the assembly and of nominating military and naval commanders.[26] The second dictatorship of Dion was very different. He had no colleague, and he continued to hold office until his death, maintaining it by force against the opposition of the democratic party, whose distrust of him must have been widely shared in the assembly. This second dictatorship of Dion is parallel in most respects to those exercised by the elder Dionysius throughout his tyranny[27] and by Agathocles before he became a Hellenistic king.[28] Under such dictatorships the semblance of a republican constitution was maintained, the council and assembly continuing to meet and in theory to perform their normal functions.[29] But the annual election of a col-

[24] The more autocratic measures of Timoleon are summarised by Hüttl, *Verf. v. Syrakus*, 127.

[25] D. 10.3; Plut. *Dion* 29.4.

[26] This is proved by the story about the appointment of Heracleides as navarch (Plut. *Dion* 33.1–3).

[27] Most scholars disbelieve the statement of Plato (*Ep.* 8.353a) that Hipparinus was colleague to Dionysius (Beloch, *Gr. Gesch.* ii. 1. 410 n. 1; Hüttl, *Verf. v. Syrakus*, 99 n. 2).

[28] Agathocles first held a limited dictatorship of an unusual kind (Hüttl, *Verf. v. Syrakus*, 130 n. 7) for one year, during which he was apparently hampered by colleagues, whether associates in his office or members of a board of *strategi* (Diod. 19.9.3–4). In the following year he attained a full dictatorship.

[29] Hüttl, *Verf. v. Syrakus*, 100–1 (Dionysius) and 131 (Agathocles). Schwahn,

lege of *strategi* was suspended. The dictator presided over the assembly, enjoyed full control of finance and of the army and navy, and had the power to redistribute public land and to direct foreign policy as he pleased. Since the plenary powers of Timoleon, as will be seen when his reforms are examined, were no less wide and he certainly had no colleague, it must have been to a dictatorship of this character that he was elected. He was not the servant of the Syracusan state, but entered into a partnership with it, in which he was evidently the predominant partner.[30]

It is impossible to decide with certainty whether his office was limited in the first instance to a single year and thereafter renewed annually, or whether he was appointed for an undefined period. Conclusive evidence is lacking concerning the limitation of tenure imposed upon other Syracusan dictators, and modern scholars disagree on this point.[31] It seems, however, that the dictatorship of Dion and Megacles, which merely filled a gap until the next election of normal *strategi*, was exceptional, and that usually there was no specified time-limit. A στρατηγὸς αὐτοκράτωρ, like a Thessalian *tagus*, was elected to deal with a dangerous situation which demanded that the government should be more centralised than under normal conditions. Since unscrupulous dictators, such as Dionysius, were able to prolong their tenure of office indefinitely, no constitutional means of terminating a dictatorship appears to have existed, and the dictator was probably expected to lay down his office as soon as his special task was accomplished.[32] Dion courted assassination by retaining his second dictatorship when he was no longer acceptable to the assembly; he imitated the methods of Dionysius

R.-E., Suppl. vi. 1131, maintains that a σ. α. at Syracuse could not legitimately carry out reforms unless they were ratified by the assembly. This may be true, though the evidence is inconclusive. But in practice the assembly evidently had no means of rejecting the proposals of the dictator whom it had appointed, as is clear from Dion's second dictatorship.

[30] The phrase ἔδοξε τῷ Τιμολέοντι καὶ τοῖς Συρακοσίοις (P. 22.7) may be compared with the well-known inscription Ἱάρων ὁ Δεινομένεος καὶ τοὶ Συροκόσιοι (Tod, *Greek Historical Inscriptions*, 22).

[31] Beloch, *Gr. Gesch.* iii. 2.197, is inclined to believe that Dionysius I was appointed for life, Glotz, *Histoire grecque* iii. 387, that he had himself re-elected annually.

[32] So Schwahn believes (*R.E.*, Suppl. vi. 1130), but the evidence which he adduces (Diod. 19.5.5) refers to the first dictatorship of Agathocles, which was of an unusual and limited character (see n. 28).

without protecting himself adequately against the odium which they must incur. On the other hand, Timoleon faithfully respected the needs of the Syracusan state, resigning his office either because he believed his mission fulfilled or, more probably, because his age and growing blindness prevented him from continuing his duties. The populace deeply regretted his resignation from an office which he alone had held without forfeiting confidence or respect. He had shown himself to be a genuinely democratic dictator.

The conclusions of this section may be summarised in a few words. Though Timoleon carefully fostered friendly relations between Corinth and Syracuse, he was not στρατηγὸς αὐτοκράτωρ of Corinth. He was appointed στρατηγός αὐτοκράτωρ by the Syracusan assembly after the liberation of the city was completed in 343, and he held this office until his resignation in the winter of 337/6. His powers were unlimited, being as wide as those enjoyed by Dionysius I throughout his tyranny and by Dion in his second dictatorship.

II. THE POPULATION

One of the most serious obstacles which lay in Timoleon's path was the depletion of the citizen-body at Syracuse. Some means of remedying this had to be found if he were to succeed in restoring, even to the most limited degree, the political greatness and economic prosperity of the city. Casualties in war and civil strife, executions and banishments, voluntary withdrawals of citizens unable to make a livelihood in conditions of insecurity had reduced the population, which is believed to have exceeded 100,000 at the death of Dionysius I,[33] to a figure perhaps below 10,000.[34] Owing to shortage of labour agriculture in eastern

[33] Beloch, *Gr. Gesch.* iii. 1.304. The figures of Hochholzer, *Klio*, 1936, 164–70, are arbitrary.

[34] Hackforth, *Cambridge Ancient History*, vi. 293 n. 1, infers a population of 10,000 in 354–3 from Plato, *Ep.* 7.337c, but the interpretation of the passage is uncertain (Harward, *The Platonic Epistles*, n. ad loc.), and the figure may be given *exempli gratia* without special reference to Syracuse. Nevertheless, it is confirmed to some extent by the size of the Syracusan contingent at the battle of the Crimisus, which was 3,000 (P. 25.4). At that time (341) the programme of colonisation, though begun, had not yet proved very successful (see below), but the proportion of men of military age would be abnormally high among the colonists. If Timoleon took with him some three-quarters

Sicily had long been neglected (D. 83.1; P. 22.8), and if the more fertile areas were to remain uncultivated, this retrogression would become irreparable. Plutarch's vivid description of the material and social decay at Syracuse and elsewhere cannot be dismissed as a rhetorical exaggeration (P. 22.4–6, cp. 1.2–3 and Nepos, *Timol.* 3.1). As Plato had pointed out some years earlier (*Ep.* 8.353e), there was a real danger that Greek language and culture might be obliterated by barbarian domination, whether Carthaginian or Italian.[35] Plato had therefore advised the partisans of Dion to swell the Greek population by attracting settlers from every available source, though he doubted whether this step would be practicable in the immediate future.[36] The need was now even more pressing and could not be wholly met by the expedient so often adopted by the tyrants of transferring the inhabitants of one Sicilian city to another. Settlers were required in large numbers and must be sought to a large extent outside Sicily.

As soon as Syracuse became a free city, the population was in some degree increased without official inducement. Many who had fled to places of safety in the vicinity during the struggles between Dionysius II and his successive opponents must have returned to resume their occupations. But even these refugees showed some disinclination to return at once, especially those who had been living in fortresses (φρούρια) and had learned to distrust city-life. The mention of φρούρια at this point by both Plutarch and Diodorus raises a minor difficulty, which may be briefly discussed here. These φρούρια were fortified posts held by garrison troops of the tyrants, and the office of φρούραρχος was an influential one under the elder Dionysius.[37] The largest

---

of the available citizen-militia, the total population would then be about 13,000–15,000.

[35] The Oscans to whom Plato refers are surely the mercenaries recruited from Italy by the tyrants. Most were settled in Sicily after their discharge and proved a menace to Greek civilisation.

[36] *Ep.* 7.336d–e. The younger Dionysius claimed to have entertained a similar design (*Ep.* 3.315d). A precedent had been established long ago by Hieron, when 5,000 Peloponnesian colonists were brought to Sicily to form half of the population of Aetna (Diod. 11.49.1).

[37] Beloch, *Gr. Gesch.* iii. 2.199; Hüttl, *Verf. v. Syrakus*, 107. The limited dictatorship of Agathocles was a command ἐπὶ τῶν ἐρυμάτων τῶν ἐν Σικελίᾳ (Hüttl, *Verf. v. Syrakus*, 130 n. 7).

φϱούϱιον was the castle of the tyrant on Ortygia, but others were established at points of strategic importance in country districts. It is not, however, at all obvious why refugees from anarchy caused by the tyrants should be living, as Plutarch records, in φϱούϱια normally occupied by mercenaries of the tyrants, or what Diodorus means by his statement that Timoleon 'restored freedom to the φϱούϱια'.[38] The explanation seems to be this. The term came to be applied to any garrisoned locality; many of these had now passed out of tyrant hands, and their mercenary garrisons either were withdrawn or deserted, some joining Timoleon (D. 69.4). Civilian refugees must have swelled the populations of these strongholds, finding protection similar to that which the hill-top villages of modern Sicily formerly afforded against bandits. Some of the mercenaries, now unemployed, may have remained and provided further safeguard for the refugees. When Timoleon demolished the castle of the tyrants on Ortygia, he also dismantled the lesser φϱούϱια elsewhere and invited their occupants to return to the city.

The programme of colonisation on which Timoleon now embarked attained ultimate success only after some years of failure. The relatively detailed narrative of Plutarch (22.7–24.1) creates the misleading impression that it was an unqualified success almost from the outset, but the short notices of Diodorus (82.3, 5) serve to dispel this illusion. The chief divergence between the two versions is chronological, and here that of Diodorus, though his annalistic system is not strictly maintained, is certainly preferable. According to Plutarch (24.1) the scheme had already made good progress when Timoleon began his campaign against the tyrants in 342, and he censures the people of Syracuse because ἀπὸ τοσούτων μυϱιάδων only 3,000 citizens could be induced to follow Timoleon to the Crimisus in 341 (25.4). But the threat of an impending struggle against the huge armament which was known to be assembling at Carthage (22.8) would scarcely

<hr/>

[38] P. 22.6, τῶν ἐν τοῖς ἐϱύμασι καὶ φϱουϱίοις κατοικούντων (cp. Nepos, Timol. 3.3, propugnacula); D. 70.4, τοῖς δὲ φϱουϱίοις ἀπέδωκε τὴν ἐλευθεϱίαν. Stier, R.E., viA. 1283, believes that in the latter passage Diodorus refers to the discharge of the tyrant's mercenaries (τὰ φϱούϱια, a not uncommon use) by Timoleon. But mercenaries were not slaves, and ἀπέδωκε τὴν ἐλευθεϱίαν is a very strange phrase to use of their discharge. Moreover, the composition of Timoleon's army at the Crimisus suggests that he did not discharge these troops but took them into his own service.

286

encourage prospective colonists. The series of events which Plutarch describes cannot have been completed in a few months, as he appears to assume, and must have occupied several years. Cephalus and Dionysius, the Corinthian lawgivers, who arrived in the middle of the campaigning season of 342 (24.3), were doubtless members of a small vanguard, whereas a large number of the colonists must have come to Syracuse only after the conclusion of peace with Carthage in 339.[39] Plutarch implies that 10,000 settlers crossed from Greece to Sicily in a body, but this is a palpable error, as may be seen from the version of Diodorus. The latter, who mentions the programme of colonisation for the first time towards the end of his account of Timoleon's career, states that shortly before peace was concluded with Carthage the number of colonists sent from Corinth amounted to 5,000.[40] Since the total number of colonists from Greece reached 10,000 (P. 23.5), the programme evidently gathered impetus after peace was signed.

Timoleon probably issued a local appeal for settlers from other parts of Sicily towards the end of 343, and some, including Carcinus, the father of Agathocles,[41] emigrated to Syracuse almost at once. The letter and the Syracusan embassy which Timoleon sent to Corinth may have arrived before the end of 343, but the games and festivals at which the Corinthians issued their proclamation inviting all Sicilian exiles to return home are

[39] Clasen, *Jahrbücher* 1888, 168; Hüttl, *Verf. v. Syrakus*, 126.

[40] D. 82.3. Some scholars believe Diodorus to mean that 5,000 of the settlers from Greece were Corinthians, i.e. half of the total of 10,000 given by Plutarch (cp. Hackforth, *C.A.H.* vi. 293). This is surely a misinterpretation of the passage. The Corinthians sponsored the enterprise, and the colonists were embarked at Corinth (hence τοὺς ὑπὸ Κορινθίων ἐκπεμφθέντας); but it is most improbable that half of the 10,000, which includes returning exiles, were Corinthians. Colonists were normally drawn for the most part from backward districts such as Arcadia.

This chapter in Diodorus (82) is a conglomeration of disconnected notes on events which covered a number of years, but there is no reason to doubt that these notes are arranged in the correct sequence. Thus at some time between the battle at the Crimisus and the peace with Carthage the programme of colonisation, so far as settlers from Greece are concerned, was only half completed. He gives further figures later (82.5).

[41] Carcinus left Thermae when his son was about eighteen, i.e. about 343 (Timaeus, *F. Gr. Hist.* 566 F 124b). He was, however, influenced by exceptional circumstances (Diod. 19.2.7).

those of the spring and summer of the following year (P. 23.2). Though plots of land and free transportation were offered, the response to these appeals and to others sent to the Aegean islands and to Asia was most discouraging. There had been 1,000 exiles from Syracusan territory alone living in Greece in 357 (Plut. *Dion*, 22.7), and the number must have increased substantially since that date. The total of those now willing to return was insufficient, as even Plutarch is compelled to admit. The menace from Carthage and the Sicilian tyrants had still to be removed, and the prospects of success cannot have been considered very bright. Many of the Sicilian exiles, who had prospered in their new homes, must have felt disinclined to sacrifice their present security in exchange for the dubious blessing of repatriation. Accordingly, Greeks from Corinth and other parts who had not hitherto lived in Sicily were invited to emigrate and offered Syracusan citizenship.[42] Again the result was disappointing, and indeed the final total of 10,000 settlers (including exiles) who came from the Greek homeland during the dictatorship of Timoleon cannot have afforded him any great satisfaction at a time when many factors encouraged emigration. In this period the Greek peninsula was apparently suffering from over-population,[43] for which no outlet was found before Alexander opened the way to the East. Factional disorders were being caused in many cities by the diplomacy of Philip when the Syracusan programme of colonisation began, and before it ended, Chaeronea had destroyed Greek autonomy. A total of 10,000 from Greece is scarcely impressive when it is remembered that colonial enterprises of the fifth century to Ennea Hodoi and Heraclea in Trachis—new foundations liable to attack by neighbouring tribes—both attracted an equal number in a short time and apparently without difficulty.[44]

[42] The promise of citizenship appears to have been fulfilled only after the battle at the Crimisus (Diod. 19.2.8). But, as has been shown above, very many of the colonists emigrated after this date. Syracusan citizenship may have been offered to some Sicilians who were not colonists. There was some doubt in antiquity whether Timaeus was a Tauromenian or a Syracusan (Laqueur, *R.E.* viA. 1076–7), and this may have arisen because the Tauromenians, or, more probably, the house of Andromachus alone, received Syracusan citizenship in recognition of their services to Timoleon.

[43] Beloch, *Gr. Gesch.* iii. 1.267.

[44] Ennea Hodoi: Thuc. 1.100.3, 4.102.2; Diod. 11.70.5. Heraclea: Diod.

The success of the Syracusan scheme was achieved owing to the more enthusiastic response of Sicily and Italy, which together contributed 50,000 colonists.[45] Among those who came to Syracuse from other parts of Sicily were many who took advantage of the clause in the terms of peace between Syracuse and Carthage whereby Greeks domiciled in the Carthaginian province were permitted to emigrate with their families and property. Under the regime of Dionysius I Greeks had drifted from the east into the Carthaginian province (Diod. 14.41.1), where they hoped to enjoy greater security and better trading conditions, and a reverse movement was now initiated by Timoleon. Greeks living in the west would be encouraged to come to Syracuse not only by the promise of citizenship but also by the consideration that they would no longer be liable to the tithe which the Carthaginians exacted from subject populations throughout their empire. Many settlers from Sicily were doubtless of Sicel stock; for the Sicels were now very largely hellenised, and the distinction between them as the Siceliots had become blurred. The ratio of Sicilian to Italian colonists is not recorded, but the latter perhaps formed a majority. At this time the Italian Greeks were hard-pressed by the Bruttians, Lucanians and Messapians,[46] and many evidently foresaw that as citizens of Syracuse they were likely to suffer less acutely from barbarian invasion than if they remained in Italy. But here too the influx was no doubt gradual and was probably greatest after the defeat and death of Archidamus at Mandonium in 338.

There is no serious discrepancy between the versions of Plutarch and Diodorus on the number and distribution of the colonists. Plutarch's total of 60,000 from all sources, which has the authority of Athanis, is probably accurate; but whereas he

---

12.59.5 (Thuc. 3.92–3 gives no numbers). For Thurii no figure is available, but it must have been high.

[45] P. 23.6. Hackforth, *C.A.H.* vi. 293, believes that Plutarch's 60,000 (10,000 from Greece, 50,000 from Italy and Sicily) excludes women and children, but in that case the armies of the Agathocles period would have been larger and the economic recovery of Sicily more striking. On the other hand, the scepticism of Beloch, *Bevölkerung der gr.-röm. Welt*, 277 n. 8, who considers that the colonists amounted to only 10,000 in all, is entirely unwarranted.

[46] Ciaceri, *Storia della Magna Grecia*, iii. 1–9.

implies that all were settled in the immediate vicinity of Syracuse, Diodorus states that 40,000 were received at Syracuse and 10,000 at Agyrium (82.5). It may be assumed that a wider distribution of the colonists followed the final liberation of eastern Sicily from the rule of tyrants, but there remains a difference of 10,000 between the two estimates, for which the treatment of Leontini by Timoleon is probably responsible. The transference of the Leontines to Syracuse, which belongs to the close of his career (D. 82.7), is inconsistent with his agricultural policy, since Leontini commanded the richest corn-growing area of eastern Sicily. But Diodorus seems to have recorded only half of a process which was in reality an exchange of populations. Leontini, which in the lifetime of Timoleon issued a coinage closely resembling that of Syracuse and was a town of some importance at the beginning of Agathocles's career,[47] cannot have been left uninhabited and must have been re-peopled by a section of the colonists. The former inhabitants, being descended from the mercenaries of Dionysius I and till lately subjects of Hicetas, were under some suspicion, and Timoleon therefore removed them from a city whence so many revolutionary movements against the Syracusan government had originated. The majority of the 10,000 missing from the brief account of Diodorus thus probably formed the new population of Leontini, while the remainder may be those sent to Camarina (D. 82.7). Civic pride has certainly misled Diodorus when he ascribes 10,000 colonists to the territory of his native Agyrium alone (82.5); for this small hill-top city could not maintain so large a supplement to its population.[48] This body of 10,000 must have been distributed widely over the fertile area watered by the Symaethus and its tributaries, which embraced Adranum, Aetna, Centuripa, Enna and Morgantina. All these towns issued coins in this period and enjoyed considerable prosperity,[49] and the support which they

---

[47] Justin, 22.2.2. It was from the new elements of the population that Agathocles received most support, and if, as seems likely, Leontini surrendered voluntarily to him, there is a further reason for believing that a section of the colonists was settled there.

[48] Diodorus states (14.95.4) that in the time of Agyris (392) the citizen-body numbered 20,000. But his references to his native town are invariably suspect, and this figure, even if it includes neighbouring villages dominated by Agyris, is much exaggerated.

[49] The colonisation of this district was of course posterior to the expulsion

subsequently gave to Agathocles against the Syracusan aristocrats suggests that they contained a large number of immigrants hostile to the rule of the Six Hundred.[50] Since all the colonists were apparently granted Syracusan citizenship, whether settled at Syracuse or elsewhere (cp. n. 42), the Symaethus basin was now largely peopled by citizens of Syracuse.[51]

When the programme of colonisation was initiated, it was stated in the proclamation issued at Corinth that plots of land would be allocated ἐπ᾽ ἴσοις καί δικαίοις.[52] This promise was fulfilled (P. 23.6), but the distribution cannot have been so equitable in practice as is claimed. It must have taken place long before the majority of the colonists arrived, as is clear from the statement of Diodorus that οἰκήτορες ἀπεδείχθησαν εἰς μὲν τὴν Συρακοσίαν τὴν ἀδιαίρετον (sc. γῆν).[53] Since it would be uneconomical to leave large tracts of the best land uncultivated for subsequent division among an indeterminable number of colonists, latecomers received somewhat inferior plots. Former citizens certainly enjoyed an advantage over colonists, and although every acre of Syracusan territory, with the exception of sacred land, was apparently confiscated for redistribution (P. 23.6), in almost every case an occupant regained the estate hitherto owned by him. Confirmation of this view is provided both by the brief

---

of the Campanians from Aetna, of Apolloniadas from Agyrium, and of Nicodamus from Centuripa (D. 82.4). The prosperity of Agyrium is attested by Diodorus (83.3), that of Centuripa by archaeological evidence (Ziegler, *R.E.*, xi, 180; Pace, *Arte e Civiltà della Sicilia antica*, 1.206). Morgantina undoubtedly lay in this area (its site was long uncertain but has now been located at Serra Orlando).

[50] Diod. 19.5.4, 6.2–3; Justin, 22.2.1.

[51] Beloch, *Gr. Gesch.* iii. 2.190, concludes from Diod. 19.6.3 (καὶ καθόλου τὸν δῆμον ἐμίσουν, ἀναγκαζόμενοι ποιεῖν τὸ προσταττόμενον) that the inhabitants of Morgantina and other inland towns did not enjoy Syracusan citizenship. But here, as often, Diodorus uses δῆμος very loosely (cp. n. 62 below), and it merely means 'the present government'. With similar vagueness Justin defines the enemies of Agathocles and of the Morgantines as 'the Syracusans' (22.2.1, 5–6).

[52] P. 23.2; cp. Thuc. 1.27.1, ἐπὶ τῇ ἴσῃ καὶ ὁμοίᾳ (the projected Corinthian ἐποικία at Epidamnus).

[53] Hüttl, *Verf. v. Syrakus*, 19 n. 22, was the first to explain this phrase, which had previously been considered corrupt. He cites a parallel use in an inscription of Black Corcyra, a Syracusan colony (Dittenberger, *Sylloge Inscriptionum Graecarum³*, 141 l. 10).

account of Nepos[54] and by the conditions regulating the allocation of houses. Though these too were treated as public property, they were not distributed gratuitously but sold at an assessed figure with the stipulation that every householder was given the option of re-purchasing the house in which he lived (P. 23.6–7). This procedure is unintelligible in the case of country or suburban estates unless the householder had also the opportunity of regaining some part of the land which surrounded his house. As the sale of houses produced only 1,000 talents, prices were modest, and the richer of the colonists doubtless bought houses which had been left deserted during the period of anarchy. But most would be poor and would have to endure such makeshift accommodation as they could devise until the cultivation of their plots began to show a profit. Of the conditions to which landholders were subject nothing is recorded, but it may be assumed that, as at Locri,[55] the plots of land were inalienable except under abnormal circumstances. The system of tithe-payments instituted long ago, perhaps by Gelon,[56] and later elaborated by Hieron II, certainly remained in abeyance during this period. A heavy produce-tax would have hindered the revival of agriculture, and a new Syracusan state without imperialistic ambitions[57] could dispense with the large armaments which under the tyrants absorbed most of the income from tithe.

Settlers were also sent to Acragas and Gela, but these are probably not included by Plutarch in his total of 60,000. The colonisation of these cities was the work of leaders whose names and provenance he mentions, and it appears to have received little more than encouragement from Timoleon himself (P. 35.1–3). Acragas and Gela had suffered even more severely than other cities, probably remaining under the direct control of Carthage

[54] *Timol.* 3.2. His words summarise the practical result of the distribution without reference to its avowed intention.

[55] Arist. *Pol.* 2.1266b 19. At Black Corcyra a limited degree of alienation was permitted (Dittenberger, *S.I.G.*[3], 141 l. 8).

[56] Carcopino, *La Loi de Hiéron et les Romains*, 50–6; Hüttl, *Verf. v. Syrakus*, 139–40. The Syracusan δεϰάτη, a property-tax proverbially associated with Syracusan prosperity (Hüttl, *Verf. v. Syrakus*, 104 n. 48), cannot have been levied at a time of widespread poverty. On the other hand, export-dues, which would enrich the treasury chiefly at the expense of foreign traders, were retained (see n. 118).

[57] See below, p. 302–4.

until liberated by the peace of 339,[58] so that their colonists perhaps arrived after the resignation of Timoleon or even after his death. Whereas the Corinthians had been invited to act as *oecists* to the new Syracuse (P. 23.1), the Acragantines and Geloans adopted Timoleon himself as their *oecist*, and this may have been a posthumous compliment parallel to that paid to Brasidas by the Amphipolitans (Thuc. 5.11.1). Acragas became once more a city of some importance, but it never regained its former prosperity, as is attested by its coinage and archaeological remains.[59]

The liberation of a Greek city from tyranny often led to outbreaks of violence such as those experienced at Syracuse after the overthrow of the Deinomenids and after the expulsion of Dionysius II by Dion; and the introduction of new and mixed elements into the citizen-body is included by Aristotle in his list of the causes of revolution (*Pol.* 5.1303a 25). The period of Timoleon's dictatorship was therefore a doubly dangerous one, and it is remarkable that serious disturbances were avoided. Nevertheless, his system of land-distribution was far from flawless and lacked adequate safeguards against abuse. Within twenty years there had arisen a Solonian situation, in which the old cry for a cancellation of debts and grants of land to the poor was raised.[60] As at Thurii (Arist. *Pol.* 5.1307a 27), the upper classes had contrived to appropriate large areas of land illegally, thereby evoking the hostility of the masses (including most of the colonists), whose rights had been infringed. From this discontent sprang the tyranny of Agathocles.

III. THE CONSTITUTION

It was imperative that the motley citizen-body of the new Syracuse should be united under a stable constitution. In some respects conditions were now more favourable for constitutional reform than under the dictatorship of Dion. The abdication of Dionysius had discredited and dissolved the party which supported the tyrant-house, and the gradual influx of colonists uninfluenced by party loyalties might assist the breakdown of

[58] Beloch, *Gr. Gesch.* iii. 1.581 n. 4.
[59] Coinage, see below, p. 305–8; archaeology, Marconi, *Agrigento*, 108–13.
[60] Diod. 19.9.5, where Agathocles promises both. There is no evidence to show whether his promise was fulfilled.

factional feuds. Yet conflicting interests were many, and some form of compromise was manifestly desirable. If the new constitution were too oligarchical, it might become a δυναστεία; if too democratic, there might be a recurrence of tyranny.[61] Efforts were made to strike a balance satisfactory to all, but the success of Timoleon and his collaborators proved only temporary.

In spite of the scantiness of the evidence there can be little doubt that the outward form of the new constitution was democratic. The terminology of Diodorus and Plutarch, who define it as a democracy (D. 70.5; P. 22.3, 37.1), cannot be accepted as conclusive evidence, since δημοκρατία had come to be used in a very wide and indefinite sense.[62] It is rather from the glimpses which their narratives afford of the constitution in operation that its democratic character is discernible. Supreme authority was vested in the popular assembly, whose vote decided the most important questions both during the dictatorship of Timoleon and after his resignation. It was responsible for the condemnation of Hicetas' family and of Mamercus, for the decree that in the event of war with a foreign enemy a Corinthian general should be employed, for the decree (which is almost equivalent to documentary evidence, since Diodorus and Plutarch reproduce it verbatim with inconsiderable differences) granting posthumous honours to Timoleon.[63] At the beginning of the career of Agathocles it elected the *strategi* and formed the court before which he impeached his oligarchical opponents (Diod. 19.3.4–5). Moreover, every freeborn Syracusan, including the colonists (D. 82.5), appears to have enjoyed a share in the government without the restriction of a property-qualification, and the outspokenness with which debates in the assembly were conducted implies the right of each citizen to express an opinion.[64] Finally, the new legal code of Syracuse was based upon that of Diocles, which can scarcely have been less radical than his constitutional reform. Hence, even though the alterations introduced

---

[61] Plato, *Ep.* 8.354e, remarks that the passion of the Siceliots for unrestricted freedom led to the tyranny of Dionysius I.

[62] In the opening chapters of Diodorus 19 δημοκρατία is used with some inconsistency (4.3, 5.4, 6.3; cp. n. 51 above). In P. 5.2 δημοκρατία is used as the converse of tyranny; the constitution of Corinth was in fact an oligarchy at the time.

[63] P. 33.1, 34.6, 38.4; D. 90.1, ὁ δᾶμος τῶν Συρακοσίων, cp. P. 39.5.

[64] P. 37.3, 38.6–7; Nepos, *Timol.* 5.3.

by the legislators of Timoleon may have been drastic, as will later be shown, the principles of the new code, and presumably of the new constitution, are likely to have been those of a democracy.

Yet Timoleon did not restore the extreme democracy of Diocles. A radical party, whose views were voiced in the assembly by two demagogues, remained dissatisfied with his constitutional reorganisation,[65] and the very restricted use of sortition in appointment to the only magistracy on which information survives is inconsistent with the principles of advanced democracy. Compromise was the keynote, and this element has led some scholars to see in the new constitution an example of the 'mixed' type which Greeks defined as πολιτεία.[66] This confusing term is associated chiefly with Aristotle, though he was not its inventor, and proved convenient to him in that it enabled him to include in a single category unusual constitutions which would otherwise defy classification.[67] Thus he cites as examples the constitutions of Sparta and of the *Laws*.[68] The constitution outlined by Plato in the *Eighth Epistle*, being deeply influenced by the latter and resembling the former in some respects, might perhaps be defined as a πολιτεία, but it has almost nothing in common with that of Timoleon,[69] which was far more democratic. Two features of Aristotle's πολιτεία are that magistracies should be wholly elective and that membership of the assembly should be restricted by a moderate property-qualification (*Pol.* 4.1294b, cp. 1297b). But under the system of Timoleon sortition played a small part in the process whereby the highest magistrate was appointed, and, as noted above, very probably every citizen, whatever his property, was entitled to attend meetings of the assembly.

The constitution of Timoleon was a democracy, but it belonged to the most moderate type, which in the opinion of

[65] P. 37.1–3; Nepos, *Timol.* 5.2–3.

[66] Hüttl, *Verf. v. Syrakus*, 121; Stier, *R.E.* viA. 1287.

[67] The theories of Aristotle on 'mixed' constitutions are severely criticised by Busolt and Swoboda, *Gr. Staatskunde*, ii. 310–11.

[68] Sparta, *Pol.* 4.1294b 19; *Laws*, *Pol.* 2.1265b 27. He is not always consistent: the constitution of Syracuse between the expulsion of the Deinomenids and the reform of Diocles is described first as πολιτεία (5.1304a 27) and later as a democracy (5.1316a 32).

[69] Timoleon had perhaps more sympathy with the political doctrines of Isocrates than with those of Plato.

Aristotle was the best as well as the oldest.[70] Such democracies were essentially agricultural, the demos being composed largely of small farmers, who were seldom at liberty to attend meetings of the assembly and had little political ambition (*Pol.* 6.1318b–19a, cp. 4.1292b). Hence 'the government was administered according to law', and the executive was not prevented from effective performance of its duties by frequent interference on the part of the assembly, whose meetings were rare. The establishment of a democracy of this limited character is consistent with the agrarian policy of Timoleon. The citizens of the new Syracuse were to enjoy full political rights, but under his scheme of land-distribution, which had a political as well as an economic aim, few could spare time for regular attendance at the assembly, and those whose farms were distant could come to the city only on the greatest occasions. The colonists settled in the Symaethus basin, though granted Syracusan franchise, can have had scarcely any share in the administration of the city, and their status was little removed from that of Perioeci. The populace, therefore, was not in any practical sense the governing body of the state, and, as in Hellenistic Rhodes and Republican Rome, the democratic constitution was little more than a façade. The personal sympathies of Timoleon and his two legislators, all natives of oligarchical Corinth, may have inclined towards oligarchy, but the lesson of Dion's failure led them to adopt a form of compromise calculated to satisfy all but the most extreme democrats and to obviate the danger of immediate party strife. Unfortunately, as Aristotle points out,[71] the sound and powerful middle class upon which moderate democracies depended was usually split apart by defections into the ranks of rival extremists, so that it seldom afforded a lasting safeguard against revolutionary movements. This disintegration of the middle class seems to have become gradually more acute at Syracuse in the two decades which followed the dictatorship of Timoleon.

No evidence is extant showing the existence of a council during the lifetime of Timoleon, but the Syracusan state in other periods

---

[70] Busolt and Swoboda, *Gr. Staatskunde*, i. 440, summarise from scattered passages in the *Politics* the main features of this moderate democracy. Its ideal was ἄρχειν τοὺς ἐπιεικεῖς ἀναμαρτήτους ὄντας μηδὲν ελαττουμένου τοῦ πλήθους (*Pol.* 6.1319a 3), which seems to have been the aim of Timoleon.

[71] *Pol.* 4.1295b 35–96a, cp. Hüttl, *Verf. v. Syrakus*, 127.

seems never to have been without this important link,[72] whose omission from any constitution would have been most unorthodox. There is every reason to believe that a council existed and that it was a powerful body recruited largely from οἱ βέλτιστοι καὶ γνωριμώτατοι (P. 1.6) who had been responsible for the appeal to Corinth and therefore considered themselves to be the saviours of Syracuse. Timoleon was likely to have greater faith in men who had supported him staunchly from the outset and had a common tradition than in the demos, in which many conflicting outlooks were represented. What he needed was a conservative and not unwieldy body which, like the Roman Senate, should be the driving force of a theoretical democracy during the critical period in which his system would be put to the test. Material for such a body could best be found among the wealthier classes who had aided Dion against Dionysius, though tactful handling would be necessary if they were to be reconciled to an influx of colonists and the establishment of an outwardly democratic constitution.

The creation of such a council by Timoleon is *a priori* likely, and when some twenty years later the government is under the control of a body defined by Diodorus as τὸ τῶν ἑξακοσίων συνέδριον,[73] it is reasonable to assume that this is the council of Timoleon now degenerated into an oppressive oligarchy, though retaining the official status of a constitutional senate.[74] But since Diodorus later describes this Six Hundred as ἑταιρεία (19.6.4), opinion is sharply divided on the question of its status, some scholars believing that it was merely a political club and therefore unconnected with any council instituted by Timoleon.[75] The latter view is surely mistaken. The legitimately constituted council of a democracy might gradually transform itself into an oppressive oligarchy without serious disturbance, but a political club could usurp control of the state only by a revolutionary

[72] Hüttl, *Verf. v. Syrakus*, 75 and 101 n. 14.

[73] 19.5.6; cp. Justin, 22.2.10–11, *senatus*.

[74] Beloch, *Gr. Gesch.* iii. 1.590, and iv. 1.180; Hüttl, *Verf. v. Syrakus*, 124 and 128 (cp. 76 n. 55); Wickert, *Gnomon*, 1933, 22; Glotz, *Hist. gr.* iii. 416, cp. iv. 376 (by Roussel). A body known as ἀνδρῶν ἑξακοσίων συνέδριον formed a very important part of the Massaliot constitution (Strabo, 4.179); the date of its inception is not recorded.

[75] Freeman, *History of Sicily*, iv. 514–17; Tillyard, *Agathocles*, 92–3; Cary, *C.A.H.*, vii. 618; Scheele, *Strat. Autokr.*, 51 n. 72.

coup. Syracusan history is almost unknown for some twenty years after the death of Timoleon, but if his constitution had been overthrown by violence, Diodorus would surely have made some reference to this event in recording the rise of Agathocles, confused as his narrative is at this point.[76] It has been maintained that the Six Hundred is correctly defined first as συνέδριον and later as ἑταιρεία, as it was originally a constitutional council but was dissolved after the second return of Agathocles from exile and thereafter existed only as a political club.[77] This may be true, but it is perhaps preferable to attribute the inconsistency of Diodorus' terminology to the composite character of his narrative. In Book 19 he made use of authorities both favourable and hostile to Agathocles;[78] to the former the Six Hundred would be ἑταιρεία, to the latter συνέδριον. The case of the Four Hundred at Athens is roughly parallel: its supporters regarded it as the council of an alleged πάτριος πολιτεία, its opponents as an illegal association.

In accordance with democratic principle members of the council probably served for one year only.[79] But the activities of the Six Hundred suggest that virtually the same body could serve for a number of successive years and that regulations restricting re-election did not exist or could be circumvented. Timoleon perhaps nominated the members of his first council himself, following the precedent of Solon, or at least secured the election of men whom he could trust.

The only executive institution on which any information survives is the Amphipolia of Olympian Zeus.[80] A priesthood which already had a long history but had hitherto remained divorced from politics was transformed by Timoleon into the highest magistracy of the new state.[81] This innovation is not to be attributed to his religious feeling, which has been exaggerated by

---

[76] De Sanctis, *Rivista di Filologia*, 1895, 289 n. 3 (who, however, maintains that Timoleon instituted an oligarchy). The crimes of two leaders of the Six Hundred, which Diodorus (19.3.3) claims to have recorded in his previous book (falsely, unless they were included in a lost part of Book 18), seem to have been a series of violent acts rather than the overthrow of the constitution.

[77] Hüttl, *Verf. v. Syrakus*, 128 n. 3.

[78] Laqueur, *R.E.* viA. 1162–3.

[79] Busolt and Swoboda, *Gr. Staatskunde* i. 467–8.

[80] Hüttl, *Verf. v. Syrakus*, 121–4, gives a very full account; cp. Ziegler, *R.E.* xviii. 191–2.

[81] D. 70.6, τὴν κατ' ἐνιαυτόν ἐντιμοτάτην ἀρχήν. Though the priesthood had

literary tradition, nor merely to a desire to parallel the honours paid to Zeus Eleutherios after the liberation of the city from the Deinomenids, though this was certainly among his motives.[82] A priest, being debarred from military command, would find it almost impossible to establish himself as tyrant, even if he were to entertain such an ambition, and his sacrosanctity afforded some protection against assassination by aspirants to tyranny or other revolutionaries. The Amphipolos held office for one year and was eponymous, and the process whereby he was appointed has fortunately been preserved by Cicero. The final selection was made by lot, but candidature was restricted to members of three aristocratic families or classes, one candidate from each being chosen by popular vote.[83] Yet this monopoly of candidature added little to the authority of the upper classes. The Amphipolia is of great interest to the student of constitutional history; its creation is described with some care by Diodorus (70.6), whereas little is known of the remainder of the system; it reappears in the *Verrines* of Cicero, who had occasion to name two Amphipoloi of his day. Hence it has been allowed to assume in accounts of Timoleon's reforms a prominence which is entirely unwarranted. The Amphipolos was the nominal head of the state, but he was not its leader, and he exercised an authority scarcely superior to that of the eponymous archon in the fully developed Athenian democracy. The method of electing the Amphipolos provided a safeguard that he should be a man of some repute but not that he should be among the foremost statesmen of the day. *Novi homines* were excluded, and even if the three selected candidates were men of ability, sortition might lead to the appointment of the least competent. Although the office survived for at least three and a half centuries, the names of very few Amphipoloi are preserved,[84] and none left his mark on Syracusan history. This silence can hardly be accidental, for at times of unrest, such as

---

been instituted long ago, there is no evidence that it bore the title of Amphi-polia before this time.

[82] Hüttl, *Verf. v. Syrakus*, 121–2; Stier, *R.E.* viA. 1288.

[83] Hüttl, *Verf. v. Syrakus*, 122–3 with full references. The exact significance of the statement that the three candidates were elected *ex tribus generibus* (*Verr.* 2.51.127) is not altogether clear, but the above explanation is generally accepted (cp. ibid., 4.61.137, *homo nobilis*).

[84] Hüttl, *Verf. v. Syrakus*, 123, gives a list.

that which preceded the tyranny of Agathocles, the Amphipolos of the year would surely have taken some action to maintain the constitution, had his powers been more than formal. The survival of the office when the rest of Timoleon's constitution had long passed into oblivion shows that it was in no way incompatible with the Hellenistic monarchies of Agathocles and Hieron or with the subsequent Roman administration.[85] Even Callimenes, who according to Diodorus was the first holder of the Amphipolia, finds no place in the more detailed narrative of Plutarch, and his year of office evidently falls within the period of Timoleon's dictatorship.[86] Dictator and Amphipolos stood side by side, the latter being little more than a picturesque figurehead.

The functions and even the designations of the other magistracies established or revived by Timoleon may only be conjectured. His resignation must have been followed by the annual election of a board of *strategi*,[87] which formed the chief executive body whenever Syracuse was not under a dictator. The existence of such a board some twenty years later may be inferred from the refusal of Agathocles to accept office if he were to have any colleagues (Diod. 19.9.3–4). When the Syracusan army took the field, it was normally commanded by one or more of the *strategi*: Damas, the patron of Agathocles, was apparently in sole command of an expedition against Acragas, but Antander, the brother of Agathocles, was one of several *strategi* in a campaign at Croton.[88] In the military sphere the powers of the *strategi* were limited by the proviso that for wars against a barbarian enemy

[85] Verres seems to have gained no substantial advantage by securing the appointment of his creature Theomnastus to the Amphipolia. The part played by the latter in the depredations of his patron was in a private capacity or in concert with others (*Verr.* 2.21.50, 3.43.101). Cicero describes the office as *sacerdotium* (ibid., 2.51.126–7) and implies that it conferred more distinction than authority (ibid., 4.61.137).

[86] Diodorus imagines that Timoleon instituted the Amphipolia immediately after the liberation of Syracuse (70.6). This is improbable, since constitutions cannot be framed and put into operation without some delay (cp. P. 24.3). Yet the election of Callimenes must belong to the first years of Timoleon's dictatorship.

[87] Schwahn, *R.E.* Suppl. vi. 1129–30. The size of the board cannot even be guessed, as the number of *strategi* in other periods of Syracusan history fluctuates considerably (Hüttl, *Verf. v. Syrakus*, 77).

[88] Diod. 19.3.1 (Damas), 3.3 (Antander). The *strategi* probably did not appoint their subordinates: Damas nominated Agathocles to be *chiliarch*, but

a commander-in-chief should be summoned from Corinth.[89] Their civil functions are unknown. The duty of presiding over the assembly, which had once devolved upon the *strategi*, was transferred, probably by Diocles, to the archons, and some scholars maintain that this practice was continued under the system of Timoleon.[90] But the inscription which is believed to substantiate this view, since it refers to a προστάτης and a body of archons,[91] probably belongs to the end of the third century B.C. Changes of procedure may well have taken place since Timoleon's time, especially as Agathocles followed the example of Dionysius I in maintaining the outward form of an advanced democracy.

A revision of the legal code, a corollary to the creation of the new constitution, is mentioned three times by Diodorus and once by Plutarch; but these notices are confusing and in some respects contradict one another.[92] Timoleon did not himself occupy the position of νομοθέτης, this office being entrusted to the two Corinthian experts, Cephalus and Dionysius, who in addition to their legislative activities doubtless assisted him in drafting the constitution. Just as Protagoras apparently adapted the old systems of Zaleucus and Charondas for use at Thurii,[93] so the Corinthian legislators used the 'Laws of Diocles' as the foundation of the new code. If the principles of Diocles had been acceptable, little change would have been required in order to adapt his comparatively recent code to existing conditions. Thus when Diodorus states in Book 13 (35.3) that Cephalus was merely an interpreter of the archaic dialect in which the code of Diocles was

---

this was an exceptional case in which a *chiliarch* had died in the course of a campaign. Normally *chiliarchs* were appointed by the demos (ibid., 3.4).

Timoleon must have built up a new army organisation, gradually disbanding his mercenary force. But evidence is lacking. The ιλάρχαι who distinguished themselves in the final defeat of Hicetas (P. 31.4) were certainly Syracusan citizens and not mercenaries.

[89] P. 38.4. See above, p. 267.

[90] Hüttl, *Verf. v. Syrakus*, 124 n. 35.

[91] Kern, *Inschriften von Magnesia am Maeander*, 74 ll. 1–4. The word ἄρχοντες is supplied only by restoration.

[92] Diod. 13.35.3 and 16.70.5, 82.6–7; P. 24.3 (cp. Hüttl, *Verf. v. Syrakus*, 92–3, 98.125).

[93] Glotz, *Hist. gr.* ii. 175, but the extent of Protagoras' debt is disputed (Ciaceri, *Stor. Mag. Gr.* ii. 354).

written, he or his authority must be guilty of some misunderstanding. In Book 16 (82.7) Cephalus is more correctly described as ἐπιστάτης καὶ διορθωτὴς τῆς νομοθεσίας. The task of the legislators was one of revision not of interpretation, and a further statement by Diodorus suggests the motive and direction of this revision. Laws regulating private contracts and inheritances were left unaltered, whereas those relating to matters of public interest were revised (82.6). This distinction is consistent with the principles of the new constitution, which have been noted above. The rights of the individual, which had been so much abused by the tyrants, were to be restored and protected, but the new demos was not to be allowed to exercise the oppressive despotism which was a feature of extreme democracies deplored by Aristotle. Thus legislative and constitutional reforms had a single aim.

The two accounts of the legislative reform of Timoleon which appear in Book 16 (70.5; 82.6–7) are almost certainly drawn from two distinct sources,[94] but they are not necessarily parallel versions of the same reform. There may well have been two stages, the first a stop-gap to further the restoration of law and order immediately after the liberation of Syracuse, the second a permanent system evolved with the aid of the Corinthian experts considerably later. In the first stage the code of Diocles, which was conveniently available, was perhaps revived in its entirety, and the modifications of this code mentioned in the second passage were later introduced to accommodate it to the new moderate democracy. Additional legislation of a kind normally required by the foundation of a colony, even where it was only an ἐποικία, would naturally follow the influx of settlers. How far the legal code instituted by Cephalus and Dionysius proved acceptable to the demos cannot be determined, but at least their mission seems to have been welcomed, whereas Dion had increased his unpopularity by seeking advisers from Corinth (Plut. *Dion*, 53.2).

Some further light may be thrown upon the character of the new state by seeking to determine whether Timoleon established, or tried to establish, a Syracusan hegemony over Greek cities liberated by him from tyranny or barbarian domination. The evidence, though once again very scanty, is not entirely inconclusive. In the decree issued at his death the demos of Syracuse assumes the right to express gratitude to him on behalf of all

[94] Laqueur, *R.E.* viA. 1159; Hammond, *C.Q.* 1938, 140–1.

Greek Sicily; but he could scarcely be honoured as the man 'responsible for the liberation of the Siceliots' if these Siceliots had merely exchanged the yoke of tyrant or barbarian for the yoke of Syracuse.[95] Numismatic evidence, which will be treated more fully in the next section, suggests that Syracusan influence upon other cities was profound but did not amount to annexation. In this period many cities produced new issues whose types, though akin to those of Syracuse, are symbolic of freedom. Relations with Acragas and Messana in the time of Agathocles show that both were wholly independent of Syracuse,[96] although Timoleon freed the former from Carthage and the latter from a tyrant. A clause contained in the peace treaty of 339 which guaranteed freedom to all Greek cities (D. 82.3) was probably included not to safeguard the Greeks against Carthage but to prevent the re-establishment of a Syracusan empire, which would be a menace to Carthaginian interests.[97] The existence of a συμμαχία under the leadership of Syracuse is twice mentioned by Diodorus (73.2, 82.4) and is confirmed both by the composition of the Greek army at the Crimisus[98] and by coins bearing the inscription ΣΥΜΜΑΧΙΚΟΝ, which were struck on Syracusan blanks for the use of several small towns chiefly of Sicel origin.[99] This alliance, however, while doubtless offensive at the outset, probably became an ἐπιμαχία after the conclusion of peace with Carthage and the expulsion of the tyrants. Timoleon seems to

[95] D. 90.1; cp. P. 39.5. The restoration of freedom and autonomy to Sicilian cities is mentioned several times (cp. D. 72.5, 73.2; P. 24.1), but this refers primarily to liberation from tyranny without much regard to their subsequent status.

[96] Acragas: Diod. 19.3.1 (probably an imperialistic venture by the oligarchial party). Messana: ibid. 65.1–5.

[97] This is the inference of Meltzer, *Gesch. der Karthager*, i. 336–7, from the circumstances recorded in Diod. 19.65.5. Since their defeat at the Crimisus the Carthaginians had gained some successes, and it is difficult to understand why they should have agreed to renounce their association with the tyrants unless they were promised substantial advantages. Plutarch (34.2) omits a clause which was in reality a concession to Carthage. Timoleon was probably glad that Syracuse should be formally debarred from pursuing a policy of which he himself disapproved.

[98] Parke, *Greek Mercenary Soldiers*, 173 n. 4.

[99] Head, *Historia Numorum²*, 117 and 125–6; Giesecke, *Sicilia Numismatica*, 69–70. Issues of a later date which retain ΣΥΜΜΑΧΙΚΟΝ (Giesecke, *Sic. Num.*, 81, 167) shows that the alliance was not wholly dissolved.

have used it not to cloak a Syracusan hegemony but to establish a comprehensive settlement of the type known in Greece at this time as κοινὴ εἰρήνη, whereby the autonomy of all states was guaranteed.[100] The Symaethus basin was bound to Syracuse by closer ties than other districts, as the 10,000 colonists settled there enjoyed Syracusan citizenship, but the cities of this area, and even Leontini, issued independent coinages. It was only the selfish rule of the Six Hundred that led them to support the revolutionary movement of Agathocles.

It is impossible to determine how far Timoleon interfered in the local government of the cities which he liberated. His advice and patronage were sought wherever constitutional and legislative reform was undertaken (P. 35.4), and he doubtless attempted to prevent both the recurrence of tyranny and the disorders which frequently followed the expulsion of a tyrant. But he can scarcely have imposed upon all cities a replica of the constitution which he established at Syracuse. Traces of an Amphipolia at other Sicilian cities many years later[101] afford no evidence of Syracusan pressure; for there is nothing to show when this institution, which is also found outside Sicily, was introduced and whether it resembled that of Syracuse in having a political significance. Because Syracuse was the centre from which the liberation of Greek Sicily was conducted, Syracusan influences were naturally strong, but during the dictatorship of Timoleon and for many years after his death this predominance was not abused. In this respect he stands alone among dictators of Syracuse.[102]

The principal conclusions which I have sought to establish in this section are these. The constitution of Timoleon was a democracy in which every citizen enjoyed full political rights, but it was a democracy of the most moderate kind. Thus the assembly, which was nominally supreme, seems to have played a less active part in the government than the council, probably a body of 600 persons. The Amphipolia of Olympian Zeus was little more

[100] Griffith, *Journal of Hellenic Studies*, 1939, 71 with notes, explains the character of this κοινὴ εἰρήνη and gives a full bibliography. A settlement of a somewhat similar nature had been advocated by Hermocrates (whether sincerely or not) in the epilogue of his speech at Gela (Thuc. 4.64).

[101] Hüttl,*Verf. v. Syrakus*, 123.

[102] The consideration which he showed for all Sicilians, whether Greek or barbarian, is emphasised by Pace, *Arte e Civiltà*, i. 243–4.

than a sinecure, and its importance has been much overrated. After the resignation of Timoleon from the dictatorship the practice of electing a college of *strategi* annually was evidently resumed. The legal code drafted by the two Corinthian legislators was based upon the code of Diocles, but considerable modifications were introduced in order to accommodate it to the new constitution, which was far less radical than that of Diocles. Finally, there is no reason to believe that any attempt was made to rebuild the Syracusan empire or to interfere in the local government of Sicilian cities.

IV. ECONOMIC REVIVAL

For some years after his arrival in Sicily Timoleon was in financial difficulties. The Corinthians, whose resources had long been declining, were unwilling at first to support him generously, and it was only when he seemed likely to succeed that they sent out a supply of money with the reinforcement under Deinarchus and Demaratus (D. 69.4). Liberated but impoverished, Syracuse could contribute little to the maintenance of his mercenary troops (P. 23.7), and on at least two occasions their pay was dangerously in arrear (D. 73.1, 78.5–6). Shortage of metals hindered the provision of an abundant currency demanded by the programme of reconstruction and by the wars with the tyrants and Carthage. The 1,000 talents realised from the sale of houses was perhaps paid largely in plate or miscellaneous coin hoarded during the period of anarchy, and this supplied a useful foundation for a new coinage-system. But the story that the statues of the tyrants were melted down for use in the minting of a bronze coinage[103] illustrates the continued and pressing need of metals. A dearth of silver is apparent from the issue of heavy bronze coins by Syracuse and smaller cities in the period preceding the battle at the Crimisus.[104] The spoils of victory then relieved this acute embarrassment, and the sale of prisoners also realised a large sum for the treasury (P. 29.1–2). Thereafter military operations became less costly, since Timoleon was not so dependent upon expensive mercenaries when the citizen-army

[103] Dio Chrys. 37.20–1. According to Plutarch (23.7) the statues were sold by auction, but this seems less likely.
[104] Giesecke, *Sic. Num.*, 66–70 (cp. the minting of gold mentioned below).

of Syracuse increased in strength and efficiency.[105] It is to the years after 341, when agriculture and trade were beginning to revive—though Syracuse was still by no means a wealthy city[106] —that the majority of issues of coinage throughout Greek Sicily certainly belong.

The coinage of Syracuse at this time reflects the course of political and economic recovery and is a valuable supplement to the literary authorities. Yet this evidence must be used with caution, for the large number of series issued within a short period has led to some confusion, and numismatists disagree in dating and interpreting them. That the Syracusan coinage underwent a transformation at some time not far removed from the middle of the fourth century is beyond doubt: the types of the fifth century, which were continued under Dionysius I, are replaced by new types whose most distinctive feature is the Pegasus. The adoption of this Corinthian emblem suggests that the influence of Corinth was strong, and indeed the earliest Syracusan Pegasi were struck from imported Corinthian dies. The monetary systems of the two states were easily equated, as the Corinthian stater corresponded to the Sicilian decalitron. Some scholars believe that Dion was responsible for the earlier series of these Pegasi,[107] but there appears to be no numismatic evidence in support of this view, while historical considerations are certainly against it. Relations between Syracuse and Corinth had not been cordial prior to the mission of Timoleon: the support granted to Dion amounted to little more than sympathy,[108] and his only

---

[105] Since Deinarchus and Demaratus became agents of Philip (Parke, *Gr. Merc. Sold.*, 173 with notes), they must have returned to Greece soon after the battle at the Crimisus and were perhaps accompanied by part of the mercenary army.

[106] A fleet would have been valuable to Timoleon both for the suppression of piracy and for the conduct of his later campaigns. Yet naval operations are mentioned only once, and these took place just before his resignation and were apparently on a small scale (P. 34.4, cp. 37.9). The maintenance of a navy—an expensive luxury, as Dion had found (Plut. *Dion*, 50.1)—was beyond the financial resources of the new Syracuse.

[107] Freeman, *Hist. of Sic.* iv. 349 (by Evans); Giesecke, *Sic. Num.*, 64–6. The electrum coinage of Syracuse, which used to be assigned to Dion (Head, *Hist. Num.*², 178), is now believed to have been a military issue of Dionysius I continued by his son (Seltman, *Greek Coins*, 187–8; cp. Giesecke, *Sic. Num.*, 60–3, who is inclined to assign most of the electrum issues to Dionysius II).

[108] Giesecke, *Sic. Num.*, 64, exaggerates the extent of Corinthian aid,

attempt to re-establish contact with the metropolis after he became dictator was the design, which has already been mentioned,[109] to summon Corinthian advisers who might assist him in drafting a new constitution. Another series of Pegasi has been ascribed to Hicetas, who is believed to have minted these coins while he was besieging Dionysius.[110] A lion's head, which had appeared on earlier coins of Leontini, occurs on some of this Syracusan series, but this is very slender evidence of any connection with Hicetas. It is hard to believe that this self-seeking adventurer, who strove to prevent the intervention of a liberator from Corinth, can have issued coins which were essentially Corinthian. In view of the efforts made by Timoleon to develop ties of intimacy between Syracuse and Corinth it is far more likely that the various series of coins bearing the Pegasus and types associated with it were all issued under his influence.[111] If all are attributed to him, many varieties must have appeared within a few years, but this is by no means improbable and suggests that, like some Roman emperors, he used coinage as an instrument of propaganda. Apart from the predominating Pegasus, the most notable of the new types is that of Zeus Eleutherios, which is believed to celebrate the victory over Carthage.[112] It seems, however, more probable that the bestowal of honour upon the Zeus to whom Syracuse had erected a statue after the expulsion of the Deinomenids[113] was designed to mark a similar deliverance from tyranny. The free horse, another frequent type, is a symbol of liberty, and the ear of corn reflects the recovery of agriculture. The new coinage was mainly of silver and bronze; the rare gold coins of this period suggest that silver was sometimes lacking, for Greek states seldom coined gold if silver was available.

The significance of this new coinage should not be exaggerated. With the coinages produced when Syracuse was a great commercial centre it will not bear comparison, but at least it reflects a remarkable rate of progress in the restoration of economic

---

relying presumably upon a vague and non-committal statement by Diodorus (6.5).

[109] See above, p. 301–2.   [110] Giesecke, *Sic. Num.*, 73.

[111] Seltman, *Gr. Coins*, 191–2.

[112] Giesecke, *Sic. Num.*, 75; Seltman, *Gr. Coins*, 193.

[113] Diod. 11.72.2; cp. the honours paid to Zeus Eleutherios at Samos, Hdt. 3.142.

stability. Other cities participated in the recovery so carefully fostered by Timoleon, many producing new issues and several now coining for the first time in their history. Silver Pegasi were issued by Leontini and possibly Messana, as well as by Italiot Rhegium. The majority of Sicilian coinages issued in this period had to be confined to bronze, but the number of small towns which produced coins obviously modelled on those of Syracuse is surprisingly large and includes several whose population was largely Sicel or Campanian. The coinages of small silver and of bronze minted by Acragas and Gela probably belong to the period between the death of Timoleon and the rise of Agathocles.

In an interesting chapter, of which the substance must derive from Timaeus,[114] Diodorus uses the evidence of building activities in later years at Syracuse and Agyrium to illustrate the return of prosperity to Sicily initiated by Timoleon. This economic revival is attributed to the resumption of the export trade in Sicilian agricultural produce, which had formerly been extensive.[115] The enthusiasm of two over-patriotic Sicilians, Timaeus and Diodorus, is not above suspicion, but evidence from impartial sources shows that Greece, and especially Athens, imported corn from Sicily during the reign of Alexander the Great. In a scientific work written perhaps not long after the death of Timoleon Theophrastus states that Sicilian wheat was 'heavier than most of those imported into Greece' (*H.P.* 8.4.5, Hort); and two Heracleots are honoured by an Athenian decree for providing corn which, if a probable restoration is accepted, was Sicilian.[116] A private speech of Demosthenes, delivered about 332–330,[117] is concerned with the purchase of a cargo of corn at

[114] D. 83; cp. Hammond, *C.Q.* 1938, 138–9 and 144–5. Plutarch is content with vague eulogy (36.8–9) and supplies no details about economic recovery.

[115] Knorringa, *Emporos*, 98–9, collects the literary evidence for the export of Sicilian corn to Greece down to the time of Demosthenes, the most instructive passage being Thuc. 3.86.4. He might have added Theopomp. (*F. Gr. Hist.* 115) F 193, where the principal gift of many sent by Hieron I to a Corinthian is a shipload of corn.

[116] *Inscriptiones Graecae*, ii.² 408; cp. Heichelheim, *R.E.* Suppl. vi. 849. Ziebarth, *Beiträge zur Gesch. des Seeraubs und Seehandels*, 70, refuses to accept the restoration, but there seems no reason why Heracleots should not have traded in Sicilian corn.

[117] Dem. 32. Cosman, *Demosthenes' Rede tegen Zenothemis*, 30, gives this date.

Syracuse and with its shipment to Athens.[118] In a speech of somewhat later date contained in the Demosthenic corpus the arrival of a convoy bringing the Sicilian harvest is regarded as a seasonal event which automatically lowered corn-prices at the Piraeus.[119] The demands of Alexander's army much reduced the amount of Pontic and Egyptian corn available for export to Greece, and between 330 and 326 a famine ensued, which was particularly acute at Athens.[120] An attractive market was thereby offered to Sicilian corn-exporters, though the prevalence of piracy in Italian waters prevented them from taking full advantage of their opportunity.

Piracy was indeed an obstacle to the restoration of commercial contacts between Sicily and Greece. It had gradually increased when the navy built by the elder Dionysius was allowed to decay and ceased to police the seas. No state except Carthage[121] took any effective steps to suppress it until Rome became a naval power. Agathocles, who might have used his fleet to protect commerce, preferred to ally himself with the pirates of Calabria, lending his ships to them and receiving a share of their profits in return.[122] Pirates from the Italian coasts are usually described as 'Tyrrhenians' in this period, but the term is a comprehensive one, which became current owing to the reputation of the Etruscans for piracy. Many so-called Tyrrhenians were of Italic stock.[123]

[118] In addition to Cosman's monograph, Ziebarth, *Beit. zur Gesch. des Seer. und Seeh.*, 50–2, and Clerc, *Massilia*, i. 301–6, deal with the circumstances of this speech. The payment of export-dues on the cargo (18, probably the regular two per cent imposed by most states) indicates one source from which the new Syracuse derived its revenue (cp. Diod. 26.8, where immunity from dues is granted to Rhodian corn-transports by Hieron II). That the ship-owner engaged in this transaction and his accomplices were Massaliots and not Syracusans may well be fortuitous; but much of the Syracusan merchant-navy must have been lost during the years of civil strife, and little money was available to make good these losses.

[119] Dem., 56.9, ὁ Σικελικὸς κατάπλους. The date is about 323.

[120] Tarn, *C.A.H.* vi. 448–9; Glotz, *Hist. gr.* iv. 209–11 (by Cohen); Michell, *Economics of Ancient Greece*, 275–8. In the third century another Athenian famine was relieved by corn from Syracuse (*Supplementum Epigraphicum Graecum*, iii. 92).

[121] Gsell, *Histoire ancienne de l'Afrique du Nord*, iv. 125–7.

[122] Diod. 21.4. Other tyrants had indulged in buccaneering: shortly before the arrival of Timoleon in Sicily the west coast of Italy was plundered by Greek raiders thought to be Sicilian tyrants (Livy, 7.25–6).

[123] Ormerod, *Piracy in the Ancient World*, 129–30.

It was largely with the object of protecting their corn-transports from these Tyrrhenians that the Athenians in 325/4 established a colony and naval station at an unknown site on the Adriatic coast,[124] but nothing further is heard of this enterprise. The attitude of Timoleon towards pirates is illustrated by his treatment of Postumius, described as a Tyrrhenian, who sailed to Syracuse expecting to be welcomed as a friend and was promptly executed.[125] He may have come to claim a reward for harrying Carthaginian shipping, but Timoleon probably feared that he would become a danger to Sicilian commerce, which must be protected as far as was possible. Since, however, Syracuse could not afford to maintain a considerable fleet,[126] piracy continued unchecked.

No evidence relating to this period is available of Sicilian exports other than corn or of markets other than Athens. Salt-fish and wool were evidently staple exports in the time of Hieron II, since these together with corn were chosen to form the bulk of the cargo of his famous ship.[127] As in other periods, wine, pottery, lard, skins and cheese[128] were doubtless among the commodities exported.[129] Commercial contacts were maintained with districts as distant as the Bosporan kingdom,[130] but it is impossible to name the principal markets to which Sicilian products were sold. In the case of corn the problem of markets is very puzzling. When the Romans began to import corn in large quantities, Sicily remained their chief source of supply for more

[124] *I.G.* ii². 1629. especially ll. 217–20. Some scholars believe this colony to have been situated far up the Adriatic, but it would be in a better position to protect traffic-routes if it were nearer to the straits of Otranto.

[125] D. 82.3. His name is Italian, and he may have been a native of Antium. The incident is not recorded by Plutarch and was probably discreditable to Timoleon, who seems to have acted treacherously. Tyrrhenian coins resembling those of towns allied with Timoleon (Giesecke, *Sic. Num.*, 69) suggest that he employed men whose normal occupation was buccaneering.

[126] See above n. 106.

[127] Moschion, *F. Gr. Hist.* 575 F 1.5.7.

[128] Sicilian cheese was still famous at the close of the fourth century or beginning of the third (Philemon fr. 76, Kock).

[129] Pace, *Arte e Civiltà* i. 367–418, gives a detailed survey of Sicilian products and trade in antiquity. The evidence is very disappointing in volume. Sicilian exports to Egypt in the Hellenistic period included horses, pigs and sulphur.

[130] Rostovtzeff, *C.A.H.* viii. 577.

than a century,[131] and Cato described the island as *cellam penariam rei publicae nostrae, nutricem plebis Romanae* (Cic. *Verr.* 2.2.5, cp. 3.5.11). Although they are said to have damaged the soil by over-production,[132] they cannot have caused the surplus available for export to be suddenly multiplied. This surplus was already very substantial before the Roman conquest of Sicily[133] and, though expanded by the enlightened policy of Hieron II,[134] must have been considerable in the later years of the fourth century and at the beginning of the third. In what directions was Sicilian corn exported before Roman exploitation under the tithe system began? To the Athenians Sicily was only a secondary source of supply, while the Peloponnese does not appear to have imported corn on a large scale in normal times. Italy may already have been a moderately good market, but a far better one was probably Carthage.

Northern Africa later became one of the principal granaries of the Mediterranean world, but it was only after the Carthaginians had begun to be shut out by Rome from their overseas sources of supply that they developed intensively the corn-production of their Libyan possessions.[135] In the fourth century the large population of Carthage was dependent in some degree on imported corn, and in the time of Agathocles corn-transports sailed thither from the Carthaginian district of Sicily and from Sardinia (Diod. 21.16.1). The terms of the second treaty with Rome, concluded in 348,[136] suggest that foodstuffs and raw materials were imported from lands outside the Carthaginian empire: for whereas the Carthaginians secured a monopoly for their industrial products by excluding the Romans, and presumably other peoples also,[137] from trade with Sardinia and almost all

[131] Scramuzza, *Roman Sicily* (in Tenney Frank, *Economic Survey of Ancient Rome*, iii), 253.

[132] Tenney Frank, *C.A.H.* vii. 800.　　　[133] Pace, *Arte e Civiltà* i. 371.

[134] Carcopino, *Loi de Hiéron*, 1–75; Hüttl, *Verf. v. Syrakus*, 137–40.

[135] Gsell, *Hist. anc. de l'Afr. du Nord*, iv. 10; Toutain, *Economic Life of the Ancient World*, 190. The soldiers of Agathocles were impressed by the richness of the countryside near Carthage, but in the highly coloured description of Diodorus (20.8.3–4) corn-fields are not mentioned.

[136] Polyb. 3.24; for the date see Last, *C.A.H.* vii. 861.

[137] As Schachermeyr shows (*Rh. Mus.* 1930, 361), this policy of maintaining a *mare clausum* would be pointless unless the shipping of all commercial states were excluded.

Libya, the port of Carthage itself was open to foreign shipping. Before the vine and the olive were cultivated on a large scale at home, wine and oil had been bought in bulk from Greek Sicily (Diod. 13.81.4–5), and the same process was probably followed in regard to corn, though developing more slowly. When the tithe payable throughout their possessions had been collected and the remaining surplus from these districts bought up, further needs were doubtless met by purchases from Greek Sicily.[138] Transport was not difficult, as the narrow strip of open sea between Sicily and Africa, if often stormy, offered few opportunities to pirates. Commercial relations between Carthaginian and Siceliot have been obscured by the tradition established by Timaeus, who hated Carthage and therefore sought to convince his readers that the two races were at all times irreconcilable enemies.[139] In reality the Carthaginians were far better neighbours to the Siceliots than were the Lucanians and other Italic peoples to the Italiots. At times the Carthaginians may have been tempted to obtain the agricultural produce of the Greeks by plunder rather than by peaceful trading, but most of the wars in Sicily were precipitated by the imperialistic ambitions of individuals. Neither race had any sustained desire to drive the other from the island.

The progress of economic recovery in Sicily was necessarily slow, and towards the end of the fourth century it was further retarded by political unrest. Had agriculture and commerce not been carefully fostered by Timoleon, they could hardly have survived the cumulative effect of the very severe dislocations which both preceded and followed his career. He must be given credit for having rescued one of the most productive of Mediterranean lands from economic ruin.

[138] It may be objected that Agathocles received 200,000 *medimni* of corn from the Carthaginians by the treaty of 306 (Diod. 20.79.5, cp. Gsell, *Hist. anc. de l'Afr. du Nord*, iv. 11 n. 1). But conditions were then abnormal. Military operations of preceding years must have so ruined Siceliot harvests that production failed to meet the demands of home consumption, and the corn surrendered by the Carthaginians was very probably drawn from their overseas possessions and not from Africa, which had itself suffered invasion.

[139] Laqueur, *R.E.* viA. 1194. There is some archaeological evidence of commercial relations between Carthage and Greek Sicily (Gsell, *Hist. anc. de l'Afr. du Nord*, iv. 151–2), but, like all archaeological evidence of Carthaginian commerce, it is unimpressive.

18

Eumenes of Cardia

The opening of the Hellenistic Age is a period in which the number of leading characters is unusually, even confusingly, large. Almost all these were Macedonians, but among them was Eumenes, a native of the Greek city of Cardia, whose fortunes in the six and a half years that elapsed between the death of Alexander and his own are more fully recorded than those of any Macedonian. He was neither the most powerful nor the most successful leader of his time, and the reason why relatively abundant information about his actions in these years has survived is that the standard history of the Successors was written by his fellow-townsman Hieronymus of Cardia, who served under him throughout his campaigns in Asia. It is for the same reason that the careers of Antigonus and Demetrius Poliorcetes, whom Hieronymus subsequently served, are more fully described in extant works dealing with this period than those of their rivals, Ptolemy, Cassander, Seleucus and Lysimachus. Hieronymus was able to study his successive masters at close quarters, and he enjoyed access to their official documents and confidential correspondence. He evidently made good use of these advantages, and the high quality of his work is clearly visible even through the mediocrity of Diodorus.

How far Hieronymus allowed his historical judgement to be influenced by loyalty to Eumenes, Antigonus and Demetrius is a question that cannot be determined with any certainty because the surviving fragments of his work are so meagre.[1] Clearly, however, his work did not consist of mere propaganda on behalf of his successive employers, and there is reason to believe that his treatment of Antigonus and Demetrius was not wholly sympathetic.[2] There is a different reason why he might have exaggerated both the importance and the ability of Eumenes, namely,

---

[1] They are collected in *F. Gr. Hist.* 154 F 1–19.
[2] This problem, as well as the general character of his work, is ably discussed by T. S. Brown, *Amer. Hist. Rev.*, lii (1946–7), 684–96. My own view, which cannot be developed here, is that he believed Antigonus and Demetrius

that they were both Cardians and may possibly have been related.[3] It is, however, difficult to imagine how either the importance or the ability of Eumenes could have been greatly exaggerated without blatantly falsifying historical facts, and these facts were well-known to the contemporaries of Hieronymus, especially at the court of the Antigonids. On the other hand, Hieronymus is surely responsible for the fact that the literary tradition is almost wholly favourable towards Eumenes and generally unfavourable towards persons with whom he was in conflict, such as Neoptolemus and Peucestas.[4] It is possible, though unprovable, that, like Thucydides, he strove to achieve impartiality but failed where his own feelings were deeply stirred. His prejudice may perhaps have taken the form of creating the impression that the motives of Eumenes were invariably unselfish and that he was wholly uninfluenced by personal ambition, a point that will be discussed later. He can scarcely have expressed any opinion on the moral character of Eumenes. Extant literary authorities based largely on his work suggest that he was not much given to passing moral judgements on his characters: his yardsticks were rather ability and the acquisition of power, and he apparently admired unscrupulous and even underhand measures whereby a leader was enabled to get the better of his rivals.[5]

It is in the parts of Diodorus Books 18–20 dealing with the struggles between the Successors that the work of Hieronymus is most clearly reflected. The chapters describing the last campaign of Eumenes, in which he commanded the army of the 'kings' against that of Antigonus, are especially instructive. Here Diodorus achieves a standard perhaps unequalled in any other

---

to have failed to gain their major objectives through their own errors of judgement.

[3] The suggestion that they were related rests solely on the fact that the father of Eumenes bore the name Hieronymus (cf. Brown, op. cit., 684 with n. 4, who is, however, mistaken in his statement that Eumenes had a son named Hieronymus).

[4] It is significant that Diodorus refers with approval to Peucestas at two points, laying emphasis upon his popularity in his satrapy: the first occurs just before his uneasy partnership with Eumenes began (19. 14.4–5), the second immediately after it ended (ibid., 48.5). In the intervening narrative he is frequently mentioned with disapproval.

[5] Cf. for example, Diod. 19. 23–4, Plut. *Eum.* 12.2–4.

section of his voluminous history. The narrative is remarkably vivid, showing at many points the hand of an observant and discerning eye-witness, while the detailed accounts of major battles are clearly based on those of a military expert, though Diodorus has been guilty of some omissions.[6] The narrative dealing with the earlier struggles of Eumenes in Asia before he embarked upon his last campaign, though for the most part less detailed, is scarcely less impressive. There is, however, an exception: a part of Book 18 where he describes how Eumenes contrived to escape from an almost desperate situation when besieged at Nora and then unexpectedly found himself more powerful than ever before, is strangely uneven. The reason for the unevenness of these chapters undoubtedly is that at several points Diodorus has followed his source less closely than usual and has chosen to develop his own ideas, as he occasionally does when writing on a subject in which he is especially interested. In this instance the remarkable change in the fortunes of Eumenes provides Diodorus with an opportunity to preach his own uninspired theory of history, namely, that τύχη is fickle and unpredictable.[7] Nevertheless, even in this part of Book 18 the bulk of the narrative is of good quality and based upon information supplied by Hieronymus, who himself played an important part in the negotiations between Eumenes and Antigonus.[8]

Considerably less valuable is the *Eumenes* of Plutarch, which is also largely, though not exclusively, dependent upon information derived from Hieronymus. It is not among the best of the *Lives*. The career of Eumenes after the death of Alexander was almost entirely military, and Plutarch, who insists elsewhere that he

[6] Cf. the observations of Kahnes and Kromayer in J. Kromayer and G. Veith, *Antike Schlachtfelder*, iv. 3 (1929), 424, on the account of the battle of Paraetacene.

[7] W. W. Tarn, *Alexander the Great*, ii (1948), 64, describes this theory as 'a convenient doctrine which can be invoked to cover any improbability or inconsistency'.

[8] The clearest examples of passages in Book 18 where Diodorus has temporarily deserted his source are 53.1–6 (where he recapitulates the career of Eumenes from his appointment as satrap of Cappadocia, stressing his changes of fortune) and 59.4–6 (where he expounds his own theory). There are, however, other references to the fickleness of fortune, and the substance of the passages in which they occur may, in some cases at least, have been contributed by Diodorus himself and not derived from his source (cf. 42.1–2, which will be discussed below, p. 325 n. 50).

writes biography and not history, seems to have felt himself handicapped by a dearth of personal anecdote. His first two chapters, dealing with the period before Alexander died, contain some personal detail mostly discreditable to Eumenes. This material can hardly have been derived from Hieronymus because the starting point of his work is believed to have been the death of Alexander. A story that Eumenes was of poor and humble origin, which Plutarch rejects, is ascribed by him to Duris,[9] whose sensational history may well be the source of other highly suspect stories included in these two chapters. The influence of Duris may also be responsible for the extravagantly rhetorical tone of a few episodes elsewhere in the *Eumenes* which are not mentioned by Diodorus. Examples are the encounter between Eumenes and the dying Craterus[10] and the address by the former to the Silver Shields after they had betrayed him:[11] the authenticity of both is doubtful. That Plutarch was not much attracted by Eumenes, and indeed misjudged him, is clearly seen in the latter part of his *Comparison between Sertorius and Eumenes*:[12] cleverness in a Greek was in his day regarded with suspicion by many, and with worse than suspicion by Juvenal. What interested Plutarch was whether his principal characters were good rather than whether they were able and intelligent, and, as has already been noted, Hieronymus does not seem to have concerned himself much with moral issues. Plutarch apparently grew tired of Eumenes: he describes the final campaign in central Asia rather briefly and somehow contrives to omit entirely the great battle of Paraetacene. On earlier events, however, he provides much valuable information not recorded by Diodorus, so that the two most important authorities for the career of Eumenes are conveniently complementary.

Minor authorities supply a few additional points. The *Eumenes* of Nepos is somewhat fuller and better than most of his brief biographies: unlike the *Eumenes* of Plutarch, it strikes no note of censure and is in general agreement with the account of

[9] *Eum.* 1.1–2.

[10] *Eum.* 7.13, cf. Nepos, *Eum.* 4.4, and Suda, s.v. Κρατερός.

[11] *Eum.* 17.5–18.2, cf. Justin, 14.4.1–18. R. Schubert, *Die Quellen zur Geschichte der Diadochenzeit* (1914), 204–9, maintains that much of *Eum.* 14–15, is derived from Duris.

[12] *Comp. Sert. et Eum.* 2.1–8. The accusation of cowardice in the face of death (2.8) appears to be false.

Diodorus. The work of Arrian known as τὰ μετ᾽ Ἀλέξανδρον dealt in considerable detail with a period of little more than two years starting from the death of Alexander, but it survives only in an epitome by Photius and a few fragments,[13] including a recently published papyrus.[14] In epitomising the account of Eumenes' career by Trogus contained in Books 13 and 14 of the *Historiae Philippicae* Justin is as inaccurate and as prone to empty rhetoric as elsewhere. Polyaenus includes in his collection of *Stratagems* a few used by Eumenes[15] and a few used against him.[16] A striking feature of these lesser sources is their unanimity: despite minor divergences all present substantially the same picture of Eumenes, which must be that of Hieronymus. This unanimity is evidence of the extent to which his account dominated the literary tradition.

The surviving authorities for the career of Eumenes are in general agreement in differentiating him from most of his principal contemporaries for three main reasons. The first is that he was outstandingly clever, resourceful and persuasive; the second that he was handicapped by being a Greek and not a Macedonian; the third that single-minded loyalty to the Macedonian royal house governed his actions. So prominent are these factors in the works discussed above that all three were surely stressed by Hieronymus. The extent of their influence must obviously be considered if the policy and aims of Eumenes are to be fully understood. While all three must be largely authentic, they have been accepted somewhat uncritically in modern times: in the case of the second and third at least, if the character of the evidence be taken into account, important reservations should, in my opinion, be made.

That Eumenes was clever is beyond dispute if there is any truth whatever in the record of his actions.[17] On many occasions the cleverness of his strategy served to counterbalance the weakness or disunity of forces under his command. In the military sphere, however, he was not perhaps more resourceful than

---

[13] *F. Gr. Hist.* 156 F 1–11, and in vol. ii. of the Teubner Arrian (ed. Roos, 1928), 253–86.

[14] V. Bartoletti, *Papiri greci e latini*, xii. 2 (1950), 1284. The arguments of K. Latte, *Gött. Nach.* (1950), no. 3.23–7, for assigning the papyrus to Arrian seem to be conclusive. [15] 4.8.2–5 (cf. 4.3, which may be authentic).

[16] 4.6.9–13, 19 (9 contains valuable information not recorded elsewhere).

[17] References to his cleverness and examples of it occur in all the authorities mentioned above; cf. also the *Heidelberg Epitome* (*F. Gr. Hist.* 155) 3.1.

Antigonus, who sometimes succeeded in outwitting him.[18] The advantage that he enjoyed over his contemporaries lay rather in the exercise of diplomatic skill, in exploiting to the full the favourable features of his relations with others and in so working upon their feelings that he was able to implement policies which he had no power to enforce. During his long association with Macedonians he had acquired an unrivalled knowledge of their temperament, which he often used with advantage. These qualities are seen most clearly in the accounts of his last campaign when as supreme commander for the 'kings' in Asia he somehow succeeded in holding together as an effective fighting force an army in which the disloyalty, insubordination and contentiousness of officers and men were perhaps unequalled even in the Hellenistic Age. However great his difficulties he always found some expedient whereby he was able to surmount them.

The best and most interesting example of his ingenuity is perhaps his establishment of what is known as the 'Alexander tent'. Acting on the authority of a dream which he professed to have had, he proposed that the insignia of Alexander should be placed on a golden throne and that daily offerings should be made by the principal officers, who should then meet in council in the tent in which this cult was observed as though Alexander were himself presiding.[19] Eumenes made this proposal soon after he assumed command of the Silver Shields, who gladly accepted it. The device proved very valuable when union with the forces of the eastern satraps had enlarged his army but at the same time intensified its discord. He was able to mitigate some causes of friction, including that of his own appointment as supreme commander. To entrust to a committee the direction of operations by an army in the field has obvious drawbacks. Eumenes seems normally to have secured the adoption of his own plans, but in one important and perhaps decisive instance he did not, namely, when the eastern satraps refused to agree to his proposal to march down to the Mediterranean coast.[20] Nevertheless the 'Alexander tent' was a brilliant conception, and without it the

[18] Cf. Diod. 19.26.5–8 and 32.1–2.

[19] Diod. 18.60.4–61, 3, 19.15.3–4; Plut. *Eum.* 13.4–8; Nepos, *Eum.* 7.2–3; Polyaen. 4.8.2. M. Launey, *Recherches sur les armées hellénistiques*, ii (1950), 945–7, points out that this military cult has no parallel in the age of the Successors.   [20] Diod. 19.21.1–2.

end would probably have come much sooner. On a subsequent occasion, shortly before the battle of Paraetacene, Eumenes showed psychological insight in telling his Macedonian troops a rather childish fable. Other audiences might well have felt insulted, especially as the fable is not even entirely apposite, but Eumenes rightly foresaw its effect upon his Macedonians, who received it with acclamation.[21]

It may be that Hieronymus somewhat overstressed the cleverness of Eumenes. In the course of his long life he must often have heard Macedonians expressing their claim to be superior to Greeks; perhaps deriving some satisfaction from recording episodes in which Macedonians were outwitted by a Greek, he may unconsciously have allowed such episodes to assume in his work a greater prominence than their importance warranted. It is also easy to believe that, because Hieronymus was personally involved in the difficulties which beset Eumenes, he may have exaggerated them and correspondingly over-estimated the cleverness of Eumenes in extricating himself. There is, however, no doubt that in this respect the general impression created by the extant sources is authentic.

References to the disadvantage suffered by Eumenes in being a Greek and not a Macedonian are much fewer than those to his cleverness. This disadvantage is, however, mentioned in a number of different connections by Diodorus, Plutarch and Nepos,[22] and at least some of these passages are doubtless derived ultimately from Hieronymus. How far it was open to the ablest Greeks to compete with leading Macedonians in the first years of the Hellenistic Age is an interesting question. Alexander had normally made appointments involving the command of troops from Macedonians alone, but it was his practice to judge men by their quality rather than their nationality, and a few Greeks were included among his Companions and most favoured subordinates. Examples are the Cretan Nearchus,[23] distinguished both as admiral and writer, and the Thessalian Medeius,[24] a very intimate

[21] Diod. 19.25.4–7.
[22] Diod. 18.60.1 and 3, 62.7, 19.13.1; Plut. *Eum.* 3.1 and 8.1 (cf. 18.2, where the Silver Shields are said to have referred to him as Χεϱϱονησίτης ὄλεθϱος); Nepos, *Eum.* 1.2–3 and 7.1.
[23] H. Berve, *R.E.* xvi (1935), cols. 2132–5.
[24] F. Geyer, *R.E.* xv (1931), cols. 103–4.

friend of Alexander in the last months of his life. Medeius subsequently commanded some mercenaries for Perdiccas, and both served under Antigonus and Demetrius, but neither attained the position to which his close relations with Alexander might seem to have entitled him. Several lesser Greeks who had served under Alexander are known to have played a part in the struggles that followed his death without securing any significant advancement.[25] These examples might seem to show that it was impossible for any Greek to break down the jealous exclusiveness of the Macedonians. Yet Eumenes was not the only Greek entrusted with a satrapy after the death of Alexander. Laomedon of Mytilene was appointed to the satrapy of Syria, which he held until his expulsion about three years later.[26] A Cypriot from Soloi named Stasanor, who had been in charge of Areia and Drangiana, two of the eastern satrapies, before Alexander died, had his appointment confirmed, and when after two years he was transferred to Bactria and Sogdiana, his successor was Stasander, also a Cypriot and perhaps his relative.[27] The most striking case is that of Lysimachus, satrap and eventually king of Thrace. There is no adequate reason for rejecting the tradition that his father was a Thessalian who migrated to Macedonia. It is true that some authorities describe him as a Macedonian and a citizen of Pella, but citizenship was doubtless conferred upon his father while living at the Macedonian court.[28] Of these Greeks entrusted with satrapies, Eumenes, Laomedon and Lysimachus —as well as Nearchus, who had been satrap of Lycia and Pamphylia for a time when Alexander was alive—are all known to have lived in Macedonia for a number of years.[29] Hence it is clear that such naturalised Macedonians, as they may be termed, were granted a privileged status not enjoyed by other Greeks and were much less sharply differentiated from native Macedonians because their loyalty was believed to have been proved.[30]

[25] Examples are Aeschylus of Rhodes (H. Berve, *Das Alexanderreich*, ii (1926), 17) and Andronicus of Olynthus (ibid., 39–40).

[26] E. Bux, *R.E.* xii (1924), cols. 756–7 (the longer of two articles devoted to the same person).

[27] E. Honigmann, *R.E.* iii A (1929), cols. 2152–3 (on Stasanor); K. Fiehn, ibid., col. 2152 (on Stasander).   [28] F. Geyer, *R.E.* xiv (1928), col. 1.

[29] Laomedon and Nearchus lived at Amphipolis which became a Macedonian city after its annexation by Philip.

[30] Stasanor was evidently a man of outstanding ability, but it is not

For any Greek to have attempted to usurp the throne of Macedonia by sweeping aside the 'kings', an ambition imputed rightly or wrongly to Leonnatus, Perdiccas and Antigonus, would have been an act of folly doomed to failure from the outset. A king of Macedonia had to have his succession to the throne formally recognised by the general assembly of the army,[31] and the attitude of the Silver Shields towards Eumenes shows that Macedonians would not, at any rate at this time, have contemplated accepting a Greek as their king. To this extent Eumenes was undoubtedly in a different position from that of his Macedonian contemporaries, to this extent the limits of his potential advancement were circumscribed.[32] On the other hand, there is no justification for assuming that a Greek so long and so intimately associated with the Macedonian court as he had been was automatically disqualified by his origin from competing with Macedonians for responsible positions conferring a substantial measure of independent authority. Polyperchon actually proposed that Eumenes should participate with himself in the guardianship of the 'kings'.[33]

It is therefore somewhat surprising to find so much emphasis laid on the disadvantage suffered by Eumenes in being a Greek. It might be suggested that Hieronymus, who served the house of Antigonus for three generations without attaining high distinction except as a historian, believed himself and other Greeks to have been unjustly denied advancement because of their nationality. Hieronymus can, however, scarcely have invented episodes mentioned in some of the passages cited above[34] from which the Greek origin of Eumenes is seen to have been an important issue in his own lifetime. His enemies are stated to have used it as an instrument of propaganda when seeking to undermine the loyalty of his Macedonian troops.[35] Even more significant are two passages in which Eumenes is said to have referred in public utterances to the consequences of being a Greek. According to

altogether clear why he and Stasander were singled out for appointment to satrapies.

[31] F. Granier, *Die makedonische Heeresversammlung* (1931), 15; W. W. Tarn and G. T. Griffith, *Hellenistic Civilisation*[3] (1952), 47.

[32] Cf. Diod. 18.60.1.

[33] Diod. 18.57.3 (cf. Plut. *Eum.* 13.1 for a similar suggestion by Olympias).

[34] See above, p. 319 n. 22.   [35] Diod. 19.13.1, cf. Nepos, *Eum.* 7.1.

x *   321

Plutarch he declared, when acting as negotiator between the cavalry and the infantry at Babylon, that 'being a foreigner he had no right to interfere in the disputes of Macedonians'.[36] Diodorus attributes to him a statement made apparently in the speech in which he proposed the establishment of the 'Alexander tent', that he could 'expect no position of authority ($\dot{a}\varrho\chi\dot{\eta}$) because he was a foreigner and debarred from the powers native to the Macedonians'.[37] If these statements are authentic, Eumenes with characteristic adroitness took advantage of a handicap. A later passage of Diodorus points in the same direction. When Antigonus tried to bribe Antigenes and Teutamus, the commanders of the Silver Shields, to betray Eumenes, Teutamus was ready to accept until Antigenes persuaded him to change his mind by arguing that, whereas Antigonus would deprive them both of their satrapies, Eumenes would treat them generously 'because being a foreigner he would never dare to pursue his own interest ($i\delta\iota o\pi\varrho\alpha\gamma\tilde{\eta}\sigma\alpha\iota$)'.[38] It is remarkable that the substance of this secret conversation should have become known even to Hieronymus, especially as Antigenes was executed immediately after the battle of Gabiene.[39] The most probable explanation seems to be that Antigenes disclosed the treacherous intentions of Teutamus to Eumenes, who then suggested the cogent argument whereby Antigenes successfully appealed to the self-interest of his colleague.

It is thus perhaps legitimate to conclude that Eumenes in his lifetime and Hieronymus after his death were somewhat disingenuous in stressing the handicap imposed by his Greek birth, which debarred him only from the pursuit of ambitions that he had no right to pursue. Exaggeration of this handicap seems to have proved useful to Eumenes by helping him to allay the jealousy of his Macedonian rivals and to secure obedience from those under his command, while Hieronymus was perhaps enabled thereby to represent Eumenes as more unselfish than he actually was.[40]

[36] Plut. *Eum.* 3.1.
[37] Diod. 18.60.3.
[38] Diod. 18.62.4–7.
[39] Diod. 19.44.1.
[40] The view of A. Vezin, *Eumenes von Kardien* (1907), 125–6, that the ultimate failure of Eumenes was due to his Greek birth seems to me to be based on an insufficiently critical acceptance of the impression created by the sources.

That Eumenes was exceptionally loyal to the royal house of Macedonia is mentioned in a number of passages[41] and is very frequently implied. His loyalty is a cardinal assumption throughout the detailed narrative of Diodorus describing his last campaign against Antigonus. In modern times it has evoked even more admiration than his military talents or diplomatic skill,[42] and with good reason. It is not my intention to deny either that he was loyal or that his loyalty was admirable. The confidence in him felt by members of the royal house is attested by the summary of a letter written to him by the masterful Olympias in which she described him as the most faithful of her friends and asked him to advise her.[43] It does, however, seem legitimate to question whether his aim was at all times solely to promote the interest of the royal house and whether he was wholly indifferent to his own prospects except as its servant. Decisions made by him both before and after the death of Perdiccas suggest that these doubts are not unwarranted.

When Perdiccas left him to defend Asia Minor against the invading army of Antipater and Craterus, they sent an embassy to invite him to change sides and join them. This offer he rejected, making a counterproposal that he should negotiate a reconciliation between Craterus and Perdiccas. Now Antipater, Craterus and Ptolemy had taken up arms against Perdiccas on the ground that he was plotting to usurp the throne. The validity of this charge, as well as the legal status of Perdiccas at this time, is uncertain. It may be that, because Perdiccas had the 'kings' in his charge, Eumenes felt himself obliged to carry out his orders faithfully.[44] Yet of all the leading Macedonians Antipater and Craterus were the most obviously loyal to the royal house and

[41] Specific references are: Diod. 18.53.7, 57.4, 58.4; 19.42.5, 44.2; Plut. *Eum.* 1.4; Nepos, *Eum.* 6.5; *Heidelberg Epitome* (*F. Gr. Hist.* 155), 3.1–2. Diod. 18.29.2, 42.2, and Plut. *Eum.* 5.8, refer more generally to the trustworthiness of Eumenes, while Nepos, *Eum.* 3.1 stresses his fidelity towards Perdiccas (who was, however, at this time in charge of the 'kings').

[42] Cf. Vezin, op. cit., 126, and the brief but eloquent tribute of Tarn, *C.A.H.*, vi (1927), 479–80.

[43] Diod. 18.58.2–3, cf. Nepos, *Eum.* 6.1–4 and Plut. *Eum.* 13.1. Hieronymus must have seen this letter. The negotiations between Eumenes and Cleopatra, the sister of Alexander, show that she too trusted him (Arrian (*F. Gr. Hist.* 156), F 9.21 and 26, 10.7–10, 11.40, cf. Plut. *Eum.* 8.6–7 and Justin, 14.1.7).

[44] Cf. Nepos, *Eum.* 3.1.

the least suspected of harbouring personal ambitions. It is also clear that, had Eumenes accepted their offer, he would have had his satrapy enlarged but would have lost what was virtually an independent command. Strangely enough, the account of these negotiations by Plutarch, who alone records them in any detail,[45] contains no mention of the 'kings', whereas much is made of the personal enmity between Eumenes and Antipater and the personal friendship between Eumenes and Craterus.

More significant than this episode, which may have been inaccurately transmitted, is the fact that from the death of Perdiccas to that of Antipater, a period of nearly two years, Eumenes was actually fighting against the forces of the 'kings'. It is arguable that he had no choice. He had been sentenced to death by the assembly of the Macedonian army, which held him responsible for the death of the popular Craterus, and he was a personal enemy of Antipater, now regent and more powerful than any other Macedonian leader. The actions of Eumenes at this time are inadequately recorded and their motives obscure. Presumably he maintained that the 'kings' had been illegally entrusted to Antipater and that it was his duty to fight for the restoration of the position as it had stood before the fall of Perdiccas.[46] There was, however, very little hope of achieving this aim, especially as the surviving adherents of Perdiccas were disunited. Alcetas, the brother of Perdiccas, and other leaders persisted in their refusal to co-operate with Eumenes, whose own forces, though large, were unlikely to, and in fact did not, fight wholeheartedly for a cause that was meaningless to them. If Eumenes had been willing to subordinate all other considerations to the interests of the royal house, which would certainly be damaged by further bloodshed, he could have surrendered unconditionally and faced the consequences. Alternatively, he could have sought to secure the cancellation of the death sentence passed on him by undertaking to put himself and his troops at the disposal of the 'kings'. He did neither.

That the opening of negotiations with his enemies at this stage might well have led to a settlement is shown by subsequent events. When his position had been much weakened by his defeat

[45] *Eum.* 5.6–8, cf. Arrian F 9.26.

[46] His attempt to win the support of Cleopatra (Arrian F 11.40) seems to indicate that he claimed to be still in the service of the royal house.

at Orcynia, which cost him the loss of almost all his forces, and he had taken refuge with the remainder in the fortress of Nora, Antigonus made overtures to him as soon as measures for establishing a blockade had been completed.[47] Diodorus declares that Antigonus, being now in control of the most powerful army in Asia, was already pursuing personal ambitions on a very large scale and was no longer content to obey the 'kings' and Antipater.[48] It is, however, highly questionable whether at this stage, while Antipater was still alive, Antigonus had already formed plans to defy the central authority and make himself independent.[49] The attitude of Eumenes in making demands that virtually amounted to a rejection of the offer was probably adopted because he was unwilling to become a mere servant of Antigonus and not because he suspected him of disloyalty to the 'kings'.[50] Later, when Antigonus again sought a settlement, the position had changed: Antipater was dead, the authority of the new regent Polyperchon was most insecure, and the surviving supporters of Perdiccas had been eliminated. Hence it is rather more likely, though by no means certain, that on this occasion Eumenes evaded the conclusion of an agreement because he was convinced that Antigonus was disloyal to the royal house.[51] The

[47] Diod. 18.41.6–7; Plut. *Eum.* 10.3–8.

[48] Diod. 18.41.4–5.

[49] P. Cloché, *Mélanges Charles Picard*, i (1949), 189–90. The ambitious plans of Antigonus are mentioned only at a later stage by Plutarch (*Eum.* 12.1).

[50] Some observations of Diodorus on the general aims of Eumenes at this juncture (18.42.1–2) are highly suspect. They are incompatible with a later passage (see the next note), and the implication that Eumenes was ready to sell his services to the highest bidder conflicts with the picture of him drawn by the narrative of Diodorus. If he had felt as he is said to have felt, he would surely have accepted without hesitation the terms offered by Antigonus. The sentiments here attributed to Eumenes foreshadow the subsequent homilies on the mutability of fortune which, as stated above (p. 315), are almost certainly original contributions by Diodorus himself. This passage also is very probably the fruit of his own surmise and not adapted from material supplied by his source.

[51] Diod. 18.50.1–4; Plut. *Eum.* 12.1–2. It is noteworthy that Hieronymus communicated the proposals of Antigonus to Eumenes on this occasion. A passage in which Diodorus (18.58.4) further discusses the reasons why Eumenes refused to listen to Antigonus is very probably derived from Hieronymus. It stresses the devotion of Eumenes to the cause of the infant Alexander and, unlike the passage mentioned in the previous note, is in entire harmony with the general impression created by the narrative.

significant fact remains that none of the attempts made by his opponents to come to terms with him led to the conclusion of a peaceful settlement.

During the first years after the death of Alexander most Macedonians and many Greeks in Macedonian service evidently desired that the Empire should be held together under the Argead house and that the young Alexander IV should, when he came of age, succeed to the heritage of his father.[52] Loyalty to the memory of Alexander remained strong, as is shown by the success of the 'Alexander tent', but self-interest probably exerted an even more powerful influence in favour of maintaining unity under the royal house. The Macedonian rank and file, because they had become professionals, were normally willing to serve anyone who could offer them generous terms and opportunities of winning booty. Often, however, they showed a disinclination to fight each other and evidently much preferred to be left to garrison the conquests of Alexander. The lesser nobles in charge of the smaller or more remote satrapies, who, like the satraps of the Persian Empire, enjoyed a considerable measure of independence, were more likely to be left undisturbed if the Empire were to remain united under the royal house and therefore favoured the maintenance of unity. Hence the cause of the royal house was not inevitably doomed from the outset. On the other hand, the extreme weakness of this cause was manifest, threatened as it was by the ambitions and jealousies of the greater Macedonian leaders. This threat was very grave indeed: it came not only from those believed to be aiming at the establishment of a personal sovereignty over the Empire as a whole but also, perhaps even more acutely, from those who, like Ptolemy, pursued limited objectives and sought for themselves separate and independent kingdoms in a dismembered Empire. While their numbers were small, these men controlled vast resources and enjoyed the enormous power that the principal barons always have enjoyed under a feudal system when the monarchy has been virtually in abeyance. None of them could hope to achieve his ambition if the boy Alexander were allowed to grow to manhood, and he lived to the age of about thirteen only because while a

[52] The half-witted and illegitimate Philip Arrhidaeus, the nominee of the infantry, was a mere stop-gap, who would doubtless have been eliminated or ignored.

minor he was a useful pawn and because even the most un-scrupulous Successors hesitated to incur the odium of having put him to death.

These considerations must have been fully appreciated by the clear-sighted and experienced Eumenes. Was he then content to expose himself to endless perils and trials, especially when as supreme commander in Asia he was in constant danger of betrayal, solely for the sake of the rather slender chance that young Alexander might become master of a united empire? The impression created by the history of Hieronymus seems to have been that he was. Hieronymus, however, for all his merits cannot be considered to be a wholly impartial witness, and the remarkable decisions of Eumenes mentioned above provide some grounds for believing that he constantly kept in mind the problem of his own future if, as was likely, the Empire were to break up.

The leaders of the cavalry in the dispute with the infantry at Babylon immediately after the death of Alexander are listed by Arrian in two categories.[53] The first consists of Perdiccas, Leon-natus and Ptolemy; the second, containing the names of five leaders who ranked after these three, includes Eumenes. Al-though some important personalities were not at Babylon, the passage provides evidence of the status enjoyed by Eumenes in relation to other leaders when Alexander died.[54] The record of his actions, at any rate from the point at which the challenge to the authority of Perdiccas brought the first clash of arms, shows how determined he was to maintain this position. If the Empire had remained united under the royal house and Alexander IV had grown to manhood, Eumenes would have had strong claims to be ranked among the principal subordinates of the young king on the same footing as the foremost Macedonians. Whatever the outcome, however, he was evidently not content, as Nearchus and other Greeks seem to have been, to become merely the tool of another's ambition. He could at almost any time have secured an honourable but subordinate command, with plenty of scope

---

[53] F 1.2.

[54] It might be argued that the inclusion of Eumenes is due to the bias of Hieronymus (Jacoby, n. ad loc.), but he had been appointed to a *hipparchy* by Alexander and was not obviously unworthy to be classed with Lysimachus and Seleucus.

for the exercise of his talents, under one of the leading Macedonians whose equals he had been when Alexander died, but he was adamant in refusing agreements whereby he would have found himself committed to an inferior position of this kind.[55] Had the regency collapsed before his own death, he would certainly have competed with other leaders for the independent kindgoms into which a dismembered Empire would naturally fall. Macedonian troops were not likely to fight wholeheartedly for a Greek, but the limitations of Macedonian manpower were becoming evident, and increasing numbers of Greeks and even Asiatics were being armed and trained in the Macedonian style.[56] Eumenes himself showed, when he built up an effective force of Cappadocian horse soon after assuming control of his satrapy, that Asia Minor could produce cavalry of high quality.[57]

What Eumenes planned to do in a situation which, partly through his own efforts to avert it, arose only when he was dead can only be guessed. There is, however, one curious feature of his relations with the regent Polyperchon which is perhaps to be explained on the assumption that he was believed to have personal aims of the kind tentatively suggested above. When he was appointed supreme commander in Asia, the sentence of death passed on him after the fall of Perdiccas was not annulled.[58] It seriously weakened his authority, being used by his enemies in attempts to undermine the loyalty of his troops,[59] and eventually it enabled Antigonus to have him put to death with some semblance of legality. The omission of Polyperchon to have the sentence annulled can scarcely have been a mere oversight: even if he failed to appreciate that his appointment of Eumenes as supreme commander in Asia did not automatically cancel the death sentence passed by the army, Eumenes must surely have claimed to be absolved from all charges, a claim that he made in his negotiations with Antigonus at Nora.[60] No explanation

[55] Cf. the severe and somewhat unjust criticisms of Plut. *Comp. Sert. et Eum.* 2.3–5.

[56] G. T. Griffith, *Mercenaries of the Hellenistic World* (1935), 40–2.

[57] Plut. *Eum.* 4.4–4, cf. Diod. 18.29.3 and 30.1.

[58] According to Diodorus (18.59.4, the principal passage on the fickleness of fortune) the Macedonians 'forgot' their condemnation of him.

[59] Diod. 18.62.1 and 19.12.1–2 (also apparently Diod., 18.63.2 and Plut. *Eum.* 8.11).

[60] Diod. 18.41.7.

of this strange omission on the part of Polyperchon seems to have been offered in modern times.[61] It may be that he deliberately refrained from taking steps to have the death sentence annulled because he saw in it a valuable means of maintaining his own authority and of curbing any attempt by Eumenes to make himself undesirably independent.[62]

If there is any validity in the suggestions made in this essay, the traditional picture of Eumenes should be somewhat modified. There is, however, much to admire in the part that he played in the struggles between the Successors during the last years of his life, especially after his appointment as supreme commander for the 'kings' in Asia. He was essentially a realist, and in the many difficult situations in which he was involved he showed a remarkable sense of what was practicable. He determined what his policy should be and pursued it with undaunted persistence. Few of his Macedonian contemporaries seem to have understood the altered world in which they found themselves. They had acquired vast power too rapidly. A few decades earlier Macedonia had been a feudal backwater, and not many Macedonians had crossed its frontiers. When the dominating personality of Alexander was suddenly removed, the Macedonian nobles instinctively reverted to the traditional practice of their ancestors, who, whenever the monarchy was weak, had tended to disrupt the unity of the kingdom by self-seeking turbulence and intrigue. It is not surprising that the Successors strove for the prizes of empire without appreciating its responsibilities, that they succumbed so easily and so shortsightedly to the lure of personal ambition. The fault lay less in their national character than in the limitations of their political experience. Although Eumenes was probably

[61] The literary tradition is very unsympathetic towards Polyperchon— possibly because Hieronymus considered that he had given insufficient support to Eumenes—but his decree recalling Greek exiles (Diod. 18.56) was a shrewd move, and perhaps he was abler than is generally believed.

[62] In discussing the loyalty of Eumenes to the royal house I have not taken into account the fact that in the spring of 317 he appears to have lost his status as supreme commander in Asia because Polyperchon was deposed by a decree issued in the name of Philip Arrhidaeus (Justin, 14.5.1–3, discussed by H. Bengtson, *Die Strategie in der hellenistichen Zeit*, i (1937), 87–8 and 110–11). Even if Eumenes received a clear picture of the confused situation in Macedonia, which is doubtful, he must have refused to recognise the regency of Cassander: his loyalty was to Olympias and the legitimate branch of the royal house.

less indifferent to his own interests than Hieronymus seems to have allowed, he did differ from most of the leading Macedonians in being less easily corrupted and therefore more loyal to the house of Alexander. One reason may have been that, as has already been pointed out, the highest prize of all was not open to him. A stronger reason, however, was that he enjoyed the very great advantage of having been born and brought up in the politically and intellectually more advanced atmosphere of a Greek city-state.

Index